CHRISTIAN THEOLOGY IN CONTEXT

SERIES EDITORS

Timothy Gorringe   Graham Ward

CHRISTIAN THEOLOGY IN CONTEXT

Any inspection of recent theological monographs makes plain that it is still thought possible to understand a text independently of its context. Work in the sociology of knowledge and in cultural studies has, however, increasingly made obvious that such a divorce is impossible. On the one hand, as Marx put it, 'life determines consciousness'. All texts have to be understood in their life situation, related to questions of power, class, and modes of production. No texts exist in intellectual innocence. On the other hand texts are also forms of cultural power, expressing and modifying the dominant ideologies through which we understand the world. This dialectical understanding of texts demands an interdisciplinary approach if they are to be properly understood: theology needs to be read alongside economics, politics, and social studies, as well as philosophy, with which it has traditionally been linked. The cultural situatedness of any text demands, both in its own time and in the time of its rereading, a radically interdisciplinary analysis.

The aim of this series is to provide such an analysis, culturally situating texts by Christian theologians and theological movements. Only by doing this, we believe, will people of the fourth, sixteenth or nineteenth centuries be able to speak to those of the twenty-first. Only by doing this will we be able to understand how theologies are themselves cultural products—projects deeply resonant with their particular cultural contexts and yet nevertheless exceeding those contexts by being received into our own today. In doing this, the series should advance both our understanding of those theologies and our understanding of theology as a discipline. We also hope that it will contribute to the fast developing interdisciplinary debates of the present.

Augustine

CHRISTIAN TRUTH AND FRACTURED HUMANITY

Carol Harrison

OXFORD

UNIVERSITY PRESS

OXFORD
UNIVERSITY PRESS

Great Clarendon Street, Oxford OX2 6DP

Oxford University Press is a department of the University of Oxford.
It furthers the University's objective of excellence in research, scholarship,
and education by publishing worldwide in

Oxford New York

Athens Auckland Bangkok Bogotá Buenos Aires Calcutta
Cape Town Chennai Dar es Salaam Delhi Florence Hong Kong Istanbul
Karachi Kuala Lumpur Madrid Melbourne Mexico City Mumbai
Nairobi Paris São Paulo Singapore Taipei Tokyo Toronto Warsaw

and associated companies in Berlin Ibadan

Oxford is a registered trade mark of Oxford University Press
in the UK and certain other countries

Published in the United States
by Oxford University Press Inc., New York

© Carol Harrison 2000

The moral rights of the author have been asserted
Database right Oxford University Press (maker)

First published 2000

British Library Cataloguing in Publication Data
Data available

Library of Congress Cataloging in Publication Data
Harrison, Carol.
Augustine : Christian truth and fractured humanity / Carol Harrison.
p. cm.—(Christian theology in context)
Includes bibliographical references and index.
1. Augustine, Saint, Bishop of Hippo. I. Title. II. Series.
BR1720.A9 H337 2000
270.2′092–dc21   99-048182
ISBN 0–19–875220–2
ISBN 0–19–875219–9 pbk

1 3 5 7 9 10 8 6 4 2

Typeset by Best-set Typesetter Ltd., Hong Kong
Printed in Great Britain
on acid-free paper by
TJ International Ltd,
Padstow, Cornwall

To

Keith Harrison
(1935–1995)

with love and gratitude.

Note on Abbreviations and Editions

References to Augustine's works follow those used in the Augustinus Lexicon, Würzburg.

Abbreviations for Reviews and Journals have been kept to a minimum and are listed at the head of the Bibliography.

For the editions of the works of Saint Augustine (and other Latin Fathers) see E. Dekkers, *Clavis Patrum Latinorum* 2nd edn., Louvain, 1961. More up-to-date, but less comprehensive, is the A. Mandouze, *Prosopographie chrétienne du Bas-Empire: L'Afrique 303–533* Éditions du CNRS, Paris, 1982. Where available I have used the *Bibliothèque Augustinienne: Oeuvres de saint Augustin* (Paris, 1933 f.), abbreviated in the notes as *BA*.

There are many English translations available (notably the *Library of the Fathers*, the *Nicene and Post Nicene Fathers*, the *Ancient Christian Writers*, the *Library of Christian Classics* and the New City Press *Works of Saint Augustine* series) which I have consulted and modified where necessary.

Biblical references are given to the text of the Latin Vulgate.

Abbreviations of Augustine's Works

Acad.	*De Academicis libri tres*	Against the Academics
c. Adim.	*Contra Adimantum Manichei discipulum liber unus*	Against Adimantus
c. adu. leg.	*Contra aduersarium legis et prophetarum libri duo*	Against Adversaries of the Law and the Prophets
agon.	*De agone christiano liber unus*	On Christian Struggle
an. quant.	*De animae quantitate liber unus*	On the Greatness of the Soul
bapt.	*De baptismo libri septem*	On Baptism
beata u.	*De beata uita liber unus*	On the Happy Life
b. coniug.	*De bono coniugali liber unus*	On the Good of Marriage
b. uid.	*De bono uiduitatis*	On the Good of Widowhood
breuic	*Breuiculus conlationis cum Donatistis libri tres*	Brief Meeting with the Donatists
cat. rud.	*De catechizandis rudibus liber unus*	On Teaching the Uninstructed
ciu.	*De Ciuitate dei libri uiginti duo*	City of God
conf.	*Confessionum libri tredecim*	Confessions
con. Max.	*Conlatio cum Maximino Arrianorum episcopo*	Discussion with Maximus
cons. eu.	*De consensu euagelistarum libri quattuor*	On the Harmony of the Gospels
cont.	*De continentia liber unus*	On Continence
corrept.	*De correptione et gratia liber unus*	On Admonition and Grace
Cresc.	*Ad Cresconium grammaticum partis Donati libri quattuor*	Reply to Cresconius
dial.	*De dialectica*	On Dialectic
disc. chr.	*De disciplina christiana*	On Christian Discipline
diu. qu.	*De diuersis quaestionibus octoginta tribus liber unus*	Eighty-three Diverse Questions

doctr. chr.	*De doctrina christiana libri quattuor*	On Christian Doctrine
c. Don.	*Contra Donatistas liber unus*	Against the Donatists
duab. an.	*De duabus animabus liber unus*	On Two Souls, against the Manichees
Emer.	*Gesta cum Emerito Donatistarum episcopo liber unus*	Proceedings with Emeritus
en. Ps.	*Enarrationes in Psalmos*	Explanations of the Psalms
ench.	*De fide spe et caritate liber unus*	Enchiridion
ep.	*Epistulae*	Letters
ep.* (Divjak)		Letters edited by J. Divjak
c. ep. Don.	*Contra epistulam Donati heretici liber unus*	Against the Letter of Donatus
ep. Io. tr.	*In epistulam Iohannis ad Parthos tractatus decem*	Homilies on the First Epistle of John
c. ep. Man.	*Contra epistulam Manichaei quam uocant fundamenti liber unus*	Against the Basic Letter of the Manichees
c. ep. Parm.	*Contra epistulam Parmeniani libri tres*	Against the Letter of Parmenianus
c. ep. Pel.	*Contra duas epistulas Pelagianorum libri quattuor*	Against two Pelagian letters
ep. Rm. inch.	*Epistulae ad Romanos inchoata expositio liber unus*	Incomplete Explanation of the Epistle to the Romans
exc. urb.	*De excidio urbis Romae*	On the Fall of Rome
exp. Gal.	*Expositio epistulae ad Galatas liber unus*	Explanation of the Epistle to the Galatians
exp. prop. Rm.	*Expositio quarundam propositionum ex epistula apostoli ad Romanos*	Explanation of a Passage from the Epistle to the Romans
c. Faust.	*Contra Faustum Manicheum libri triginta tres*	Against Faustus
c. Fel.	*Contra Felicem Manicheum libri duo*	Against Felix
f. et op.	*De fide et operibus liber unus*	On Faith and Works
f. et symb.	*De fide et symbolo liber unus*	On Faith and the Creed
f. inuis.	*De fide rerum inuisibilem*	On Faith in Things Invisible

c. Fort.	Acta contra Fortunatum Manicheum liber unus	Against Fortunatus
c. Gaud.	Contra Gaudentium Donatistarum episcopum libri duo	Against Gaudentius
gest. Pel.	De gestis Pelagii liber unus	Proceedings with Pelagius
Gn. litt.	De Genesi ad litteram libri duodecim	Literal Commentary on Genesis
Gn. litt. inp.	De Genesi ad litteram liber unus inperfectus	Unfinished Literal Commentary on Genesis
Gn. adu. Man.	De Genesi aduersus Manicheos libri duo	On Genesis against the Manichees
gr. et lib. arb.	De Gratia et libero arbitrio liber unus	On Grace and Free Will
gr. et pecc. or.	De gratia Christi et de peccato originali libri duo	On the Grace of Christ and Original Sin
gr. t. nou	De gratia testamenti noui ad Honoratum liber unus (=ep. 140)	On the Grace of the New Testament
imm. an.	De immortalitate animae liber unus	On the Immortality of the Soul
Io. eu. tr.	In Iohannis euangelium tractatus	Homilies on St John's Gospel
adu. Iud.	Aduersus Iudaeos	Against the Jews
c. Iul.	Contra Iulianum libri sex	Against Julian
c. Iul. imp.	Contra Iulianum opus imperfectum	Unfinished work against Julian
lib. arb.	De libero arbitrio libri tres	On Free Will
c. litt. Pet.	Contra litteras Petiliani libri tres	Against the Letter of Petilian
mag.	De magistro liber unus	The Teacher
c. Max.	Contra Maximinum Arrianum	Against Maximian
mend.	De mendacio liber unus	On Lying
c. mend.	Contra mendacium liber unus	Against Lying
mor.	De moribus ecclesiae catholicae et de moribus Manicheorum libri duo	On the Morals of the Catholic Church and the Morals of the Manichees
mus.	De musica libri sex	On Music
nat. b.	De natura boni liber unus	On the Nature of the Good

nat. et gr.	*De natura et gratia liber unus*	On Nature and Grace
nupt. et conc.	*De nuptiis et concupiscentia ad Valerium libri duo*	Marriage and Concupiscence
op. mon.	*De opere monachorum liber unus*	On the Works of Monks
ord.	*De ordine libri duo*	On Order
orig. an.	*De origine animae*	On the Origin of the Soul
c. p. Don.	*Contra partem Donati libri duo*	Against the Donatist Sect
pecc. mer.	*De peccatorum meritis et remissione et de baptismo paruulorum ad Marcellinum libri tres*	On Punishment and Forgiveness of Sins
perf. iust.	*De perfectione iustitiae hominis liber unus*	On the Perfection of Justice
perseu.	*De dono perseuerantiae liber ad Prosperum et Hilarium secundus*	On the Gift of Perseverance
praed. sanct.	*De praedestinatione sanctorum liber ad Prosperum et Hilarium primus*	On the Predestination of the Saints
ps. c. Don.	*Psalmus contra partem Donati*	Song against the Donatists
qu. an.	*De quantitatae animae*	On the Greatness of the Soul
q. Hept	*Quaestionum libri septem*	Questions on the Heptateuch
reg.	*Regula*	The Rule
retr.	*Retractationum libri duo*	Retractations
c. Sec.	*Contra Secundinum Manicheum liber unus*	Against Secundinus
s.	*Sermones*	Sermons
c. s. Arrian.	*Contra sermonem Arrianorum liber unus*	Against an Arian Sermon
s. Denis	*Sermones a M. Denis editi*	Sermons edited by M. Denis
s. Guelf	*Sermones Moriniani ex collectione Guelferbytana*	Sermons from the Codex Guelferbytanus edited by G. Morin
s. Lambot	*Sermones a C. Lambot editi*	Sermons edited by C. Lambot

s. Morin	*Sermones a G. Morin editi*	Sermons additional to the Codex Guelferbytanus edited by G. Morin
Simpl.	*Ad Simplicianum libri duo*	To Simplicianus
sol.	*Soliloquiorum libri duo*	Soliloquies
spir. et litt.	*De spiritu et littera ad Marcellinum liber unus*	On the Spirit and the Letter
trin.	*De trinitate libri quindecim*	On the Trinity
uera rel.	*De uera religione liber unus*	On True Religion
uid. deo	*De uidendo deo liber unus*	On Seeing God
uirg.	*De sancta uirginitate liber unus*	On Holy Virginity
un. bapt.	*De unico baptismo contra Petilianum ad Constantinum liber unus*	On One Baptism
util. cred.	*De utilitate credendi liber unus*	On the Usefulness of Belief
util. ieiun	*De utilitate ieiunii*	On the Usefulness of Fasting

Other abbreviations

BA—*Bibliothèque Augustinienne: Oeuvres de saint Augustin* (Paris, 1933 f.)
CCL—*Corpus Christianorum Latinorum*
Cicero, *de finibus*—*De Finibus Bonorum et Malorum*
  tusc. disp.—*Tusculanes Disputationes*
  de Rep.—*De Re Publica*
Cod. Theod.—*Codex Theodosianus*
Jonkers—E. M. Jonkers (ed.), *Acta et symbola conciliorum quae saeculo quarto habitu sunt. Textus minores* 19 (Leiden; E. J. Brill, 1974)
Mansi—J. D. Mansi, *Sacrorum Conciliarum Nova et Amplissima Collectio*, 31 vols. (Florence, 1759–98)
Plotinus, *Enn.*—*Enneades*
Virgil, *Aen.*—*Aeneid*

Foreword

Forewords are usually written last, when the author has already exceeded the agreed word limit and time is pressing. This one is no exception to that rule.

The subject of this book is a ridiculously ambitious one which I agreed to in a moment of madness because it seemed to fill such an obvious gap in the vast oceans of secondary literature on Augustine, and promised to be just the book I needed to recommend to the students who yearly enrol for the Augustine and his Age course which I teach at Durham. I can now better understand why the gap is there but hope that it will not loom so obviously for my students when they are set adrift on the seas of Augustine scholarship. If nothing else, it points out the main landmarks of Augustine's thought and time, indicates why they are there, how they might best be viewed and how to find out more about them.

Two elements of Augustine's context, which seem to have exercised the greatest influence on this theology, structure this book; these are his cultural and social context. The first three chapters examine the philosophical, literary and ethical aspects of Augustine's cultural context; the last three chapters consider the social context for Augustine's reflections upon the Church, forms of Christian life in the world and the nature of the two cities. Themes which ordinarily structure general books on Augustine, such as his biography, his conversion, his controversies with Manichaeans, Donatists or Pelagians have been immersed in this general structure and surface at relevant points. I have, however, been careful to observe a chronological perspective when dealing with specific themes, but they necessarily run alongside each other, or create cross currents, rather than forming a consecutive whole.

One theme unifies the whole book—the transition from paganism to Christianity—and it is this which I have attempted to express in its title, *Christian Truth and Fractured Humanity*. For Augustine lived at a time of transition—from a classical pagan past to a new Christian empire—initiated by the conversion of the Emperor Constantine to Christianity in AD 312. Of course, paganism and the thought world and social structures that went with it were not suddenly obliterated, rather there was a slow, unsteady, faltering and rather ambiguous process of confrontation, accommodation, rejection and coercion before an indentifiably 'Christian' culture and society, founded upon a conviction that Christianity was the true philosophy and true religion, emerged. The real extent and limits of

Christianization—in culture and society—is one of the questions which arise in both parts of this book.

Another, perhaps less well-noted, transition from a classical to a Christian culture and society, takes place in Augustine's theology of the fall of mankind. His doctrine of original sin, and the way in which it fractures and vitiates mankind's ability to know or to will the good, marks a decisive break with classical ideals of the all-sufficiency of reason or the attainability of perfection, and forms the hallmark of his theology in all its aspects. In this respect, more than any other, Augustine broke with classical thought, to propound what has become the distinctive theology of Western Christendom. How this happened, in specific contexts, is examined throughout this book.

I would like to thank T&T Clark, Edinburgh, for permission to use material from my articles 'The Silent Majority: Patristic thought on the Family' in *The Family in Theological Perspective*, ed. S. C. Barton (Edinburgh, 1996) 87–107, in chapter 5, and 'Augustine, Wisdom and Classical Culture' in *Where Shall Wisdom be Found?* ed. S. C. Barton (Edinburgh, 1999) 125–38, in chapter 1. I would also like to thank Routledge for their permission to use my contribution to their forthcoming Festschrift for Gerald Bonner in chapter 2.

Contents

Acknowledgements

I would like to thank Lewis Ayres, Gerald Bonner, David Hunter, George Lawless and Robert Markus for advice, comments, offprints and friendly encouragement. To George Lawless I am also grateful for revising the title to make it gender inclusive. He will be disappointed to find that I felt a revision of the full text would lead to too much awkwardness in expression. I hope that he, and other readers, will accept my assurance that no bias is intended by my use of the term 'man' to denote male and female humanity.

To Robert Markus I owe an especial debt: a work on Augustine in context—a giant in an age of unprecedented change—would have been a hopelessly ambitious undertaking if I had not been able to draw upon his work in so many of the areas it has to cover. A glimpse at the footnotes and bibliography will reveal just how far reaching his influence and inspiration have been: this book has been written in his shadow.

It is a pleasure to thank all past and present students of Augustine at Durham for their enthusiasm, interest and thought-provoking questions. This book would not have been the same without them and was written with them in mind.

My husband, Andrew Louth, has read and commented upon numerous drafts with unfailing patience and encouraging criticism. He has also saved me from a number of howlers (the ones that remain were probably added later!). My debt to him, my mother and friends is otherwise intangible: their love, help and support are beyond telling. To my son, Isaac, a special thank you for so much delightful and refreshing distraction: without it this book would otherwise have been written long ago but its author would not be such a happy person.

PART ONE

Christianity and Classical Culture

1

Wisdom and classical culture

The *Confessions*, in which Augustine describes his conversion to Christianity in AD 386, are undoubtedly his best known work and have become one of the classics of Western literature.[1] Although they were begun in 396, a full ten years after his conversion, and are therefore written with the benefit of retrospective interpretation and reflection, Books 1–9 have provided the Augustine scholar with the spectacles, as it were, through which the dramatic events of the years leading up to his conversion have been viewed. It is for this reason that most general books on Augustine begin with a chapter which uses the *Confessions* to trace Augustine's biography and intellectual odyssey, before the time when other documentary sources can take over. Whilst I will also have to rely on the *Confessions* to a large extent, I would like to avoid using them as a determining source, not least because they impose an interpretation and perspective which is fundamentally anachronistic and, whilst informative, can be misleading.

Furthermore, although they are not without literary antecedents in antiquity,[2] the *Confessions*, written as a sort of prayer or conversation, with God as the unseen and unheard interlocutor, are a unique work, which defies neat classification. The long history of intense scholarly debate concerning their structure and intention is a good indicator of the difficulties one encounters in using them. Books 1–9 do indeed provide Augustine's version of his life leading up to, and immediately following his dramatic conversion in the garden at Milan in 386, but then problems arise: Book 10 consists of a Neoplatonically inspired ascent of the soul towards God followed by an evaluation of just how far Augustine has attained his desired goal of *continentia* (primarily understood as single-minded and single-hearted devotion to God). Books 11–13, meanwhile, are devoted to a commentary, or at least the beginnings of a commentary, on Genesis chapter 1. Book 11 gets no further than 'In the beginning' as Augustine becomes preoccupied with the nature of time. Books 12–13 cover the six days of creation. Then the *Confessions* end. There have been many ingenious

---

[1] Clark (1993a). For an excellent introduction, text and notes, *BA* 13 and 14. For text and magisterial commentary, O'Donnell (1992) I–III. Citations are from Chadwick's 1991 fine translation.   [2] Courcelle (1963a).

suggestions as to how these at first rather disparate books hang together.[3] Those theories which find a degree of unity in the nature of conversion, both Augustine's conversion, and creation understood (as Augustine often does) as conversion towards God, perhaps bear more weight than others. The former seek to link conversion with the classical idea of the six ages of man and the six days of creation, so that Augustine's personal history becomes a sort of miniature of what is happening on the broader canvas of divine creation and world history.[4] But these ideas are still only suggestions in response to what one must finally admit is a tantalizing enigma.

In the first half of this book, therefore, rather than relying wholly upon the uniquely valuable, but problematic *Confessions*, I intend to examine three aspects of the cultural context which shaped the whole course of Augustine's life and thought. (This is, of course, an artificial division—there are innumerable topics to be covered but a threefold presentation has a venerable tradition and it is to be understood that much will be tailored to fit, or disguised under these headings!). The present chapter will therefore be devoted to philosophical context, the second to literary culture, and the third to ethical concerns. My hope is that a picture as coherent as the one which emerges from simply reading *Confessions* 1–9 will emerge, but that it will have a wider focus and frame, comprehending the course of Augustine's life and the development of his thought, thus allowing the reader to view the whole, but also to concentrate on the details, in a chronological—and cultural—perspective.

THE SEARCH FOR WISDOM

The *Confessions* will, however, prove particularly useful in this chapter, since in them Augustine chooses to present his conversion to his readers as above all a search for wisdom (Lt. *sapientia*) or philosophy (Gk. *philosophia*—lit. love of wisdom). The Greek, which Augustine knew,[5] perhaps makes clearer what he would hear in the word: wisdom is not only an object to be contemplated, but is primarily a movement towards the truth, a search for and love of wisdom, inspired by, and assisted by, wisdom itself—a wisdom he would later identify with Christ. He draws out these ideas in one of his earliest works, the *Soliloquies*, written shortly after his conversion, during the retreat he took with his family and friends at the

[3] For a summary see Solignac, *BA* 13, 19–26.

[4] The main proponent of this thesis is Pizzolato (1968).

[5] It is often said that Augustine did not know Greek. He did not enjoy learning it, was largely dependent on translations, but was not entirely ignorant of it and seems to have become more adept in later years. See Courcelle (1943), 137 f.

small northern Italian village, Cassiciacum.[6] The *Soliloquies* take the form of an interior dialogue between Augustine and his Reason and in many respects foreshadow the later *Confessions*. Following linguistic pointers, as well as Jewish and pagan tradition, he depicts wisdom as female,[7] indeed, she is described in rather erotic terms: she is the sole object of Augustine's love, he desires 'to see her, to posses her without any covering, naked, to see and to hold her in perfect chastity'[8] (well, almost erotic!) (*sol.* I.13.22. Cf. *lib.arb.* 2, 13, 35; 2, 14, 37). But reason warns Augustine that chaste wisdom, like any beautiful woman, will only grant this favour if she is sure that Augustine loves no one else. Augustine assures reason that he loves nothing—life, rest, friends—more than her, his love is without limits and knows no jealousy. He wishes to possess and enjoy her in company with as many friends as possible. Reason approves—such chaste, pure love is exactly how wisdom ought to be loved. Nevertheless, there is more than one way that leads to her, and this depends upon man's capacities. Wisdom is like the intellectual light of minds—Reason draws on Plato's allegory of the Cave (*Republic* 7.514[9]) and the analogy of light: some can look at the sun directly, others are blinded by it and seek out the shade, needing to be gradually accustomed to its brilliance by first looking at objects upon which the light shines, then, as the light intensifies, upon shiny objects like gold and silver, fire, the stars, the moon, the dawn, and then perhaps finally, the sun. In the *Confessions*, ten years later, Augustine obviously places himself among the latter group—those who need to be gradually accustomed to the dazzling light of wisdom.

HORTENSIUS

He identifies the very beginning of his search in a decisive event—his reading of a book. It was a work which he had been given to study at the age of 19, in the course of his rhetorical studies: Cicero's *Hortensius*, or *Exhortation to Philosophy* (*conf.* 3.4.7).[10] He was meant to be studying the style of the work, but what really attracted him was its substance. Cicero

[6] Cf. also the story of *philosophia* and *philocalia* in *Acad.* 2.7.

[7] Though Power (1995), 135, with a feminist agenda to pursue, ignores this earlier identification and concentrates instead on Augustine's later identification of Wisdom/*sapientia* with the masculine, as opposed to female *scientia* (on the analogy of Adam and Eve) in *De Trinitate* 12.13.21. Reason is also personified in *sol.* I.6.12; *Acad.* I.1.3.

[8] Madec (1994), 219–20, also cites *en. Ps.*33.s2.6 and *trin.* 11.9.14 and suggests that Augustine probably owes these themes to Neoplatonism.

[9] The same image also occurs in Cicero *De finibus* 3.14.48—Verbeke (1958), 71.

[10] Although the work is no longer extant see *BA* 13, 667 for what we do know about it. Also O'Donnell (1992) II, 162–7.

exhorted his reader to study philosophy in order to ascend above earthly things and to attain happiness.[11] This, Augustine records,

> changed my feelings. It altered my prayers, Lord, to be towards you yourself. It gave me different values and priorities. Suddenly every vain hope became empty to me, and I longed for the immortality of wisdom with an incredible ardour in my heart. I began to rise up to return to you. (3.4.7) . . . My God, how I burned, how I burned with longing to leave earthly things and fly back to you. I did not know what you were doing with me, for 'with you is wisdom' [Job 12: 13, 16]. 'Love of wisdom' is the meaning of the Greek word *philosophia*. This book kindled my love for it . . . the one thing that delighted me in Cicero's exhortation was the advice 'not to study one particular sect but to love and seek and pursue and hold fast and strongly embrace wisdom itself, wherever found'. (*conf.* 3.4.8)

Augustine's identification of wisdom with the Christian God here is largely due to the retrospective nature of the *Confessions* where he presents his journey towards wisdom as one played out against the ever-present back-drop of Christianity—the religion to which he had been born, which he had drunk in with his mother's milk (3.4.8), to which he had been dedicated as a child, and to which he was but seeking to reconcile himself. So he rejects Cicero because the 'name of Christ was not there' (3.4.8); Manichaeism is attractive because it claimed to be a purer form of Christianity; the Acade-mic philosophers are rejected because he could not find 'the saving name of Christ' in them (5.14.24); the Neoplatonists are measured against Christian teaching and found lacking (e.g. 7.21.27) . . . . This has led scholars to suggest that Augustine was never not a Christian[12]—and it is an attractive idea with much to recommend it, not least in terms of fourth-century culture, but it is one which cannot really be conclusively proved.

CONVERSION TO PHILOSOPHY

What *is* clear is that Cicero inspired in Augustine such an enthusiasm for philosophy, of whatever type, that Augustine might be said to have under-gone his first 'conversion', for, as Gillian Clark observes, a 'decision to follow philosophy could, at any time from the fourth century BC, amount to conversion, a radical change of lifestyle in favour of simplicity and study'.[13] The philosopher, like the ascetic, traditionally led a life of self-denial, of withdrawal from society, in order to purify himself morally and intellectually for the task he had undertaken—the pursuit of wisdom. This

---

[11] Thus foreshadowing and preparing him for his later encounter with the Neoplatonists.

[12] Notably Madec (1994), 73; (1989), 23.

[13] Clark (1993a), 15. For the idea of 'conversion' to philosophy see Nock (1933), 173. Marrou (1949), 161 f. considers Augustine's conversion in its cultural context, from rhetor to philosopher, i.e. from a literary to a philosophic culture.

philosophical, ascetic ideal—and by Augustine's time, as we shall see in Chapter 5, they overlapped to a large extent in the ideal of the Christian martyr and then of the Christian monk—was deeply influential on Augustine.[14] It was often expressed in celibacy, an ideal he would have found in Cicero's *Hortensius* and which he later valued and embraced as the acme of the Christian life, but which he strangely—given its prominence in his account of his conversion—does not mention here. Nevertheless, he was conscious that the search for wisdom carried with it high ideals as to how one ought to live in the world. Later on, in *City of God* Book 8 he mentions Plato's division of philosophy into three branches: the practical, concerned with conduct of life and morals; the theoretical, concerned with the discovery of natural principles and truth in its purest form; the rational or logical, which undertakes to distinguish truth from falsehood. The practical element often meant that the philosopher belonged to, or established, some sort of community, consisting of men who shared the same goal. Hence *philosophia* was traditionally linked with *philia* (friendship).[15] We shall see that this link is well demonstrated in Augustine's own life—he always sought the company of like-minded friends in order to share his life in wisdom.[16] Indeed, this probably accounts for the next step in his journey towards it, as recounted in the *Confessions*.

Having, he tells us (*conf.* 3.4.8), found that the only drawback with Cicero was that the name of Christ was missing, he turned, significantly, to examine the Christian Scriptures. They were, at this stage, a great disappointment, 'unworthy in comparison with the dignity of Cicero' (3.5.9). Presumably he found them comparatively crude, badly written, and rather vulgar—the translation of the Old Latin Bible, which he almost certainly referred to, left a lot to be desired. And so he turned to the Manichees and was to remain a member of their sect for the next nine years of his life. Who were they?

MANICHAEISM

The Manichees[17] were a religious sect, based on revelations granted to the prophet Mani (born AD 216 in Babylonia) and his teachings. It was universal and missionary in intention, and very close to earlier Gnostic thought (the Manichees are often referred to as fourth-century Gnostics) in its

---

[14] Markus (1990), 72–4, 'The distance between the philosopher, the *mousikos aner*—the "man of the Muses", of cultivated intellect and devoted to the life of the spirit—and the *theios aner*—the "divine man", close to the divinity—was never very great and could easily be crossed' (74). [15] A point made by Madec (1989), 223.

[16] See Chapter 5. *conf.* 6.14.24 is a good early example of Augustine's attempts to establish such a philosophical community even before his conversion.

[17] *BA* 13, 118–38; Brown (1972), 94–118; Lieu (1985), 117–53; Bonner (1963), 157–236; O'Donnell (1992) II, 174–5.

syncretism, dualism, and its claim to a superior knowledge which explained everything within a vast and complicated system of cosmological myths. In Manichaeism, as in Gnosticism, matter is evil; the soul, a spark of the divine, is trapped within it and seeks to be liberated by realizing its exile, obtaining knowledge of itself and of the truth, and by adopting specific practices, such as eating selected foods which contain a high concentration of particles of light, which were thereby liberated. The Manichaean élite, the 'elect', therefore practised celibacy and severe asceticism in an attempt to avoid contact with matter as much as possible, and were helped in this by the lower grade of 'hearers' who prepared their food and attended to their needs. It was to this latter group that Augustine belonged—for, importantly for him, they were allowed to marry (though strongly urged to avoid having children, as this would simply be introducing more evil matter into the world) and he wished to live with his recently acquired concubine. But what was it that attracted him to this sect?

Having been fired with an enthusiasm for philosophy it seems strange that Augustine should then almost immediately go on to embrace Manichaeism, which was not so much a philosophical system, concerned with wisdom (*sapientia*) as a mythological system concerned with truth (*veritas*). (They did not, so far as I can see, adopt any of the sapiential features of Valentinian Gnosticism.) But Augustine, as many Gnostic devotees before him, was attracted by their claim to truth, to a comprehensive, satisfying explanation of the universe, of man's place in it, of evil, salvation, and so on. Their literature was impressive, if only because of its awesome quantity and its beautifully illustrated and illuminated tomes (*conf.* 3.6.10). Above all, if we can conjecture on the basis of Augustine's retrospective account in the *Confessions*, they satisfied the desire to reconcile himself to the Christianity he felt was such an integral part of himself and which he could not easily cast off: that which he had 'piously drunk in with my mother's milk, and at a deep level . . . retained the memory' (3.4.8). The Manichees claimed to be a true and purified form of Christianity—*integri christiani*. Mani claimed to be the Paraclete, and the figures of Jesus and God the Father—indeed, the Trinity (3.6.10)—were central to their myths. Above all, they criticized just those features of traditional Christianity that Augustine also found troublesome: the emphasis on faith (which seemed like credulity) (*On the Usefulness of Belief*); the anthropomorphic conception of God so characteristic of African Christianity (*conf.* 5.10.19); the deficiencies of Scripture which were ruthlessly taken apart by the Manichees' literal, rational criticism—for example the incredible account of creation in Genesis 1 (*On Genesis against the Manichees* I.2.3 f), the dubious morality of the Patriarchs (*conf.* 3.7.12–10.18) and the contradictory genealogies of Matthew and Luke (*Sermon* 51, 4.5), to cite but a few examples. The Manichees enabled Augustine to reconcile himself, or so it seemed, to a more coherent, rationally defensible, superior form of Christianity, than that bequeathed to him by his long-suffering and at this stage, despairing, mother (*conf.* 3.12.21).

The strong emphasis on asceticism, which Augustine accepted as inherent in any attempt to pursue wisdom, was also central to the Manichees as part of their denial of evil matter. Their emphasis on celibacy, food regulations and so on, would command his respect (if not his participation) and reassure him of their superiority. The social, communal aspect which often accompanied such philosophical asceticism was, as we shall see in Chapter 5, also deeply attractive to Augustine and in the Manichees met, at least for a while, a deeply felt need, which would impose itself throughout his life, to live in community; with them, Augustine found himself in the company of friends with a common goal. The Manichees formed a distinctive group, to a large extent at odds with society (which always lends itself to a high degree of cohesiveness), and subject to laws against heretics (which Peter Brown[18] suggests led to their becoming more Christianized and to the Church taking a greater part in their suppression, at least in the West). Although they began in Persia—and were popularly loathed because of their origins[19]—their missionary enterprises ensured that their presence was soon felt throughout the eastern part of the Empire. In Africa they were very much a fourth-century phenomenon, but in Italy they seem to have been more entrenched. Whenever someone seemed too extreme in his world-denying asceticism it was customary to charge him with Manichaeism. (Indeed, as we shall see, Augustine found it difficult to avoid the label even later, as a Christian bishop, in his teaching on original sin.)

But the Manichee's hold on Augustine did not last—the startling and inexplicable thing is that Augustine remained a Manichee for so long. (Though it is ironic that it is his own later, extensive and fierce criticism of the sect and its doctrines, which largely prompts this reflection.)

It is not clear at what stage Augustine began to entertain doubts concerning the Manichees, or whether his mind was ever entirely free from them. At any rate—as one might expect—the *Confessions'* account dwells on their deficiencies, not least the contradictoriness and inadequacy of their supposedly 'scientific' teaching which Augustine found was largely contradicted by the 'scientists'—the astrologers and philosophers—of his day (5.3.3–5.8) and of their interpretation of Scripture (5.11.21). Furthermore, he became increasingly aware that the Manichees' admirable asceticism and morality was in fact more a matter of theory than of practice for

---

[18] Brown (1972), 110.
[19] Brown (1972), 107 cites Ambrosiaster *Commentarius in II epistulam ad Timotheum*. 3.6 which refers to it as a 'new and unexpected monstrous birth from Persia'.

many individuals (*On the Morals of the Manichees* 19.67–70). And their dualism, which had at first offered a very attractive solution to the problem which had, above all others, preoccupied Augustine—the problem of evil—in turn raised further problems concerning the sovereignty of a God who could be affected by the forces of evil (*conf.* 7.2.3–3.4).

The Manichees Augustine questioned could not provide satisfactory answers to these problems but urged him to await the arrival of the well-known Manichee, Faustus,[20] in Carthage. He came in about 382 (Augustine's twenty-ninth year—5.3.3) but although Augustine obviously warmed to him personally and very much admired his rhetoric, he found that his legendary learning left much to be desired and that his knowledge of philosophy and the liberal arts, so essential in any attempt to justify the Manichaean system, was of a very elementary kind and fell far behind his winning eloquence (*conf.* 5.6.11). This encounter seems to have dealt the final blow to Augustine's diminishing confidence in the Manichaean system and he lost hope of ever reconciling himself to it.

The closing chapter of Book 5 of the *Confessions* is revealing here, not so much of Augustine's state at the time as of his retrospective appreciation of what was happening and what was about to happen. In it he seems to be setting the stage for the next, crucial, step in his search for wisdom—his encounter with Neoplatonism. Lacking, he tells us, a conception of spiritual substance (which is what the Neoplatonists could uniquely provide) he could not, at this stage, decisively prove the Manichees wrong. He was still troubled by anthropomorphic images of God, the question of evil and exegetical questions in relation to Scripture which left him sitting on the fence concerning Christianity (*conf.* 7.3.4–9.13). However, 'in regard to the physical world and all the natural order accessible to the bodily senses', he tells us, 'consideration and comparison more and more convinced me that numerous philosophers held opinions much more probable than theirs [the Manichees]' (5.14.24).

SCEPTICISM

Leaving the Manichees, Augustine describes himself as a sceptic, one who doubted everything.[21] The 'other philosophers' he refers to presumably

---

[20] Faustus of Mileu, against whom Augustine later wrote the long *Contra Faustum*, on exegetical questions.

[21] His first work was written against them: *Acad.* (AD 386). Cf. *ciu.* 11.26; *trin.* 15.12.21; *vera rel.* 73; *lib. arb.* 2.7; *sol.* 2.1. On Augustine and scepticism: *BA* 13, 94–100; Rist (1994), 41–91; Kirwan (1989), 15–34. His sources were probably Cicero *Academica* and Varro *Liber de Philosophia*. Rist (1994), 42 comments: 'Unlike almost every other thinker of late antiquity, Augustine took radical scepticism seriously and was driven by his own experiences to attempt to find answers to it.'

included those he would have encountered in the course of his traditonal classical education, in the work of Cicero,[22] Varro and other scholarly manuals of the time,[23] and which he later lists, or at least mentions, in his survey of ancient philosophy in *City of God* Book 8: the Pre-Socratics, Socrates, the Platonists, the Stoics,[24] the Epicureans (though he is highly critical of them), the Academics (or sceptics, whom he was later to refute), the Peripatetics, and Aristotle (whose *Ten Categories*[25] he read with some admiration at the age of twenty). But the philosophers, he observes, 'were without Christ's saving name ... I therefore decided for the time being to be a catechumen in the Catholic Church, which the precedent of my parents recommended to me, until some clear light should come by which I could direct my course' (*conf.* 5.14.24).

The 'clear light' soon appeared to clarify matters in two decisive encounters: with Ambrose and with the Neoplatonists. Augustine moved from Rome to Milan, the Imperial capital, in 386, to take up the municipal chair of rhetoric, a prestigious job which had been secured through the influence of Manichaean friends (5.13.23) and which he probably rightly regarded as the next rung on the ladder to a provincial governorship or even senatorial rank.[26]

NEOPLATONISM

'And so I came to Milan to Ambrose the bishop.'[27] The words are ominous, but the *Confessions* retain a studied distance in describing the somewhat conventional, rather formal and guarded meeting of the young rhetor, enthusiastic for philosophy, and the older, mature bishop. Ambrose received Augustine kindly, Augustine warmed to him, and was charmed by his rhetorical skills. The substance of what he said was less inspiring, but even so it far surpassed what Faustus had to say and, in retrospect, Augustine realized that Ambrose's preaching, the 'sound doctrine of salvation', was 'drawing him closer' (*conf.* 5.13.23).

---

[22] Testard (1968).

[23] *BA* 13, 85–112; Solignac (1958), 113–48 who mentions Favonius Eulogius *De somno Scipionis*; Varro *De Principiis numerorum* and *De Arithmetica*; Nichomachus of Gerasa *Introductio Arithmetica*.

[24] See Verbeke (1958), 67–89 who concludes that Augustine did not have a profound knowledge of Stoicism but that the ideas he adopts or refutes, especially concerning wisdom, virtue, reason, the soul, seminal reasons, evil ... belonged to a common heritage possessed by all cultured men of his time, and was usually based on ancient Stoicism. Cf. Spanneut (1973); Baguette (1968) who suggests that on leaving the Manichees Augustine passed through a period influenced by Stoic thought.

[25] Read in Victorinus' translation. *conf.* 4.16.28. See *BA* 13, 87.

[26] Lepelley (1987).

[27] See Madec (1974); McLynn (1994); Williams (1995); Ramsay (1997).

Neoplatonism was in the Milanese air. Ambrose, a Christian aristocrat and former governor, who became Bishop of Milan rather suddenly, in 373 at the age of 34, was, unlike Augustine, familiar with Greek culture and thought. His allegorical or spiritual exegesis of Scripture enabled Augustine to resolve some the exegetical problems which still troubled him (*conf.* 5.14.24). It has also been suggested[28] that, although he was no great philosopher, Ambrose's use of Plotinus,[29] the main representative of Neoplatonic philosophy, in his sermons prepared Augustine's mind for his subsequent encounter with the 'books of the Platonists', though Augustine nowhere suggests this. In fact, Ambrose's attitude to philosophy contrasts sharply with Augustine's. He does indeed borrow freely from Plato, Cicero, Philo, and Plotinus but he is also highly critical of them, invariably preferring the authority of Scripture which he believed was anterior to them and the source of their teaching. As Madec observes[30] he seems to use the language and ideas of the philosophers more as literary ornamentation than as substantial arguments.

There were other men in Milan who were also reading the Neoplatonists in a Christian context,[31] among them the learned priest Simplicianus, Ambrose's mentor, and later successor, at Milan, who was to be so influential in Augustine's conversion and in clarifying his perception of Neoplatonism, and who no doubt mediated the influence of his close friend from Rome, Victorinus, the famous African rhetor and, later, convert (*Conf.* 8), who was responsible for the translation of numerous Neoplatonic works.[32] There was also the Christian layman Manlius Theodorus, a powerful figure who held a number of high-ranking posts and took a mid-

---

[28] E.g. by Courcelle (1968), 136, 311–82, who demonstrates that Ambrose paraphrases entire pages of the Enneads in his sermons *De Isaac vel anima* and *De bono mortis*. He cites further bibliography to support his case in Courcelle (1963b), 191, notes 150–4. This is contested by Theiler (1953) and Mohrmann (1951). See *BA* 13, 146–9. Ambrose also made use of Philo and Basil of Caesarea.

[29] Madec (1974), 61–71 on the difficulty of ascertaining what Ambrose actually knew of Plotinus and how he obtained this knowledge.   [30] Madec (1974), 175.

[31] With these individuals, and presumably others (perhaps pagans) whose names have not come down to us, scholars have often referred to a 'Neoplatonic circle' at Milan (*BA* 14, 529). However, the circle, as Madec (1994), 38 suggests, only really appears insofar as Augustine forms its centre and relates to the various individuals, with their very different understandings of Neoplatonism.

[32] Though the only evidence we have for his translating the *platonicorum libri* is *conf.* 8.2.3—O'Donnell (1992) III, 13–15 who also notes that there is practically no evidence that Augustine read anything by Victorinus. Before his conversion Victorinus wrote on physics, logics and rhetoric. As a Christian he wrote numerous Neoplatonically inspired works on Christian theology, especially on the Trinity, and commentaries on Paul's epistles. Augustine does, however, include him in the list of those Latin Christian authors (Cyprian, Lactantius, Optatus of Milev and Hilary of Poitiers) who have used pagan philosophy—or spoiled the Egyptians of their treasure—in *doctr. chr.* 2.40.61.

career retreat to write on philosophy. In a work dedicated to him, Augustine describes him as a fervent admirer of Plotinus (*beata u.* 1.4).[33] As with his reading of Cicero's *Hortensius*, Augustine's reading of a text (or texts) was to mark a decisive turning point. But his account of it is decidedly obscure: 'Through a man puffed up with monstrous pride (perhaps Manlius Theodorus, who later lost enthusiasm for Christianity[34]), you brought under my eye some books of the Platonists, translated from Greek into Latin' (*conf.* 7.9.13).

Augustine's tantalizing vagueness has led, as one might expect, to intense scholarly activity to determine just what it was he did read: was it simply Plotinus, or just Porphyry, or Plotinus and Porphyry, or Plotinus first and then Porphyry? The debate is still very much alive, with different methods and arguments continually being proposed.[35] What we can conclude, with some degree of certainty, is that Augustine most probably read some Plotinus (AD 204–270), an Egyptian Greek who taught in Rome, and who is best known for his *Enneads*, and maybe some Porphyry (AD 232–?300), Plotinus' disciple and editor, who was a vehement critic of Christianity (*ciu.* 19.22) and author of *Against the Christians*.[36] To describe them as 'Neoplatonists', however, is a nineteenth-century anachronism. They regarded themselves as followers and interpreters of Plato, and it is in this context that Augustine presents them in *City of God* Book 8: 'The best known philosophers of more modern times who have chosen to follow Plato have refused to be spoken of as Peripatetics or Academics, but call themselves Platonists. The best known of them are Plotinus, Iamblichus (whom Augustine almost certainly had not read) and Porphyry . . .' (8.12).[37] Augustine describes Plotinus as 'Plato revived' (*Acad.* 3.18.41). But to speak of Christian Platonism or Christian Neoplatonism, or indeed, Neoplatonism, in Augustine's time is in reality to speak of something which did not exist. Different people interpreted, used, appropriated or rejected ideas from the Platonists and their 'recent interpreters' in different ways, in relation to the Christian faith. And the Platonists, in their turn, criticized and evaluated Christianity.

---

[33] Courcelle (1943), 122 ff.

[34] Courcelle (1968). Though there have been other suggestions—O'Donnell (1992) II, 419.

[35] The literature is vast. For a summary bibliography see Harrison (1992), 8, n. 32; O'Donnell (1992) II, 421–4; Madec (1996), 38, an excellent book on Augustine and philosophy with an extensive bibliography.

[36] Very few of Porphyry's works survive and most of what does is fragmentary. For a list see Hadot (1968) I, 456, n. 1; Wallis (1972), 98–9.

[37] It might at first seem odd, given their crucial importance for Augustine's thought, that they appear here almost as an afterthought. We must remember that in *City of God* Augustine is writing for pagans, in the traditional way, by appealing to their classics—in other words to Plato, not some new-fangled Plotinus!

Whatever the precise identity of the works, they had a profound effect. He writes to his patron and friend, Romanianus, that 'a few drops of their precious essence . . . stirred up an incredible conflagration—incredible, Romanianus, incredible, and perhaps beyond even what you would believe of me—what more shall I say?—beyond even what I would believe of myself' (*Acad.* 2.25).

The revolutionary thing about the Neoplatonists was that they taught that true reality was spiritual. This insight alone enabled Augustine to break free from the philosophical materialism which characterized most thinkers of his day[38]—the vast masses under which he had suffocated as a Manichee—into the 'pure and simple breeze' of the truth of Christianity (*conf.* 5.11.21). It freed him from difficult physical conceptions of God which tied Him down to space, measurement and mutability (5.10.19; 7.1.1–2) and enabled Augustine to conceive of Him as true 'Being' (7.10.16),[39] spiritual, incorporeal, and immutable. It likewise liberated him from the unacceptable Manichaean notion, to which he had hitherto found no alternative, that evil is an independent physical entity, inherent in matter, which could somehow impinge upon the good (*conf.* 7.3.4–5.7). Rather, he was able to follow Plotinus in teaching the initiative of the good in giving form to matter, and evil as a declining from this order whilst being comprehended by it—a sort of *privatio boni* (or privation of the good) (*conf.* 7.12.18)[40] which could be attributed, in man, to the free will.

The 'books of the Platonists' also allowed Augustine to 'return into' (*conf.* 7.10.16, cf. *Ennead* 5, 1) himself, to appreciate himself as a spiritual being; to find God, true Being, as the foundation of himself, within, and to realize that God transcends him (7.10.16): 'interior intimo meo et superior summo meo'(3.6.11). The 'ascent' Augustine describes in Book 7 (17.23) forshadows a number of other, similar, ascents.[41] Such passages have prompted some scholars[42] to speak of Augustine's 'spirituality' or 'mysticism', and to evaluate how much this owes to Neoplatonism, for they are undeniably Neoplatonic in form (introversion, ascent from creation, to the soul, to the mind, and above the mind to God[43]), though his emphasis on divine initiative and help (see the opening lines of *conf.*

---

[38] Fortin (1959); Holte (1962), 98; Brown (1967), 84.

[39] Rist (1994), 257–8 who notes that in Neoplatonism God is 'being itself' or 'beyond being'. Augustine does not use the latter, probably because of difficulties in translation; Madec (1994), 71–89.

[40] An idea derived from the Neoplatonists—*BA* 13, 687–8—and then corrected by Augustine. Kirwan (1989), 60–81.

[41] Before conversion 7.17.23 and after 9.10.23–25; 10.1.1–27.38.

[42] E.g. Louth (1981), 132–58.

[43] *Ennead* I.6; I.8; 5.1. Porphyry *De regressu animae.* Madec (1994), 151–62 for sources of idea of conversion, interiority and intentionality, esp. Porphyry's *Zétémata* in *De Immortalitate Animae*.

7.10.16), and the later emphasis on the need for a mediator,[44] give them a definite Christian colouring.

We will examine Augustine's actual conversion in Chapter 3. Here we might note that the general question of Augustine's debt to Neoplatonism and just how far his conversion was indeed one to Christianity, and not to some sort of Neoplatonically inspired philosophy, has exercised scholars for the past hundred years.[45] The fact that Augustine describes his journey towards conversion as inspired by Cicero's *Exhortation to Philosophy* and as then progressing through various philosophical schools—the Manichees, Academics, and Platonists—to arrive finally at Christianity, both in his early works and later, in the *Confessions*, has done much to mislead.

THE TRUE PHILOSOPHY

The very spiritual, world-denying emphasis of Augustine's earliest works, which are written in the form of philosophical dialogues and have philosophical themes—*Against the Academics, On the Happy Life, On Order, Soliloquies*—do indeed reveal Augustine's excitement and enthusiasm for the 'books of the Platonists' he had just read. Their predominant concerns—refuting Manichaean materialism; the search for happiness; the attainment of truth or wisdom; the nature of the soul and its superiority; a low estimate of the senses of the body and sense perception; introversion and ascent from the corporeal to the incorporeal by exercise in the rational disciplines of the liberal arts[46]—might indeed suggest that Augustine's adoption of Christianity was in fact simply another stage in his conversion to a philosophy based on his enthusiasm for the Platonists and his rejection of Manichaeism. At the beginning of *On the Happy Life* he describes Cassiciacum as the 'haven of Philosophy'—the end of a long and tempestuous journey across the tumultuous sea of the philosophical schools.

In some senses, of course, this is true. What we find in the earliest works is, indeed, a 'Christian philosophy'—and they are none the worse for that. But they are, scholars would now generally agree, distinctively Christian.[47] And this emphasis comes to the fore as Augustine's theological reflection, experience, and practice of the Christian life develop; as his attack on Manichaeism is stepped up, and his burning enthusiasm for Neoplatonism

---

[44] As O'Donnell points out in reference to 7.17.23, not so much because the Neoplatonic ascents had failed, rather that they did work, but were not enough—they were only momentary and transient.

[45] Again, the literature is immense. For a near exhaustive review, Madec (1994), 51–69.

[46] Harrison (1992), 12–31.   [47] Henry (1934), 96; Marrou (1949), 176.

begins to die down and be modified in the light of these developments. At Cassiciacum, and increasingly, in the works written soon afterwards—at Rome (where he was forced to spend most of 387 because of a blockade of the Mediterranean[48]) and then in his home town of Thagaste (388–391, where he went, following his mother Monnica's death, to take up the family property[49])—the reader finds a growing preoccupation with distinctively Christian concerns: the relation between faith and reason (or philosophy); the authority of the Church; the temporal revelation of God in Scripture, creation, divine providence, salvation history, and the incarnation; Christology; interpretation of Scripture.

In considering the relation between Christianity and philosophy in Augustine's conversion—and his later thought—we perhaps also need to remind ourselves, if it has not already become clear, that philosophy was an integral and essential part of Augustine's cultural milieu and of his own intellectual mindset.[50] It was unthinkingly adopted as the means to examine, discuss, and evaluate truth. This was as true of Christianity, at least from the second century onwards, as it was of pagan society in general. There were, of course, those Christian thinkers who, on reflection, rejected its use in expounding Christianity (such as Tatian, Irenaeus, and Augustine's African predeccesor, Tertullian[51]); others, the majority, were more constructive, if critical and eclectic, in their use of it; whilst a further minority embraced it with open arms (e.g. Minucius Felix). And the same is true, vice versa, of pagan thinkers.

Augustine's search for wisdom, through the various philosophical schools, to eventually arrive at the truth of Christianity, was nothing new. One only has to think of the second-century Apologists, and in particular of Justin Martyr,[52] to find very similar conversion stories. It was natural for Christians to describe Christianity as the 'true philosophy' or 'true wisdom', the place where the highest wisdom is to be found. (Clement of Alexandria is a good example of this, and in fact parallels Augustine in many respects, though Augustine cannot be supposed to have known his work.) In order to do this, however, Christians had to justify and defend their claims. The Apologists went about it in various ways. Justin claimed that all men, including the philosophers, possessed the natural gift of reason, or 'seeds' of the Logos, but that truth itself is only finally and fully revealed in Christ, the Logos incarnate. Or they argued that all truth is

---

[48] *qu. an; lib. arb.* I; began *mor.*   [49] *Gn. adu. Man.*; begins *diu. qu.; mag; vera rel.*

[50] Vogel (1985), 1–62 for an excellent discussion of this question.

[51] Though this is not to say that Tertullian, especially, lacked a sound knowledge of philosophy but rather that he was wary of popular syncretism and of the way philosophy was used by the heretics—see Fredouille (1972), 239 f.

[52] *Dialogue with Trypho the Jew.* Cf. Hilary *De Trinitate* 1–14; *BA* 13, 40–41 for pagan references.

found in Christianity, in the prophets of the Old Testament, from whom the philosophers borrowed their ideas—though this involved them in rather complicated calculations to give chronological priority to the Old Testament.[53] Although he thinks the latter improbable (*ciu.* 8.11), Augustine stands in much the same line of thought in discussing the relation between classical, pagan philosophy and Christian thought: he freely admits that wisdom is found in the philosophers but is convinced that it is only found in its fullness in Christianity.

How does Augustine set about defending this claim? It is clear from the early works that he was at first very optimistic about being able to reconcile Platonism and Christianity—or reason and authority, as he puts it (*Acad.* 3.7.37–19.42). He felt confident that if Plato were to come to life again, he would become a Christian, with the change of a few words or phrases (*uera rel.* 4.7). The two systems were fundamentally the same (*uera rel.* 5.8), not least because what the Platonists know (like Justin's seeds of the Logos) they know through God's illumination (*ciu.* 8.7).[54] Wherever truth is found it has the same source, therefore using philosophy is like claiming back the truth for its rightful owner—the Israelites spoiling the Egyptians of their treasure (*conf.* 7.9.15).[55]

Although he is later much less optimistic about reconciling Platonism and Christianity and criticizes himself for his earlier, rather over-enthusiastic comments (*retr.* I.1.12), he is still generous in his praise of the Platonists and is convinced that they, of all the philosophers, come closest to the truth—in other words, Christianity. We have already seen just how attractive Augustine found the emphasis on spiritual reality and ascent in the 'books of the Platonists'. In particular, he is convinced that Plato had discovered the threefold nature of philosophy—natural, logical, and moral—and had related this to God, the 'cause of physical existence, the ground of rational thought, and the pattern of life' (*ciu.* 8.4; 11.25. *vera rel.* 3.3).[56] In *City of God*, Book 8, he observes:

So these philosophers have come to the above [he is summarizing what he has just discussed] conclusions about the true and most high God, namely that he is the author of created things, the light by which things become known, and the good for which things are done, and that we derive from Him the origin of our substance, the truth of our instruction and the happiness of our life, whether these

[53] Chadwick (1966), 1–30; Holte (1958).

[54] O'Daly (1987), 206–7 on illumination as natural to the mind.

[55] In reference to the 'books of the Platonists' he states 'And I had come to you from the Gentiles and fixed my attention on the gold which you willed your people to take from Egypt, since the gold was yours, wherever it was'. Cf. *doctr. chr.* This idea had a long tradition—Pépin (1955), 105–22; Holte (1962), 126.

[56] Hadot (1979), 272–9; Rist (1994), 257—Augustine probably got this, historically false, notion from Varro.

philosophers are more appropriately termed Platonists or else attach some other name to their school . . . these we set above any others and avow that they are closer to us. (8.9)

In *Epistle* 118 he likewise praises the Platonists in these three respects: for placing God *above* the soul or mind (rather than finding the Supreme God in the mind, as the Stoics do); for teaching creation by uncreated Wisdom (rather than the Stoic materialist view); for asserting that knowledge is beyond the senses (against the Epicureans) and is unchangeable and eternal, perceived only by the understanding. He is also convinced that the Platonists have knowledge of the Word of John's Prologue (*conf.* 7.9.13).

In evaluating the relation between the philosophers' insight into truth and the truth of Christianity, Augustine often quotes Romans 1: 19–23,[57] to illustrate the Platonists' knowledge of God, which God has revealed to them through creation (illumination): 'For what can be known about God is plain to them; because God has shown it to them. Ever since the creation of the world, his invisible nature, namely, his eternal power and deity, has been clearly perceived in the things that have been made.' But the limitations of the philosophers, and their culpability, are also made clear by this passage: although they thereby knew God, they 'did not honour him as God, or give thanks to him as God, but became futile in their thinking, and their senseless minds were darkened. Claiming to be wise they became fools and exchanged the glory of the immortal God for images resembling mortal man or birds or animals or reptiles.' The reason they did this, Augustine adds, is their pride in failing to acknowledge God as Creator, and most especially, the creator Word in the incarnate Word, and to worship Him as God.

Augustine does not doubt that the philosophers know the 'truth and the life', but they do not know the 'way' to it (John 14: 6) (*s.* 141.1), for that way is Christ. They see the goal and the homeland (*conf.* 7.21.27) but are not humble enough to follow there, for there is only one way, the way of Christ's cross (*Io. eu. tr.* 28.5)—a plank to which the believer must cling in the sea of this world in order to reach the distant shore (*Io. eu. tr.* 2.4; *en. Ps.* 118.xxvi.9; *trin.* 4.15.20). In other words, the philosophers have philosophized without a mediator, and will therefore never reach the Truth or Wisdom which is their goal (*trin.* 13.1.24). In the *Confessions* Augustine sees it as providential that he encountered the books of the Platonists *before* the Scriptures, so that he could appreciate the difference between 'presumption' and 'confession'; between 'those who see what the goal is but not how to get there and those who see the way which leads to the home of

---

[57] E.g. *Io. eu. tr.* 2.4. Madec (1962).

bliss, not merely as an end to be perceived but as a realm to live in' (*conf.* 7.20.26).

The contrast is essentially one between pride and humility; reliance upon reason, and dependence upon faith [authority]. In *City of God* Augustine turns to Porphyry to illustrate this opposition: although Porphyry acknowledged that the *patrikos nous*—the mind or intellect of the father, which knows the father's will—was the only cure for ignorance (rather than theurgy, which we will examine later), he refused to identify this with Christ (*ciu.* 10.28). Likewise, whilst admitting God's grace he lacked the humility to identify it with the Son, whom he despised, because of his virgin birth, his possession of a body and his death on the cross (*ciu.* 10.29)[58]—all things which were deeply inimical to late antique philosophy. Instead, his pride made him a follower of Plato.

The authority of the Platonic philosophers is also at stake here. Even though they come closer than all other philosophers (Augustine particularly has in mind the Stoics and Epicureans) to grasping wisdom, they lack the authority to lead other philosophers to it. *Epistle* 118 is a key text here: following the appearence of Christianity Augustine notes that the philosophical sects obviously feel they cannot measure up to Catholic authority and therefore dare not teach or gather followers without taking the guise of Christianity.[59] Meanwhile,

The Platonists, at the time when the errors of false philosophers were raging around them, had no divine person in whose name they could demand faith . . . they chose to hide their true belief as something to be sought out rather than exposed to dishonour; when at length the Name of Christ became well known, to the wonder and consternation of earthly powers, they began to show themselves and to publish and expound Plato's doctrines. That was when the school of Plotinus flourished at Rome, and had as disciples many extremely shrewd and clever men. But some of them were led astray by an attraction for the practices of magic while others learned that the Lord Jesus Christ is the embodiment of absolute Truth and unchangeable Wisdom, and they came over to his service. (p. 293)

Augustine is obviously convinced that the only true philosophy is found in Christianity and that all other philosophies, in so far as they have attained the truth, are fulfilled in Christianity. What is necessary is that the philosophers themselves realize this, and cease to proudly rely on their own reason, but rather humbly confess faith in Christ and acknowledge the authority of his teaching.[60]

---

[58] Augustine refers to Porphyry's *De Regressu Animae* in this respect.

[59] *ep.* 118 p. 292 and p. 281 on Stoics and Epicureans who dare not oppose the faith except by taking the name of Christian.

[60] Augustine often uses the expression *cedat auctoritatis*, e.g. *ciu.* 10.31.

THE TRUE RELIGION

In the above quotation Augustine refers to those of the school of Plotinus who were 'led astray by the practices of magic'. The particular person he probably has in mind is Porphyry, and the practice is doubtless that of theurgy—an illegal practice in Augustine's day, (though here, as elsewhere in *City of God*, Augustine is arguing with the pagan past). Plotinus himself may not have been acquainted with the literature relating to theurgy (in particular the *Chaldean Oracles*) and certainly does not use the expression *theourgia*. He expresses no interest in magic and did not think it had any role to play in the moral and intellectual purification of the soul in its ascent towards the One.

Porphyry, his pupil, editor, and disciple, is, however, rather more ambiguous. *Theourgia* was a technical term, coined by a certain Julian, who lived in the time of Marcus Aurelius, who seems to have intended an opposition between *theologia*, or mere talk about God, in contrast to 'divine work' or *theourgia*. Porphyry is familiar with the principles of its practice, which were based on the widely accepted assumption that the parts of the world are all related in such a way that they mirror one another, that material things were types of an archetype, and that use of material objects in a particular way might enable the theurgist to make contact with a divine force.

In his *Letter to Anebo*,[61] in true polemic style, he is fiercely critical of the claims of theurgy. But his attitude seems to have softened. Dodds refers to his 'incurable weakness for oracles' and supposes that after Plotinus's death his reading of the long-neglected *Chaldean Oracles* modified his views.[62] Indeed he wrote a commentary on them[63] and Augustine is one of our main witnesses for his 'continual mention of them' in his *On the Return of the Soul*.[64] In *City of God* he notes Porphyry's wavering hesitation and embarrassment in propounding these ideas: at times he warns that they are delusive and dangerous, at others he teaches that, for those who do not belong to the philosophic élite (and who cannot therefore reach the truth in the way prescribed by Plotinus) it can purify the spiritual (though not the intellectual) part of the soul,[65] making it capable of seeing the gods, but not of being made immortal and eternal (*ciu.* 10.9.26–27).

Porphyry's hesitation was not shared by the other well-known Neoplatonist, Iamblichus (*c.* 250–*c.* 330) who positively affirmed, defended, and

---

[61] Now lost. Eusebius refers to it in his *Praeparatio Euangelica* 3.4; 5.8–10. It is also referred to in Iamblichus' reply, *De Mysteriis* (and can be largely reconstructed from it).

[62] Dodds (1951), 287.   [63] Marinus *uita Procli* 26.

[64] Probably translated by Victorinus. Augustine knew it and refers to it, here at *ciu.* 10.32.

[65] Porphyry took this distinction between spiritual and intellectual from Plotinus *Enn.* I.1 and 5.3.9. It is developed further by Augustine in *Gn. litt.* 11.17.34 f.

cultivated the practice of theurgy. But, though acquainted with his name, Augustine did not know his work. His refutation of theurgy, which we will examine later in this chapter, is therefore reserved for Porphyry. Here we might simply observe that, in contrast to his positive attitude to much of pagan philosophy, and in particular to Platonism, Augustine's attitude to pagan religious practice is unreservedly negative.

Having placed Augustine, as it were, in relation to the philosophical thought of this time, we are now, I think, in a position to examine the distinctively Christian understanding of wisdom which determined his judgements of it. In order to do this we need to ask why Augustine became much less optimistic about the unaided power of human reason to reach the truth and came, increasingly, to emphasize the importance of humility, in contrast to pride, and of faith and authority, in contrast to reason.

There are, in fact, a number of rather different answers to this question.

FAITH AND REASON

First of all, when Augustine returned to Africa from Italy, following his conversion, he also returned to his past life. Whereas Cassiciacum had been a retreat, in Thagaste, his home town, he was still remembered as an ardent, positively crusading, Manichee. How was it, people would ask, that he was now a zealous Christian? Where was his concubine? What about his career as a rhetor? Augustine found himself in the position of attempting to reconvert friends he had persuaded to become Manichees, and to follow him in embracing Christianity. An emphasis upon faith and the authority of the Church as against Manichaean claims to reason (and implicitly, one must suppose, those of the philosopher) was one of the arguments he used.[66]

An emphasis on faith, hope, and love, and on the role of authority in relation to reason is not absent from Augustine's earliest works.[67] At Thagaste the latter is specifically discussed in *On True Religion* (24.45–38.71), a startlingly mature work for such an early date, which Augustine wrote to reconvert his patron, Romanianus. But it is in the slightly later *On the Usefulness of Belief* (AD 392) written soon after Augustine's ordination (AD 391) and directed specifically against the Manichees, that the importance of faith and authority is given its fullest treatment.

---

[66] He also interpreted Genesis allegorically (*Gn. adu. Man.*) against the Manichees' rational, literal interpretation; affirmed the goodness of creation against Manichaean theories of evil (*nat. b.*; *vera rel.*); corrected Manichaean exegesis, especially of the Old Testament (*c. Faust.*; *util. cred.*); attacked the Manichees claim to superior morality (*mor.*).

[67] E.g. *ord.* 2.26; *beata u.* 5.35; *Acad.* 3.20.43; *sol.* I.12.

He argues on a general level: faith is essential, he observes, if human beings are to relate to one another: we cannot see the thoughts of another person, but we must believe in his goodwill and friendship (*util. cred.* 10; 24. Cf. *Ep.* 2.1; *Solil.* 1.9). It is the basis on which society works. For example, we must believe our parents when they tell us that they are our parents; we must have faith in a doctor when he prescribes medicine or in the captain of a ship when we undertake a voyage (*util. cred.* 26). Most importantly, all men would agree that we cannot begin to seek the truth without first relying on a worthy authority which can tell us what the truth is—indeed, that it exists (28–9), since some past events cannot otherwise be known (25). Augustine identifies this authority with the Catholic Church, its Scriptures, doctrines, teaching, and tradition. (It is these which the Platonists lack and will therefore never have access to the truth.) Christ's miracles, he observes, attracted a following which would then pass on the tradition (32); his incarnation and the history and growth of the Church witness to God's providence and command man's faith, hope, and love (34). The Church's authority is further confirmed 'on the grounds of a report confirmed by its ubiquity, by its antiquity and by the general consent of mankind' (31). These he sets in opposition to the Manichees' claim to possess the truth through reason.[68]

It is worth noting, however, that even at this stage Augustine can entertain the possibility that some men might be able to attain the truth through reason, without faith, but advises that they should be held back and 'forced for a little . . . while to walk on a way which is safe for others', so as not to lead the less able astray (*util. cred.* 24).

TEACHING THE UNINSTRUCTED

There were, however, perhaps more pressing reasons than a desire to distance himself from the Manichees which determined Augustine's emphasis on the role of authority and faith. His return to Thagaste and his subsequent ordination as priest at Hippo, was, as Bonner makes clear,[69] a movement away from the intellectual stimulus and company which Italy had provided, where knowledge of philosophy and the liberal arts could be taken for granted. It was, rather, an encounter with the simple, uneducated faithful who made up the majority of the Christian Church and who had little or no knowledge of classical culture. Their grasp of wisdom, the truth of Christianity, was founded directly upon their faith, which was mediated by the authority of the Church.

---

[68] Cf. the later famous definition of belief in *praed. sanct.* 2.5 as 'thinking about something with assent'. Rist (1994), 61–2.   [69] Bonner (1987a), IV, 12.

Peter Brown has commented upon the 'authoritarian cast' of African Christianity.[70] Augustine suggests that it was in reacting against the demand for obedience to authority without rational questioning that he was thrown into the hands of the Manichees: 'For what else forced me . . . to follow these men and diligently to listen to them, save that they said we were terrified by superstition and that faith was demanded of us before reason' (*util. cred.* 2).[71] His mother, Monnica, had ensured that Augustine was never totally unaware of, or completely distanced from, this aspect of the faith. Even in the early works Augustine is aware of the sharp contrast between his own, newly acquired, philosophically inspired faith, and the simple, unquestioning devotion of his mother. He is deeply appreciative of her insights into the faith (*beata u.* 10; 16; 27; *ord.* 2.1), but finds them, at first, very difficult to reconcile with her lack of education. A passage in one of Augustine's first works, written at Cassiciacum, where Monnica was present, obviously represents the sort of reflection such a contrast inspired. In *On Order* (2.26), he distinguishes a twofold path: reason and authority. Reason, he observes, teaches the first principle of things, authority teaches that the first principle is God, the Trinity; reason is first in the order of reality, authority is first in operation; reason is the way to truth, authority is the cradle of truth; reason is first in theory, authority is first in reality. He concludes that reason is the way for the few; authority is the way for the many (*ord.* 2.30).[72] Indeed, authority provides a shortcut through what is often perplexing and obscure, and eliminates the hard work involved in attaining the truth by rational means (*ord.* 2.7. Cf. *qu. an.* 12; *mus.* 6.1.1; 17.59). The Church's rites are part of this authority: 'In these mysteries the life of a good man is purified with the utmost ease, not by the circumlocution of disputation but by the authority of the mysteries' (*ord.* 2.19.27).

A little later on, concluding the long and involved work on metrical composition, *On Music*, Augustine seems to be more than aware of the secondary, and ultimately superfluous nature of such tedious academic work: 'If any read this talk of ours', he comments, 'they must know that these things have been written by persons much weaker than those who having followed the authority of the two Testaments, by believing, hoping and loving, venerate and worship the consubstantial and unchangeable Trinity . . . For they are purified, not by flashing human reason, but by the effective and burning fire of charity' (*mus.* 6.17.59. Cf. *Acad.* 3.19.42; *qu. an.* 7.12).

And yet, as one might expect, Augustine cannot bring himself wholly to relinquish reason. Despite the concluding comments, *De musica* is in fact

---

[70] Brown (1967), 42–3.   [71] O'Connell (1968), 223.

[72] Which leads some to suggest the influence of Porphyry's *De regressu animae*—O'Meara (1954), 143–55.

one of a series of works he had undertaken on the Liberal Arts[73] at the time of his baptism in 387. These were the disciplines—grammar, dialectics, rhetoric, number, geometry—of classical education and were generally studied as preliminary training for philosophy. They trained and exercised the mind, leading it from corporeal to incorporeal—material to immaterial, inferior to superior—things, and eventually enabled it to grasp truth.[74] Augustine's enthusiasm for them is evident throughout the early works[75] and is ironically most obvious in *On Order*, the other work we referred to above on faith and reason. Here he describes an ascent through the disciplines and concludes that if a man rightly uses the 'shadows and vestiges' of reason in sensible reality, and looks to their unity, by analysing and synthesizing them, then, 'without being rash, he can search after things divine—not merely as truths to be believed, but also as matters to be contemplated, understood and retained' (*ord.* 44).

Augustine is later rather guarded and dismissive of the projected series of books,[76] indeed, as we have seen he expresses reservations about their usefulness even in the early works. But their presence, Augustine's reaction against the *superstitio* of the African Church, and his optimism about the possibility of attaining truth in this life, should still be noted as a counterweight to his early teaching on the usefulness of faith. He was still not prepared to admit that reason could not attain the truth unaided[77]—this observation had to wait until he had worked out a doctrine of the fall—and yet he is increasingly aware of the superiority and necessity of faith, not least for those who are blinded by their sins (*Acad.* 3.42; *uera rel.* 73). It was to be the shared, Neoplatonically inspired, ascent with his mother, which he describes in *Confessions* 9 (10.23–25) which truly vindicated the pre-eminence and sufficiency of faith.[78]

Such reflections are then, to some extent, autobiographical—and they do not disappear from Augustine's work. He was sensitive to the distance which education and culture, or the lack of it, could impose between Christians, and how different people needed to be met at their different levels, if they were not to be excluded from, or at least, put off, the Christian faith. The most obvious example of this is his attitude to Scripture, which we will investigate in the next chapter. But it is also evident, in practice, in his sermons (which vary in level according to where, and to whom, they were

---

[73] *Retr.* 1.6. *BA* 12.565; Solignac (1958), 120; I. Hadot (1984); Marrou (1949) chapters 3 and 4. In fact, he only completed *mus.* and *dial.*

[74] Solignac (1958), 120–2 for sources in Varro; Svoboda (1933), 29–34 for sources in Varro, Cicero, Stoics and Poseidonius.

[75] E.g. his use of geometry in *qu. an.*; grammar in *mag.*; metre in *mus.* Marrou (1949), 229–327.   [76] *retr.* 1,6; *ep.* 101.2; *serm.* 70.2; 133.4; *ciu.* 22.5.

[77] That some can reach vision in this life, see *util. cred.* 25.

[78] An insight I owe to a former student in Durham, Craig James.

preached) and catechetical works—especially *On Teaching the Uninstructed*, where he attempts to give practical advice concerning the teaching of the faithful, and the different strategies to be adopted with, for example, the learned nobleman, trained in the liberal arts, the moderately learned rhetor or the illiterate farmer from Carthage (*cat. rud.* 8.12–9.13).

He thus places some significant question marks against his acceptance of traditional, philosophically based, classical culture and points to the unease and ambiguity he felt in relating it to the Christian faith. This wider issue is something Peter Brown thinks was particularly raised when Christian bishops, who were unquestionably products of traditional, classical culture, began to exercise their pastoral role. They, like the monks and philosophers before them, challenged and broke the mould of the élite, governing classes who were essentially identified and unified by their common possession of *paideia*—a classical education. Whereas before this had served as a sort of cultural glue, to hold together the tremendous diversity which made up the ruling class of the Empire, and had provided a cultural *koine* which allowed men who were otherwise total strangers to understand, and be understood by, one another,[79] the bishops, some of whom still belonged to this class and to some extent continued to avail themselves of its privileges, had much to say that rather undid the cohesiveness of the glue which rhetoric had cemented. Like the philosophers and monks ('The monks could utter the *gros mots* that broke the spell of paideia'[80]) they could ignore convention, if necessary, and were in a position to speak freely; they were able directly to confront and challenge the reigning *mores*. Ambrose, and his active involvement in the political relations between Church and State is an excellent example of how the balance set up by a cultured élite could be changed. Whilst not rejecting classical culture, or *paideia*, what Augustine had to say about the importance of faith and humility—the role of fishermen in the divine plan—also challenged and altered the balance of that culture. This is, of course, saying no more than that the Christianization of the Empire inevitably changed, or at least challenged, its identity and self-understanding, and that relations were not always straightforward.

THE FALL

It is Augustine's growing conviction of man's sinfulness, and his development of a doctrine of the fall of man, which are, I think, the main reason why he emphasizes the need for humility, as against pride, and faith in

---

[79] Brown (1992), 39 f.   [80] Ibid. 73.

authority, rather than reason. They are also the key to understanding the way in which Augustine finally diverges from classical philosophical culture.

In *On True Religion* Augustine observes that it is faith which enables the man who is blinded by his sins to hold to what he cannot grasp with his understanding. This is characteristic of his early understanding of man's sinfulness. We encountered the Platonic idea of gradually becoming accustomed to the light of wisdom, or truth, at the beginning of this chapter. The impurity of man's mind means he cannot gaze directly upon the full radiance of God's light. This and other Platonic ideas to describe man's position in the world, such as the cave, the body as a dark prison, the wings of the soul held back by the birdlime of the senses and its home in the heavens, were probably mediated to Augustine by Cicero.[81]

Throughout the early works Augustine tends to follow philosophical tradition in attributing man's sin to his attachment to external things, to the senses and the body, and his failure to place the soul and reason above them. He explains this as at least partly due to man's restricted viewpoint: like a statue placed in the corner of a building, he can only see what lies in his immediate vicinity, he can see parts but not the whole (*ord.* 1.1–2; 2.15). His soul is therefore 'turned away from contemplation of higher things', and is distracted by curiosity and love of lower things (*mus.* 6.13.39), taking creation for its Creator (*uera rel.* 67–8). It is in the context of the activity of soul among lower things that pride belongs: 'the general love of action turning away from the true arises from pride by which vice the soul has preferred imitating God to serving God' (*mus.* 6.13.40). What is clear from the early works is that the agent of sin is not the body or the senses but rather the soul, because of its weakness, and failure to order its love and action, with regards to lower reality.[82] Sin is a breach of right order.[83]

It is useful to remember that the early works were written against the background of Augustine's break with Manichaeism. We have seen that the Manichees' dualistic solution to the problem of evil was, for a while, a great attraction to Augustine, but that, on further reflection, it seemed to raise more problems than it solved. In the *Confessions*, written some time later, he describes his final resolution of the problem in an understanding of evil as originating in the action of man's free will (*conf.* 7.16.22; *ench.* 23), of evil as a *privatio boni* or detraction from an essentially good creation (*conf.* 7.12.18; *ench.* 12–13), and in an 'aesthetic' justification for evil as providentially comprehended by, and contributing to, a good whole (*conf.*

---

[81] Teselle (1970), 68–9.

[82] *uera rel.* 67. Cf. 39; 41; Plotinus *Enn.* 1.6.5, for a description of the soul which has fallen because of its involvement in the sensible realm.

[83] Markus (1994a), XVIII, 23 citing *Simpl.* 1.2.18.

7.13.19; *ench.* 11).[84] He had evidently gradually come to see evil as an intrinsic part of man's fragmented self, inevitable in the soul's creation from nothing,[85] but comprehended by God's providential order, as against the Manichees' dualistic separation of evil from the good. The key to the working out of these ideas, however, which appear rather anachronistically in the *Confessions*, in Augustine's description of events leading up to his conversion in 386, lies in Augustine's reading of St Paul, beginning in the 390s.

Augustine, had, of course, been acquainted with Paul's work well before the 390s but he hardly refers to him before this and what he did read was presumably in a Manichaean context, or later, in the spiritual, philosophically inspired anti-Manichaean context characteristic of the early works.[86] Others were also reading St Paul—Peter Brown has observed that 'the last decades of the fourth century in the Latin Church could well be called the "generation of St Paul"'[87]—and were to influence Augustine's reflections: the Manichees (who regarded Paul as one of the prophets), the Roman Ambrosiaster,[88] the Donatist, Tyconius,[89] Victorinus and Pelagius.[90]

As we have seen above, Augustine's return to Africa in 389 was also a return to the scene of his Manichaean past and precipitated a number of works directed against various aspects of their doctrines. The series of works on Paul's letters which Augustine produced from 395 onwards are illuminatingly placed by Paula Fredriksen in this context, as attempts to work out the question of moral evil, and the interplay of grace and free will, as against Manichaean dualism and determinism (*ep. Rm. inch.*; *exp. Gal.*; *exp. prop. Rm.*).[91] Thus, for example, in 395—perhaps under the influence of Tyconius[92]—we find him emphasizing that salvation is based on the merit of the sinner's free response, in faith, to God's call (*exp. prop. Rm.* 44. 3).

Two years later, however, in the important work *To Simplicianus: On Diverse Questions* he completely overturns this interpretation and states that everything which man receives, including faith, is the unmerited and

---

[84] This Stoic idea is sometimes expressed in terms of God's providential action in bringing good out of evil; punishing sin and rewarding virtue, e.g. *uera rel.* 44; *lib. arb.* 3.26–27 and illustrated by the contrast between light and dark so that the light is made to seem more brilliant when juxtaposed with the dark, e.g. *ep.* 29.11; *ciu.* 11.23.

[85] Expressed most clearly in *ciu.* 14.13.   [86] Delaroche (1996), 77–92.

[87] Brown (1967), 151.

[88] Though Augustine did not use his commentaries on Paul or series of questions on the Old and New Testament until later (*c. ep. Pel.* 4.7) and then he thinks he is Hilary.

[89] see p. 200 n. 22 below.   [90] He wrote a *Commentary on Romans*. De Bruyn (1993).

[91] Fredriksen (1980); (1986); Delaroche (1996), 60, nn. 51 & 52; 302, n. 2 for further bibliography on Augustine on Paul.

[92] Fredriksen (1988). She suggests that by 396 (*ep.* 41.2) Augustine had read his *liber regularum* on exegesis. Rule 3 makes much the same point as Augustine makes here.

gracious gift of God. Here, it is no longer Manichaeism which seems to be at the forefront of his mind, rather he is preoccupied by an attempt to make sense of his own experience of conversion and the Christian life, as a priest and newly appointed bishop. That he found the ideas and words to do so in Paul suggests that at this stage, Romans revealed, and perhaps articulated, what he had hitherto been trying to understand; he could now read Paul in a new light and found in him deep resonances with his own personal convictions and was able to claim his authority in expressing them.[93]

Whatever the case, the letter *To Simplicianus*, with its clear teaching on the fallenness of man—of mankind as a *massa peccati*, 'one lump in which the original guilt (of Adam) remains throughout' (*Simpl.* 2.17; 20), the culpability of all men (2.17), the impotence of man's will to do the good (2.2; 12) and the unmerited grace of God which can alone (and regardless of faith, reason or works) inspire in man a delight in the good (2.21)—marks a watershed in Augustine's thought which was profoundly to effect its subsequent course.

It is a turning point which scholars have not been slow to note. Robert Markus, for example, places it alongside Augustine's rejection of Manichaean dualism as the next crucial stage in Augustine's progressive 'disillusionment' (understood in a positive sense of ridding oneself of illusions) with ideas of 'human self-determination in a rationally ordered, comprehensible and manipulable world'. Rather it accompanied his growing appreciation of social existence 'which sprang from a sense of uncertainties of direction, of conflicting purposes and irresolvable tensions'.[94] The consoling, confidence-inspiring certainties of a rationally ordered universe, controlled by and subject to man's free will, which Augustine had enjoyed in the early works, were now taken from under his feet.

It is easy to over-dramatize the importance of what may, at first sight, seem a very revolutionary change in Augustine's thought, if one does not carefully consider the evidence of the early works. The explicit and uncompromising nature of Augustine's teaching on man's fallenness and God's grace in *To Simplicianus*, does indeed mark a decisive stage in his reflections on the sinfulness of man and his need for divine assistance, but the groundwork for it had been clearly laid in the early works. These are essential reading if one is not to regard the change of emphasis in the 390s as arbitrary and unprecedented, as due to some some sort of mid-life crisis, or, indeed, simply the result of the frustrations of Augustine's biographers

---

[93] See Fredriksen (1986), 24.

[94] Markus (1994), XVIII, 39. Bonner (1987), IV, 5 refers to it as his 'other conversion'. Brown (1967) makes much of it in the chapter entitled 'The lost future' (146–57)—though see Madec's (1989, 18) reservations on this.

when dealing with a period which lies just beyond the rich detail provided by the *Confessions*.[95] As we have seen, he is preoccupied in the works written before this date with the role of faith and authority, the nature of evil, of man's will and his ability (or failure) to do the good, the need for humility, temporal revelation, Scripture, and God's descent, in Christ, in order to lead man back to himself. And we must remember that these questions were considered not only in relation to Neoplatonism, or in the context of a refutation of Manichaeism, but against the background of the Christian faith, to which Augustine (if the account of the *Confessions* is to be followed) had always, in some sense held. His interpretation of Paul in the 390s, though it takes some previously held ideas to the extreme and seems to overturn others, is, I would argue, of a piece with Augustine's previous work and thought, rather than in total and startling contrast to them, and seems to bring Augustine's reflections over a number of years to their inevitable conclusion.

The influence that a fully evolved doctrine of the fall had on his subsequent thought cannot, however, be overestimated: from 396 onwards it is central, and determinative of practically everything he wrote. We will have occasion to reconsider its influence at numerous points throughout the rest of this book and in particular in Chapter 3, where we will examine the nature of the fall in more detail in relation to classical notions of virtue and his controversy with Pelagius.

THE EFFECTS OF THE FALL

In the context of philosophical thought and the attainment of wisdom, an understanding of the fall, such as it appears in *To Simplicianus*, means that truth is, in fact, unattainable without divine help, and that the one who seeks wisdom must acknowledge this if he is not to be frustrated in his search. A passage in a relatively early treatise, *On Genesis against the Manichees* (389) which in fact pre-dates *To Simplicianus*, vividly expresses this insight: in proudly turning away from God, from the fountain which had welled up to refresh his soul within, towards external, material things, man, Augustine comments, now finds himself dependent upon the rain which falls from the dark clouds of human words, doctrine and teaching (2.4.5–5.6). Having turned away from the inner illumination of God, man now finds himself dependent upon God's exterior, temporal revelation, which meets him in the realm into which he has fallen; having been blinded

---

[95] Madec (1989), 18; (1996), 69 as against Brown (1967), 146–57.

by pride, he must now humbly confess his dependence upon divine revelation and his faith in its authority.

The essential continuity of Augustine's thought in this respect is confirmed by the fact that this is an insight which is made numerous times in the early works (e.g. *Acad.* 3.19.42; *ord.* 2.27; *lib. arb.* 3.30) and is then constantly reiterated throughout the works of his maturity (e.g. *trin.* 4.18.24; *cons. eu.* 1.35.53). It does, however, mark a break with his earlier confidence in the power of reason to attain the truth in the few who are capable of exercising it. He will now observe, quoting Isaiah 7: 9, 'Unless you believe, you will not understand' (*lib. arb.* 2.2.6). Although the Platonists might have seen the truth, faith in God's revelation is indispensable in understanding it. For the Christian faith and reason are ultimately complementary but the latter cannot be had without the former: we believe in order to understand but it is reason which acknowledges that it is reasonable to accept an authority: 'Everyone who believes thinks; for by believing he thinks, and by thinking he believes' (*praed. sanct.* 2.5. Cf. *ep.* 120.3). These insights are best expressed in what Augustine has to say about the incarnation of God.

INCARNATION

It is significant that Augustine did not write a work specifically on the incarnation or Christology.[96] What he has to say appears in diverse works and contexts, which in fact give us some indication as to when, where and why the doctrine of the incarnation became important to him. The controversial element, which so often predominates in others, is subordinate in Augustine to reflections on Christ's exemplary, paedagogic, healing, sacramental and salvific role. He seems to have been largely unaware of the eventful christological debates taking place in the east and died just before the Council of Ephesus met in 431. But this is not to say that he did not have to argue on a number of fronts—for Christ's full humanity against the Docetists (Christ only seemed—*dokeo*—to be a man), and especially the Apollinarians (Christ did not possess a human soul), and for Christ's full divinity against the Arians and Eunomians (Christ was a creature), Photinians (Christ was not pre-existent and only wise through God's inspiration) and Sabellians (Christ did not possess separate existence but was simply a mode of the Father's being).[97] He could not have been unaware

---

[96] On Augustine's Christology: van Bavel (1954); Grillmeier (1975); Studer (1975); Geerlings (1978); Rémy (1979); Verwilghen (1985); Madec (1989).

[97] *ep.* 183 (*c.* AD 417) for Augustine's awareness of christological heresies. He also lists Donatists, Pelagians, pagans and Jews.

of Ambrose's battle against the Arians which was still very much in full flood when he arrived in Milan in 386.

The opponents Augustine most frequently has in mind, however—whether they are explicitly mentioned or not—are in fact the Platonists. As we have seen, the attitude of the pagans towards Christ varied—from Celsus's violent repudiation of him (in *True Doctrine*) to a more general, though somewhat vague and guarded, admiration of him. Augustine may have encountered some of the latter in the 'Neoplatonic circle' at Milan. Like Porphyry, they denied Christ's divinity but were prepared to accept that his doctrine came from Plato and to see in him a type of *theios aner*—a wise man or magician, like Pythagoras, Socrates, Plato, or Apollonius of Tyana, who venerated the pagan gods.[98] Their influence on Augustine is probably reflected in the description of his early, defective, understanding of Christ, in *Confessions* 7 (19.25) 'as a man of excellent wisdom which none could equal'.[99] The influence of the heretic Photinus, who affirmed Christ's Virgin birth and his authority as a teacher, but denied his pre-existence or his possession of wisdom, except through God's inspiration, is also clear in this passage. To Alypius, on the other hand, Augustine attributes, at this stage, an Apollinarian Christology: he 'held that in Christ there was only God and flesh. He did not think they [Catholics] held him to possess a human soul and mind'.

The *Confessions* proceed to recount Augustine's movement towards an orthodox Christology of the incarnate Christ *before* his conversion in 386. He makes clear his disillusionment with the books of the Platonists in almost the same breath as he describes his encounter with them: he found in them the Word of John's Prologue, but no mention that the Word became flesh; they taught that the Son was 'in the form of the Father', but not that he humbled himself and took 'the form of a servant' (Phil. 2: 6–11); they stated that the only-begotten Son immutably abides with God (John 1: 16), but not that 'at the right time he died for the impious' (Rom. 5: 6). They lacked the meekness and humility characteristic of Christ and those who he came to save. (*conf.* 7.9.13–14).

Augustine's attempts at Neoplatonic ascents also made him conscious of the need for grace, and a mediator between God and man, if the wisdom the Platonists described is ever to be fully attained (7.10.16; 17.23–18.24). He now realized that Scripture was to be preferred: in St Paul

[98] They are mentioned in Ambrose's, now lost, *De sacramento regenerationis sive de philosophia*. We find Augustine at pains to refute such ideas in the first book of *cons. eu.* (1.7.11–15.23) c. AD 400; Cf. *ciu.* 19.23; *doct. christ.* 2.28.43.

[99] See O'Donnell (1992) II, 464–5 for the pagan background and evidence in Augustine's works, especially *ep.* 233 (from Longinianus) and Augustine's reply, *ep.* 235. Also *ep.* 135 (from Volusianus) and *ep.* 136 from Marcellinus, with Augustine's reply, *ep.* 137. BA 13, 693 'La Christologie d' Augustin au temps de sa conversion'.

he found what he read in the Platonists along with a commendation of God's grace (7.21.27). But is this wishful retrospective interpretation or an accurate reflection of events? What did Augustine think in 386? Madec, following Courcelle, suggests that the key to answering this question lies in the conversation Augustine tells us he had with the Milanese priest, Simplicianus (8.2.3), who, they maintain (though there is no direct evidence here), enabled Augustine to identify the logos of the Neoplatonists with the incarnate Logos of St John's Prologue.[100] O'Connell, on the other hand, who sees a rather longer evolution in Augustine's thought in this respect, would disagree.[101]

We are on more certain ground if we examine the works Augustine wrote soon after his conversion where there is, in fact, much to support the orthodoxy of his early understanding of Christ in contradistinction to pagan, philosophical views. Philosophical influence is evident in Augustine's description of Christ as supreme Measure, the measure of the soul (*beata u.* 32–3), supreme Truth, Unity, Form, and Number (e.g. *uera rel.* 66), all of which are known by the mind. But in his first work, *Against the Academics*, observing that it is difficult, indeed impossible, for souls 'blinded by the manifold darkness of error and stained deeply with the slime of the body' to see Wisdom with their own eyes, he states that God has 'bent and submitted the authority of the divine intellect even to the human body itself' (3.19.42. cf. *qu. an.* 76). Elsewhere he talks of Christ's outward deeds, miracles, and authority (*util. cred.* 33. cf. *ord.* 2.27), his work as a doctor (*sol.* 1.12.27) and teacher (*uera rel.* 33[102]), all of which purify man by faith. These passages alone suggest that Augustine's early Christology, though not a central concern, was at least orthodox. It is summed up in the somewhat later (391–5) work, *On Free Will* (though even this antedates the *Confessions*):

The food of the rational creature became visible, not by changing his own nature but by adapting it to ours, in order that he might recall those who follow visible things to embrace him who is invisible. So the soul, which in its inward pride had forsaken him, finds him again in humble guise in the outward world. By imitating his visible humility it will return to its invisible superiority.

Philosophy, however, and in particular the Platonists, had had a sufficiently dramatic effect on Augustine's thought, and was such a prominent

---

[100] As evidence, Madec (1989), 42 cites *ciu.* 10.29 which does make this identification in relation to Simplicianus in terms similar to *confessiones* and perhaps evokes earlier conversations. No doubt Simplicianus took this identification from Victorinus in whose works it appears—Henry (1934), 44–62. See also Van Bavel (1954), 5–12; Madec (1979); Mallard (1980).

[101] E.g. O'Connell (1984).

[102] Madec (1989), 67–75 cites a number of passages from *uera rel.* which could easily have made up a christological treatise if Augustine had wished.

part of the culture he was addressing that it continued to pose problems in relation to Christology which simply could not be ignored. Pagan thinkers had not been slow to criticize Christianity and its beliefs.[103] Their main objections, represented by Celsus's *True Doctrine* and described in Arnobius's *Adversus Nationes*, in fact resemble those of the Manichees: they ridiculed the creation account of Genesis; they wondered why God allowed his own creation to disobey him; they questioned the morality of the Patriarchs, the contradictions between Old and New Testament, the Old Testament Law, discrepancies between the Gospels. In particular, they objected to Christian doctrine of incarnation and the resurrection of the body. The very spirituality of the Platonists, which had resolved so many problems for him, seemed to be totally irreconcilable with a doctrine of the Word made flesh, of his bodily resurrection and of faith in him as the only means for fallen man to grasp the truth. In these respects, Augustine found himself at odds with the philosophers and in a position of having to defend Christianity against them.

DEVALUATION OF THE BODY

The Manichees thought the body was evil. The Platonists at least attributed its creation to a good God (*Timaeus* 41c). Nevertheless, it was, for them, a miserable prison (*ciu.* 14.3), a punishment (*ciu.* 12.27), from which the soul sought freedom. Against both Manichees and Platonists Augustine emphasized the goodness of Creation, including man's body (*nat. b.* 15–18; *ench.* 12–13).

The Christians' decisive argument against the Platonists' denigration of the flesh, however, was to insist on the—for the Platonists, paradoxical and absurd—notion of the resurrection of the body.[104] Underlying this insistence was a conviction—in the event somewhat difficult to express—of the *unity* of body and soul. Augustine sometimes talks of a 'mixture' (*permixtio Gn. litt.* 3.16.25), in which body and soul retain their individual identities and yet are inseparable, of a *contemperatio* (*qu. an.* 30.59) or conjunction (*coniunctum—ciu.* 13.24.2), or even more crudely, of 'a kind of intimacy of gluing and fastening together' (*en. Ps.* 68.3). Elsewhere he describes the *intentio* (intention, extension, concentration) of the soul which unites it to the body (*ep.* 166.4; *mus.* 6.9; *Gn. litt.* 3.5.7; *trin.* 11.2.2). Rist argues that what Augustine intends by these awkward expressions becomes clearer in those passages (from *c.* 400) in which he refers to Ephesians 5: 29, 'No one

---

[103] See Courcelle (1963b), 151–66.
[104] *ciu.* 13.18–20; 22.19. Cf. *s.* 24.2; 242.2; 257.3; *ep.* 205.2; *doct. chr.* 1.24.24–27; *Io. eu. tr.* 52.11. Marrou and La Bonnardière (1966).

hates his own flesh' (*doctr. chr.* 1.24.25; *s.* 244.4) and speaks of the soul's love of the body,[105] and even of 'a kind of conjugal union of flesh and spirit' (*util. ieiun.* 4.5).[106]

Lying behind Augustine's obvious difficulties with language here, and to some extent explaining them, is his consciousness that what he says about the relation of body and soul, united and yet not confused, within the one person of man, to some extent must also refer (at least analogically) to the unity of the Word (Godhead) and manhood (body and soul) in Christ. In some texts, most notably *ep.* 137, they are directly linked in such a way that Augustine has been said to have worked out a doctrine of the hypostatic union before Chalcedon.[107]

In comparison to his Eastern counterparts, however, he has very little of any technical import to say in this matter. Debates as to whether Augustine was Antiochene or Alexandrian are generally irrelevant and anachronistic. His thought is deeply rooted in traditional Latin ideas. So, for example, he follows Tertullian, Minucius Felix, and Lactantius in emphasizing the role of Christ as teacher; Hilary, Victorinus, and Ambrose in describing Christ's role within the Trinity; he repeats Tertullian's teaching in *Adversus Praxean* (27) on one person in two substances (*s.* 294);[108] he frequently uses Novatian's distinction between what Christ does as man and what he does as God;[109] he speaks of the two births of Christ—from the Father, and from Mary—in relation to the two natures of Godhead and manhood,[110] so that Mary's womb becomes a sort of bridal chamber for the union of the Word (the bridegroom) with flesh (the bride) (e.g. *Io. eu. tr.* 8.4). Even passages in works written after 410, in which he appeals to Christ as the supreme example of unmerited antecedent grace (*pecc. mer.* 2.17.27; *ep.* 187), do not, McGuckin argues, mark him out as an Antiochene, but rather suggest the influence of Porphyry mediated by the likes of Victorinus, Simplicianus, and Ambrose.[111] More generally Augustine simply describes Christ's flesh as a 'cloud' (*Io. eu. tr.* 34.4–5) or 'veil'[112] which

---

[105] Rist (1994), 110–11.

[106] Similarly, when he speaks of care for the dead: 'The actual bodies are certainly not to be treated with contempt, since we wear them in a much closer and more intimate way than any clothing. A man's body is no mere adornment, or external convenience; it belongs to his very nature as a man' (*ciu.* 1.13).

[107] Madec (1989), 232 f, thinks the expression 'union without confusion' of *ep.* 137 is inspired by Porphyry's theory of *asugchutos enosis* and is amused to be able to attribute a role to Christianity's most hostile critic in making Augustine a Chalcedonian before Chalcedon. Cf. *ep.* 219 concerning Leporius—a pre-Nestorian whom Augustine corrected when he fled to Hippo from Gaul, where he had been condemned, Madec (1989), 234–7; 244–5. On the same analogy see *ep.* 169.8; *Io. eu. tr.* 19.15; 47.12; 78.3; *trin.* 13.22.

[108] McGuckin (1990), 45.   [109] McGuckin (1990).   [110] Studer (1972).

[111] McGuckin (1990), 49–50.

[112] A very common image used, e.g. in *Io. eu. tr.* I.19; 2.16; 3.6; 14.12; 17.1.

serves to cover his Divinity and temper its brightness, so that fallen man
can look upon him.

Christ's body, like man's, will also be raised; even after the resurrection
his body is called 'flesh' (*ench.* 23.91), he will take his seat at God's right
hand in his 'glorious humanity',[113] the angels will adore his risen flesh
(*s.* 225.2.2). It is difficult to overestimate how utterly paradoxical and
incomprehensible such statements would be to a Platonist: 'that after
having fought so much against the body and its annoying tendencies one
must—and that for eternity—rejoin this miserable companion, this tat-
tered garment!'[114]

PRIDE

The example of Christ's humility in assuming a human body in order to
teach fallen man, and lead him back to the truth through faith in himself,
is often used by Augustine to counter the pride he ascribes to the Platonists for relying on their own rational insights to attain the truth. We have
already encountered some of his arguments earlier in this chapter. In
speaking of the incarnation in this respect the text he most often turns to
is Philippians 2: 6–11: 'though He was in the form of God, He did not
count equality with God to be grasped, but emptied Himself, taking the
form of a servant, being born in the likeness of man . . .'[115] The Platonists
would immediately understand the idea of Christ *in forma Dei*–a term
which Augustine equates with Christ as Word, Wisdom, Creator, Son of
God[116] and the 'I Am' of Exodus 3: 14.[117] The idea that he could retain his
divine form and yet empty himself, humble himself, in order to take on
humanity and all its infirmities would, however, be wholly alien to them.
And yet it is this which Augustine emphasizes incessantly: 'this way is first
humility, second humility, third humility . . . if humility does not precede
and accompany and follow every good work we do, and if it is not set
before us to look upon, and beside us to lean upon, and behind us to fence
us in, pride will wrest from our hand any good deed we do while we are
in the very act of taking pleasure in it (*ep.* 118).' This humility is directly
opposed to the 'ignorant knowledge' of the philosophers. Their study of

---

[113] *c. s. Arrian.* 2.9; *en. Ps.* 85.21; *trin.* I.10.21; 13.28; *Io. eu. tr.* 19.16; 21.13.

[114] Marrou and La Bonnardière (1966). It is not at all certain that Augustine knew
Tertullian's treatise *De carne Christi* though his arguments recall certain passages from this treatise. Tertullian writes, for example, 'God's son was crucified—this is not a matter for shame,
because it is a disgrace; and God's Son has died—this is credible because it is a foolishness; and
he was buried and risen again—this is certain, because it is impossible' (5.4). Cf. *ciu.* 10.28.

[115] Verwilghen (1985).   [116] See Verwilghen (1985), 163–7 for references.

[117] *BA* 71, 845–7 n. 10.

ancient philosophy is a 'waste of time', 'empty ostentation', undertaken merely 'for the sake of appearing learned and well informed' (*ep.* 118 (p282–91)) when compared with the wisdom revealed by Christ.

THE ONE MEDIATOR

As we have seen above, the Platonists were also associated in Augustine's mind with the pagan practice of theurgy and its doctrine of demonic mediators. It is not until the mid-390s, however, that we find him taking over the word 'mediator' (Lt. *mediator*; Gk. *mesites*) and emphasizing texts such as 1 Tim. 2: 5: 'For there is One God, one Mediator between God and Man, Jesus Christ.' From this time onwards, however, his appeal to 1 Timothy, Galatians 13: 19–20 and Romans 11: 36 becomes much more frequent. In *Confessions* we find him appealing to Christ as Mediator following his failed attempts at Platonic ascents (e.g. 10.43.69).

The doctrine is fully worked out in *City of God* 9–10 in contradistinction to pagan theurgy. Here the immortal mediators of pagan rites, who had tried to lure man astray by promising immortality, are shown to have actually prevented man from passing to immortal blessedness and happiness since there is only one way and this is through the mortal mediator, Christ. The demons and their rites are no longer needed because 'a God who is blessed and bliss creating has become a participator in our humanity and so provided a short and easy path towards our participation in his divinity' (9.15). He is the true Mediator who, in the form of a servant, is the sacrifice itself and in the form of God, accepts the Sacrifice along with the Father; he is both the priest, who offers the sacrifice, and the offering (*ciu.* 10.20). This is the 'supreme and true sacrifice' now continued by Christ's body, the Church, and in the shadow of which 'all false sacrifices have yielded and vanished' (*ciu.* 10.20). In fact, Imperial action supports Augustine's arguments: Constantine had prohibited public, though not private, sacrifices in the temples[118] and Theodosius later proscribed both on pain of treason.[119]

Christ's role as mediator is best expressed in the *loci classici* for Augustine's doctrine of the incarnation: *On the Trinity* Books 4 and 13. Here, Christ is shown to be the only true mediator between man and God because as man and God he holds the two together in Himself: he is both the One and the many; truth and faith; eternal and temporal; wisdom and knowledge. By faith in the latter man is led back to the former. The ultimate origin of such pairs is Pythagorean, where they appear as opposites,

---

[118] Eusebius *Uita Constantini* 2.45; *Codex Theodosianus* 16.10.2.
[119] *Codex Theodosianus* 16.10.10–12.

the one good, the other bad. Here they appear in more Platonic form, so that the second is understood as deriving from the first and as leading back to it: many is many ones; the temporal is a moving image of eternity, faith is a shadow of the truth. Augustine goes one step further than the philosophers in demonstrating that the first of the pairs is in some way concealed in the second, which can then disclose it. What he had in mind, of course, is the incarnation: 'lest the faith of mortal life should be at discord with the truth of eternal life—the Truth itself, co-eternal with the Father, took a beginning from earth when the Son of God so came as to become Son of Man, and to take to himself our faith, that He might thereby lead us on to His own truth, who so undertook mortality, as not to lose His own eternity' (*trin.* 14.18.24).[120]

Most importantly, Christ holds together within himself wisdom (*sapientia*) and knowledge (*scientia*).[121] Wisdom is the highest faculty of the mind, that which is concerned with contemplation of immutable and eternal truth, directly and intuitively, in a manner unmediated by temporal things (12.14.21). This is, of course, what fallen man has lost; he is now restricted to the realm of *scientia*, to knowledge derived from temporal realities. *Scientia* is that which distinguishes man from the beasts and enables him to engage with temporal reality, to judge it and act in relation to it (12.3.3). It is also that which gives birth to and sustains his faith (14.1.3) so that he does not simply become engrossed in the temporal (12.12.17). It is faith in Christ, pre-eminently, which allows man to move from the realm into which he has fallen to that from which he has fallen: from *scientia* to *sapientia*; knowledge to wisdom. This is so because 'Christ is our knowledge (*scientia*), and the same Christ is our wisdom (*sapientia*). He Himself implants in us faith concerning temporal things; He Himself shows forth the truth concerning eternal things. Through Him we reach out to Himself: we stretch through knowledge to wisdom; yet we do not withdraw from one and the same Christ, 'in whom are hidden all the treasures of wisdom and knowledge (Col. 2: 1–3)' (*trin.* 13.19.24).[122]

The centrality, indeed the indispensability, of Christ as mediator of wisdom marks the decisive break between Platonism and Christianity. It is also the dividing line between Augustine's past optimism concerning the relation between philosophy and Christianity and his later conviction that true wisdom can only be found in Christianity (*ciu.* 10.28).

Above all, the centrality of Christ as mediator sets Christianity apart as

---

[120] Harrison (1992), 207 for Augustine's relation of this passage to *Timaeus* 29c.

[121] See Madec (1975).

[122] Derived from Scripture (1 Cor. 12: 8; Job 28: 28; Col. 2: 1–3). Camelot (1956), suggests that in *trin.* 14.1.3 the philosophical definition is taken from Cicero's *Hortensius*. Solignac (1958) suggests the influence of Nichomachus of Gerasa's *Introductio Arithmetica*.

the 'Universal Way' to wisdom, which the philosophers had sought, but not found (*ciu.* 10.32).[123] As Augustine states in the culminating chapter of the first half of the *City of God*, Christianity 'is the religion that embodies a universal path to the liberation of the soul, since no soul can be liberated by any other but this. For this is the royal road that alone leads to the kingdom, a kingdom not doomed to sway uneasily upon a pinnacle of time but solidly founded on eternity' (*ciu.* 10.32).

THE TRINITY

The two christological texts which we examined from *On the Trinity*, in order to demonstrate Augustine's break with ancient philosophy, are in fact pivotal texts in the work as a whole, for in this long work Augustine is above all concerned to make clear that it is only on the basis of a true faith in, and love for, Christ, that man can be reformed in the trinitarian image.

Although the work might at first appear to be a purely intellectual, Neo-platonically inspired discussion of a fundamentally unknowable mystery, written for the further reflection of erudite scholars, the inherent difficul-ties of the subject obscure the fact that it was intended as a work on the Christian life as it should be lived in relation to man's creator, reformer, and redeemer, and that it was composed in a traditional, often polemical context which has little time for purely philosophical speculation or Neo-platonically inspired ascents. Rather, the emphasis is clearly placed upon the need for orthodox faith in the Trinity, reasoned reflection upon that faith, and love for its origin and object: it is this that determines the struc-ture and content of the work.

Augustine wrote *On the Trinity* over a period of twenty years (399–419).[124] It is clear from book one (1.4.7) that he attempted to read as much as possible of the work of his predecessors and that his first concern was to demonstrate the congruence of orthodox trinitarian doctrine with the account of Scripture (1;2;4); only so, he believed would the tradition carry authority and merit acceptance, and only so could the problems which both tradition and Scripture raise be tackled.

---

[123] Augustine mentions Porphyry here, who states at the end of *De Regressu Animae* (now lost) that 'no one system of thought has yet embraced a doctrine that embodies a universal path to the liberation of the soul'. See Vanderspoel (1990), who suggests that Porphyry's failure to find a 'universal way' perhaps rested on his affirmation of religious plurality—an assertion increasingly made by pagans in the fourth century.

[124] As he tells Aurelius of Carthage (*ep.* 174), he began it as a young man and completed it in his old age. Progress was interrupted when an incomplete version (probably up to book 12) was stolen and subsequently published. This meant that the completed work, which he finished at the insistence of others, could not be subject to the sort of final revision he would have liked.

SOURCES AND BACKGROUND

Whom had he read? The only person he mentions by name is Hilary of Poitiers (*On the Trinity* (see *trin.* 6.10.11; 15.3.5)). Among the Latins we might speculate that he had read Tertullian (*Against Praxeas*), Novatian (*On the Trinity*) Ambrose (*On the Holy Spirit*) and Victorinus.[125] It is less clear, however, whom he might have read among the Greeks. Although, as we shall see in our examination of Books 5–7, he had a working knowledge of Greek technical terms for the Trinity, it is generally thought–and Augustine confirms this (*conf.* 1.13.20; 14.23; *trin.* 3 prologue)—that his lack of Greek forced him to rely on translations. If this was the case, then Rufinus' translation of Origen's *On First Principles* (mentioned in *ciu.* 11.23), Victorinus's translation of nine homilies by Gregory Nazianzen and Jerome's translation of Didymus the Blind's *On the Holy Spirit* (mentioned in *q. Hept.* 2.25) were perhaps available to him. He may also have read Athanasius, Basil and Ephiphanius.[126] Whatever it was he did read, he is conscious that what he deems to be the insufficient attention paid by the Latin fathers to the Trinity, and the very small amount of material available in Greek for the Latin-speaking reader, necessitates his own work (*trin.* 3 Prologue).

Most of Augustine's predecessors had written polemically in order to refute heretical doctrines of Christ (Arianism and, to orthodox eyes, its later manifestations in Homoianism and Eunomianism), the Holy Spirit (Macedonianism) or the Trinity (Sabellianism). Although Augustine's work is less overtly polemical and rarely names particular heresies, his awareness of them clearly informs the subjects he chooses to address and what he has to say about them. The East had fought these battles from a much earlier date, but Arianism in the West was still a cause for genuine concern, not least because of its prevalence among the Goths who were evangelized by Ulfilas.[127] In *On the Trinity*, Augustine consciously stands in a line of anti-Arian, pro-Nicene polemic (6.1.1), initiated by Athanasius's exiles to the West and represented by the likes of Hilary, Phoebadius of Agen, Lucifer of Cagliari, Gregory of Elvira, Ambrose and Victorinus.[128] Likewise, following Tertullian and Hippolytus in the West, he was acutely aware of the threat of Sabellianism (7.4.9) (otherwise known as modalism or Monarchianism—a doctrine which saw no division within the Godhead but

---

[125] His work on the Trinity includes *De Generatione Verbi Divini*; *Adversus Arium*; *de homoousio recipiendo* and three hymns on the Trinity.

[126] Chevalier (1940).   [127] Bonner (1987a), V, 52.

[128] D. H. Williams (1995); M. R. Barnes (1993); (1999) (forthcoming) for the anti-Homoian character of the polemic (I owe these references to Ayres 1998). See Chapter 4 for Augustine's confrontation with Arian thinkers. Bonner (1987), V, 52 also notes that Jerome mentions that Donatus had written a work on the Holy Spirit which was Arian in tone (*uiris illustribus* 93).

taught that the Son and Holy Spirit were regarded simply as 'modes' or temporal appearances of the One God).

SCRIPTURE AND TRADITION

What exactly was the tradition which Augustine was at pains to defend and which determined his reading of Scripture and his elucidation of trinitarian terminology in the first part of *On the Trinity*? He provides a concise summary at 1.4.7, when he writes,

The purpose of all the Catholic commentators I have been able to read on the divine books of both testaments, who have written before me on the trinity which God is, has been to teach that according to the scriptures Father and Son and Holy Spirit in the inseparable equality of one substance present a divine unity; and therefore there are not three gods but one God; although indeed the Father has begotten the Son, and therefore he who is the Father is not the Son; and the Son is begotten by the Father, and therefore he who is the Son is not the Father, and the Holy Spirit is neither the Father nor the Son, but only the Spirit of the Father and of the Son, himself coequal to the Father and the son, and belonging to the threefold unity.

Earlier on, as Lewis Ayres has pointed out,[129] Augustine similarly appeals to Catholic tradition to underline the fundamental basis for this doctrine of trinitarian unity and relation in the doctrine of the inseparable operation of the Trinity. In *ep.* 11.2 (389) he writes, 'For according to the Catholic faith, the Trinity is proposed to our belief and believed . . . as so inseparable that whatever action is performed by it must be thought to be performed at the same time by the Father and by the Son and by the Holy Spirit . . .' This doctrine is again taken as a basic axiom of the Catholic faith and expounded at length, Ayres demonstrates, in the important sermon on the baptism of Christ in Matt.3: 13 f, *s.* 52 (410–12). The scriptural account seems to suggest that the three persons are present and active at the baptism in separate manifestations with different functions. Catholic tradition, however, teaches the inseparable operation of the persons: 'Now someone may say to me, "Demonstrate that the three are inseparable." Remember you're speaking as a Catholic, speaking to Catholics. Our faith, after all, that is to say the true faith . . . which is not a bundle of opinions

---

[129] Ayres, (as yet unpublished article) 'Remember that you are Catholic (*serm.* 52.2): Augustine on the unity of the Triune God'. He refers to Ambrose *Expositio in Euangelium Secundum Lucam* Prologue 5 and Gregory of Nyssa *On the Holy Trinity* to illustrate the traditional emphasis on inseparable operation which Augustine is reiterating here. I must record an enormous debt of gratitude to Lewis Ayres for his invaluable help and encouragement in writing this section.

and prejudices but a summary of biblical testimonies, not riddled with heretical rashness, but founded on apostolic truth . . . insists on this (52.2).

Augustine proceeds to reconcile tradition and Scripture by demonstrating, from the scriptural account of the Son's birth, death, and resurrection, that whatever the Son does is brought about by and is the work of, the Father, and the Son: 'You have the persons quite distinct, and their working inseparable' (52.14).

It is with the elucidation (Books 1–4), definition (5–7) and illustration (8–15) of this Catholic consensus concerning the unity and equality of substance and persons within the Trinity, their inseparable operation, and their differentiation only at the level of origin and relationship that Augustine's *On the Trinity* is concerned. And it is the role of the incarnate Christ, as we saw in relation to Books 4 and 13, to provide for fallen man the means of believing, knowing and loving the ineffable Trinity as his Creator and redeemer, so that he might be reformed and ultimately, in the life to come, arrive at full knowledge and love of the Trinitarian God.

There is insufficient space here to provide anything but the most summary illustration of *On the Trinity* as an elucidation, definition, and illustration of a clearly defined Catholic tradition concerning the Trinity, written against its heretical detractors and primarily intended for the spiritual reformation of its readers. A few examples must suffice.[130]

BOOKS 1–4

Against Arian subordinationism, in Books 1–4 Augustine considers the way in which God, the Trinity, has appeared to men in the history of salvation as recounted in the Old and New Testaments. He departs from a good deal of traditional reflection (Apologists, Tertullian, Hippolytus, Novatian, Clement) which had ascribed God's theophanies in the Old Testament to the Son, or Logos, and which seemed inevitably to lead to subordinationism, in denying that God appeared in the Old Testament in any of the persons of the divine substance, who are all equally invisible. Rather He was present through created intermediaries which were the work of the whole Trinity (4.21.30–1).[131] The eternal relations and inseparable operation of the divine Trinity itself was only manifested in the temporal mission of the Son in the incarnation (4.1.3–20.28) and in the Holy Spirit at Pentecost (4.20.29). He avoids the Arian charge that the one sent is

---

[130] The bibliography on *De Trinitate* is immense. Standard works are Schmaus (1927); Sullivan (1963); Schindler (1965); du Roy (1966). For more recent criticism and comment on the approach of these works see Bourassa (1977) and (1978); Williams (1990); M. Barnes (1995a and b); Ayres (1995) and (1998).   [131] Maier (1960).

subordinate to the sender by arguing that in the case of the divine Trinity the temporal missions of Son and Holy Spirit simply reveal their eternal relation of being *from* the Father; of being begotten and proceeding from the Father respectively (4.20.29) and therefore of being co-eternal, consubstantial and coequal. All other, seemingly subordinationist passages of Scripture, are attributed, following tradition, to the humanity of the Son, in contradistinction to his divinity (i.e. *in forma servi* rather than *in forma Dei*).

BOOKS 5–7

In books 5–7 of *On the Trinity* Augustine turns to examine and define the philosophical terminology by which the doctrine of the Trinity has been articulated. Tertullian, his African predecessor, had used the Latin term *substantia* to refer to the divine substance, and *persona* to refer to the three divine persons. The Greeks, faced with the task of articulating what the Nicene *homoousios* (that the Son is *of one substance* with the Father) meant, had gradually moved towards a trinitarian definition of one *ousia* and three *hypostaseis*, such as we find in the Cappadocians in the second half of the fourth century.[132] Augustine is aware of these developments and is conscious of their rather difficult transposition into Latin: *mian ousian* and *treis hypostaseis* would be 'correctly' translated, rather nonsensically, into Latin as *una essentia* and *tres substantiae* (5.8.10). Although he prefers to use *essentia*, or *natura* (7.6.11) for the divine substance, Augustine was well aware of the traditional use of *substantia* (5.8.9) in this respect. He therefore adopts the formula *una substantia et tres personae*. *Persona*, in its common meaning, indicated a mask, role or actor, and was therefore somewhat inadequate. Augustine adopts it, as he puts it, 'in order not to remain silent' (5.9.10), whilst remaining acutely aware of the inadequacies of language to express the ineffable and invisible Trinity.[133]

But verbal formulation was necessary, not least to overcome heretical misrepresentions: talk of three persons is indispensable to counter the Sabellians. And yet the inseparability, consubstantiality and full divinity of the three must also be maintained. In order to do this, and to counter the extreme Arianism of Eunomius—who argued in Aristotelian terms that since God is simple being, without accidents, all that is said of Him must refer to His substance; therefore the Son, who is begotten, must be alien from the Father's substance—Augustine, as we have seen, uses the language of relationships—of being unbegotten, begotten, or proceeding[134]— *within* the Godhead, in order to distinguish between the persons whilst

---

[132] E.g. Basil *Letters*. 38; 236.   [133] E.g. *s.* 117.3; *ep.* 120.3.13 (Bonner (1987) V, 55).
[134] For references see *BA* 15, 570. Cf. Bonner (1987) V.

retaining their substantial identity. In this he was following (knowingly or not) Gregory Nazianzen (*s.* 29.16; *33.9*) and Didymus (*De trinitate* 1.2).

What he says about the procession of the Holy Spirit from the Father *and* the Son was later to become something of a *bête noire* between Western and Eastern theologians (the latter held that the Holy Spirit proceeded only from the Father). Augustine, however, was unaware of the Greek creed of the Council of Constantinople (AD 381) already formulated on this matter (usually called the 'Nicene' creed) and therefore of the potentially controversial nature of his assertion. As far as he was concerned he was merely following pointers in Epiphanius (*Ancoratus* 6; *Panarion* 76) and Ambrose (*On the Holy Spirit* 1.11) which tended towards the idea of a double procession.

It is only in terms of relation within the Trinity—of begetting and proceeding (Book 5) (*gigno* and *procedo*)[135]—that Augustine will allow any distinction between the persons. In every other respect, in mind, will, substance, attributes, and actions, the Father, Son, and Holy Spirit are inseparably identified (Book 7). As Augustine illustrates from numerous New Testament texts, the Trinity is therefore one according to essence and three according to relation (Book 6).[136]

BOOKS 8–15

It is this insight—the inseparable identity and operation of the three interrelated persons in the One Trinity—which Augustine goes on to express in Book 8[137] when he says he wishes to examine what has already been said in 'a more inward way'. What he describes in Book 8 is a trinity of relations, of the lover, the beloved, and the love which joins them (the language of love to describe the Holy Spirit is a new and striking contribution to trinitarian theology). He then proceeds to examine various similitudes, or analogies[138] of the inseparable operation and identity of the three persons which are inspired by the insight that man is said by Scripture to

---

[135] In *ep.* 148.2.10; 10.15 Augustine says that he has read Ambrose, Jerome, Athanasius, and Gregory (presumably Nazianzen) on this topic.

[136] As Ayres (see note 129), M. Barnes (1995a and b) and Williams (1990) have cogently demonstrated, the now classic assertion that Augustine works from the unity of God to the threefold Trinity, whereas the East works from the three to the One, is fundamentally flawed and misleading. [137] On books 8–15 see Louth (1981), chapter 7.

[138] As Ayres (see note 129) points out, Augustine never uses *analogia* to describe relations between God and his creation, but rather uses *similitudo*, *imago* (only for likenesses found in human beings), *indicium* or *uestigium*. Our use of analogy as a translation of these terms can be misleading. He comments, 'Generally, *similitudo* almost always serves to indicate the sort of aesthetic resemblance between a model and copies, or between two things of disparate nature, that does not carry with it the technical sense of actual continuity of nature that is so central to *analogia* or *proportio*.'

be created in the three-fold image of God—'Let *us* make man in *our* image and *our* likeness' (Gen. 1: 26). Since it is man's capacity for self-awareness, reason and love which sets him apart from the rest of creation, and places him closest to his creator (11.5.8), it is here that Augustine locates the image[139] of God in man. In a highly original way, he attempts both to illustrate from the image in man similitudes of the inseparable, threefold operation of the one Trinity[140] and, more importantly, to demonstrate how the deformed image of God in fallen man might be reformed in awareness, knowledge, and love of the gracious redemptive activity of his trinitarian Creator, revealed to Him in the incarnation of the Son, and loved in the inspiration of the Holy Spirit.

Although much of the second part of *On the Trinity* might therefore at first appear as an exercise structured and informed by the Neoplatonic ascent of the image or soul, seeking to return to that from which it is derived, it must be remembered that for Augustine the image or soul is *created* by God, from nothing, it does not derive from Him; similarly its return is not a matter of its own striving but is only possible by God's revelation and grace. Augustine is, however, able to find vestiges or traces of the Trinity in its creation, likenesses of it in the external activity of man, and its closest image in the mind of man and its operations. It is a hierarchy, as we saw, of self-awareness, knowledge and love, ultimately not of oneself or of temporal created things, but of one's dependence upon and gracious redemption by the trinitarian creator as revealed in the incarnate Christ.[141] Thus Augustine outlines threefold images such as the mind (*mens*), knowledge (*notitia*) and love (*amor*) (9.2.2–5.8), or, at a more spiritual level, memory (*memoria*—awareness of oneself), understanding (*intelligentia*—of self) and will (*voluntas*—of self) (10.11.17–12.19) as first attempts at defining the trinitarian nature of the image in man.

In order to illustrate how difficult it is for fallen man to direct his awareness, understanding and love from himself to God, Augustine demonstrates, by means of threefold similitudes based on sight and memory (Book 11) just how much these spiritual faculties rely on external, temporal perception and experience. In other words, how much they operate at

---

[139] On the distinction between *imago* and *similitudo* see *diu. qu.* 51; 74; *qu. Hept.* 5.4; *trin.* 11.5.8. See Markus 1964b; *BA* 15, 589–90. Augustine's understanding of *similitudo* as inferior likeness or vestige (e.g. of the Trinity in creation or man's outer senses) is in sharp contrast to Greek ideas, where *similitudo* (*homoiosis*) is a kind of perfection of the image, lost at the fall, and restored in the life to come.

[140] For a table of references to likenesses of the Trinity in creation, external images and psychological images, see *BA* 15, 570–1. Gregory Nazianzen tentatively suggested, but did not develop, a comparison between man's spiritual faculties and the Trinity. Victorinus had also used Neoplatonic ideas on the structure of the soul to examine the Trinity.

[141] Williams (1990); Ayres (1995); (1998).

the level of *scientia*, or sense knowledge, and how difficult it is for man to enjoy *sapientia*, or the inner contemplation of truth he enjoyed before the fall (Book 12). It is in this context that Christ's role as both man and God, as *scientia* and *sapientia*, in Book 13 is placed. In order to embrace Christ's mediation between the temporal and eternal Augustine observes—by means of another trinitarian image—that man must have faith in His temporal revelation. Thus the image of God in man might be reformed in attending to, understanding and loving its Creator (Book 14).

Of course, this reformation will never be perfected, and God can never be fully known in this life; man can only see 'through a glass darkly'. Like the search for wisdom which we have examined in this chapter in relation to classical philosophy, it is, rather, a continual process whereby God's grace and love enables man to turn to Him, respond to Him, and be progressively formed in His image. Thus Augustine can only conclude *On the Trinity* with a prayer: 'May I remember you, understand you and love you. Increase in me all these things until you conform me to your perfect image' (Book 15).

2

Res non verba: *Christianity and pagan literary culture*

Even in the backwaters of his native town of Thagaste Augustine's social, cultural, and intellectual horizons were determined by the same, long established, unquestioned, norms which held throughout the length and breadth of the Roman Empire. The monolithic nature of the Empire has often been commented on and various attempts have been made to explain the extraordinary cultural homogeneity which its educated citizens shared. Recent studies[1] tend to converge in their focus upon the formative and cohesive role of the Roman's distinctive educational system in moulding and identifying the most influential stratum of cultured society. It was a system which had barely changed since the time of the Republic, when the Romans drew upon Hellenistic models to shape an educational system and culture which might best be described as literary: one founded upon the study of grammar which reached its apex in the practice of rhetoric—the art of speaking, of teaching, moving, and persuading one's listener. Thus it prepared men to exercise the highest functions in government and law—to practise their rhetorical skills in framing policies and convincing a jury of their case—and effectively created a ruling élite. A shared education which was the same throughout the Empire, which was universally respected, and which invariably produced the same type of man, provided the obvious—but no less tacit and subtle—means of identifying and unifying a certain influential class regardless of geography, profession—or even religion.[2]

What did this education consist of?[3] Most of the population, if they had any formal education at all (levels of illiteracy were staggeringly high[4]) would simply attend a school of letters and obtain basic, functional literacy. The élite, however, would be effectively insulated from them at the very outset, by instruction either at home, or in a town school. Here a trained *grammaticus* would begin the long course of study which often lasted into

---

[1] Marrou (1949); Kaster (1988); Brown (1992).

[2] See Brown (1992), 39–40 on a common educational *paideia*.

[3] For a bibiliography on Roman Education in Augustine's day see Marrou (1949), 9, n. 3.

[4] Kaster (1988), 35–6; Humphrey (1991).

the students' twenties, and initiate them into the intricacies of reading a text,[5] of accent, poetry, metre as well as some of the disciplines of the liberal arts, in preparation for the more advanced school of rhetoric (though not all progressed to this). They would begin to study rhetorical theory[6] and to read the standard classic authors—beacons of aristocratic distinction and privilege: Cicero (the historian, philosopher, and rhetor), Virgil (the poet), Sallust (the historian), and Terence (the dramatist). These four, commonly referred to as the *quadriga*, were venerated, known and studied by all.[7] Seneca, Apuleius, Ovid, Catullus, Juvenal, Horace, Lucian, Persius, and Varro might follow (at least in *florilegia* or collections).[8] In Africa Augustine may also have encountered the less well-known Manlius (first-century verse handbook on astrology), Fronto (second-century tutor to Marcus Aurelius), Apuleius of Madura (author of *The Golden Ass* and handbooks on Platonic philosophy), and Aulus Gellius (author of *Attic Nights*, which has been described as a 'a kind of readers digest to effective dinner party conversation').

The further disciplines studied were generally known as the liberal arts, the *disciplinae liberales*,[9] those studies which were appropriate for—indeed, which distinguished—free men:[10] grammar, rhetoric, dialectic, arithmetic, music, geometry, astronomy (or, sometimes, philosophy).[11]

Such an education, preoccupied with authoritative, classical rules, categories, definitions, and divisions did not lend itself to spontaneity or independent thought, to the cultivation of overarching views, syntheses, or judgements, and scarcely seems geared to the practical necessities of effective government—but then this was not its aim. Its function was primarily social rather than academic: it was intended to create, foster, and protect a governing élite, and its success in this respect is unquestionable.[12] It was Patrick's social ambition for his son, rather than purely intellectual

---

[5] *lectio, emendatio, ennaratio, judicium*—Marrou (1949), 20–1.

[6] E.g. the five parts of oratory—invention, disposition, style, memory, and delivery; the five divisions of speech—introduction, statement of facts, proof, refutation, and conclusion; the three kinds of style—the grand, the moderate, and the simple. Laistner (1951), 12.

[7] Marrou (1955), 405 f.

[8] Of whom Augustine makes extensive use—*ciu*. 6.2, 'he will teach the student of things, as much as Cicero delights the student of words'.

[9] Marrou (1949), 187–275 for detailed discussion.

[10] They are contrasted by Plato, in *Republic* VII, 522b, with the servile or mechanical arts.

[11] Though the number and precise nature of the disciplines varies: Philo lists six; Seneca, five; Cicero, seven; Varro , in *The Nine Books of the Disciplines* which Augustine knew (Solignac (1958), 120–1) added medecine and architecture; Quintilian added history, law, and philosophy. See Marrou (1949), 216–17 for a table of how the liberal arts were classified before Augustine. Augustine himself varies on the specific disciplines to be included, Marrou (1949), 189.

[12] Kaster (1988), 12–14—to whom I am much indebted for these insights; Brown (1992), 39–40.

interests, which motivated him to ensure that, despite financial difficulties, Augustine received the best education available. This meant, of course, the school of grammar at Thagaste and, thanks to a wealthy patron, the school of rhetoric at Madura and then Carthage. Thus, Augustine was able to climb the social ladder into the ranks of the élite—an aristocracy, not of birth, but of educational formation. He was now able to speak the right language with all the right allusions and overtones, to the right people. His chosen profession—a teacher of rhetoric—led him ever closer to the centre of power and influence, from Carthage (371/376–83), to Rome(383–4), and finally, to an appointment to the municipal chair of rhetoric in Milan (384), the Imperial capital, where, on occasion, he had the Emperor's ear.[13] He might not unreasonably have aspired to still further advancement—perhaps, in the manner of Arnobius or Ambrose, to a provincial governorship. In 386 the future was open and it shone with promise.

What beckoned Augustine, however, was not promotion but conversion to a radically new life in which the liberal arts, those markers of aristocratic power and prestige, which had enabled him to progress so far, would be wholly re-evaluated. We see the roots of Augustine's new identity taking hold, tentatively, and with difficulty, in the very foreign soil of the Christian Scriptures. His gradual acquaintance with these Scriptures, and his overcoming of the immense difficulties which they posed to his cultured mind, mark his transition from—or perhaps better, transformation of—classical culture to a Christian culture.

THE SCRIPTURES

To examine these roots we need to turn to the *Confessions*. As we have seen in the previous chapter, Augustine's first (recorded) encounter with Scripture came when, after reading Cicero's *Exhortation to Philosophy* and regretting that Christ was not mentioned in this otherwise excellent book, he turned to examine the Scriptures. His first reaction was profound disappointment: they 'seemed (to me) to be unworthy in comparison to the dignity of Cicero' (*conf.* 3.5.9. Cf. *s.* 51.4–5). And well they might: although Greek was used throughout the Mediterranean (Tertullian, in Africa, wrote in Greek and Latin) and was used by the Roman church until the third century, the version Augustine consulted was no doubt the Old Latin or *Vetus Latina*,[14] an early third-century Latin translation of the New Testa-

---

[13] He proclaimed the official panegyric on the death of the consul Bauto in the presence of Emperor Valentinian II, *conf.* 4.2.2 .

[14] See Petitmengin (1985) for an examination of extant MS. It is generally accepted that the African bible was the earliest version. The best early evidence is Cyprian's *Ad Quirinum*

ment and the LXX characterized by its extremely literal, none too careful translation. It had no aspirations to literary style but rather contained so many vulgarisms and solecisms that it could not fail to offend the sensitive ears of cultured readers and make them recoil in distaste. Arnobius, Lactantius, and Jerome predictably shared Augustine's feelings, and similarly made no attempt to hide them, when considering the literary merits of Scripture.[15] Pagan, and especially Manichaean, criticisms of Scripture would only serve to heighten Augustine's sensitivity to its defects and endorse his religious affiliation to the latter: they were merciless in pointing out Scripture's inconsistencies, its dubious morality, its contradictions, discordances, and all too human depiction of God.[16] Christianity failed to meet the requirements of civilized discourse; it was an alien, foreign, unsympathetic, somewhat rebarbative culture which presented itself to educated readers in illiterate, crudely written prose. This was the very real obstacle which Augustine, and other cultured late antique men, had to surmount in their conversion to Christianity.

Ambrose's pleasing rhetoric, and above all, his spiritual, allegorical, figurative interpretation of those very passages of Scripture which had been the target of the Manichees' criticisms when read literally, was the catalyst for Augustine's change in attitude (*conf.* 5.14.24. Cf. 6.3.3–4). Here was someone he could relate to; a cultured, educated, immensely impressive man who inspired deep respect and admiration, who had yet embraced Christianity; 'who asserted its claims and refuted objections with abundant argument and without absurdity' (*conf.* 5.14.24). Augustine was gradually persuaded that faith in Scripture was to be preferred to the Manichees' claim to truth by reason. It possessed pre-eminent authority; was diffused through all lands; was persuasively coherent when interpreted spiritually: 'Already the absurdity which used to offend me in those books, after I had heard many passages being given persuasive expositions, I understood to be significant of the profundity of their mysteries' (6.7.8); it was accessible to all in its simple style while also exercising the minds of the more educated (ibid.). It was in Scripture that he learnt the way of humility, of Christ incarnate, which counteracted the Platonists' pride, and which enabled him 'to discern and distinguish the difference between presumption and confession' (7.20.26). With a new enthusiasm and respect he began to read

I–III which contains long quotations from a practically complete Latin Bible. Traces of this version are also found in the *Acts of the Martyrs*, the work of the Donatists, Hilary, Victorinus, Ambrosiaster, and Ambrose, but the latter often also work with the Greek and correct the Latin in reference to it, so that it is difficult to establish a text. For this, see the painstaking work of the Institute at Beuron, *Die Reste der Altlateinischen Bibel*.

[15] Arnobius *Adversus nationes* 1.58–9; Lactantius *Institutiones* 3.1.11; 5.1.15–18; 6.21.4–5; Jerome *Ep.* 22.30.2; 53.10.1. Referred to by Fredouille 1985a, 29 n. 12.

[16] Courcelle (1963) I, 158–60. Fredouille 1985b, 479–98.

St Paul, not with cultured distaste, but joy and trembling at his commendation of God's grace (6.21.27). It was St Paul that he took up to read in the garden of Milan and whose words precipitated his conversion.

Thus, as a literary text, and as an authoritative witness to truth, Augustine embraced Scripture as central to, and definitive of, Christian faith and culture. The ideas we have seen taking root in the *Confessions* evolve within the environment of the Church, where Augustine's role as priest and bishop necessitated frequent attention to them, and find their full flowering in his work, *On Christian Doctrine*, which we will be examining later in this chapter.

Following the advice Simplicianus had offered when he consulted him before his conversion, Augustine realized that to acquaint himself with Christianity he must study the Scriptures. Although he seems to have been more preoccupied with reading Virgil and discussing philosophical questions during the retreat he took at Cassiciacum, immediately following his conversion in 386, he would no doubt have learnt a good deal of the Bible during the period immediately following, when he received instruction as a *competentes*, a candidate for baptism, under Ambrose at Milan in 387. Here he would doubtless have heard what we can now read in Ambrose's *On the Sacraments* and *On the Mysteries*. He makes numerous references to how limited his knowledge of Scripture was when he left Italy for Africa (*ep.* 55.38; 73.5; 104) in 388, and from the time of his return, at pains to answer his critics, Scripture becomes his sole text. It is frequently cited in the works he immediately felt compelled to write against the Manichees[17] and was evidently the inspiration and foundation of the works which occupied his time at Thagaste (388–91).[18] On being appointed priest at Hippo in 391, Augustine immediately asked his bishop Valerius for time to study the Scriptures, the fruits of which are seen in the veritable torrent of commentaries on Scripture—the *Unfinished Literal Commentary on Genesis*; *The Sermon on the Mount*; *Exposition of Various Queries on Romans*; *The Epistle to the Galatians*; *Unfinished Exposition on Romans*—which precede his consecration as bishop in 395. In this year he wrote to Jerome, concerned about his duty to interpret Scripture from such a prominent position (*ep.* 9.2) and asked for some translations of Greek commentaries on Scripture. He also began work on *On Christian Doctrine*.

Augustine stands in a long line of Western Christian reflection upon the Bible.[19] Perhaps the most significant development in biblical exegesis in the

---

[17] Especially *mor.* (AD 390) and *Gn. adu. Man.* (AD 389). Also *lib. arb.* I (AD 388); *util. cred.* (AD 392) and *duab. an.* (AD 392).

[18] *uera rel.* (see, particularly, chapter 99 where Augustine demonstrates his awareness of the complexities of exegetical questions and methods); the earlier *diu.qu.*

[19] Simonetti (1994). In the West there was Hippolytus (though he wrote in Greek), Novatian, Cyprian, Ps. Cyprian, Victorinus of Pettau, Reticius of Autun, Hilary, Marius Victorinus, Ambrosiaster, Ambrose, Jerome, Tyconius, Julian of Eclanum, Rufinus, Gregory of Elvira, Zeno of Verona, Chromatius.

West was Jerome's initiation of a Latin translation of the Hebrew Old Testament—*hebraica veritas*, or what has come to be known as the Vulgate—rather than relying upon the LXX or Origen's revision of it in the *Hexapla*, as Augustine tenaciously insisted upon doing. Lacking Jerome's linguistic ability, conscious of the weight of authority and tradition which the inspired translation of the LXX carried, especially in countering hostile criticism, Augustine could not bring himself to relinquish the LXX or wholeheartedly to accept Jerome's new translation which threatened to undermine it. And yet his embattled correspondence with Jerome shows a marked weakening in Augustine's attitude, to the point where, ever respectful of Jerome's biblical scholarship, he acknowledges the usefulness of Jerome's translation alongside the LXX.[20]

Thus Scripture assumed its central place in Augustine's thought. How easily did it sit with his earlier formation and education? We have already examined how far-reaching the effects of this formation were—both intellectually and socially. We have hinted at some of the frictions which might arise from any attempt to read Scripture as a work of literature comparable to the pagan classics and how Ambrose, in both his person and work, seemed to smooth these over.

But Augustine had to resolve the frictions for himself. At first, as with philosophical questions, he seems to have been optimistic about the possibility of simply synthesizing Christianity and classical thought. This is especially evident in what he has to say about the role of the liberal arts in his early works. These useful disciplines, which trained the mind, and led it away from the concrete, sensible and corporeal to the abstract, intelligible and incorporeal, he still maintained were the best way of attaining the truth (e.g. *sol.* 2.32). It was for this reason that Augustine tells us in the *Retractations* (1.6) he planned a series of books on the liberal arts in 387, following his baptism. The project did not progress very far[21]—only *On Music* and *On Dialectic* were completed[22]—but his confidence in the liberal arts and his desire to give them a key role in his newly adopted religion, is clearly evident in the works he composed at Cassiciacum. *On Order*, in particular, gives them a central place in the Christian's attempt to apprehend the truth: they correct any deceptive impressions which the mind might receive from corporeal things (1.1); they cultivate it to receive the seeds of divine truth (1.4), and bring clarity to those who are confused by the 'great obscurity and maze of affairs' (2.15). Thus the soul ascends through the disciplines (2.35–44), from the reasonable pleasure and delight of the senses, to the communication and expression of its meaning in

---

[20] White (1990) provides a translation of the correspondence and an illuminating introduction.   [21] *BA* 12, 565; Marrou (1949), 570–9.

[22] He perhaps also began a *De grammatica* and a *De rhetorica*—see Madec (1996), 51; Law (1997).

grammar, to teaching and learning this message in *dialectics*, to persuading and convincing of its truth in *rhetoric*, to the use of *number* which looks beyond the transient, rhythmically ordered sounds of the rhetor to what they signify, and finally, to *geometry*, which looks beyond corporeal beauties to the rational unity of design and number by which they are governed. Thus, the soul can search after divine things, 'not merely as truths to be believed, but also as matters to be contemplated, understood and retained' (2.44).[23] Although he was later to regret such passages (*retr.* 1.3.2; *ep.* 101.2; *conf.* 4.16.30; *mus.* 6.17.59; *s.* 70.2; 133.4; *ciu.* 5.) and to dismiss the disciplines as 'theatrical and poetic trifling' (*uera rel.* 100) in comparison to diligent study of Scipture and dependence on faith rather than rational enquiry, it should not surprise us to find they were so ingrained in his ways of thinking, arguing, and making sense of reality that they could not be wholly abandoned. Rather, they continually appear in the service of his attempts to interpret, defend, and preach upon Scripture and expound Christian truth. In this respect, he was to remain a grammarian, a dialectitian, and a rhetor for the rest of his life. He would continue to use Cicero,[24] Virgil and a host of other classical authors[25]—not least apologetically; to use the divisions and definitions of the grammarians;[26] to practise the art of dialectics[27] and pre-eminently, the art of rhetoric.

Henri Marrou's classic book, *Saint Augustin et la fin de la culture antique* (1948) initiated what was to prove a far-reaching and influential debate concerning Augustine's relation to late antique literature and culture. Its subsequent, rather unconventional appendix, or—in Augustinian fashion—*retractatio* (1949), in which Marrou sought to revise or temper some of his original opinions, is a measure of the liveliness of the debate which followed its first publication: was Augustine simply a typical product of late antique culture—*un homme de la décadence*—someone whose education, work, and written style betrayed all the marks of an over-ripe culture, a culture which had, as it were, gone to seed; its preoccupation with eloquent presentation largely obscuring any attention to content and truth? Or was he one of the first representatives of a new Christian culture, in which style was sacrificed on the altar of truth and concern for eloquence was strictly subordinated to a desire to instil the message of the gospel? Of course, Augustine, like all the fathers, belonged to both cultures. The question really was, and is, just how far he achieved, or failed to achieve, the difficult, almost amphibious movement, between them.

---

[23] See I. Hadot (1984) for the possible Porphyrian influence and Madec (1996), 52 n. 43 for reservations. There are close parallels to this sort of appreciation of the liberal arts in Basil *To Young Men on the Manner of Profiting from Hellenistic Writings*, 9.86 ff.—see Kaster (1988), 77–80.   [24] Testard (1958).

[25] Hagendahl (1967).   [26] Marrou (1949), 15–16.   [27] Pépin (1976).

Are we therefore to speak of a transition, a crossing over, from one culture to another? Of an abandonment of classical culture? Of an eclectic mix of classical and Christian? Of a transformation of classical culture by a Christian culture?

A CHRISTIAN CULTURE?

These questions are all, to some extent, relevant: we find them being raised and discussed by those Christians—and they include all the fathers—who found themselves inescapably part of classical culture: those who, in their intellectual and social formation, had been trained and cultivated by it. Classical culture was, along with the Bible and philosophy, one of the 'intertexts',[28] which they shared with their educated readers, and which they could allude to in the certain knowledge that they would be understood.

It was for this reason that the Eastern fathers were generally very positive in their attitude to, and use of, pagan literature and culture. It proved an invaluable apologetic and catechetical tool, enabling them to appeal to generally accepted authorities and thereby find common ground with critics as well as fellow Christians, in their defence and exposition of the Christian faith. Such is the attitude of Justin, Origen, Clement, the Cappadocians. There were, of course, aspects of pagan culture which they unanimously rejected as hostile to, and wholly incompatible with, Christianity, such as idolatry, sacrifices, the mysteries and ethical standards. Their general attitude, however, is characterized by a positive eclecticism towards those aspects of pagan culture—the disciplines, philosophy, moral rules, monotheist affirmations, and aspirations—which seemed to have so much in common with Christianity that, as we saw in the previous chapter, they frequently concluded that in fact they were *derived from* earlier teaching in Moses and the prophets that Christians claimed for themselves, or through the gift of insights into the truth granted by the *logos spermatikos*.

The Western fathers adopt much the same approach, but with greater reservations and more studied criticisms. The reason for their reticence and reserve, which at times amount to outright rejection, seems to lie in the fact that Greek was not their native tongue; they were not direct heirs of the Greek philosophical tradition and Greek literature and culture, which had quite easily become part of the expression of Christianity in the East, but were forced to reflect far more carefully on what place they had in a Latin Christianity which, although it could also draw upon its own classical literature, was characterized far more by the popular, idiomatic

---

[28] Clark (1993a), 73.

Christianity represented by the *Vetus Latina*. Here, as Kaster puts it, 'the polished speech of the few continued to be incompatible with the spiritual understanding of the many'.[29] Western Christianity had developed relatively late, with a popular literary culture which was at odds with the more cultured version which had naturally developed in the East but which, in the West, was very much the preserve of an élite. This is, of course, to generalize, but it is clear that the Western fathers found it much more difficult to bridge the gap between their educational culture and the distinctive Christian culture which had developed in the West. The fine line between 'holy rusticity' and 'sinful eloquence',[30] the common good and individualistic pretention, humility and pride, sound instruction and rhetorical display, was the precarious one which the educated bishop had to tread. We generally find that the Western fathers are much more self-conscious in their use of, and criticism of, classical culture; they are more acutely aware of its dangers, and more sensitive to the needs of their fellow Christians in this respect, than their Eastern counterparts, though exactly why this is the case is not clear.

Their reactions to the 'holy rusticity' represented by the *Vetus Latina* differ: Minucius Felix, a famous advocate at Rome, firmly rejects it in his attempt to find a literary expression closer to the classical tradition; Tertullian (whose profession is debated but who, according to Barnes, belonged by birth and upbringing to Christian literary circles in Carthage[31]) and Cyprian (a former teacher of rhetoric) make no comment on the quality of biblical Latin but take up developing Christian idiom to make it part of Latin literature; Arnobius (a former rhetor), Lactantius (a teacher of rhetoric) and Hilary obviously sympathized with Minucius Felix but found it impossible to avoid what had now become an intrinsic part of Christian idiom and syntax. Augustine, as we shall see in examining book four of *De Doctrina Christiana*, attempts to define exactly what this new Christian idiom and style is.[32]

The other side of this question returns us to our original query: what role did the Latin fathers assign to the various aspects of the classical tradition in a Christian context? It might be worth noting, first of all, that according to Barnes, Latin Christian authors in Africa far outnumbered African Latin pagan writers,[33] whose work, such as it was, provided a pitiful contrast to the East and to the 'Golden Age' of the late Republic and the reign of Augustus.[34] There were very few notable pagan writers in any of

[29]   Kaster (1988), 76.

[30]   Jerome *Letters* 52.9; 27.1; 53.3; 57.12; *In Ezekielen* 2.7—cited by Kaster (1988), 82.

[31]   Barnes (1971), 58.   [32]   Mohrmann (1958), I, 8.

[33]   Barnes (1971), 192, who points out that they themselves outnumbered all other Latin writers of this period.   [34]   Ibid. 189.

the well-known genres, rather it fell to the likes of Minucius Felix, Cyprian, Arnobius and Lactantius, as the first growth of the great flowering of Christian Latin literature in the West, to continue the Latin literary tradition. Alongside an ingrained respect for the authority of antiquity, this also explains why the fathers invariably had in mind the classical past, rather than the present, in considering its relation to Christianity.

RES NON VERBA

Tertullian, who is usually put forward as a representative of the extremist wing of Christianity's rejection of pagan culture (along with Tatian and Aristides), is, in fact, a good example of the general ambiguity of the fathers' attitude. Certainly, he is more vociferous than most in denouncing those aspects of pagan culture which he deemed incompatible with the Christian life, such as its polytheism, idolatry, sacrifices, shows, and festivals[35] (though such rejection of pagan culture is a polemical *topos* common to all the fathers[36]) and is the famous author of the oft-quoted, 'What has Athens to do with Jerusalem? or what has the Academy in common with the Church?' (*Praescr. Haer.* 7). Yet Tertullian concedes that a pagan education is desirable in the absence of a Christian alternative and, like all the fathers, uses his own education, and its rhetorical expression, to great effect in defence of Christianity.[37]

Western authors shared with the Greeks the experience that an elegant literary style carried more weight in expounding the Christian faith, both to its opponents and its cultured adherents, than straightforward, unadorned, prose. Many of them, as we have seen above, were either former rhetors or still teachers in the rhetorical schools. We frequently find them using all the techniques of their art—rather ambiguously—both to set forth the truth of Christianity, *and* to criticize rhetorical excesses.

Arnobius, for example, cogently—with great rhetorical style—makes clear that what matters is *what* is said, not *how* it is said; that the reader should learn, not be entertained (*Adv. nationes* 1.59).[38] Another excellent, rather self-conscious example of this genre can be found in Lactantius' *Divine Institutions*: it is a carefully crafted literary piece in the classical style, intended to expound and defend Christian teaching—but then he feels obliged to add that the simple, undisguised truth is sufficient ornament in itself (3.1.3–4); that the wise man has no need for rhetoric, rather, the seat of wisdom is not the tongue but the heart (3.13.4–5).

---

[35] See *De Spectaculis*; *De Idolatria*; *De Cultu Feminarum*.
[36] E.g. Madec (1974), 349–98.   [37] Barnes (1971), 210; Fredouille (1972).
[38] See Simmons (1995).

Ambrose, likewise, though theoretically hostile to classical culture, uses it almost unconsciously in his interpretation and preaching upon Scripture[39]—though he too obviously feels he must justify his use of rhetoric by pointing out that it is also used in Scripture. And, like the other fathers, he is keen to stress the virtues of simplicity and clarity (*De officiis* 1.22.101); that the preacher should keep to the inner meaning of the words, rather than being too theatrical (ibid. 1.23.104). For Jerome, the ambiguities, or conflicts we have noted between the fathers' use of classical culture and their attitude to it, surfaced in his famous, fevered dream, where his fondness for the pagan classics, his inability to leave behind his library, led to the charge 'Ciceronianus es, non christianus'—'You are a Ciceronian, not a Christian' (*ep.* 22.30). He too appreciated the powers of rhetorical expression but was also well aware of how it could be misused, especially by heretics (*In Osee* 5.11; 12.7–8; *In Isaia* 11.40.18; 18.65.3.). So, along with the other fathers, we find him stressing simplicity rather than rhetorical fireworks (*In Galatis praefatio*; *In Amb. praef.*; *ep.* 36.14.1–2.); the meaning of a passage, rather than the words which express it (*hom. orig. in Jer. et Ezech. prol.*; Cf. *In Isaia* 2.45–6); literary faithfulness, rather than elegance in translation (*In Isaia* 8.327–8); clarity rather than grammatical correctness (*In Ezechielen* 14.590). 'What' he asks, 'has Horace to do with the Psalter, Vergil with the Gospels and Cicero with the Apostle? . . . we ought not to drink the cup of Christ and the cup of devils at the same time' (*ep.* 22.29.6–7).[40] We will find the same ambiguities and the same arguments in Augustine's consideration of classical rhetoric in *On Christian Doctrine* Book 4.

The importance Christians attached to classical learning is evidenced in their violent reaction to the Emperor Julian's edict of 362 which attempted to forbid Christians to teach in pagan schools—thus, as the Christians saw it, depriving them of the only culture they knew and all that that meant in terms of social standing and recognition. At a time when the two most important chairs of rhetoric were occupied by Christians—Prohaeresius at Athens and Victorinus at Rome—and numerous Christians were employed in the secular schools, sensitivity to Christianity's position was obviously heightened. The Christians seem to have made no attempt to establish an educational system of their own, which might be seen to rival the classical pagan one: even Basil's *To Young Men on the Manner of Profiting from Hellenistic Writings* simply deals with Christian use of traditional education

---

[39] Madec (1974), 341 writes: 'Sa prose s'orne comme naturellement de mille réminiscences virgiliennes qui consonnent avec sa sensibilité poétique.'

[40] I owe this quotation, together with some of the others in this section, to Ellspermann (1949).

and does not envisage a new Christian system.[41] The only exception seems to be the work of the two Apollinarii, father and son, who, in response to Julian's edict, composed Christian manuals of grammar and collected together explanatory texts inspired by the Bible to take the place of the pagan texts they were now forbidden to teach: they adapted the Pentateuch into epic hexameters; the historical books of the Old Testament into tragic verse; the Gospels and Acts into Platonic dialogues.[42] But such efforts were hardly necessary: the edict did not outlive Julian, who died in 363. That a pagan should so readily have identified literature and religion was an unprecedented, highly unusual move, which disconcerted pagans as well as Christians.[43] It temporarily brought the issue of pagan and Christian culture to a head but, as Kaster suggests, it should probably be regarded more as a legacy of Julian's Christian upbringing[44] than as representative of a general pagan attitude. It was not to be repeated.

The Christians, meanwhile, as we have seen, had developed a well-established set of arguments to justify and defend their use of pagan culture: the argument that the Old Testament and its prophets were prior to pagan authors so that all pagan learning could be argued to be ultimately borrowed or derived from it; the theory of the seeds of the logos, or *logos spermatikos*, which held that all men naturally enjoyed insights into the truth by virtue of their possession of reason, or *logos*, and that the full truth was to be found in the revelation of the *Logos*, the Word of God incarnate, Jesus Christ. Thus, pagan literature could legitimately be read as containing insights into the truth; it could be plundered for the truth it had appropriated from Christian sources; the truth could be reclaimed by its rightful owner, once cleansed of the dross which had become attached to it in its pagan dress. A number of biblical texts were adduced to elucidate these views: the most popular was the Exodus story of the Israelites spoiling the Egyptians of their treasure (3: 22; 11: 2; 12: 35). The gold and silver which the Israelites plundered, had been taken by the Egyptians, Augustine comments, from 'the mines of divine providence' (*doct. chr.* 2.40.60[45]). So,

---

[41] This is not to deny the existence of Christian works of instruction, such as Chrysostom's *On Vainglory and the Right Way for Parents to Bring up their Children* (see Laistner (1951), 75–122), and of catechetical instruction, such as Cyril's *Catechetical Orations*, Theodore of Mopsuestia's *Sixteen Addresses*; Gregory of Nyssa's *Great Catechism*; Ambrose's *On the Sacraments* and *On the Mysteries*.

[42] Socrates *Historia Ecclesiae* 3.16 (who is critical of their actions); Sozomen *Historia Ecclesiae* 5.18 (who supports them).

[43] Cf. Ammianus Marcellinus *Res gestae* 22.10.7.   [44] Kaster (1988), 73 n. 168.

[45] Cf. *conf.* 7.9.15; *c. Faust.* 22.91. Origen *Epistula ad Gregorium* 1–2; Gregory of Nyssa *De Vita Moysis* 2.115–116.

'When the Christian separates himself in spirit from their [the pagans']
miserable society, he should take this treasure with him for the just use of
teaching the gospel' (ibid.). He praises Cyprian, Lactantius, Victorinus,
Optatus, and Hilary, who, following the example of Moses (who 'was
instructed in all the wisdom of the Egyptians' (Acts 7: 22)), have done
precisely this (ibid. 2.40.61). The 'treasure' Augustine has in mind he
identifies with some of the liberal disciplines, certain moral precepts and
'truths concerning the worship of the one God'. The 'clothing' which the
Israelites also took he interestingly identifies with 'those human institutions which are accommodated to human society and are necessary to the
conduct of life' (ibid. 2.40.60).

ON CHRISTIAN DOCTRINE 2.19.29–42.63

The passage we have referred to above from *On Christian Doctrine* Book 2,[46]
is in fact part of a much more extensive consideration of exactly what
attitude the Christian should adopt towards the various aspects of pagan
culture, which runs from 2.19.29 to 42.63.[47] It is this that Luc Verheijen, in
a seminal article on this section, has described as a 'charte fondamentale
pour une culture chrétienne'—a 'fundamental charter for a Christian
culture', in contradistinction to the rest of *On Christian Doctrine* which he
describes as a manual of hermeneutics (*modus inveniendi* or *inventio*) and
Christian expression (*modus proferendi* or *elocutio*—following the classical
terms).

His distinctions cut across, and thankfully serve to defuse, a long history
of scholarly debate as to the nature and purpose of this work:[48] it is primarily a work on the interpretation of Scripture which includes a handbook of Christian rhetoric and a charter for a Christian culture: Book 1
sets forth the *res* or truths of the Christian faith; Book 2 discusses the *signa*
or signs in which they are expressed in Scripture and how they should be
interpreted; Book 3 deals with difficult, ambiguous signs; Book 4 examines
how to express what has been discovered in Scripture, in preaching. The
section on the nature of Christian culture (2.19.29–42.63) lies between the
general discussion of signs and the later consideration of ambiguous or
difficult signs.

---

[46] A work begun in AD 396 but only completed (taking up from 3.35.51) in AD 426/7.

[47] Verheijen (1974a).

[48] The debate, primarily between H.-I. Marrou (who thought it was a blueprint for a Christian culture) and F. X. Eggersdorfer (who thought it was primarily concerned with the
methods and principles of Christian education), is summarized in Kevane (1966). Madec
(1989), 119–21 also suggests it was written because of the urgent need to form Christian teachers, probably at the request of Aurelius of Carthage, to serve as a manual for young clergy.

This apparent digression is in fact intrinsic to, and complements, the work as a whole, since Christian culture is primarily defined by its Scriptures and classical culture is taken over and used, insofar as it facilitates the interpretation and expression of the truth of Scripture. The much debated *doctrina* of the title therefore primarily means 'doctrine' or 'teaching' (and is used in this sense, in the singular, throughout the main body of the work, in Book 1 of the content of Christian faith; in Books 2 and 3 of the contents of Scripture; in Book 4, of Christian rhetoric). The fifteen instances where it appears in the plural, *doctrinae*, occur, significantly, in the section on Christian culture, where it refers to those aspects of pagan culture, the 'Egyptian spoils', which Christians might take over and use.[49]

Let us examine this section more carefully: Augustine begins his discussion by distinguishing two categories: those 'things which men have themselves instituted' and those which 'they have seen to be firmly established or divinely ordained' (2.19.29). The first category, things which have been instituted by men, includes both things that are superstitious and those that are not. Superstitious things are those that are characteristically pagan: making and worshipping idols; divination; amulets, charms, and superstitious practices; astrology; fortune telling; pacts with demons (2.20.30–24.37). All these aspects of pagan culture are to be wholly repudiated, feared, and avoided by Christians. Such practices work, not because of any innate value, but because they are commonly agreed upon by a group of men, in this case pagans: 'signs are not valid among men except by common consent' (2.25.38). But there are other practices which are similarly a matter of general consent, which are not superstitious. Some of these are dismissed as superfluous to the Christian, such as the gestures used by actors in the theatre, or the conventions of artists and sculptors, or imaginative fables (2.25.38). Others are more useful, such as the conventions which help distinguish sex and rank, which regulate weights and measurements, the value of coinage and above all, letters, signs, shorthand. These, he concludes 'are useful; they neither are learned in an illicit way, nor do they enmesh anyone in superstition, nor enervate through extravagance, if they occupy us only so far as they do not interfere with more important things to which we should devote our attention' (2.26.40).

The second category comprises those things that men have not instituted themselves, but that have been observed by them in the course of time or that occur through divine institution (2.27.41). There are, first of all, those pertaining to the senses: the faithful narration of events in history (which enables the Christian to say that Plato borrowed from the Old Testament! 2.28.43); the observation of natural phenomena in herbal

---

[49] Verheijen (1974a), 12–13.

medicine, geography, geology, which are sometimes useful in interpreting Scripture (2.29.45), and astronomy, which has little use for the Christian 2.29.46; the human 'arts' in which men work either to make something— to build a house, a bench or a dish—or to assist the work of God, in medicine, agriculture, and navigation, or simply work themselves in the act of dancing, running, and wrestling (though we do not need to know how to *do* any of these things, it is useful to be able to understand what Scripture implies when it bases figurative language on them). Secondly, there are those things not instituted by men which pertain to reason: the science of disputation, or the art of dialectic (of valid inference, definition, division, partition, and of eloquence, which is extremely useful in solving many of the questions which appear in Scripture—though its practitioner must use them in the cause of truth and beware of pride, ostentation and sophistry—since all its rules are given by God (2.31.48–37.55)); the science of numbers, of arithmetic (the source of which men should seek out, so as to rise from the mutable to the immutable truth of God). These too have their utility, but only if rightly used and directed—*ne quid nimis* (2.39.58).

The readers Augustine has in mind are 'studious and intelligent youths who fear God and seek the blessed life' (2.39.58). They are to use the social conventions, education, and disciplines of pagan society—their *doctrinae*— insofar as they prove useful in their search for Christian truth, and especially in the interpretation of Scripture. However, they should reject pacts with demons and the superfluous, extravagant institutions created by men. The passage which we have already examined concerning the Israelites spoiling the Egyptians concludes the digression.

Augustine has been criticized for his narrow[50] and 'utilitarian, extremely reductivist viewpoint',[51] in relation to classical culture in this section— for being simply preoccupied with the exegesis of Scripture.[52] There is a measure of justice in such observations, especially if we bear in mind Augustine's sweeping rejection of the arts of the theatre, painting, sculpture, poetry, and story-telling in 2.25.38–39. In their pagan manifestations these arts may well have tended towards idolatry, immorality, lies, and deception (*ord.* 2.34; *ep.* 91.3; *c. Faust.* 13.15; *ciu.* 2.8; *conf.* 1.13.20; 16.26; 3.2.2.), and were for this reason traditionally rejected—but is this sufficient ground to repudiate them completely? Could they not have been transformed and used positively, in a Christian context? Indeed they were—one need only think of the art of the catacombs, early Christian mosaics, the hymns of Ambrose, the Latin Christian poetry of Prudentius and Paulinus of Nola to give the lie to Augustine's outright condemnation.

---

[50] Bonner (1987a) IV, 14.   [51] Schäublin (1995), 53.   [52] Ibid.

Whereas Augustine could praise these arts—albeit as a stage to be transcended in the soul's ascent—in *On the Greatness of the Soul*, and continued to read Virgil at Cassiciacum; whereas he encouraged Licentius in his reading of Pyramus and Thisbe (*ord.* 1.8.24), tells us in the *Confessions* that he wept on reading Virgil's description of the death of Dido (1.13.20), that he prefers the fables of the poets to the errors of the philosophers (the Manichees, *conf.* 3.6.11) and that the music he heard in Church profoundly affected him (10.33.49), yet he still rejects them. It was not that he did not appreciate their beauty, but rather that they were too inextricably bound up with paganism—and too beguilingly distracting—to be acceptable: quoting a passage of Terence when recounting his schooldays in the *Confessions*, he writes, 'I bring no charge against the words which are like exquisite and precious vessels, but the wine of error is poured into them for us by drunken teachers' (1.16.26).

There is, at the same time, a licit and an illicit delight: 'A sacred psalm sung sweetly delights the hearing; the songs also of actors delight the hearing—the first licitly, the second illicitly' (*s.* 159.2.2). We will examine Augustine's Christian aesthetic later on in relation to Scripture and preaching. Here we might simply note that in the course of its evolution Augustine could not wholly ignore or dismiss its counterparts in pagan literature.[53] Apart from these sensitive areas, the digression in Book 2 demonstrates clearly that Augustine is generally prepared to plunder pagan culture of everything that is of value, on the understanding that in fact it rightfully belongs to Christianity, and to reject anything that is alien to it. His criteria for selection seem to be based on whether something is of use in understanding and interpreting the Scriptures. If it is, it might legitimately be taken over, studied, taught, and used by the Christian. But, although useful in interpretation, pagan wisdom pales into insignificance when compared with Scripture itself, which contains all knowledge (2. 42.63).

This procedure might indeed, at first sight, seem somewhat blinkered. However, we must now ask why Scripture and its interpretation is so crucial. The answer is, in fact, clear: it is Scripture which contains the *res*, the truths of the Christian faith; it is Scripture which is the norm, the rule, the blueprint, for Christian life in the world; it is Scripture upon which Christian society or culture is founded.

Augustine is clear in *On Christian Doctrine* that societies are founded upon convention; upon a common understanding as to what certain signs and rituals signify. This agreement enables societies to identify themselves, to validate the signs they use, and to use them within generally agreed

---

[53] See H. J. Westra in Meynell (1990), 87–100; Pollmann (1996), 159–73.

parameters. The worship of demons, for example, works on the basis of a pact between the demons and men, as to the meaning and function of magical practices and signs. Greeks are able to communicate because they have a commonly agreed set of signs which function as language in order to convey information which will be understood by another Greek. The Latins have another language, and another set of conventions, by which they can communicate and be understood, but this is not the same as the Greeks, so 'the single sign *beta* means a letter among the Greeks but a vegetable among the Latins' (2.24.37). Understanding therefore varies according to the society one identifies with and upon acceptance of its conventions and practices. Rituals and signs, conversely, are only valid if they are agreed upon: 'signs are not valid among men except by common consent'.

What does this mean for a Christian society, a Christian culture? As we have seen, the digression in Book 2 falls into two parts, the first dealt with those things instituted by men and the second with those which are not instituted by men. The latter is comparatively straightforward and unproblematic. There are certain things which can be observed, or which God has made part of the nature of things, which are generally accepted, practiced and known by *all* men, for example, history, natural history, geology, geography, astronomy, human skills, the disciplines. They belong, as it were, to a general human culture, and insofar as they are useful and appropriate, are also part of a Christian culture. But the first, the things which men institute themselves, is much more problematic: Christianity differs from all the other social groupings Augustine describes in that it is *not instituted by men*, it is not just a matter of common agreement on, and acceptance of, a particular language, or specific rituals: it is *given* to men by God. In other words, it is authoritative in a way that classical culture, pagan culture, demonic worship, Greek or Latin culture, was not. And central to its authority is the text of Scripture[54] (*mor.* 2.3; 7.11; *c. ep. Man.* 5.6; *c. Faust.* 11.2; 11.5; *ciu.* 11.3; *c. Cresc.* 2.31.39). This explains a number of the characteristic features of Christian culture as Augustine describes it.

First of all, it explains why Augustine works from the narrow, eclectic, position we find him adopting in *On Christian Culture*: there are certain institutions, social groupings and practices which are not inimical to Christianity and with which it has much in common; there are others, however, which are quite alien to it. These can be rejected from an authoritative position which cuts through the ambiguity and relativity of things based on social convention—and this is precisely what Augustine does.

Secondly, it is not so much a Christian education that matters as a Christian way of living in the world. Because Augustine considers the disciplines

---

[54] On the Canon of Scripture and Augustine's attitude to problematic/marginal books see *doctr. chr.* 2.8.12–13 and A.-M. La Bonnardière (ed.) (1986), 287–301.

of pagan education and their relative usefulness for the Christian exegete in Book 2, *On Christian Doctrine* has sometimes been misconstrued as a treatise on Christian education.[55] In fact, Augustine's purpose in this part of the work is very similar to St Basil's in his *To Young People on the Manner of Profiting from Hellenistic Writings*: he simply discusses, rather less positively than Basil, the use a Christian might make of a traditional education. Nowhere do we find him attempting to outline the elements of a distinctively Christian education such as Jerome sets forth for Paula's primary education in *ep.* 107 (cf. *ep.* 128).

RES AND SIGNA

More importantly, it means that there are certain realities, or *res*, which impose an order upon social relations, rituals, language, or *signa*[56]—all the aspects of human culture—thereby making them relative and subject to the truth of Christianity. This is what Augustine sets forth in the tightly argued, systematic, first book of *On Christian Doctrine*. The argument revolves around a distinction between *res* (or 'things' which signify nothing other than themselves), and *signa* (or 'signs' which do signify something beyond themselves). God, the eternal, immutable Trinity, is the *res* which is to be loved and enjoyed (*frui*) for its own sake; everything else—creation, man, God's temporal revelation—is to be used (*uti*[57]) and referred to this end. Man's attitude to created reality, his love, is therefore ordered by the created and revealed order of God: it is to be used towards, and referred to, its maker and orderer, and created reality only enjoyed, if at all, in God, and towards the final end of love and enjoyment of Him.[58] It is this which Scripture authoritatively states in the double commandment of love of God and neighbour (Matt. 22: 37–40. Cf. *ep.* 55.21.38; *s.* 350.2.2.):

it is to be understood that the plenitude and end of the Law and of all the sacred Scriptures is the love of a Being which is to be enjoyed and of a being that can share that enjoyment with us . . . that we might know this and have the means to

---

[55] E.g. Eggersdorfer (1907).

[56] These are classical terms referring, respectively, to the objects of *inventio* and *elocutio*—Quintilian *Instituto Oratoria* 8, prooemium 6.

[57] These are also classical terms. The 'eudaemonisitic tradition' originates with Aristotle's *Nichomachean Ethics*, transmitted through Peripatetic and Academic philosophy to Cicero, who interpreted morality as a pursuit of the *finis bonorum* or *summum bonum* (*De Finis Malorum et Bonorum*). See *ciu.* 19.1–4 for a summary and evaluation of the different schools of thought. For Augustine the desire for happiness is an *a priori* certainty, and is used, as here, as the basis for his arguments which lead towards God as the source of all reality and the *beata vita*.

[58] The problems this raises in relation to love and 'use', especially of oneself, one's neighbour and God's love for us, are discussed in detail at 1.22.20–33.36. The discussion is long, involved and somewhat convoluted—see O'Donovan (1980); Harrison (1992), 247–53.

implement it, the whole temporal dispensation was made by divine Providence for our salvation. We should use it, not with an abiding but with a transitory love and delight . . . so that we love those things by which we are carried along for the sake of that toward which we are carried (1.35.39).

The double commandment is also the key for the interpretation of Scripture: 'Whoever, therefore, thinks that he understands the divine Scriptures or any part of them so that it does not build the double love of God and of our neighbour does not understand it at all. Whoever finds a lesson there useful to the building of charity, even though he has not said what the author may be shown to have intended in that place, has not been deceived' (1.36.40). And yet it is the authority of Scripture which makes interpretation possible: we must first believe, on the basis of its authority, before we can truly love, and we can only hope to attain what we love if we first believe and love it (1.36.41). Indeed, 'a man supported by faith, hope, and charity, with an unshaken hold upon them, does not need the Scriptures except for the instruction of others' (1.39.43).

Here, then, is the theoretical background against which Augustine's comments on Scriptural interpretation, the Christian community of interpretation (better, perhaps, than Christian culture), and the expression of the truths of Scripture, are worked out in Books 2–4 of *On Christian Doctrine*, in contradistinction to secular literature, culture, and rhetoric. What distinguishes Christianity is its possession of the truth, or *res*; its authoritative statement of the truth in the *signa* of Scripture; its fundamental orientation in faith, hope, and love towards ultimate enjoyment of God. The clarification of these distinctive characteristics serves to determine and order a proper attitude to all temporal reality, to all *signa* (including Scripture as well as secular culture), which treats them as ultimately inconclusive, as pointing beyond themseves, as finding their meaning only in God, the Trinity.[59] This is reflected in Augustine's frequent reiteration of the admonition we found to underlie the attitude of all the fathers to the expression of the Christian faith in Scripture and preaching: *res non verba*—things not words: it is the meaning of the passage, not the expression that is important; the truth, not appearance; the intention, not literal statement.[60]

In was in this context that Augustine sought to overcome the problems

[59] See Madec (1996), 80–2 for scholarly debate on the meaning of *res/signa*. See Williams (1995), to whom this section is indebted.

[60] E.g. the basic argument of *cons. eu.* is to overcome apparent discrepancies in the accounts of the various evangelists. See eg. *s.* 71.13, 'there is no other reason why the Evangelists do not relate the same things in the same way but that we may learn thereby to prefer things to words, not words to things, and to seek for nothing else in the speaker, but for his intention, to convey which only the words are used.'

which the text of Scripture raised both in the minds of its opponents and for the Christian exegete: its 'rusticity', its contradictoriness, its obscurity. These were simply the *verba*, the *signa* which all pointed beyond themselves to the same *res*—the truth of God, the Trinity—if interpreted according to the rule of the double commandment. Thus, Augustine could allow for a plurality of meaning, for differing interpretations of the same text, for allegorical and figurative readings, so long as they cohered with this basic rule.[61] Indeed, he could urge that not just everything that is *contrary* to faith and morals should be read figuratively, but rather that everything that is not directly related to it, should be interpreted in this fashion.

Such openness or freedom of interpretation also enabled the exegete to make the authoritative text of Scripture relevant and appropriate to his hearers, just as the interpreters of Virgil or Homer had done, by allowing him to interpret it allegorically. Again, so long as the allegory did not contravene the basic rule of the double commandment, it was acceptable.[62] And as we shall see, it not only enabled Augustine to tolerate and explain the obscurities and difficulties of the text at a literal level but also to develop a literary aesthetic which makes sense of Scripture's ability to point beyond itself by engaging man's delight and love for what it says. The text itself, with all its apparent contradictions and difficulties, is both secondary to, but also instrumental in leading the interpreter to seek for its inspiration and truth.

Moreover, there is no divorce between style and substance, words and meaning, signs and signification, in a Christian context, because the former are sacraments of the latter. In this sense too, then, the former cannot be taken as ends in themselves, as they perhaps were in classical practice, but are to be 'used' so that their truth can ultimately be 'enjoyed'. The inconclusive, open-ended, eschatological nature of Augustine's attitude to language and literary artistry is therefore grounded in his theological understanding and interpretation of them, and sets him apart from classical theory and practice.

THE LANGUAGE OF LOVE

A further consequence of the fact that Christianity and its Scriptures are not simply based on arbitrary social convention and agreement but upon the authoritative truth of God and his revelation is that it succeeds in

---

[61] We see Augustine working most openly with these difficulties and considering the problems they raise for interpretation in *conf.* 12. See O'Donnell (1992) III, 328 on 12.20.29.

[62] Markus (1996), 9—though Markus notes growing reservations about the use of allegory.

communicating the truth where other social groupings fail. This is not least because, as we have just seen, Christians cohere as a group, and their Scriptures make sense, because they are based upon truth and love, rather than the idolatry or self-seeking pride characteristic of so many other social groupings. It is love which overcomes and transcends the inherent difficulties of language following the fall and which provides the motivation of the Christian teacher.

Whereas language was a possibility, but by no means a necessity before the fall, since Adam and Eve intuitively knew the truth of God and each other's thoughts (*Gn. litt.* 8.18.37–27.50), it is now the burdensome, but unavoidable way in which man must seek to articulate an idea in his mind, so that it can be known by another.[63] That it now risks misunderstanding, is characterized by ambiguity and obscurity, is capable of hiding man's true thoughts rather than revealing them, and takes the form of many different languages, is a mark of man's fallenness (*Gen. adu. Man.* 2.4.5–5.6).[64] Nevertheless the identity and cohesion of a society succeeds or fails by its ability to communicate linguistically—through authoritative texts, speeches, laws, teaching.[65] Now that individual men and women, and human society in general, is divided by language, what Augustine has to say about the role of Scripture, of divine communication with mankind, is central to his demonstration of what sets the Christian linguistic community apart and how it can function successfully in this fallen context.

His paradigm is the descent of the Word of God, in love, in order to assume flesh to communicate with fallen man (*fid. et sym.* 3.3–4; *s.* 119.4.4–7.7 Io. eu. tr. 37.4). So, when we speak, 'our thought is not transformed into sounds; it remains entire in itself and assumes the form of words by means of which it may reach the ears without suffering any deterioration in itself' (*doc. chr.* 1.13.12. Cf. *trin.* 9.7.12). These are the conventional signs which all men use 'for the purpose of conveying, in so far as they are able, the motion of their spirits or something they have sensed or understood' (ibid. 2.2.3). And they include the signs given by God in Scripture, since they are presented by the men who wrote them (ibid.). If these signs are given, heard and interpreted in love, then they will be truly understood.

This is a note which is frequently sounded throughout Augustine's work—in the Prologue to *On Christian Doctrine* he observes that, 'charity itself, which holds men together in a knot of unity, would not have a means of infusing souls and almost mixing them together, if men could teach nothing to men' (6)—but it is orchestrated most fully in *De Catechizandis Rudibus*, On Teaching the Uninstructed. An awareness of language as a

---

[63] On how language works and for Augustine sources, see Rist (1994), O'Daly (1987), Kirwan (1989), Markus (1996).

[64] Harrison (1992), 59–63.   [65] See Markus (1996), 32–43.

result of the fall is not far from the surface. He discusses the discouraging frustrations and difficulties of the preacher, who may not feel inclined to speak but who must nevertheless labour to articulate his understanding of the faith and descend from an inward enjoyment of the truth to find words suitable to the level of his hearers (who are themselves all too prone to fail to grasp or be moved by what he says).

Augustine gives the example of Christ's descent to man in love. This ought to be the true motive of the preacher's efforts: the more inspired by love his discourse is, the more irresistibly it finds its way into the heart of the hearer (10.15). What matters is not so much what the preacher says but his state of mind, whether he takes pleasure and delight in what he is saying—if he does, he will be heard with pleasure. For, 'so great is the power of sympathy' Augustine acutely comments in Chapter 12, 'that when people are affected by us as we speak and we by them as they learn, we dwell in one another and thus both they, as it were, speak in us what they hear, while we, after a fashion, learn in them what we teach.' *De Catechizandis Rudibus* might aptly be described as a treatise on the nature of love: it is love which ought to dictate the preacher's attitude and words; love which forms the subject of his discourse and is the central lesson of Christian history as it is narrated in Scripture and expressed in the Church; love which the discourse inspires and which motivates man's actions. Love therefore informs the nature, practice, content, and goal of exegesis and preaching.[66]

Like any other linguistic, interpretative community,[67] Christianity is determined by its acceptance of certain customs, traditions, conventions, authorities, and texts. These possess validity and value precisely because they are accepted and agreed upon (*doctr. chr.* 2.24.37). Thus, words signify because there is agreement as to what they mean; conversely, they determine the nature, practice, and self-understanding of the community as they become traditional, authoritative, and customary. As we have seen, Christianity's distinctive emphasis upon the practice and rhetoric of love in its Scriptures and preaching enabled it to create a linguistic community in which the central message of the faith could both be understood and communicated in such a way that it was then practiced and lived. In other words, the central message of love of God and neighbour was interpreted and preached in such a way that it inspired and moved the hearer to love. We cannot therefore underestimate the social and cultural function of exegesis of Scripture, and preaching upon it, in the formation of Christian culture and society.[68]

---

[66] Pollmann (1996), 121–46. Cf. *mor.* 1.17.31—'It is love that asks, love that seeks, love that knocks, love that reveals, love, too, that gives continuance in what is revealed.'

[67] See Markus (1996), 105–24, to whom I am indebted for these insights.

[68] Nor should one ignore its influence in the wider context of Latin culture. Mohrmann (1961); Fontaine and Pietri (1985), 129–42.

CHRISTIAN RHETORIC OR
CLASSICAL DECADENCE?

Scripture's centrality to Christian culture provides the context for Book 4 of *On Christian Doctrine*. In this book, written near the end of his life,[69] Augustine turns to the question of preaching—of how to express, to communicate the message of Scripture. We therefore find him attempting to come to terms with the Christian practice—or art—of public speaking, or rhetoric.

The questions we raised earlier on concerning the exact relationship between classical culture and Christianity become especially relevant, and sensitive, when Augustine turns in Book 4 to consider the literary, aesthetic value of the Christian Scriptures and preaching upon them, largely because of unresolved tensions in Augustine's own work and practice. In a sense, Book 4, written so late on, seems to mark Augustine's coming full circle. If late antique culture was defined by anything it was the art of rhetoric, the art of public speaking, of teaching, moving and persuading an audience. All education—the liberal disciplines or arts—were simply a preparation for this, the highest achievement, the most desirable and influential profession, of late antique culture. And Augustine, as we know, had followed this well-trodden path to advancement to become the municipal rhetor of Milan, the imperial capital, before his conversion in 386. From 392, for the rest of his life, he was to be similarly involved, as a priest and bishop, in the art of speaking: in teaching, preaching to, and advising his congregation. In Book 4 he is able to reflect on a lifetime's experience of the art of public speaking—though, of course, the texts and hearers changed rather dramatically during its course. Here, more than at any other point in his work, the meeting of classical and Christian culture is seen in all its complexity—and Augustine is more than aware of the need to articulate the nature of their relation.

His main concern in Book 4 is to discuss how the Christian teacher or preacher should go about expressing the message of Scripture. The discussion proceeds almost entirely within the frame of classical rhetoric, in order to evaluate its aims, practices and rules and their usefulness for the Christian preacher.[70] Augustine obviously regards it as a norm, a yardstick, an unavoidable rule against which Christian practice is to be evaluated and defined. In this respect he has been blamed for too freely and willingly adopting its criteria and techniques, its literary artistry, so to speak, in order to engage the interest and delight of his listener—with unfortunate results. His figurative, allegorical exegesis, most especially, is frequently criticized

[69] For suggestions as to why there is such a gap in the composition of this work see Kannengiesser (1995), 4–14.   [70] Discussed in Pollmann (1996), 215–44.

in this context for its artificiality and arbitrariness.[71] Eloquence which aims to please, seems to take precedence, for some of Augustine's critics, over content; the means of expression over the true meaning of the passage. In fact, as we shall see, Augustine is keenly aware of, and highly sensitive to, these criticisms; he both articulates them, appreciates their force, and seeks to counter them by attempting to justify his own practice and that of the biblical authors—though some of his justifications are more convincing than others.

Before we examine them a number of general observations need to be made. First of all, we have noted the cultural significance of rhetoric: it carried with it social respect, prestige, power, authority. In this sense Christianity could not ignore it, rather, it was an important instrument in establishing its own position within society.[72] Secondly, the fathers themselves were products—educationally and socially—of late antique culture. They naturally adopted its methods of understanding and communication in order to frame and preach their new Christian identity, however critical they were of it in theory—indeed we often see them using classical rhetoric to inveigh against it![73] Furthermore, they justified their practice by appealing to Scripture—that rather disappointing, strange, somewhat crude and badly written text, which they rendered acceptable, both to themselves and its pagan critics, by reading it according to classical exegetical practices, such as allegory—the technique, we have seen, which pagans used to render their own classics, Virgil or Homer, relevant and acceptable.

In Book 4 of *On Christian Doctrine* Augustine cautiously, at times, contradictorily, attempts to define just what the Christians' use of eloquence should be: what *its* aims, practices and rules are in relation to, and in contradistinction to, classical practices. At times they follow the same path, motivated by the same aims; at others the fundamental principles of the one are seen to be in opposition to the other; in some instances they follow the same practices for different ends. Augustine moves rapidly between acceptance, rejection, and modification of classical eloquence. The argument is therefore far from straightforward, but as I suggested earlier, this probably has more to do with the unresolved tensions—even at this late stage, near the end of his life—within Augustine's own person and mind: between his past, but still enduring, educational and intellectual formation, and his present identity as a Christian bishop. The biggest tension seems to lie in what he has to say about rhetoric or eloquence—the linguistic or literary artistry of the written or spoken word. Arguments for its usefulness, indeed its indispensability, are juxtaposed throughout Book 4

---

[71] Comeau (1930), chapter 6; Finaert (1939), 94; O'Connell (1978), 146; Markus (1996), 12.
[72] Brown (1992); Cameron (1991), 123.
[73] See example given by G. Clark (1993a), 77.

with arguments for its irrelevance and redundancy in Christian exegesis and preaching.

For example, Augustine is at pains to demonstrate that the Christian Scriptures can be analysed according to the rules of classical 'eloquence' and that they will not be found wanting in this respect—'For where I understand these authors, not only can nothing seem to me more wise than they are, but also nothing can seem more eloquent' (4.6.9). The exercise is a rather artificial one—passages from 1 Corinthians and Amos are subjected to a throughly classical critique, in terms of *caesa*, *membra*, and *circuitus*; their ornaments, figures, and expressions are detailed, as it were to show their pedigree. Later on, in a similar vein, Augustine betrays an educated rhetor's niggling concern that the authors of Scripture lack the rhetorical ornament of rhythmic closings. Perhaps, he suggests, this is the fault of their translators, or perhaps—and he has to admit, he thinks this more likely—they avoided them themselves. The fact worries him, so much so that he rather desperately resorts to the suggestion that if someone skilled in rhetoric rearranged their endings by changing a few words here and there they could then be shown not to lack anything which is 'so highly regarded and taught in the schools of grammarians or rhetoricians' (4.20.41). Further, he appeals to Jerome who had found rhythmical metre in the prophets. Then, perhaps realizing these concerns are inappropriate for a Christian bishop he concedes that although he does not himself neglect rhythmical endings insofar as they can be used moderately, it pleases him to find them very rarely in the authors of Scripture.

How much does this owe to Augustine's sensitivity to pagan criticism and to his own desire to make the Scriptures palatable to himself and other refined, educated minds? He openly admits that the former is indeed a matter for concern: 'I am ashamed to be tainted by this boasting when I discuss these things in this way' he writes at the end of his rhetorical analysis of Paul, 'But ill-informed men are to be answered when they think to condemn our authors, not because they do not have, but because they do not show that eloquence which such men love too well' (4.7.14). But his sensitivity to criticism is obviously stronger than his shame: in the next paragraph he proceeds to analyse Amos according to classical rules in order to defend himself from the criticism that he has chosen Paul because he is the only eloquent speaker Christianity possesses!

And yet his embarassment continues to surface: he is more than tacitly aware that what he is doing might be perceived as a rather decadent selling out to pagan critics and the over-refined sensibilites of an educated, cultured rhetor, in a manner which is inimical both to the aims, and the methods, of the biblical writers. Both his analysis of the passage from 1 Corinthians and his analysis of Amos are immediately followed by very similar retractations: he is at pains to make clear that the eloquence he finds in Scripture is not contrived or deliberate, but is rather the natural, spontaneous accompaniment of words which are true: 'like wisdom coming from her house (that is, from the breast of the wise man) followed by eloquence as if she were an inseparable servant who was not called' (4.6.10). And following the Amos passage: 'But a good listener warms to it not so much by diligently analysing it as by pronouncing it energetically. For these words were not devised by human industry, but were poured forth from the divine mind both wisely and eloquently, not in such a way that wisdom was directed towards eloquence, but in such a way that eloquence did not abandon wisdom' (4.7.21). When he turns to examine how Christian authors have used the most elaborate and extravagant 'grand style' of rhetoric, (as opposed to the subdued or moderate styles) he is likewise careful to modify any impression that they might have deliberately and consciously worked upon their style as a sort of decoration for what they have to say, rather, it is attributable to an unconscious enthusiasm, to an 'ardour of the heart', to the inherent force of the things being discussed, rather than careful choice (4.20.42). So the biblical authors are indeed eloquent—naturally and unconsciously eloquent—even though they did not mean to be!

This attempt to exonerate the authors of Scripture, or those who preach upon it, from being overly concerned with decadent rhetorical eloquence, is also evident in the passages where Augustine discusses how eloquence is to be acquired. He is quick to point out, at the very beginning of Book 4, that he will not be giving the rules of eloquence that he learnt in the secular schools—not that they are not useful in the service of truth but that they are to be learnt elsewhere. Besides, methodical study of rules, he hastens to add, is of secondary importance. What is more important is the unconscious acquisition of eloquence which occurs when one reads or hears it in a text or speech which one is reading for other purposes: for *what* is said, rather than *how* it is said. This happens in the natural course of study of ecclesiastical literature or of Scripture (4.5.7) and in the practice of writing, dictating or speaking upon them. Here, eloquence is not a matter of rules; the rules are observed *because* someone is eloquent, they are not applied that they might be eloquent (4.3.4). It is rather like the way a child acquires language: the child is not taught to speak, but learns by hearing and practice. Similarly, a boy does not need to learn the art of grammar if he grows up and lives among men who speak correctly (4.3.5).[74]

---

[74] The gender exclusive language is Augustine's, not mine; girls were not usually educated to the same degree as boys in his day.

Eloquence is therefore not a matter of rules, it is not directly learnt, but somehow picked up intuitively and unconsciously. Indeed, it is very much a gift: the preacher is effective 'more through the piety of his prayers than through the skill of his oratory' (4.15.32). It is not acquired, but given.

The above arguments, which I have suggested arise from Augustine's ambiguous attitude towards classical rhetoric and its use in a Christian context, and which serve, to a large extent, to distance the Christian preacher and writer from deliberate, direct, conscious use of it, whilst still holding on to the idea that Christianity possesses rhetorical eloquence, are in fact the arguments of classical rhetors themselves. They too, whilst formulating, teaching and analysing according to rules, taught that rules do not lead to eloquence; that eloquence is better acquired by reading and listening to the classics; that eloquence naturally accompanies truth; that it is a gift. These observations were no doubt made from experience and were doubtless used to defend the practice of rhetoric in the face of long-standing criticism—especially from the philosophers who viewed it with distrust and distaste: how could it be said to teach the truth when its primary concern seemed to be to utilize rules of speech in order to please, to delight and to persuade the listener of a merely plausible opinion—of what might seem to be true (*ueresimiliter*)—in other words, 'the ability to persuade without teaching'.[75]

It might therefore be argued that in Book 4 Augustine is continuing the defence of rhetoric—in this context, Christian rhetoric—against its detractors. He is aware of the criticisms which have been made of classical rhetoric, and of the arguments deployed by classical authors to counter these, and can be seen using them on two fronts: first to demonstrate that Christian literature and preaching *is* rhetorical against pagan criticisms which focused on its lack of literary sophistication; secondly, to defend its use against the criticisms which were commonly made of classical rhetoric—and especially of the Sophists, or the Second Sophistic of Augustine's day—that it was merely verbal fireworks, a technical display of virtuosity performed to please and thus, to sway, its hearers, whatever its relation to truth or the good. What he seems to want to say is that Christian literature *is* rhetorical, in a way which takes up the best of classical practice but which is not subject to its failings.

This becomes evident if we examine the ways in which he distinguishes the Christian practice of rhetoric from classical practice, and especially from Cicero.[76] Unlike the arguments we have discussed above, in which he was concerned to demonstrate that Christianity does indeed possess

---

[75] Plato *Gorgias* 454e. Cf. the contrast Plato draws between eloquence based on plausibility and philosophical eloquence founded on the truth which it aims to teach. See Fortin (1974).

[76] For a discussion of Augustine's use of Cicero see Fortin (1974); Primmer (1995), 68–87.

rhetorical eloquence, Augustine is less wavering, and far more forceful in his criticisms of classical 'eloquence' and the way in which Christian eloquence diverges from it.

In Chapter 12 Augustine refers to Cicero's classic definition of the three aims of rhetoric: to teach (*docere* or *probare*), to delight (*delectare* or *conciliare*), and to move (*movere* or *flectere*) (*S*. 21.69). For Cicero, as for all classical rhetors, teaching and delight were subordinate to the ultimate goal of persuasion. After all, rhetoric's primary forum was the law-court. Augustine, however, reverses these aims: the first and determining aim, the ultimate goal of the Christian preacher, is to teach. Delight might indeed be useful in this context to persuade the listener of the truth and move him to act upon it—we will return to this later—but Augustine can see that, in fact, this need not always be the case. Sometimes the bald unadorned statement of the truth is sufficient to move the listener to act upon it, it is pleasing in itself, and causes the hearer to act upon it, precisely because it is the truth (4.12.28). In a sense it is the substance of what is said, the content, which is pleasing and motivating, rather than the manner and style in which it is expressed. As Augustine observes of the preacher: 'In his speech itself he should prefer to please more with the things said than with the words used to speak them; nor should he think that anything may be said better than that which is said truthfully; nor should the teacher serve the words, but the words the teacher' (4.28.61).

Thus, in sharp contrast to how rhetoric was popularly perceived, he subordinates eloquence to truth; a desire to please, to clarity and concern that one be understood (4.8.22–9.23), to the extent that if a word in good Latin is obscure or ambiguous the preacher should not be afraid to use vulgarisms (4.10.24). In this sense, Christianity can be seen to overcome the philosophers' criticism of rhetoric in teaching its own understanding of the truth, and might well claim to be the true philosophical rhetoric (just as it claimed to be the true philosophy).

It is because of his overriding emphasis on teaching the truth, that, in examining the three styles of rhetoric—the subdued to speak of small things; the temperate to speak of moderate things; the grand to speak of grand things—Augustine inclines in favour of the subdued as the basic style to be adopted by the Christian preacher. This style most easily lends itself to teaching. The simple exposition of the truth of the faith should, as we noted above, be sufficient in itself to move and persuade. Writing on the equality of the Holy Spirit with the Father and the Son, for example, Ambrose, Augustine notes, uses the subdued style, for 'the thing discussed does not need verbal ornaments, nor motions of the affections to persuade, but evidence as proof' (4.21.46).

Augustine recommends the employment of the other two styles, which were usually associated with delight and persuasion, respectively, only when they too further the aim of teaching: to praise, and to persuade of, what is taught. Thus, the great truths of the faith, which would ordinarily demand the grand manner, are best taught in the subdued manner, praised in the temperate manner and instilled for acceptance and action in the grand manner. As in his demonstration of the rhetorical eloquence of the Scriptures, Augustine provides scriptural and patristic illustrations of the use of the three styles in accordance with his revised recommendations as to their use (4.20.39–21.50). The three styles complement each other and are best varied and intermixed in a single passage (4.22.51–23.52) so as not to tire the hearer. But in his relative evaluation of them Augustine has introduced a radically new note which overturns classical practice—whilst still, as is often the case, using its terminology—and has more in common, once again, with the philosophical critics of rhetoric. The unadorned, unarmed, naked truth (albeit with a certain uncontrived beauty, and a few unostentatious rhythmic closings, not of course deliberately sought, but rather, in some way natural—Augustine cannot entirely give up his predilection for the old 'eloquence'!) comes forth to 'crush the sinews and muscles of its adversary and overcomes and destroys resisting falsehood with its most powerful members' (4.26.56).

The ethical dimension of rhetoric, which had effectively been sidelined by the rhetors of Augustine's day, but which was very much emphasized by the philosophers, is also made central in Augustine's observation, towards the end of Book 4, that 'the life of the speaker has greater weight in determining whether he is obediently heard than any grandness of eloquence' (4.27.59). His life is, as it were, as eloquent a witness to the truth as his words; but if his life is a lie it undermines the force of his words (4.29.62).[77]

But it is not when Augustine is attempting to demonstrate the eloquence of Christian literature; nor when he is desperately trying to show that this eloquence is somehow 'natural', unintentional, and uncontrived; nor when he is at pains to criticize classical rhetoric and to set it in contradistinction to Christian aims and practices, that he is at his most convincing. Rather, it is when he turns to actually *justify* his use of rhetoric, to explain why it is necessary and effective for the Christian writer and preacher, that what he says seems most cogent, ingenuous, and true to his own experience.

The key term here is one which recurs frequently in Book 4: delight or *delectatio*. In this context it refers to Cicero's second aim of rhetoric, to please or delight, which follows teaching, and by engaging the listener's assent enables the speaker to persuade and move them to act upon what

---

[77] See Howie (1969), 232–9 for commentary on this.

has been taught: 'But if those who hear are to be moved rather than taught, so that they may not be sluggish in putting what they know into practice . . . there is need for greater powers of speaking. Here entreaties and reproofs, exhortations and rebukes, and whatever other devices are necessary to move minds must be used' (4.4.6). It also belongs to the second style of rhetoric—the moderate or temperate style, which similarly aims to render what is said 'sweet' or pleasing, before the grand style moves the hearer to consent.

Ever conscious of criticism, Augustine warns that the speaker must not go too far: rather unusually, he chooses to illustrate his call for restraint with the work of another, otherwise venerated, African father, St Cyprian. Referring to an especially flowery, too allegorical passage—'Let us seek this place; the neighbouring solitudes offer a refuge where the wandering tendrils of the vines twine through loaded trellises with pendulous interlacings so as to make with a leafy roof a woody colonnade'[78]—he comments, 'that sweetness of discourse is not pleasing in which, although no iniquity is spoken, trivial and fragile truths are ornamented with a frothy nexus of words' (4.14.31). The proper and acceptable use of the moderate style is not to evoke pleasure in rhetorical eloquence—as was almost exclusively the case among classical rhetors—but understanding of, delight in, love of, and obedience to, the truth which is taught by means of it (4.25.55; 26.57). It is in this sense, I think, that we can speak of a Christian aesthetic, a new Christian literary culture; one in which rhetoric holds as central a place as it did in classical culture, but where it is transformed from a practice which primarily aims to please and persuade, to one which aims to inspire love of, and the practice of, the truth.

This assertion may make more sense if we remind ourselves of the theological presuppositions on which it is based. First, Scripture, unlike the works of classical culture, was, as we have seen, authoritative: it was held by the fathers to express the truth. This is what they believed the authors of Scripture were seeking to express, this is what the exegete seeks to find and what the preacher, in turn, attempts to teach. Secondly, we have had numerous occasions to note that what enables fallen man to act upon the truth is his ability to delight in it and love it (Cf. *mus.* 6.11.29–30; 13.38; *s.* 159.3; *sp. et litt.* 3). It is the notion of delight which transforms Augustine's very negative picture of language after the fall, to make it one of the key ways in which God reveals himself to fallen man, in a manner which inspires his delight, and which therefore pleases and moves him, so that he loves and performs the good.

---

[78] Cyprian *Ad Donatum* 1. Cf. Augustine's comments on the similar rhetoric of the Donatist bishops in *cresc.* 4.2.

These insights are perhaps summed up in the famous passage from Augustine's sermon on John 6: 44, 'No one comes to me unless the Father draws him'. He writes,

> You are drawn, not merely by the will, but what is more, by pleasure. What is it, to be drawn by pleasure? 'Delight in the Lord, and he shall give you the requests of your heart' (Ps. 37: 4) . . . Moreover if the poet had leave to say, 'Trahit sua quemque voluptas', not necessity, but pleasure; not obligation, but delight; how much more strongly ought we to say that a man is drawn to Christ, when he delights in truth, delights in blessedness, delights in righteousness, delights in everlasting life, all of which Christ is? (*Io. eu. tr.* 26.4).

In the light of these theological principles we should not be surprised to find Augustine at pains to demonstrate the rhetorical eloquence of Scripture in Book 4, or to find him enthusiastically recommending the use of the rhetorical techniques of classical culture to the preacher, in order to render the truth he teaches beautiful, delightful, love-worthy.

There is a sort of hermeneutical circle here: love is the hermeneutical principle of Scripture; delight is that which inspires love; beauty is that which inspires delight; truth is that which inspires beauty; what man loves is the truth. It is therefore essential for Augustine that Scripture be shown to be beautiful, be made delightful, if its true end is to be attained. This is not a concession to its refined, cultured critics, or to his own sensibilities, but is, rather, the keystone of a 'Christian aesthetic' which recognizes that God has chosen to motivate man's fallen will to the true and good through the delight occasioned by His beautiful revelation of Himself—and this includes, centrally, Scripture and preaching.

And so Scripture becomes that difficult entity—a work of literature. If truth is beautiful; if beauty is delightful; if delight is the way in which God chooses to orient the fallen towards Himself, there is nothing artificial, arbitrary, misleading, superfluous, or decadent about describing Scripture as a work of literature or using rhetoric to preach. To seek out the beauty of Scripture, to make preaching aesthetically pleasing, is, rather, to do full justice to their subject matter and to make it accessible. In his interpretation of it we see Augustine coming to terms with the 'fallenness' of language, its obscurities, ambiguities, difficulties—and Scripture has more than its fair share of these—by making of them something positive, indeed, something literary, artistic, fashioned in order to arouse fallen man's interest, (positive) curiosity, aesthetic delight. It meets him at an affective, rather than a rational level,[79] and demands imagination, intuition, aesthetic sensitivity, if its message is to become clear. As Marrou comments in the *Retractatio* which we mentioned at the beginning of this chapter,

---

[79] See Gillespie (1982), 199–231.

If Holy Scripture is not just the history of sinful humanity and the economy of salvation . . . if it is also this forest of symbols that through the appearences of figures suggests to us these same truths of the faith, one must have the courage to conclude that God is also a poet himself: To manifest himself to us he chose a means of expression which is also poetic, which brings into play one of the conceptions of poetry that reason and human culture have developed.[80]

As well as a general Baudelairean tendency, one presumes that what Marrou has in mind includes the fact that Scripture was thought to be inspired, to possess different levels (literal, spiritual . . .), that it uses imagery, allegory, figures, poetry, and parables as well as betraying the more formal traits of rhetorical artistry which Augustine demonstrates in Book 4 of *On Christian Doctrine*.[81]

Scripture signifies as language, but is sacramental as the inspired word of God. Thus the difficulties and obscurities inherent in language overcome man's pride, inspire humility, and cultivate a healthy sense of his limitations. They veil, honour, and guard the truth, meeting readers at their different levels, with their different approaches, to inspire, exercise, attract, and delight them, so that its meaning and its mystery might both be grasped and desired in its fullness.[82] Thus, Scripture became a work which could stand its ground against pagan literature and satisfy the cultured sensibilities of the educated (including the fathers).[83] But much more importantly, it became the means whereby God reorients and inspires the wills of the faithful, whatever their erudition (or ignorance), so that they can delight in the truth of the faith and realize the one thing necessary: love of God and neighbour.

A large proportion of the fathers' exegesis takes a homiletic form. They generally interpreted Scripture, not in the manner of modern, academic, biblical scholars (though of course one only has to think of Origen or Jerome to realize that this discipline was not wholly absent from their work) but as pastors, intent on expounding the text for the benefit of their congregations. It is in this context that the preacher's use of rhetoric finds its place. We noted Augustine's somewhat ambiguous attitude towards it and his careful adoption, and to a large extent, transformation, of it in a Christian context—not least because, like Scripture, it proved to be the best means of reorienting the will of fallen man to move him to delight in the truth, goodness and beauty of the Christian revelation and to act upon it. This is not, however, the place to demonstrate Augustine's rhetorical artistry—his use of verbal ornaments, figures, allegory, parables,

---

[80] Marrou (1949), 648.   [81] See Moreau (1986).

[82] Harrison (1992), 81–95 and Marrou (1949), 488–94 for references and a discussion of Augustine's practice of allegory.

[83] For Augustine's awareness of this problem and his recommendation of this sort of exegesis to meet it, see *cat. rud.* 9.13; *ep.*137.1.3–5.

metaphors, imagery, puns, proverbs, assonance, rhythm, word-play, anti-theses, parallelism, *abundantia*, rhythmic closures, and so on.[84] We might simply note that, as one might expect, it was influenced by classical, Cynic-Stoic, Sophistic and ecclesiastical or scriptural forms, and that practice does indeed usually follow theory (with a few gratuitous rhetorical excesses): what we find is a distinctive 'Christian aesthetic', shaped by the desire to teach and to move the listener to delight in and love the truths of the faith.

We are now, in conclusion, in a position to appreciate the nature of the convergence of classical and what we might call Christian literary culture in Augustine's own personal history and identity, and in his work and preaching. He did not leave his past behind and attempt to root out any traces of it in his new Christian identity: he was too well aware of the futil-ity of such a task and of the pervasiveness, importance, and usefulness of secular culture to make such an attempt. Rather, he attempted to come to terms with secular culture, to appreciate but also to criticize; to assimilate but also to reject—in other words, to 'convert' it to Christianity.[85]

---

[84] See Mohrmann (1961); Finaert (1939).
[85] These observations are inspired by Fredouille (1972).

3

The nature of virtue

THE HAPPY LIFE

The philosophers have engaged in a great deal of complicated debate about the supreme ends of good and evil; and by concentrating their attention on this question they have tried to discover what it is that makes man happy. For our Final Good is that for which other things are to be desired, while it is itself to be desired for its own sake (*ciu.* 19.1)

The nature of happiness, to which all man's actions aspire because in it alone is his ultimate good, was the guiding principle of all ancient philosophical thought.[1] In other words, ancient philosophy was eudaemonistic (Gk. *eudaemonia*—happiness) or teleological (Gk. *telos*—end). Different understandings of this good, of what man's happiness is, and of what was necessary in order to attain it, lay behind the different philosophical schools. It was generally agreed that the only reason for doing philosophy was the desire to be happy (*ciu.* 19.1). Augustine's education, his acquaintance with the various schools, and the fact that Christian authors were already articulating their understanding of God and the Christian life in this way, meant that he too inevitably approached questions which we would categorize under the general heading of 'ethical', within this very clearly defined intellectual context. Moreover, it was a context which he evidently found congenial: he retains its basic structure into his mature works, even though he was to discard its fundamental assumptions.

Augustine's knowledge came primarily from Latin sources: Cicero, who, in his *De finibus bonorum et malorum*, discusses the positions of the different schools and their differences and disagreements (*conf.* 6.16.26), and Varro, whose *De philosophia* Augustine cites in the famous passage in *City of God* 19 in relation to the 288 different possible schools which could be created from different combinations of certain basic eudaemonistic ideas.

Cicero's *Hortensius*, which had been so influential in initiating the young Augustine's search for truth, was written in order to counter Hortensius' view that the study of philosophy did not contribute to happiness. In it,

[1] See Holte (1962), 11–70 for an examination of teleological reflection in ancient philosophy.

Augustine found the view that all morality is the pursuit of an ultimate good—here identified with wisdom—in which man finds his happiness.

But what is the ultimate good, the *summum bonum*? In what does man find happiness? The question is a complicated one since the answer depends on a comprehensive and systematic understanding of man, his nature and his place in the universe, in order to establish that in which he will find his fulfillment or happiness. Man's rationality, spirituality and ultimate destiny are all at stake here, and as we have seen in the first chapter, Augustine's developing understanding of man and his relationship to God caused him to diverge profoundly from ancient philosophical thought in these respects. Of course, the schools themselves differed: the Epicureans, whom Cicero discusses in Book I of *De finibus* held that man's ultimate good was to be found in unending bodily pleasure. This was not least, presumably, because they had no conception of the afterlife and of ultimate reward or punishment—the grounds on which Augustine criticizes and rejects them (*conf.* 6.16.26; cf. *trin.* 13.5.8). The Stoics, Cicero tells us (Books 2–3) also disagreed with the Epicureans: man's basic instinct (*oikeiosis*) is not pleasure, rather he is a rational being who seeks perfection of soul in self-sufficiency, self-determination, and the sovereignty of his reason over the passions (*autarche*) which would otherwise disturb it; in other words he seeks *apatheia*, a state of imperturbable calm. This is achieved, for the Stoic, by a life of virtue (*arete*) which, because it is wholly a matter of will acting in accord with reason, is able to limit itself to what is within man's power and make him invulnerable to external things, thereby ensuring his happiness. As we shall see, the influence of these ideas, particularly that of invulnerability, is clear in Augustine's earliest works[2]—being, at least in part, mediated by the Neoplatonic texts he had recently discovered with such enthusiasm. But Cicero tells us (in Book 5) that the Peripatetics and Platonists also included external goods as contributing to happiness, and that their thought was taken up in the syncretistic revival of the Old Academy by Antiochus of Ascalon, who, combining their thought with a basic Stoic emphasis on virtue, viewed the happy life as one based on virtue but augmented by external things. Augustine accepts this synthesis and presents it, in *City of God* 19.1–3, drawing primarily on Varro's *De philosophia*.[3]

As we have seen in Chapter 1, Augustine singles out the Platonists for especial praise because they identified the supreme good with God and taught that happiness was to be found not in the body or material goods, or in the mind, but only in love of the supreme good for its own sake: 'Plato

---

[2] For the nature of Stoic influence on Augustine's thought see Chapter 1. Its particular influence on his ethical thought is strongly emphasised by Wetzel (1992), e.g. 55–76 (see p. 56, note 15 for bibliography) in relation to *beata u.* and *lib. arb.*

[3] Wetzel (1992), 47–8.

defined the ultimate good as living in conformity with virtue, that he held this possible only for the man who comes to know God, and to copy Him, and that he believed happiness to be due to this cause alone. For this reason he has no doubt that philosophy is the love of God, whose nature is incorporeal' (*ciu.* 8.8). The basic insights of ancient philosophy, and especially Stoicism, concerning the ultimate good, the identification of this with happiness and the role of virtue are all here. The identification of the ultimate good with God and the subjection of material things marks it out as both Platonic and Christian and demonstrates the reason for Augustine's enthusiasm for this philosophy and why Markus can rightly speak of 'an almost wholesale adoption of Platonic notions, especially in the sphere of ethics'.[4] Augustine's encounter with Neoplatonism no doubt underlined one of the other main aspects of ancient philosophical ethical reflection, which we have seen to be particularly characteristic of the Stoics, that is, the notion of man's self-sufficiency in acquiring the good. Indeed, as Holte notes[5] Plotinus attributes to his perfect man all the qualities of the Stoic sage. He was insistent that 'man's life is sufficient in itself for happiness and the acquisition of good' (*Enn.* I.4.4); that one must leave behind the body and alone seek the Alone. In this respect, above all, Platonism did not go unchallenged.

Augustine's *On the Happy Life*, one of his earliest works written at Cassiciacum in 386, clearly evidences his interest in this theme, the importance he attached to it in understanding his newly embraced religion, and his acquaintance with, and acceptance of, philosophical reflection to elucidate his thoughts. He is able to work with presuppostions which he is confident will receive unquestioned support: that all men desire to be happy (2.10); that no one is happy who does not have what he wants without fear of losing it (4.26). It goes without saying therefore that we must want the right thing in order to attain happiness, and by this Augustine understands eternal, immutable things as opposed to temporal, mutable things. In *On the Happy Life* Augustine asserts that happiness consists in possessing God (*Deum habere* 3.17) and describes virtue, by which this good is attained, in a decidedly Stoic fashion, as moderation (*modestia*), which derives from *modus* or just measure. The latter he identifies with the measure of the soul (*modus animi*), a state in which it neither allows itself to fall into excess or fails to achieve that of which it is capable—*ut ne quid nimis*. In other words it turns from temporal things, which can be lost, and loves eternal things. Such moderation, or measure, is in fact wisdom, and to possess wisdom is to possess happiness (4.33), since wisdom is found fully only in God, the Son, the Truth (4.34). Thus the virtuous activity of

---

[4] Markus (1970a), 380.   [5] Holte (1962), 55.

the soul by which it achieves measure (or as the Stoics would have it, self-determination and invulnerability), enables it to 'have' or possess God, who is the supreme measure, and thereby, the happy life (4.34). But Augustine acknowledges that while we search we have not yet attained full measure, and are therefore not yet wise or happy—or, as Monnica puts it, rather more accessibly, we attain the happy, perfect life, by praying to God, the Trinity and having confidence that we will be led there 'by a well-founded faith, a joyful hope and an ardent love' (4.35).

Augustine's awareness of the fact that most men are seeking the *summum bonum*, rather than in possession of it, should not, however, be read to imply that he did not think it possible, at this stage in his thought, for some, however few, to actually attain it in this life. *On the Happy Life*, with its distinctly Stoic emphasis on virtue, moderation of soul, and the limitation of our desires to what cannot be lost, suggests so much. The Neoplatonically inspired discussion of those who attain eternal wisdom by reason and those who seek it by authority and faith, explicitly confirms it of the former group in *On Order* (ord. 2.9.26).[6]

It has justly been observed of Augustine's early moral theory that the emphasis lies on notions of value (of the high estimate of eternal goods in contradistinction to temporal goods) and of virtue (by which the soul adheres to eternal goods) rather than upon notions of obligation, such as acting upon the authority of commandments or rules.[7] But this emphasis, together with Augustine's early optimism concerning the attainability of virtue and the ultimate good in this life, was not unaffected by the marked changes we have already had occasion to observe in the works he composed in Rome and Thagaste, in the two years following the retreat at Cassiciacum.

Two works, which were begun in 388, *On the Morals of the Catholic Church* and *On Free Will*, mark important developments in Augustine's ethical thought which, to some extent, diverge from late antique ethical reflection, and foreshadow the main lines of his later thought.

ON THE MORALS OF THE CATHOLIC CHURCH

It has been observed that[8] the question of happiness becomes, in Augustine's early thought, a matter of human love, or more precisely of two loves, both of which desire something for its own sake (*propter se—sol.*

---

[6] For a discussion of the relationship—or conflict—between Stoic and Neoplatonic influences here see Wetzel (1992), 68–76.   [7] Carney (1991).

[8] Babcock (1991)—to whom I am much indebted for the following paragraph.

1.13.22), but which have very different objects. In *On the Morals of the Catholic Church*, begun in 388, these two loves are set in a eudaemonistic context which is, in structure, very close to *On the Happy Life*, but which is expressed in the transforming language of love: *caritas* is love of eternal things, which are immutable, can never be taken away, and therefore lead to happiness and freedom; *cupiditas* is love of inferior, temporal things, which are mutable, can easily be lost, and which therefore lead to misery and enslavement (*mor.* 12.21; *sol.* 1.11.19; *div. qu.* 35.2). The first is founded upon man's humility and subjection to God, whereby he acknowledges his creaturely status and dependence upon his Creator, so that he receives God's illumination and enlightenment; the second is founded upon man's pride, whereby thinking that he possesses the same nature as his Creator, he turns to himself, cuts himself off from the truth and becomes blind (*mor.* 12.20).

Virtue, which leads us to the happy life, is therefore 'nothing other than the perfect love of God'; 'to love Virtue, to love Wisdom, to love Truth, to love with all your heart, and with all your soul, and with all your mind' (*mor.* 13.22; 25.47). Virtue, Wisdom, Truth are all titles of Christ, and it is by love of him that we are sanctified, and are able to love in such a way that we are conformed to His image, rather than to the world. The love which effects this conformation is the Holy Spirit: 'The love of God has been shed abroad in your hearts by the Holy Spirit which has been given to you' (Rom. 5: 51). Thus, Augustine concludes, as in *On the Happy Life*, that it is love of the Holy Trinity which leads man to the happy life. This is the message of Scripture (of the Old Testament—against the Manichees—as well as the New), which itself can only be known and understood by those who love (*mor.* 25.46). Quoting Matthew 7: 7 'Ask and you will receive, seek and you will find . . .', he comments, 'It is love which asks, love which seeks, love which knocks, love which finds, love which dwells in what is found' (17.31). Similarly, Augustine stresses that we must first love God whom we desire to know, in order to enjoy this knowledge in the life to come—such knowledge being the reward of the perfect. In other words, love of authority, and especially that of Scripture, precedes and enables understanding (*mor.* 25.47; cf. *uera rel.* 7.13; 24.45). So, too, does love of one's neighbour: there is no more certain way to love of God than to love one's neighbour as oneself, and to share with him one's love of God. This love is the basis of human society (*mor.* 26.48–49); its practical out-working best evidenced in the moral precepts taught by the Church (30.62). Referring to the well-known traditional fourfold form of virtue in classical thought in *On the Morals of the Catholic Church*, Augustine therefore redefines it as four different types of love: 'Temperance is love keeping itself sound and uncorrupted in God; courage is love bearing everything readily for the sake of God; justice is love serving God only, and therefore ruling all else well; and prudence is love discerning well what helps it toward God and what hinders it' (15.25; cf. 19.35–24.45).

On the Morals of the Catholic Church, whilst continuing to use the same classical language and ideas which we found in *On the Happy Life*, therefore demonstrates a marked development in Augustine's thought in rethinking these ideas in the context of a distinctively Christian morality. In contrast to Stoic thought, virtue is not held, of itself, to bring happiness. Although it is essential in leading man to happiness it is not its end; rather it serves to lead man to God, the transcendent source and object of happiness.[9] Nor is it determined in its action by the temporal order of nature but rather by God's eternal law. Augustine also makes it clear that happiness—possession of God or knowledge of God—is a reward for the perfect which will not be attained in this life (*mor.* 25.47).

Whereas the identification of beatitude with possession of an eternal, transcendent object bears obvious traces of Neoplatonic influence, Augustine also distances himself from this philosophy in a number of important ways. His emphasis upon the transcendent in *On the Morals of the Catholic Church* is made in the context of the created status of man, and the need for him to acknowledge his created dependence and subjection to God, and his duty to care for and order the lower, temporal realm, including his body. His desire for happiness thus appears as a desire to attain 'man's best' (*optimis hominis*), to fulfil that which is highest in himself, which can only be found in conformity to God. When Augustine describes what this entails he uses the language of obligation, of responsibility, of social duties, of love of authority, expressed in the Decalogue, the teaching of the New Testament, and most especially the commandment of love of God and neighbour. Conformity to God is therefore not only described by Scripture as man's good, but, in order to attain it, as his duty or moral obligation. Augustine also identifies the Wisdom to which man is to be conformed, and the love which enables this conformation to take place, with Christ and the Holy Spirit respectively. These central notions—of the created goodness of the body, of man's created dependence, of divine assistance—are all fundamentally alien to Neoplatonism and, contrary to the opinion of many scholars, leave little room for its influence in Augustine's earliest moral reflection beyond the bare traces of a theoretical structure.

---

[9] This is the argument of Colish (1985), 216 whom Wetzel (1992), 69 cites in order to disagree. He would like to retain the Stoic ideals of self-determination and autarky at the centre of Augustine's thought during this period: 'the ideal of beatitude . . . remains that of *virtuous* [sic] self-determination, or the autarky of wisdom'. A close reading of *mor.*, I think, gives the lie to his confident assertions.

ON FREE WILL

The other notable work Augustine began in 388 is another anti-Manichaean work, *On Free Will*. In this work he sought to counter the Manichees' dualistic explanation of evil, and to demonstrate that evil is not caused by God or inherent in matter, but is wholly attributable to man's misuse of his free will, in choosing to pursue mutable, temporal goods rather than the immutable, divine, eternal good. The notion of choice is not new—we have already found it in the language of love in *On the Morals of the Catholic Church*. What is new, however, is the language of will in order to express the operation of man's love. In Book 1 Augustine underlines the fact that man is a rational creature who possesses knowledge of the eternal law and who is free to choose to observe or disregard it: 'what each one chooses to pursue and embrace is within the power of his will to determine (*lib. arb.* 1.16.34)' . . . 'for what is so completely within the power of the will as the will itself?' (1.12.26). If his will errs in cupidity, loving mutable, temporal things (1.4.9), then he alone is responsible for evil, his sin is voluntary, and his present state of ignorance and inability is the just penalty for his sin (1.11.23; cf. *uera rel.* 11.21–14.27). Whereas he could have attained the happy life by exercising his will virtuously—Augustine lists the four classical virtues of prudence, fortitude, temperance, and justice—he suffers unhappiness because of his wickedness (1.13.27–14.30). Having disobeyed the eternal law he becomes subject to the temporal laws which regulate earthly peace and social life (1.15.33–16.34).

But the question remains: why did God create man with the ability to sin and why does man choose to sin? Augustine's consideration of these questions leads him to modify the argument we have just traced in Book 1 and precipitates an evolution in his thought which was to have the most dramatic consequences for his subsequent understanding of Christian ethics. He did not complete *On Free Will* until 395/7, by which time he was bishop at Hippo. Thus, when we turn to consider Books 2 and 3, we are moving into what was to prove a crucial transitional period in Augustine's thought—one which marks the end of his 'early works' and the beginning of his mature thought. The catalyst for the changes which took place is undoubtedly Augustine's reflection on the question of evil, man's sinfulness, and the fall of Adam. We have already had occasion to note the significance of the fact that Augustine's consideration of these questions during the 390s takes the form of a series of works which tackle interpretation of St Paul, and especially his letter to the Romans.

In Book 2 of *On Free Will* Augustine argues that all good things are from God and that the will, in itself, is good. In Book 3 he continues to observe that although God foreknows what his creatures will do he does not rob them of the freedom of willing; rather their actions, including sin, have a place in the perfectly ordered whole of God's universe. Although we cannot say why Adam first sinned, Augustine thinks we can explain man's subsequent sinfulness by the state of ignorance and difficulty which is the penalty for Adam's sin and which is suffered by all his descendants. Thus, as he argued in *Against Fortunatus* (392),[10] following Adam's sin of his own free will, 'we who have descended from him have been plunged headlong into necessity' (*c. fort.* 22). In contrast to Book 1, where ignorance and inability are the result of each individual's sin, and man's actions are entirely voluntary, it now appears that Adam's sin is the only instance in which man's will can be said to have acted with entire freedom; his descendants have their vitiated wills blinded, fettered, and hampered as a consequence of his sin and can never again act with complete freedom (3.18.52–19.54). In other words, whereas Adam's sin was voluntary, the sins of all other men might fairly be described as involuntary: 'From ignorance springs disgraceful error, and from difficulty comes painful effort. To approve falsehood instead of truth so as to err in spite of himself, and not to be able to refrain from the works of lust because of the pain involved in breaking away from fleshly bonds: these do not belong to the nature of man as he was created. They are the penalty of man as condemned' (3.18.52).

The marked contrast between Book 1 of *On Free Will*, with its optimistic portrait of the autonomy of man's will, and Books 2–3 is therefore a marker of how far Augustine's thought has moved in the ten years between his conversion and becoming Bishop of Hippo. The happy life is now one which man is journeying towards along the 'darkly shadowed' way of life following Adam's fall (*lib. arb.* 2.16.41), but which his vitiated, fallen will, can no longer hope to attain in this life.[11]

BETWEEN LAW AND GRACE

In other works during this period Augustine expresses his thought in the form of four stages of salvation history: before the law (when man is ignorant of sin and simply acts as he desires without any feeling of guilt); under the law (when he is conscious of sin and wishes to overcome it, but is incapable without divine help); under grace (when, with divine help, man's will is enabled to do the good); in peace (when, in the life to come, man will no longer be troubled by sinful desires) (*diu. qu.* 83.66–68; *exp. prop. Rm.*

---

[10] For discussion and bibliography on the idea of 'involuntary sin' see Wetzel (1992), 96.

[11] Augustine is careful in the *retr.* to clarify any passages in the early works which might suggest that the happy life is attainable on earth—e.g. 1.2; 1.3.2; 1.7.5.

13–18). In order to move from being under the law to under grace Augustine maintains that the individual must have been elected by God, on the basis of his freely willed faith and desire to do the good, so that he is then assisted with the help of the Spirit (*exp. prop. Rm.* 44.3). Thus, Romans 7, in which Paul describes the inner conflicts and divided will which hindered him from doing the good, is a portrait of man in the second stage, under the law, before the assistance of grace.

But in 396, in the course of writing his reply to Simplicianus' questions on the nature of election, grace, original sin and free will, Augustine's thought underwent perhaps the most crucial change of his life. Whereas the argument of Book 1 follows the lines we have just sketched above and presupposes that grace follows man's meritorious actions, in Book 2 Augustine wavers over the problems raised by Romans 9 concerning the story of Jacob and Esau, whose fates seem to have been determined before their birth, and certainly before they had any chance to respond to, or refuse faith; to act sinfully, or to will the good: 'Jacob I have loved and Esau I have hated.'

If all are called—and one must presume that this is the case if one is to uphold God's justice—why do some respond and some refuse? Faced with this dilemma Augustine seems to be convinced that fallen man's will is no longer free to do the good without God's help (*Simpl.* 2.13). The fact that some respond to God's call, therefore, is no longer attributable to man's will but to the action of God's grace in ensuring that they are called in a way which will effect a positive response: 'God has mercy on whom he will and . . . whom he will he hardens' (*Simpl.* 2.16); 'If those things delight us which serve our advancement towards God, that is due not to our own whim or industry or meritorious works, but to the inspiration of God and to the grace which he bestows' (2.21). It is therefore clear that from the *massa peccati* of mankind (2.20), from those who are universally affected by Adam's fall and who all rightfully deserve damnation, God elects some but not others (why this is the case is attributed to his 'inscrutable judgements' (Rom. 11: 33; *Simpl.* 2.22), and that neither faith or good works can any longer be said to be attributable to the free, unassisted action of man's will: 'What do you have that you did not receive? If then you received it, why do you boast as if it were not a gift' (1 Cor. 4: 7).[12] We saw Augustine coming close to this conclusion in the third book of *On Free Will*, completed at about the same time as *To Simplicianus*, when he described the ignorance and necessity which hinder the operation of man's will as the result of his sharing in the effects of Adam's fall. But it is only in *To*

---

[12] As Bonner (1987) XI, 16 observes, it was in writing this treatise that Augustine later tells us (*retr.* 2.1; *praed. sanct.* 4.8; *perseu.* 20.52) he suddenly understood these words.

Simplicianus that, in the light of man's fallenness, he takes the final, irrevocable step and attributes man's faith and any good work that he does wholly to the action of God's grace.

The far-reaching consequences of this insight were to determine the entire structure of his theology and imposed a never-ending attempt to defend and justify it in the face of his critics. Robert Markus sums up this transformation in Augustine's thought—which, as should already be obvious, marks his decisive break with classical moral theory—thus:

Salvation is no longer an ordered progression towards a distant goal, but a sustained miracle of divine initiative; confidence in human resources, moral and intellectual, is the chief of the obstacles man can place in its way. The idea of an ultimate justice comprehensible in human terms, and the possibility of attaining it through the arrangements of social living, now seemed to Augustine a dangerous illusion.[13]

How and why did this transformation come about? We have noted the immediate circumstances and the texts which precipitated it, but in order to appreciate its growth in Augustine's mind we need to examine the broader canvas of his intellectual sources and context.

PAUL: ROMANS 7

The figure of Paul seems to accompany Augustine on his intellectual journey, from reading of his works as a Manichee, through the attempt to reclaim him from the Manichees in the commentaries of the 390s with their changing perspectives on the question of evil, grace, and free will, to the adoption of his experiences as a model to understand, with theological retrospection, his own conversion in *Confessions*, Book 8. No one has traced the relationship between the two figures with more illuminating clarity than Paula Fredriksen.[14] She also points out[15] that others, such as the Donatist Tyconius, were also working on Paul and that some of Augustine's ideas may well have been influenced by their interpretation of Paul. Certainly, the third rule of Tyconius' *Book of Rules* (*Liber Regulorum*) on exegesis, which Augustine had read by 396 (*ep.* 41.2), is very similar to Augustine's early interpretation of Paul (in *exp. prop. Rm.*; *ep. Rm. inch.* and *diu. qu.* 66–68) which we contrasted with *To Simplicianus* above.[16]

Others also exercised an influence: Plotinus's *Enn.* 5.1 might well lie behind Augustine's emphasis on pride, expressed as love of self and of

---

[13] Markus (1994a), XVIII, 22–3.

[14] Fredriksen (1986) and (1988). See also Delaroche (1996), 60; 85–91 and for bibliography.

[15] Fredriksen (1988).

[16] Tyconius also, she points out, uses texts Augustine will later use, especially 1 Cor. 1: 31 and Eph. 2: 8–9.

one's own powers (including power over others), in antithesis to love of God;[17] Ambrose, Cyprian, and Tertullian are probably a source for his doctrine of original sin;[18] Ambrose could also be the source of Augustine's later emphasis on the link between sin, desire, and sexual intercourse.[19]

But it is Paul, as we have seen, to whom Augustine turns to express his own experience of the workings of original sin, the fallenness of the will, and the operation of grace, in writing his *Confessions*.[20] This work was begun about the same time as *To Simplicianus*, ten years after his conversion, and like *On Free Will*, is a valuable text in tracing the important developments which we have seen taking place in Augustine's thought during these years. Here the theology is expressed autobiographically—written, as autobiographies always are, with the benefit of hindsight, and telling us just as much about Augustine's present, in its preoccupations and interpretative stance, as it does about his past. Augustine's account of his conversion is famous, not so much for the various intellectual stages he traversed in persuading himself of the truth of Christianity, as for his very personal, moving, and human description of the conversion of his will in embracing the Christian faith.

'With avid intensity', Augustine recounts in Book 7, 'I seized the sacred writings of your Spirit and especially the apostle Paul.' Paul proved to contain all the truth he had found in the Platonists, but with the important difference that whatever is known is a gift to man who is wholly dependent on God's grace (he cites the texts we have already encountered above: 1 Cor. 4: 7 and Rom. 7: 22–24). Augustine uses Rom. 7: 22, 'for I delight in the law of God, in my inmost self, but I see in my members another law at war with the law of my mind and making me captive to the law of sin which dwells in my members', as the context to vividly depict his own fallen will: imprisoned, weighed down by the iron chain of sin which had assumed all the strength and necessity or habit; at war with the new will which was emerging towards God (*conf.* 8.5.10); twisted and turning with his half-wounded will (8.8.19), divided within himself; passive and unwilling in the

---

[17] Rist (1994), 188.

[18] Ibid. on Cyprian *ep. 64*; *Commentary on the Lord's Prayer*, *Testimonies*. Tertullian *de anima* 41 uses the term *uitium originis*. Gerald Bonner suggests that this doctrine was simply accepted by Augustine as part of Catholic teaching, Bonner (1987) X. When he was accused of inventing the doctrine of original sin Augustine retorted: 'My instructor is Cyprian . . . my instructor is Ambrose . . .' (*c. Iul. imp.* 6.21). In *On the Merits and Forgiveness of Sins* (3.5.10) Augustine refers to Cyprian, who had justified the baptism of infants on the grounds that by birth they had contracted *contagium mortis antiquae*.   [19] Teselle (1970), 265–6.

[20] O'Donnell (1992) III, 3 observes that the whole of *conf.* 8 is a reading of Paul, particularly Romans, and sets out the pattern of citations from Romans in this book which gradually work their way through the epistle.

face of ingrained habit (8.5.11), like someone unwilling to get out of a comfortable, warm bed, delaying the moment when he must leave it and get up, even though he knows that this is inevitable (8.5.12); afraid that God might 'too rapidly heal him of the disease of lust which' he 'preferred to satisfy rather than to suppress' (8.7.17). Whereas his body readily obeyed his will in moving his limbs, his will was at war with itself, unable to obey its own orders because of the way in which it had become dissociated from itself by sin (*conf.* 8.8.20–10.23). Thus, though convinced of the truth, he was unable decisively to decide for it (*conf.* 8.11.25). The root of the sinful division he acknowledges to be his inability to leave his past relations with women behind and to embrace the celibacy which for him was an essential part of conversion to Christianity. His old loves held him back, tantalizing him with memories of the past; they 'were whispering behind my back, as if they were furtively tugging at me as I was going away, trying to persuade me to look back . . . I hesitated to detach myself, to be rid of them . . . meanwhile the overwhelming force of habit was saying to me: "Do you think you can live without them?"' (*conf.* 8.11.26). Even an alluring vision of Lady Continence (*conf.* 8.11.27) could not provoke a final decision. Tortured and torn, divided and dissociated from his own will, Augustine turned to the letters of Paul he had been reading: 'I seized it, opened it and in silence read the first passage on which my eyes lit: "Not in riots and drunken parties, not in eroticism and indecencies, not in strife and rivalry, but put on the Lord Jesus Christ and make no provision for the flesh in its lusts"' (Rom. 13: 13–14). It was this divinely inspired and graced reading that effected the conversion of his will.

Before we go on to examine Augustine's mature reflections on the nature of human willing it would be useful to consider just what he understands by Paul's description, in Romans 7, of an inward law, a law of the mind, which was resisted, and held captive, by the law of sin which was in his members. First of all, what is the inward law of the mind, which in *Confessions* 8 appears as Augustine's new will towards God, at war with the old will of habit, necessity, and sin? The obvious answer is that it is Augustine's acknowledgement of the truth about God—which he had eventually realized through his reading of the Platonists and St Paul—and his desire to embrace and follow it in a life which subjects all temporal and bodily things to him, in other words, a life of virtue—expressed as celibacy. That the law of the mind is 'inward', and in a sense, inherent, rather than simply learnt and acquired from others, is made clear in *Confessions* 10 where Augustine analyses his mind or memory and details the truths it contains, the eternal laws and principles of the disciplines, the universal desire for the happy life which arises from the fact that God is found both within and above it—the mind knows Him but has not yet attained Him, and therefore loves and desires Him (10.8.12–27.38[21]). In this way knowledge of God and of his eternal law is possible, even for fallen man, and constitutes the basis of his desire to return to Him. As we have seen in Chapter 1, Augustine held that all men, by virtue of their creation by God, have some knowledge of the truth. In *On the Trinity*, this knowledge is described as the natural foundation for moral conduct: 'For He always is . . . And He is whole everywhere, and for that reason people live, move and have their being in Him (Acts 17: 28), and therefore remember Him . . . hence it is that even the godless think of eternity, and rightly condemn and praise many things in the moral conduct of men'.[22] In other texts he talks of a 'natural law' (*ep.* 157.3.15; *en. Ps.* 118 *s.* 25.4), of the 'light of reason' (*c. Iul. imp.* 1.94), an 'eternal law' (*ciu.* 15.16.2) or an 'inward law' written on the heart (*en. Ps.* 57.1), an idea of truth 'impressed' on the mind (*Gn. litt.* 8.27.49–50).[23]

Two treatises, *On Lying* (AD 395) and *Against Lying* (AD 420), therefore work on the assumption that there are absolute moral rules—against lying and killing—which must never be set aside, whatever the temporal justification; one must not tell lies or blaspheme, even though this might serve to uncover liars and blasphemers who will otherwise harm the Church (e.g. to find heretical Priscillianists, *c. mend.* 17;41); one must not commit a venial sin in order to avoid a greater sin. Such rules are laid down in Scripture and by the truth which is known to human reason (*mend.* 5). Nothing can justify mortal sin, whatever its beneficial consequences in this life, since it always entails the loss of eternal life; and even venial sin violates the order of truth, and is therefore an affront to God, who is Truth, and to the image of God in the man who commits it.[24]

Thus, in some sense, Augustine can argue that man knows the truth and is bound to act upon it. But as we have seen in our investigations into his earlier reflections on the will, culminating in his account of his conversion in *Confessions* 8, things are not, in fact, so simple for fallen man. It is possible for man to will the good which he knows but to find that he is incapable of acting upon it. This is a universal human experience and one which Augustine's understanding of the will, in contrast to ancient[25] and post-Enlightenment thinking, goes a long way to explaining.

[21] Augustine obviously has in mind Plato, for whom all knowledge is reminiscence (*anamnesis*), but modifies him by maintaining that the mind's reminiscence or memory is not of some pre-existent, pre-fallen existence of the soul, but rather of the presence of God to the soul. [22] *trin.* 14.15.21—quoted by M. T. Clark (1994), 45.

[23] See Rist (1994), 191 f; Markus (1970), 388–9.

[24] Rist (1994), 193 cites *s.* 9.15 and comments on the individual's responsibility for the well-being of his own soul, to preserve himself guiltless and undivided. He also notes the fact that certain episodes of Scripture forced Augustine to admit that God can suspend his own absolute rules if He wills (199).

[25] For bibliography on the will in antiquity see Wetzel (1992), 86 n. 1.

As inheritors of the Enlightenment the notion of will probably immediately conjures up for us that faculty or power which works independently
in man, which is able to choose, discriminate and opt for the thing or action
it has rationally deliberated. Augustine's understanding of the will
(*voluntas, liberum arbitrium*) is rather different: it is a much more dynamic
movement within man, for as long as he lives and thinks he must exercise
it for good or for ill. It is a God-given power, created with mankind from
nothing, and capable of being turned to faith or unbelief; to God and
eternal things (*conversio*) or the world and temporal things (*aversio*). When
man misuses it in turning towards himself and away from God he is actually diminishing his being; a wrong action of the will is not, as for Kant, a
choice which he can then undo, rather it is something which determines
his whole being. The fall of Adam, which has effected the will of each one
of his descendants, means that they find themselves in a state of ignorance
and inability, the sort of condition which Augustine finds vividly depicted
in Romans 7 and develops in *Confessions* 8—though we must be careful to
remember that for Augustine this state does not disappear with conversion, when man might be said to have moved from being 'under the law'
to 'under grace'. The will experiences just the same problems in the baptized Christian as it does in his pagan counterpart:

> Nor does the human soul itself stand firm. Through how may modifications and
> variations of thought it fluctuates! By how many desires is it moved! By how many
> perverse feelings is it disrupted and split apart! The very mind of man which is
> called rational is mutable, it is never the same. At one moment it wills, at the next
> it does not will; at one point it knows, at the next it does not know; at one instant
> it remembers, at the next it has forgotten, therefore no one from his own resources
> remains the same. (*en. ps.* 121.6)[26]

Whereas the Manichees explained the dividedness of the will using the
concept of two souls, one good and one evil, and the Platonists attributed
the weakness of the will to the effect that the (irrational) body has on the
(rational) soul, Augustine rejects dualistic interpretations and is clear that
sin is in reality due to the corruption of the soul, not the body. As he
observes in *City of God* 14.5, 'The Platonists suppose that souls are so
affected by their earthly joints and moribund members that they attribute
to these the diseases of desire, fear, joy and pain, the four peturbations or
passions in which is contained all the vitiation of human conduct.' Ancient
philosophical reflection was agreed in attributing the four passions,[27] which

---

[26] Rist (1994), 184 elucidates Augustine's understanding of the weakness of the will with
Aristotle's use of *acrasia* in the *Nicomachean Ethics*, and notes that whereas for Aristotle some
are acratic some of the time, and some all of the time (about some things), for Augustine we
are all acratic all of the time.   [27] Cicero *de finibus* 3.10.35; *tusc. disp.* 4.6.11.

disturb man, to the body, and in holding that they could be controlled by the will or reason in accordance with its knowledge of wisdom. Augustine's experience of the workings of the will had found the passions invading, dividing, and upturning the workings of the will in the face of its rational grasp of truth.

THE PASSIONATE INTELLECT

It is true, he admits in *City of God* 14, that Adam and Eve would not have experienced any of the passions which now afflict man, before they fell: 'They were not distressed by any agitations of the mind, nor pained by any disorders of the body . . . In this state of bliss there would have been the serene assurance that no one would sin and no one would die' (14.10). But in turning away from God to themselves, in following their own will rather than God's, their will became divided, vitiated, flawed, and they became subject to loss, suffering, and death—in other words their will began to act involuntarily and became unavoidably subject to the passions.

In reconsidering the role of the passions (Gk. *pathe*, Lt. *perturbationes, affectiones, passiones*) in the light of the fall, in *City of God* 9 and 14, Augustine fundamentally reevaluates ancient philosophical reflection so that, far from relegating the passions to the irrational soul he makes them a part of the rational soul, as forms in which the will works, and which are capable of both positive and negative applications. The two main schools he has in mind are the Stoics and the Platonists. Whereas in theory the Stoics seem to differ from the Platonists in refusing to admit that the passions can even affect a wise man, whilst the Platonists maintain that the wise man, though affected, subjects them to reason, in practice the difference is simply one of terminology: the Stoics admit that though the soul of a wise man cannot help experiencing the passions, still he resists them by rational deliberation. Such a man is Virgil's Aeneas: 'Unmoved his mind: the tears [of Dido] roll down in vain' (*Aen.* 4.449 in *ciu.* 9.4). Similarly, whilst the Stoics condemn compassion in theory, in practice Epictetus admits compassion in the soul of the wise man, without calling it a vice, since, as Augustine puts it, it 'is the servant of reason, when compassion is shown without detriment to justice, when it is a matter of giving to the needy or of pardoning the repentant' (*ciu.* 9.5). Thus Augustine unites the views of ancient philosophy in order to proceed to counter them.

Compassion is in fact a good example of Augustine's insistence that what matters is not the 'passion', whatever it might be, but the character of the individual's will: 'If the will is wrongly directed, the emotions will be wrong; if the will is right, the emotions will be not only blameless but praiseworthy.' The passions are, in fact, all acts of will: desire and joy are acts of will in agreement with what we wish for; fear and grief are acts of will in disagreement with what we reject (*ciu.* 14.6). So, all the passions might be rightly felt by a Christian: if his love, or will, is right he fears to sin, desires to persevere, feels pain over sin and gladness in good works.

Indeed, the passions are not only possible, but necessary. The Stoic ideal of passionlessness (Gk *apatheia*, Lt. *impassibilitas*), however it is under-stood—as the absence of disordered passions or the complete absence of any emotion whatsoever—is neither desirable or attainable in this life or even in the life to come (*ciu.* 14.9). In fact, Augustine observes, the Stoics do admit three sorts of 'passions' into the perfected state of reason (in accordance with the first understanding of *apatheia*[28]): they called them *eupatheiai* (Gk) or *constantiae* (Lt.)—constant states—where will replaces desire; gladness, joy; caution, fear—as opposed to the disordered *pathe* of desire, joy, fear, and grief which afflict the mind of the fool. Augustine's examination of Scripture and classical authors demonstrates, however, that the three *eupatheiai*, as well as the four *pathe*, are felt by both wise and foolish, good and bad, in this life; by the former in a good way, indicating a rightly directed will, by the latter in a bad way, indicating a wrongly directed will (14.8). The Stoic's notable exception of grief from the soul of the wise man is also unacceptable and impossible for a Christian, for whom the life he desires is unattainable in this fallen world, and sin and suffering are inevitable—all are causes of a positive grief.

Thus Augustine undermined classical moral philosophy and its assertion that the happy life can be attained here and now by the virtuous control of reason over the passions and the body. What did he put in its place? How is fallen man to act virtuously? How is he to seek the happy life? His answer draws on other aspects of ancient philosophy together with what he perceived to be the central message of the gospel: the commandment to love God and to love one's neighbour as oneself. If everything the will does is guided by these two principles then it will act rightly, in accordance with the good. That this is possible for fallen humanity is a matter of God's love—of grace.

'LOVE AND DO AS YOU WILL' (*EP. IO. TR. 7.8*)

For Augustine the will is synonymous with love; to will is not just to ratio-nally deliberate and choose to act, rather it is to love something and to be

[28] See Colish (1985), 221–5 for Augustine's treatment of *apatheia* and *eupatheia*—referred to by Wetzel (1992), 102 n. 27.

moved to act on the basis of that love. It is at the root of everything man does, it informs every movement he makes—'Man's will cannot be inactive' (*en. ps.* 121.1)—and thus constitutes his very being, making it what it is. A man whose love is directed to God and neighbour is therefore a man of good will. The various Latin terms for love are synonymous in this context: 'This attitude is more commonly called charity (*caritas*) in Holy Scripture; but it appears in the same sacred writings under the appellation love (*amor*) . . . the Scriptures of our religion . . . do not distinguish between love (*amor*), fondness (*dilectio*) or charity (*caritas*)' (*ciu.* 14.7).[29] The one who exercises his will badly in self acquisitive pride still wills and still loves, but this love is best described as cupidity (*cupiditas*), concupiscence (*concupiscentia*), or lust (*libido*). Relating these loves to the passions in *City of God* 14 Augustine makes clear that what distinguishes *caritas* from *cupiditas* is not the way the love or will is expressed, but the object towards which it is directed: 'Both upright and perverse love are will; love as longing for its object is desire; as possessing and enjoying it, it is joy; fleeing what is hurtful to it, it is fear; feeling its presence, it is pain. All these are evil if the love is evil, good if it be good' (14.7).

How is it possible for the fallen will to direct itself towards the good? We have seen that it is always naturally at work within man but that in his fallen state it is to a large degree constrained by necessity; vitiated and flawed, it finds it extremely difficult either to recognize the good, or, having done so, to act upon it. In *City of God* we found that, acknowledging the will's incapacity rationally to deliberate, choose, and act upon the good, Augustine broke with classical moral philosophy in attributing the desires and passions, which it relegated to the body and viewed merely as disturbances, to the will itself and gave them a positive role in directing the fallen will towards the good. Love, operating through the passions, therefore takes the place of reason in directing man's will towards God. As Augustine comments in *City of God* 11, 'For we are justified in calling a man good not because he knows what is good, but because he loves the good' (11.28).

Of course, no one can love the good unless he in some sense knows it (*trin.* 10.1.1)—and we have seen that Augustine held there were certain truths which are both innate to man's mind and made known to him through God's revelation of Himself in Scripture. But it is love which both

---

[29] Though Augustine inclines to use *caritas* and *dilectio* (the equivalent of the Gk. *agape*) in a positive context and *amor* (which is close to the Platonic *eros*) as a neutral term. See Pétré (1948). I do not propose to enter the debate initiated by A. Nygren concerning the meaning of Augustinian *caritas* here but refer the reader to the discussions in O'Donovan (1980) and, in particular, Holte (1962).

increases this knowledge (*Io. eu. tr.* 96.4) and enables man to act upon it and use it rightly. Nowhere is this more evident than in what Augustine has to say about the will, or love, as a weight, drawn by desire and longing towards the good.

LOVE AS A GIFT OF GRACE

The idea of love as a sort of weight or gravitational force, which pulls the will in a certain direction, is frequently used by Augustine[30] to describe the unerring way in which the will is moved by its love of a particular object: 'For the movements of gravity are, as it were, the "loves" of bodies. As the mind is carried by its love, so is the body by its weight; each to its own place ... fire goes up, a stone comes down, ... oil floats on water ... My weight is my love; by it I move wherever I move' (*conf.* 13.9.10).

What unerringly moves man's love in a certain direction is the delight which he cannot help taking in what is attractive, pleasing, beautiful, inspiring. (Again the source of these ideas is found in Plato[31].) Love (*dilectio*), desire (*desiderium*), and delight (*delectatio*) are used almost synonymously by Augustine. We only love and act upon that which delights us (*serm.* 159.3; *exp. Gal.* 49), that which we find beautiful (*mus.* 6.13.38) and which affords us pleasure.

We saw, earlier on, in reference to *To Simplicianus*, that the fallen will would have no motive to act unless something delighted it. That this happens, Augustine observes, is due to God's inspiration and grace (*Simpl.* 2.22). It is only God's gracious inspiration and revelation which ensures that man's will is moved to love Him and is not ensnared and held back by love of the beautiful for its own sake, by pleasure as a matter of personal indulgence, or corrupted by the temporal as an end in itself:[32] 'The man in whom God deals graciously is he in whom God inspires delight in the good—and that is, to speak more plainly, he to whom God gives the love of God' (*EN. ps.* 17.2). This love has its origin in God's gift of the Holy Spirit: 'The love of God is shed abroad in our hearts by the Holy Spirit which has been given to us' (Rom. 5: 5[33]). Augustine's identification of love and the Holy Spirit (which seems to be original to him) implies that all love of God is from God, that man moves and delights in God because of God's gift and grace, and is thus drawn to God by God.

---

[30] e.g. *conf.* 13.9.10; *ep.* 55.18; 157.9; *Gn. litt.* 2.1.2; 4.3.7–8; 18.34; *ciu.* 11.28.

[31] Rist (1994), 156–7, who refers to Plato's 'ethics of inspiration'.

[32] See the second half of *conf.* 10 for Augustine's analysis of the various temptations which threaten his *continentia*, or single-minded devotion to God, in terms of 1 John 2: 16 and his appeal to Christ's grace as mediator.

[33] One of Augustine's favourite texts. He cites it more than 200 times.

As we shall see, the emphasis upon God's grace, and of the Holy Spirit as the source of inward delight in righteousness and love of justice, as opposed to fearful observance of the law, come to increased prominence in Augustine's later anti-Pelagian works, as he attempts both to defend the absolute necessity of grace and also the free operation of man's will.[34]

The corollary of delight (*delectatio*) is desire or longing (*desiderium*) to attain fully that which delights us and inspires our love, for in this life fallen man can never reach it. Thus we find that Augustine's characteristic picture of a Christian is of someone in exile, on a pilgrimage, journeying towards the object of his love, meanwhile yearning and longing, uttering sighs and groans, his journey moved forward by love and delight in God's revelation, his unending desire serving to increase his capacity to receive what he longs for. These ideas find their best expression in Augustine's *Homilies on the First Epistle of St. John* which are primarily concerned with the nature of love: 'The whole life of a good Christian is a holy desire . . . by longing you are made capable, so that when that comes which you may see, you will be filled . . . God, by deferring our hope, stretches our desire . . . This is our life, that by longing we should be exercised' (4.6).[35]

'HE HAS ORDERED LOVE WITHIN ME'
(Song of Songs 2: 2)[36]

Man's fallen will is also enabled to direct itself towards the good by virtue of a God-given order which it finds in created reality and which, if his love observes it, will lead him to its Creator: 'Just as the covetous man subordinates justice to his love of gold—through no fault in the gold but in himself—so it is with all things. They are all good in themselves, and capable of being loved either well or badly. They are loved well when the right order is kept, badly when this order is upset . . . hence it seems to me that the briefest and truest definition of virtue is that it is an order of love' (*ciu.* 15.22).[37] This classical idea[38] was used by Augustine early on in his defence of creation against the Manichees: insofar as creation possesses order, expressed as measure, number, and weight, to that extent it is good and reveals its divine Creator, Orderer, and Sustainer. This ontological

---

[34] Foreshadowed in *sp. et litt.* 15.26 and clearly in evidence in *c. ep. Pel.* 1.22; 36–7; 2.21; *perf. iust.* 9; *nat. et gr.* 36; *c. Iul. imp.* 3.122; *gr. et lib. arb.* 17.33; *pecc. mer.* 1.13.27; 2.19.32. See Harrison (1993).   [35] See Harrison (1992), 259–63.
[36] Rist (1994), 51 n. 18, observes that the first quotation of this verse seems to be in *s.* 100.2 (*c.* AD 395) or *s.* 37.2 (*c.* AD 397).   [37] Cited by Markus (1970b), 386.
[38] The idea of a cosmic hierarchy was general currency. Markus notes the Ciceronian precedents for Augustine's definition of virtue as 'the disposition of the mind whereby it agrees with the order of nature and of reason' in *diu. qu.* 31.1. Markus (1970b), 387.

order is therefore a 'given'; it is one which man discovers, in which he naturally participates, and which naturally orders his love—rather than one
which he rationally imposes himself, as is often the case in classical eudaemonism.[39] As in the *conversio/aversio* model, if his love does not submit to,
and participate in this order, of which God Himself is the originator and
summum bonum, he can only decline from right order and diminish, deform,
and enslave his being in evil doing, moving back to the nothingness from
which he was formed.

Augustine's most theoretical consideration of the divinely created order
of reality to which man must conform his love in order to attain the
summum bonum, occurs in Book 1 of *On Christian Doctrine*, in the form of
the well-known distinction between use (*uti*) and enjoyment (*frui*). Its
Stoic,[40] Varronian,[41] source is clearly evident in *83 Diverse Questions* where
Augustine talks in terms of the right (*honestum*) and the useful (*utile*), that
is, of 'what is desired for its own sake (*honestum*), and what is desired for
the sake of something else (*utile*)' and comments that, 'we are said to enjoy
(*frui*) things which satisfy our desire; we use (*utimur*) those which we refer
to the acquisition of the things which satisfy our desires.' He proceeds to
elaborate on these distinctions in terms very close to *On Christian Doctrine*
Book 1 (1.3.3):

All human perversion, which we also call vice, consists in wanting to use things
which are meant to be enjoyed, and to enjoy things which are meant to be used.
And all order (*ordinatio*), which we also call virtue, consists in wanting to enjoy
what is to be enjoyed and to use what is to be used. What is right (*honestis*) is
to be enjoyed (*fruendum*), what is useful (*utilibus*) is to be used (*utendum*) (*diu.
qu.* 30).[42]

On Christian Doctrine Book 1 provides further elaboration in a directly
eudaemonistic context: 'Those things which are to be enjoyed make us
blessed. Those things which are to be used help and, as it were, sustain us
as we move towards blessedness in order that we might gain and cling to
those things which make us blessed' (1.3). The ethical implications for the
operation of man's love follow: 'To enjoy something is to cling to it with
love for its own sake. To use something, however, is to employ it in obtain-

---

[39] For the importance of this ontological perspective in (the largely Swedish) debates on
the question of the *summum bonum* see Holte (1962), 207–20; Madec (1996a), 82–3.

[40] Holte (1962), 201 cites Cicero as the source of the distinction *honestum* and *utile*, based
on the Stoic distinction between the moral good (virtue) and the objects chosen or preferred
(values). Markus (1970b), 389 notes that Augustine reduced the Stoic's threefold scheme of
classification of goods (*delectabile*—pleasant; *utile*—useful; *honestum*—right) to two.

[41] Lorenz (1950); Madec (1996), 82 n. 22.

[42] I owe this quotation to Markus (1970b), 389–90. Cf. *ciu.* 11.25; 19.10; *trin.* 10.10.13; *conf.*
7.17.23; *ep.* 140.2.4; *En. ps.* 121.3; *s.* 177.8.

ing that which you love, provided it is worthy of love' (1.4). Stated in distinctively Christian terms this implies that God, the Trinity, is the *telos*, the *res*, which alone is to be loved for its own sake (*propter seipsum*—1.27) and enjoyed (*frui*). Everything else, His temporal, mutable creation (including man, his neighbour, and all created reality below man)[43] and His revelation of Himself in His Son, the Spirit, and the Church,[44] is to be used (*uti*) towards this end, referred to (*referre ad*) it.

Problems arise—for Augustine and his critics—in relation to the question of love of self and of one's neighbour. How can these loves, set forth in the double commandment, be properly described as 'use'? Of course, all men, Augustine concedes, naturally love themselves; they seek to maintain their health and to prolong their life (1.25).[45] Over and above this, man needs to be able to assess 'the intrinsic value of things', that is, to have an 'ordinate love' (*ordinatam dilectionem*). For Augustine this means above all else that one properly loves oneself and one's neighbour by loving God:[46] this implies that man's soul, created in God's image, is to be loved above his body (1.26), his neighbour should be loved 'for the sake of God' (*propter Deum*), and God should be loved for Himself (*propter seipsum*) (1.27).

The tempering of the idea of 'use' implicit in the language of loving 'for the sake of' or 'on behalf of' (*propter*) is further developed when Augustine cites Philemon 20, 'may I enjoy thee in the Lord' and concedes that love of another person may well be described as 'enjoyment' in the sense of 'use with delight' (*cum delectatione uti*) (1.33; cf. *conf.* 6.16.26; *ep.* 26.4; *ciu.* 19.13; *trin.* 9.8.13). So Augustine can conclude this section of *On Christian Doctrine*: 'The whole temporal dispensation was made by divine providence for our salvation. We should use it, not with an abiding but with a transitory love and delight (*quadam dilectione et delectatione*) so that we love those things by which we are carried along for the sake of that toward which we are carried' (1.35).[47]

The terminological straitjacket of 'use' and 'enjoyment' has thus been cast off in favour of the language of love of God: of His creation and revelation, on the way towards the ultimate good; love of Himself, as the end and ultimate Good itself. This break foreshadows Augustine's mature reflection on the nature of human willing where the focus lies not so much

---

[43] Augustine defines four levels of reality, four kinds of things which determine the order of man's love: that which is above us (God); that which constitutes ourselves; that which is equal to us (our neighbour) and that which is below us (creation) (1.23).

[44] See 1.5–19 where Augustine gives an outline of Christian doctrine to elucidate the way in which God provides a way back to Himself through His temporal revelation of Himself recounted in Scripture.

[45] The Stoic doctrine of *oikeiosis*.   [46] Cf. *mor.* 1.26.48.

[47] This paragraph is based on my previous discussion of this question in Harrison (1992), 247–53.

upon a hierarchical order of goods, or failure to observe this order, but rather upon the polarity between love of self and love of God, pride and humility, which is developed on the broad canvas of the *City of God*. Nor must it be forgotten that the love with which man loves God is in fact the love of God Himself which he inspires in men's hearts through His Holy Spirit; of himself man can do nothing but sin.

CLASSICAL AND CHRISTIAN VIRTUE

The Christian doctrine of the fall, with its denial of man's capacity to attain the good through his own unaided efforts, of his inability to know or to do the good without God's grace, and of the unattainability of beatitude in this life marks the final break between classical and Christian understandings of virtue, the will, and the happy life. The startling optimisim of classical philosophy, with its unerring conviction of man's autonomous will, his capacity for rational self-determination and for perfectibility through knowledge (and in Neoplatonism, the ascent of the mind), has been dealt a death blow by Augustine's uncompromising picture of man subject to Original sin following the fall of Adam. Without the help of grace man can do nothing to achieve salvation, his flawed and vitiated will can no longer do anything but sin, his grasp of the truth is marred by ignorance and blindness.

This is not to say that Augustine thought that non-Christians were incapable of virtuous acts but that, without grace, such virtues really amounted to vices—albeit ones which will be punished less severely than actual vicious acts (*c. Iul.* 4.3.25; 33).[48] Only acts dependent upon grace are effective for salvation.

It is in this context that we might begin to investigate the controversy with the British layman Pelagius (350–425), which was to dominate Augustine's thought and work from at least 410, for the remaining twenty years of his life. Before going into any detail we can make plain the reasons for the conflict by simply observing that, though a devout and popular Christian preacher, Pelagius's thought was firmly rooted in the classical tradition of reflection upon man's moral and intellectual autonomy, and of his perfectibility in this life, which Augustine's understanding of the fall completely undermined and invalidated.[49]

---

[48] Pointed out by Rist (1994), 172 who also cites *ciu.* 19.25 where Augustine describes pagan virtues as 'sterile' or ineffective.

[49] In *ep.* 186.11.37 Augustine warns Paulinus of Nola that to tolerate the followers of Pelagius would be to support men who, like the pagan philosophers, thought that the happy life was attainable in this world.

PELAGIANISM

The one thing which Pelagian scholars invariably comment upon is the difficulty one encounters in trying to define 'Pelagianism', for the term covers the thought not just of Pelagius, but of numerous other 'Pelagian' thinkers, some of whom were acquainted with him, such as Caelestius, and others who were probably not, including the 'Sicilian Anonymous'[50] and Julian of Eclanum. The movement is associated with areas as far apart as Britain and Sicily, Spain and the Holy Land, but tended to centre upon Rome, and following the fall of Rome, North Africa. Its teaching also varied in its different representatives and diverse contexts. And as with all movements which were condemned as heretical, one must be critical of the manner in which its opponents choose to represent it. There are, however, a good number of 'Pelagian' texts[51] to which we can look for evidence of some homogeneity of thought against which to judge its more extreme proponents and also its detractors.

Jerome famously referred to Pelagius as 'that fathead, bloated with Scotch porridge' (*Commentary on Jeremiah*, prologue). We know that Pelagius came from Britain, and scholars have speculated on the origins of his thought here—suggesting, for example, that its roots lie in a movement of social protest against unjust direct Roman rule,[52] though such ideas are now generally discredited. What we do know with certainty is that Pelagius came to some prominence from 394 onwards, firstly in Rome and then in the Holy Land, where he was established at Jerusalem under the patronage of Bishop John. His first two works *On Nature* and *On Free Will* were composed in the context of a controversy he had entered into with Jerome,[53] then resident in Bethlehem, concerning the question of man's sinlessness and the nature of marriage. On the matter of sinlessness, each accused the other of Origenism. Pelagius, who may have met Rufinus (the

---

[50] A number of treatises emanating from Sicily, with a distinctive emphasis (e.g. on redistribution of wealth (*On Riches*; *To Fatalis*)), are commonly agreed to be the work of one anonymous author. See Rees (1991) for texts. In *perf. iust.* Augustine mentions ideas which the 'brethren of Sicily' attributed to Caelestius and in *ep.* 157 discusses questions raised by Christians in Syracuse concerning the possibility of sinlessness and the forbidding of oath taking (e.g. in *On the Possibility of Sinlessness*; *On Chastity*). Rees (1991), 165 suggests that Pelagius or Caelestius had probably passed through Sicily *en route* for Africa and established a Pelagian circle there to which the 'Sicilian Anonymous' belonged.

[51] Editions, newly discovered texts, and secondary literature are considered in Bonner's magisterial article 'Augustine and Modern Research on Pelagianism', Bonner (1987a), XI, 5–11 to which I refer the reader for details and bibliography. Rees (1991) has since published an excellent edition of the letters of Pelagius and his followers.

[52] Again, see Bonner (1987a), XI, 9–10 for a survey of the secondary literature and sound judgements. Also Brown (1972), 184.

[53] Evans drew attention to this previously neglected encounter in his book of 1968.

translator and champion of Origen against Jerome[54]), and had certainly read some of his works, probably intentionally revived Jerome's earlier controversy with him on this matter, when he found himself subjected to the same criticisms; he could therefore perhaps count on the same support from aristocratic circles which Rufinus had already received.[55] In the debate on the nature of marriage[56] Pelagius took the side of the Roman priest Jovinian, who placed the married state on a par with virginity, as against Jerome, who scornfully exalted virginity above the third-rate state of marriage. It must be noted, however, that in aligning himself with Jovinian Pelagius was not endorsing his attempt to find the ideal Christian life in that led by the married majority, but on the contrary, was advocating the ascetic life as the standard which *all* Christians ought to be aiming for:[57] he did not advocate mediocrity as the norm, but perfection.

Repercussions of the strident notes of perfectionism sounded in this early controversy are forcefully evident in Pelagius's work and teaching at Rome from 390?–409. In the first half of this chapter we examined the factors which led Augustine to break with the classical tradition of moral perfectionism and observed that it was perpetuated in the work of Pelagius and his followers. One of the main reasons for this seems to lie in the social context of Pelagianism, and in particular the social situation at Rome before 410.[58]

That part of Roman society which looked to Pelagius as a mentor, and found his teaching so attractive was an extremely conservative élite of affluent, influential, lay aristocrats who self-consciously strove to set themselves apart by enthusiastic ascetic renunciation and observance of a strict moral code.[59] He was patronized, among others, by Sixtus, a Roman priest who was later to become Pope, and by that small group of Christian *conversi* who are so prominent in the history of this period for their spectacular renunciations of their status and wealth, their correspondence with some of the major figures in the Church, and their generous benefactions. Figures such as Demetrias, the virgin (who received letters of advice from Pelagius and Augustine), her mother Juliana (who requested their advice), her grandmother Proba (the recipient of Augustine's famous Letter 130 on prayer), the young married couple Melania and Pinianus (who visited Hippo) are perhaps the most well-known representatives of the aristocratic élite for whom Pelagius's uncompromising emphasis on moral duty and ascetic perfection was so irresistible.

---

[54] His *Apology* was countered by Jerome's *Apology*.   [55] Brown (1972), 221.
[56] See Chapter 5.   [57] Markus (1990), 41.
[58] This is the subject of what have become classic articles by Peter Brown (1972), 183–226, the arguments of which have found general acceptance among Pelagian scholars.
[59] See Chapter 5.

In an age when Christianity was the religion of the State, and therefore of anyone who sought social standing and respectability, Pelagius's teaching was welcomed as a means to revive 'authentic' Christianity and to identify true Christians or *integri Christiani*[60] in contradistinction to nominal adherents for whom the faith was something they happened upon through marriage to a Christian or through professional advancement. His message was therefore by no means limited to the aristocratic élite who ensured its influence, but like all ascetic teaching, was also welcomed by all those who desired to 'set themselves apart' from the ordinary run of Christian devotion and practice, to those who felt they had seen Christian life and the Church's identity corrupted by the mediocrity inherent in its 'institutionalization'.

In his collection of the letters of Pelagius and his followers Rees comments upon the limited nature of early Pelagian literature, which largely consists of letters of advice or reprimand addressed to converts, penitents, virgins, celibates, and widows—in other words, to the sort of follower we have sketched above. Pelagius's extensive citation of biblical texts, his use of earlier Christian authors,[61] and his anti-Manichaean approach,[62] would all tend to inspire the confidence of his followers in the orthodoxy and authority of his work. And what he had to say was what they wanted to hear: that man is created in God's image and likeness, possessed of reason and wisdom, which enable him to recognize and serve God (*To Demetrias* 2.2). He is therefore free both to choose between good and evil and to act upon his choice, 'it is on this choice between two ways, on this freedom to choose either alternative, that the glory of the rational mind is based' (*To Demetrias* 3.1.)[63] Most importantly, in view of his Manichaean opponents, Pelagius was convinced that the choice of good or evil is 'voluntary and independent, not bound by necessity' (ibid. 3.2). Sin is therefore not a fault in our nature but of our will (8.1).[64] Nor can man's sin be attributed

---

[60] Brown (1972), 192. *Ep. Humanae referunt litterae* 3, Caspari p. 18: *PL* Suppl. 1378.

[61] Including Rufinus' translation of Greek monastic literature, and notably, the *Rule* of Saint Basil. Also Rufinus' translation of the *Sentences of Sextus*, which Pelagius believed to be the work of the second-century Pope Xystus, the Christian martyr. In fact Jerome attributes this collection of ethical maxims to a pagan philosopher, Sextus. Whatever the case, its teaching on man's natural goodness, his free will, the possibility of sinlessness, and on good works and faith, is very close to Pelagian ideas and might well be one of its sources. See Chadwick (1959).

[62] There was a large Manichaean population at Rome and any form of asceticism was sensitive to the accusation of Manichaeism. Much of Pelagius' teaching can be read as a refutation of Manichaeism and therefore a defence of his own brand of asceticism in contradistinction to it. In this respect his teaching, unsurprisingly, resembles that of Augustine. See Bohlin (1957).   [63] A passage obviously directed against Manichaean determinism.

[64] Cf. another Pelagian treatise, possibly by the Sicilian Anonymous, *On the Possibility of not Sinning* 3.1; 4.1 for similar teaching.

to ignorance, rather he possesses a natural knowledge of good and evil, a 'kind of inner law' in his conscience, which enables him to judge: 'this is the law the apostle recalls when he writes to the Romans, testifying that it is implanted in all men and written as it were on the tablets of the heart' (4.2). This inner law Pelagius describes as a good of nature, the natural state of all men as they are created—including the Gentiles. That it enabled some men to achieve sinlessness is evidenced in numerous Old Testament figures: Abel, Enoch, Melchizedek, Lot, Noah, Abraham, Isaac, Jacob, Joseph (5.1), and Job (6.1).

But others sinned, and having sinned, their sin became a habit, which gradually clouded their ability to know and do the good: 'Nor is there any reason why it is made difficult for us to do good other than that long habit of doing wrong which infected us from childhood and corrupted us little by little over many years and ever holds us in bondage and slavery to itself, so that it seems somehow to have acquired the force of nature' (8.3). The law of Moses was given in an attempt to remedy this situation; now, under grace, the new law frees man from sin and restores him to his natural state of freedom to do the good (8.4, quoting Rom. 6: 14, 'For sin will have no dominion over you, since you are not under law but under grace').

What is this new law? For Pelagius there is no antithesis between law and grace, rather grace *is* a new law, the law given by Christ in the New Testament, in His teaching and example, which, unlike the Mosaic Law, which was written on stone, is written on the heart. Thus, it removes the rust of habit and restores man's natural ability to know the good and to will freely. For the Christian the new law comes into operation when the benefits of Christ's unmerited death are appropriated in baptism, in the forgiveness of sins (*On the Divine Law*).[65] It is baptism which marks the decisive break for Pelagius, since by it man's sins are remitted, the new law begins to operate, and most importantly, the Christian's natural state of knowledge and freedom (his *ratio* or *lex naturae*) is restored. Baptized, the Christian is able to leave behind decisively his past life; he becomes a *tabula rasa* and it is once again possible for him to be sinless. Since he is commanded to be so in Scripture, he must obey, since nothing impossible has been either forbidden or commanded (*On the Possibility of Sinlessness* 4.2–3[66]). This is, of course, just the sort of thing Pelagius's Roman aristocrats and ascetics would warm to.[67]

But as Rees noted, the predominant concern of early Pelagian literature

---

[65] Cf. *On Bad Teachers*, which is probably by the Sicilian Anonymous, for similar teaching.

[66] Probably by the Sicilian Anonymous, though quite in keeping with Pelagius's thought.

[67] For the prevalence of the concept of habit viewed as an external, social force (identified especially with pagan society), and for the idea of breaking dramatically with one's past, in Western Christianity, see Brown (1972), 198–9.

is not so much theological as practical: Pelagius's audience wanted advice, guidance, encouragement, as to how they might live their lives in order to become *integri Christiani*. The theology demonstrated the possibility and obligation of this calling for all Christians; the practical teaching set forth the means of attaining it. What Pelagius's teaching in this respect amounted to was an exhortation to asceticism which, as we shall see in Chapter 5, is the predominant characteristic of so much fourth-century reflection on the Christian life. His letters *To Demetrias, On Virginity, On the Divine Law, On the Christian Life,* and *To Celantia* all betray the same preoccupation: to exhort the recipient to obey the commandments, to practice moderation and asceticism in the matters of everyday life, in conduct, dress, food, sexual relations, and sleep, to observe times of prayer and devotion, to read the Scriptures, to give alms, do good works, and act with neighbourly love.

Only the perfectionist thrust of the theological principles we outlined above set these letters apart from the large number of very similar contemporary works on the same themes and for the same audience. But of course, however much Pelagius believed himself to be simply reiterating orthodox teaching on the sound basis of Scripture and tradition, it was his theology which almost immediately began to attract criticism. Jerome had already found much to criticize, but then, Jerome himself had his 'orthodox' critics, including Rufinus and Jovinian, and was notorious for some of his more extreme views, especially on virginity and marriage. Although his support of Jovinian against Jerome might suggest that Pelagius was attempting to avoid exclusivism and extremism, his thoroughgoing application of the principle and requirement of perfection for all Christians in fact made even Jerome seem moderate.[68]

Matters were brought to a head when Pelagius was forced to leave Rome along with other exiles following the fall of the city in AD 410. Transplanted to the soil of Africa his thought was exposed to a climate far less conducive to its growth and where its foreignness provoked much hostile reaction. He arrived in North Africa with Caelestius in 411, on the eve of the Conference of Carthage which was being held by Catholic and Donatist factions. This in itself was ominous of the prevailing atmosphere Pelagius could expect to face in his new country. The Donatist's ardent perfectionism was determinedly opposed by the Catholic Church, which denied not just its historical foundation in the time of persecution, but above all, the theological foundations it proposed to find in the idea of a Church, priesthood, and sacraments sinless, holy, and untainted. As we shall see in the next chapter, the Catholics undermined the validity and coherence of the

---

[68] For an interesting comparison of Pelagianism and Priscillianism see Bonner (1987), XI, 73 n. 100.

Donatist Church by a doctrine of original sin which implied that no person, and hence, no institution—not even the Church—could claim to be without sin. This doctrine, which we found Augustine elaborating fully for the first time in 396, and which he proceeded to reiterate incessantly against the ever-present threat of the Donatist majority in Africa, from his elevation as Bishop of Hippo in 395/6, he will also use to cut at the roots of Pelagian theology and its claim to perfection and sinlessness in the baptized Christian. His direct confrontation with Pelagius was to come later, however; he only begins to attack his thought openly from *c.* 415 onwards. What was happening in the meantime?

THE CONTROVERSY

Caelestius stayed behind in Carthage while Pelagius went on to Palestine. He immediately drew attention to himself by making clear his views on the subject of infant baptism and the questions it raised concerning the doctrine of original sin and its transmission. No time was lost in bringing him to trial late that same year. Here, in the presence of the judge Aurelius of Carthage, and his accuser, Paulinus of Milan, he countered the consensus of African tradition which these two men represented[69] and denied the doctrine of Adam's original sin, its transmission to his descendants and therefore the grounds for the practice of infant baptism.[70] He was duly condemned on six counts[71] and excommunicated. He took himself off to Ephesus where he became a priest and continued to propound his views. It was at this stage that Augustine became acquainted with his teaching. He received a letter from the Ephesian Imperial Commissioner, Marcellinus, asking him to clarify certain questions which had obviously been raised by Caelestius: Was Adam mortal? (Though this was not one of Pelagius's doctrines, Caelestius had affirmed this at Carthage and it was included in the charges made against him.) Is his sin hereditary? Why should infants be baptized? Can man be without sin in this life? (Again, this

---

[69] Markus (1994a) IX, 198 sees the Pelagian conflict as arising 'not so much from the confrontation of a new and heretical body of ideas with an established orthodoxy as from the encounter of two theological traditions: the African, with its own sharply defined specific character, and the other, more widely diffused but far less well-defined orientation of the European Churches'. This is perhaps a good instance of this insight. See p. 89 and n. 18 above on African origins of doctrine of original sin.

[70] Bonner (1987) XI, 36–7 sees the influence of Rufinus the Syrian here. Probable author of *Liber de Fide* (a work marked by its anti-Origenism and denial of original sin—the two are probably linked) he has been identified with the Rufinus *natione Syrus* whom Marius Mercator reports corrupted Pelagius at Rome during the pontificate of Anastasius (399–401), and also with the person Caelestius mentions during his trial. See also Bonner (1987) X, 31–47.

[71] The six 'theses' of Caelestius are listed in *gest. Pel.* 35.65.

was a statement for which Caelestius had previously been condemned.) Augustine's reply, *On the Consequences of Sins and their Forgiveness* (that death and concupiscence are the consequence of Adam's sin—for him and for all his descendants—and that forgiveness is the work of God alone, so that infants should indeed be baptized), marks the beginning of his response to Pelagianism but not yet to Pelagius himself. Further rumblings of anti-Pelagian thought are evident in his subsequent elucidations to Marcellinus in *On the Spirit and the Letter* (AD 412) (against some ideas he had read in Pelagius's commentary on Romans[72]); in two sermons on original sin and the necessity of baptizing infants (AD 413) (many of Pelagius's followers would now be present in the congregations at Carthage); in letter 157 to Hilarius (414) (responding to reports of Pelagian teaching in Sicily[73]).

The reasons why Augustine refrained from directly criticizing Pelagius himself until 415, when he specifically attacked his *On Nature* with *On Nature and Grace*, are a matter for speculation. Pelagius was highly esteemed and had a great reputation for sanctity among his Roman, aristocratic followers—and these were people whom Augustine also knew and respected (Paulinus of Nola[74] and Melania and Pinianus, for example) and who would therefore predispose him in Pelagius's favour.

The rumblings against Pelagian ideas, initiated by the arrival of Caelestius and Augustine's reading of some of Pelagius's works in the two-year period between 412 and 414, suddenly became a fierce roar in 415, in *On Nature and Grace*. Was this because Pelagius presented the letter (*ep.* 146), which Augustine had written to him previously, as a sort of testimonial during his trial at the Synod of Diospolis (415)? Or was it because, as some scholars suggest, Augustine found his own earlier teaching on the will, grace, and the fall in *On Free Will*, cited by Pelagius, together with that of other Catholic authorities, in support of his own theories in *On Nature*?[75] Whatever the case, from 415 onwards Pelagius found himself at odds with the Catholic authorities in Palestine, Rome, and Africa and caught up in a seemingly unremitting battle with the African bishops for his condemnation. From the Synod of Jerusalem in 415, which, recounted by Orosius, brought the disagreements into the open for the first time, named names, and linked the various representatives of 'Pelagianism' together as one school with Pelagius at their head; through the Synod of Diospolis later that year which exonerated him owing to his disowning of Caelestius; to

---

[72] Bonner (1987) XI, 38. He refers to some arguments he has read in Pelagius's commentary on the Pauline Epistles, on Rom. 5: 12, against the doctrine of original sin, in *gest. Pel.* Book 3, but here presumes that Pelagius is simply quoting the ideas of others. See De Bruyn (1993); Delaroche (1996).

[73] See note 50 above.   [74] Suggested by Brown (1972), 217.

[75] See Evans (1968) for a careful consideration of the textual evidence for these views.

the appeal of the African bishops to Pope Innocent to endorse the decisions of the Councils of Carthage and Milev against Pelagius and to
condemn the Eastern bishops who had seen fit to support him; through
Innocent's agreement; his successor Zosimus' insistence on reconsidering
the decision under the influence of Caelestius; to the African's angry
appeal to the Emperor Honorius and the Imperial Court at Ravenna;
to the Imperial Rescript of 418 condemning Pelagius; to the Council of
Carthage which met on the day following its promulgation and which
passed nine canons systematically condemning Pelagianism, Pelagius and
his followers were buffeted between ecclesiastical councils and caught in
the cross currents of ecclesiastical politics between Africa, the East, and
Rome,[76] finally to be caught in the unyielding net of an Imperial Rescript
which was immediately and firmly tied up by the canons passed at
Carthage.

But the councils, Rescript, and Canons did not so much put an end to
Pelagianism as complete the process of identification and definition of the
movement, its adherents and its ideas so that the real battle could begin.
Forced by the Imperial Rescript to abandon any further attempts to keep
the condemnation of Pelagius and his supporters an open question, Pope
Zosimus signalled his defeat in 418 by requiring his Italian bishops to sign
a letter which clearly set out the orthodox position against Pelagius. One
of the eighteen who refused was Julian, bishop of the small town of
Eclanum in southern Italy. A well-connected, middle-aged landowner who
belonged to an ecclesiastical family, he was promptly exiled from Italy and
spent the rest of his life in the East, and later in Sicily. It was he who
pursued the cause of Pelagianism with such unremitting ardour and intellectual brilliance and who would force Augustine to defend the orthodox
position on original sin, baptism, grace, and marriage, to the end of his
life.[77]

It is not within the scope of this chapter to examine the later history of
the Pelagian controversy in any detail. Augustine's ethical thought has
already been examined in its philosophical, cultural, historical, and theological context. The characteristic theologies of Augustine and Pelagianism, and the structure of their arguments, have already been drawn. We
might conclude this chapter by briefly indicating the issues around which
the later history of the controversy revolved and the distinctive emphases
they produce in Augustine's theology. To do any more would be to write
another book.

---

[76] For a detailed discussion of the events on which this summary is based see Bonner (1987)
XI, 42–52. For its implications for relations between Africa and the Roman Episcopal See, see
Merdinger (1997), 126–30.

[77] None of Julian's controversial works survive. He prompted Augustine to write *c. ep. Pel.*;
nupt. et conc.; *c. Iul*; *c. Iul. imp.* on the questions of original sin, baptism, grace and marriage.

The basic issue was obviously the question of original sin.[78] We have seen that this was, in fact, a doctrine which Augustine simply adopted from others,[79] and later supported by Ambrosiaster's exegesis of Romans 5: 12 ('in who' instead of 'through who', e.g. *c. Iul.* 6.24.75; *c. ep. Pel.* 4.7[80]), and his own reading of 1 Cor. 15: 22 ('as in Adam all die, so in Christ all will be raised', e.g. *trin.* 4.12.15).[81] He developed it to explain the obvious facts of his own experience of the vitiated, divided state of man's will even under grace, of concupiscence,[82] and the sinfulness of human society as a whole.[83] To Pelagius and Julian the facts were not so strikingly obvious or the experience so readily identifiable—except in the dualistic, deterministic beliefs of the Manichees, or in those who wished to shirk their moral responsibilites and the radical demands of Christian life in the world (*c. Iul. imp.* 2.8; 4.114).

Implicit in the ideal of original sin for Augustine was the necessity of infant baptism in order to remit the guilt (*originalis reatus*) of the sin which they had inherited from Adam so that they would not endure damnation if they were to suffer an early death (e.g. *ep.* 217.5.16). This justification for the commonly accepted practice of infant baptism, for which Augustine often cites Cyprian,[84] touched an extremely sensitive nerve of ancient thought—the question of the origin (or fall) of the soul. Origen's adoption of the philosophical idea of a pre-existent soul which falls into man, implying thereby an inherent 'taint' in the soul, was common currency among late-antique thinkers, as was the idea of the immortality of the soul, in virtue of its derivation from the divine. Augustine's obsession with the nature of the soul in his earliest works is part of this late antique mindset. His conviction that the soul is created by God, from nothing, whilst dealing with some aspects of ancient thought, still did not solve the crucial question: How do we come to possess a soul? Throughout his life Augustine wavered between the creationist answer (that each individual soul is created by God at birth) and the traducianist solution (that the soul of each person is inherited from their parents and ultimately from Adam) (e.g. *Gn.*

---

[78] For an extensive bibliography on this question see Madec (1996), 66 n. 33.

[79] See note 18 above. Bonner (1987) VIII, 97–116.

[80] See Delaroche (1996), 310 on Rom. 5: 12 and for bibliography; 321–3 for the interesting parallels he finds in Eastern writers, especially Ephrem the Syrian, to Augustine's exegesis of it.

[81] Kirwan (1989), 131–2 lists five proof texts Augustine uses for original sin and concludes that three are mistranslations and the other two are misconstrued! Solignac (1988) suggests that the extremes of Augustine's doctrine of original sin, predestination and irresistible grace were due to an over-rational explanation of the faith butressed by defective exegesis of Paul.

[82] See Chapter 5.

[83] The two main texts for Augustine's discussion of the fall are *Gn. litt.* 11; *ciu.* 14.

[84] Bonner (1987) VIII, 113 f. for discussion and references. He notes that the idea of the damnation of infants who die without baptism was found not only in Africa, but also in Italy, and perhaps in Gaul and Spain, even before the beginnings of the Pelagian crisis.

litt. Books 7 and 10; *ep.* 166;[85] *ep.* 190). Most often, but not without much agonizing, he opts for the latter as a better way of explaining the inheritance of original sin and the practice of infant baptism.

Pelagius, of course, could see no justification for this practice: baptism was for the forgiveness of sins which the believer had himself committed and which would be remitted by his participation in Christ's death and resurrection through baptism. After it, he could begin anew: his natural capacity and knowledge of the good having been completely restored he could now move from a position of righteousness towards perfection and sinlessness.[86] For Augustine, however, it is difficult to say exactly what change baptism effects since, after it, man's nature remains impaired. Although the guilt of original sin may have been remitted through Christ's unmerited, vicarious death for man (born of a virgin he is the only one free of original sin (*ench.* 41; 51; 108)[87], its effects have not. Man is still striken by sin, still convalescing, his past is still very much a part of his present, there is no return to an original state, no new life, he still needs continual, illuminating, and inspiring grace to achieve any good action. Paul in Romans 7 (and Augustine in *Confessions* 8), torn between the flesh and the spirit, subject to their two laws at war within himself, recognizing the good but incapable of doing it, is not 'under the law' but 'under grace'.

Whereas Pelagius understood grace simply as the divinely given power (*posse*) which enables man to will (*velle*) and to act (*esse*) (*gr. et pecc. or.* 1.5.6), as man's nature created by God, and as the 'new law' which restored this nature, Augustine was convinced that the law, whether the Mosaic law, or the life, teaching, and example of Christ, avails nothing without the aid of the Spirit:

> We must refuse the argument that we can be righteous without the operation of God's grace, merely because God gave the law, instituted the teaching, delivered good precepts, for all this, apart from the Spirit's aid, is indubitably the 'letter that kills': only when the life-giving Spirit is present, does he cause to be written within us that which, when it is written externally, the law caused to be feared (*sp. et litt.* 32.19).

This is the case because Christ is not only an 'example' and the giver of a new law, but is the One Mediator, a spring of inner grace welling up within man.[88] The Spirit, too, not only informs man of the good, but also moves his will to desire it, love it, and delight in it. Obedience motivated by fear

---

[85] See White (1990), 48–53 for a careful examination of this problem.

[86] For an illuminating treatment of the role of baptism see Tugwell (1984), 59–70.

[87] See Delaroche (1996), 324–7 for Augustine's thought on this in context.

[88] On Christ as inner grace, *nat. et gr.* 40.47; *perf. hom.* 20.43; as the One Mediator, *nat. et gr.* 40.47; *s.* 169.10.12; *pecc. mer.* 1.15.19; *perf. hom.* 20. 43. See Studer (1975) from which these references are taken.

or hope of reward, such as the Pelagians urged,[89] is servile when compared with the obedience which springs from inner delight, desire, and love of God (*ep.* 194; *gr. et pecc. or.* 24.25).[90] It is in the love that grace inspires that man's true freedom is found.

But is man truly free when his every good action is attributable solely to the irresistible inspiration and operation of grace? This question was one of the main bones of contention between Augustine and Julian and has inspired the herculean efforts of numerous Augustinian scholars intent on finding some way to retain meaningful reference to the freedom of the will in the context of his theology of grace.[91] Augustine distinguishes between the freedom Adam enjoyed as a gift of divine grace before the fall (*libertas*), the sort of freedom the Pelagians maintained his descendants still enjoy, to choose between good and evil, to do the good and resist evil,[92] and the freedom (*liberum arbitrium*) which he possesses after the fall, whereby he is only 'free' to sin,[93] and only does the good by a 'greater grace' than Adam's (*corrept.* 34).[94] What sort of freedom is this?

In some contexts Augustine talks in terms of God's preparation of the will,[95] of man's co-operation with God (e.g. *gr. et lib. arb.* 33), or of God as a helper (*adjutor*), commenting that 'the very name of Helper tells you that you yourself are active' (*s.* 156.11). Although God created man without man playing any part, he cannot justify him without man having some part to play (*s.* 169.13—a rather laborious translation of the Latin, 'qui fecit te sine te non te justificat sine te'). He therefore seems to be allowing some room for man's response to God's acts of grace, in acceptance, co-operation, or love. To speak of compulsion is to invalidate the will and therefore man's ability to act at all: 'If I am compelled to will (*cogi velle*) I do not will' Augustine states against Julian (*c. Iul. imp.* 1.101).

But even these arguments do nothing to mitigate Augustine's insistence on what we might call the seemingly 'irresistible' nature of the operation

---

[89] As expressed in the Pelagian text *On Bad Teachers* 24.2.

[90] Scholars have noted that around AD 418 Augustine tends to move the operation of grace inward and speaks of it as inspiring the direction of the will rather than simply presenting it with something to which it will respond. See Wetzel (1992), 187–97 for discussion and bibliography (esp. Patout Burns 1980).

[91] Notably, Burnaby (1938), 219–52; Teselle (1970), 285–93; Rist (1969); Bochet (1982), 302–34; Wetzel (1992), 197–206; Léon-Dufour (1946). I use the substance of my article, Harrison (1993), in this section.

[92] It was an *auxilium sine quo non*—the help without which a good work would not be done by the free will, *corrept.* 29–34.

[93] *Io. eu. tr.* 5.1; *c. ep. Pel.* 1.3, 6–7; *ench.* 30; *nat. et gr.* 19.21; *c. Iul imp.* 1.109; *nupt. et conc.* 1.30–31; *gr. et lib. arb.* 34–35; *trin.* 5.9.4; 10.5.7.

[94] This is an *auxilium quo*—the help by which something is done.

[95] For references and differing ideas as to what exactly Augustine means here see Sage (1964) and Rist (1969).

of divine grace. There are indeed passages which clearly state that it is God who effects in men's hearts the movement of their wills so that He can bring about through them what he wanted to accomplish Himself (*gr. et lib. arb.* 42) and that the will is powerless to stop God doing what he wants (*corrept.* 45); that divine grace works 'indeclinabiliter et insuperabiliter' (ibid. 38). Perhaps, then, we need to ask *why* divine grace is irresistible. Is it because it overrides, coerces, and controls the will, or is it—and we have already seen much evidence to suggest this in our consideration of Augustine's doctrine of will in the first half of this chapter—because it unfailingly, irresistibly, calls forth a response which corresponds with man's deepest desires and motivations, with his true identity and being as a creature of God, so that he is able to respond to it freely, wholeheartedly, and in the way grace intends? In acknowledging its created dependence upon God 'the will is freer the more it is subject to divine grace' (*ep.* 157.7–8).[96]

We are already familiar with the language in which Augustine expresses this insight: delight, desire, love. We have seen that these are the motivating factors of the will's free action, in charity or cupidity, for good or evil, towards freedom or slavery. So how does grace bring it about that man delights in what is good? Augustine teaches that this is effected by God making what is good attractive, pleasing, delightful to man: 'the good begins to be desired when it begins to be sweet . . . therefore the blessing of sweetness is the grace of God, whereby we are made to delight in and to desire, that is, to love, what he commands us' (*c. ep. Pel.* 2.21).[97] By thus inspiring delight in the good God is effectively giving man love of Himself and enabling him to fulfil his being as it was created to be. To move man (however this is done) to act in accordance with his own nature, through love, cannot be said to deny him freedom, rather it is his only way of attaining it.

But grace manifestly does not work in this way for all men. Some may be called and saved, but others obviously are not. Why is this? Why do some believe and some do not? Why are some able to persevere in faith to the end while others cannot? For the Pelagians these problems completely undermined Augustine's doctrine of grace and made it positively offensive. For the monks at Hadrumetum, in N. Africa, for whom Augustine wrote the works we have referred to above, *On Grace and Free Will* and *On Correction and Grace*, they prompted anxious reflection on their *raison d'être*. The same might be said for many of his critics to this day. For Augustine they were simply the necessary outworking of a doctrine of the fall, of Original Sin, and of universal culpability. What gave him pause for thought

---

[96] As Augustine puts it in *Io. eu. tr.* 41.8 'Eris liber si fueris servus'.
[97] Cf. *s.* 131.2; *pecc. mer.* 2.17.26; *c. ep. Pel.* 1.13.27; *nat. et gr.* 31; *corrept.* 31.

was not that so many are not saved, but that so many are. Given that all men justly deserve damnation it is not so much God's judgement as his mercy that causes reflection. Since God is omnipotent, and everything happens according to His will, and nothing can happen against it (*ench.* 95–96), he reasoned that God either allows things to be done, or does them Himself (ibid. 96). God therefore permits evil to happen (because of his just judgement and knowing what good he will bring from it (ibid. 98; 100)), allows men to be lost (because of his judgement, ibid. 107; 112),[98] or works through grace to call and to save men (*gr. et lib. arb.* 6.15).[99]

Whereas in the works on Romans written between 394–96, Augustine briefly entertained the possibility that election was based on merit, on man's choice of faith and anticipation of God's grace, he was subsequently to hold fast to the convictions first expressed in 396, in Book 2 of *To Simplicianus*: that election, faith, and a life of virtue are wholly due to God's gracious calling and enabling; that the operation of grace and God's fore-knowledge of man's choices does not compromise man's freedom, but that without them he can do no good; that the fact that some are saved whilst others are left to God's just judgement is unfathomable but wholly just. The logical outworking of these convictions was an uncompromising doctrine of election and predestination to which Augustine was to hold fast to the end of his life. In his penultimate year (429), in response to the representations of his supporters, Prosper and Hilary (*ep.* 225; 226), who voiced the concerns of groups of monks around Marseilles, in southern Gaul, that Augustine's predestinarian theology left no room for human initiative or responsibility, he argues forcibly that both the beginning of faith (which the monks were keen to attribute to man's own choice) and the perseverance to continue in the faith until the end, are wholly the work of grace (*On the Predestination of the Saints* and *On the Gift of Perseverance*). There is no room for merit, for antecedent efforts or the choice of faith, all is of grace. As he reflects in his *Retractations* on the second book of *To Simplicianus*, the battle had been fought and victory won for grace in 396: 'In attempting to solve this question, I laboured on behalf of the free choice of the human will, but the grace of God triumphed; and not until this point was reached could I understand the apostle's clearest meaning when he said: "Who is it that sets you apart? For what do you have that you have not received? And if you have received it, why boast of it as if you had not?"' (*retr.* 2.1 quoting 1 Cor. 4: 7).

It is important to remember that Augustine's ethical thought, including

---

[98] Rist (1994) notes that Augustine interprets 1 Tim. 2: 4 'God wishes all men to be saved' in *ench.* 103, as merely meaning that all those who are saved are saved by God's will and that 'all men' must mean 'all the elect' or 'all sorts', *corrept.* 14.44; *c. Iul.* 4.8.44; *ciu.* 22.12.

[99] Cf. *gr. et lib. arb.* 6.15; *corrept.* 13.41—eternal life is 'grace for grace'.

his doctrine of the fall, original sin, grace, and free will, was well established long before his confrontation with Pelagianism, and that its defining characteristics were shaped not in the context of controversy, but in reflection upon the nature of human willing against the philosophical background of classical eudaemonism. The contours of his thought are classical; the detail is Christian, set apart by its rejection of dualism, of the idea of rationally determined human autonomy and freedom, and by its insistence upon the unattainability of perfection, the impossibility of realizing happiness, in this life. Above all, it is characterized by its insistence upon the virtue of love as the motivating force of the human will, as the source, means, and end of grace, and thereby, of human freedom.

PART TWO

Christianity and Late Antique Society

4

The Church in the world

AUGUSTINE'S AFRICA

Augustine's Africa lay at the heart of the Roman Empire. Its northern coast bordered the Mediterranean and its roads led to seaports whose busy traffic ensured that the roads ultimately led to Rome. The traffic was largely one-way, however, for Rome depended upon the fertile plains of the coastal strip for its bread—at least two-thirds of its wheat supply came from Africa—which it exacted as part of the land tax, or *annona*. Huge granaries dominated the ports, their importance evidenced by neighbouring Roman garrisons.

What Rome exported was a distinctive culture and civilization which transformed the lives of individual Africans and their towns. It controlled about 140,000 square miles of North West Africa,[1] divided originally into four, and later, under Diocletian's reforms, eight, provinces. Roman life was essentially urban and nowhere was this more the case than in Africa, which, with about 650 towns,[2] possessed a higher density of towns than almost any other region of the Western Empire. Carthage, its capital city, was one of the biggest in the Empire. Inland, away from the fertile olive and wheat plains of the coast, a village culture—one proportionately less Roman-ized—predominated, where Punic, as opposed to Latin, was still spoken,[3] and rural traditions and beliefs were more persistent.[4]

Most of the land was in the hands of the owners of large private estates which were cultivated by, or let to, tenants known as *coloni*. Almost all these estates were acquired towards the end of the third and the beginning of the fourth century, when the aftermath of severe economic difficulties made their purchase attractive. From then on their owners were a force to be reckoned with, not least because they enjoyed freedom from the onerous tax system which was needed to keep the machinery of the

---

[1] Raven (1993), 1.

[2] Jones (1966), 239. Though some of them were very small indeed and attempts to estimate population are notoriously hazard-ridden.

[3] Augustine is aware that clergy need a knowledge of Punic in rural areas, *s.* 288.3.

[4] A great deal (perhaps too much) has been made of this distinction by scholars attempting to explain the nature and rise of Donatism. We will return to it later in this chapter.

Empire working, and which constrained the lives of the less well off with its relentless and unremitting demands.

By the fourth century the duty of city councillor (*curiale* or *decurion*), who was responsible for the collection of the taxes for a particular town and its lands, was made hereditary and compulsory, as were tax-paying occupations among the peasantry. Both the collector and the debtor were constrained by the law, which became progressively harsher under Theodosius to ensure that no one could evade it by, for example, entering the Imperial service or the clergy.[5] It was the poor who paid the lion's share: it has been estimated that the cities contributed only one twentieth of the tax burden and that the rest was met by the countryside.[6] A town councillor, such as Augustine's father, Patrick, was further motivated to fulfil his duty of exacting taxes from the poor by the knowledge that he would ultimately be held responsible for any shortfall.

It used to be a commonplace to talk about the decline of the cities in the late empire, and of the fortunes of its officials, but, whatever might be the case elsewhere, Claude Lepelley has cogently demonstrated that this certainly cannot be said of North Africa in Augustine's time, or of his own family,[7] 'in fact', he writes, 'Augustine was confronted with a lively, active and structured municipal reality, a reality he knew well since he was the son of a decurion from Thagaste.'[8]

Augustine's birthplace, the small, rather insignifcant, and traditionally Berber town of Thagaste (modern Souk Ahras), in the eastern part of Numidia, had, like many provincial towns from the second century onwards, undergone a slow but sure process of Romanization in its legal, administrative, and social life.[9] Hippo (modern Annaba), where Augustine was to spend most of his life, included the regions of Thagaste, Calama, Madura, and Theveste, and belonged to the ecclesiastical province of Numidia and the administrative province of Proconsular Africa.[10] Africa's second largest seaport, it lay at the head of a large bay, at the mouth of the river Ubus (modern Seybouse), with the mountainous headland of the Djebel Edough to the West.[11] Its very un-Roman jumbled streets were witness to its Phoenician foundation 2000 years earlier; its impressive forum, theatre, baths, and temple testified to its thorough Romanization over the past 200 years or so. Its evident prosperity lay in the vineyards,

---

[5] See Cochrane (1940), 320 for details.   [6] Jones (1964), vol. 1, 464–5.

[7] Lepelley (1979), e.g. at 372–3; (1975). See also (1987), 230–3—Augustine's family had servants and land though, in common with most *curiales* or minor gentry, not much ready money.

[8] (1975), 13.   [9] Lepelley (1987), 230.

[10] Lepelley (1987), 230 n. 3 and *Augustinus Lexicon* I (1986), col. 188–94, Africa.

[11] For topography see Gsell (1911). For climate Gsell (1913–28) I, 40–99; flora IV, 9–37 and fauna I, 100–137; 216–34—referred to by Dennis (1970).

olive groves, and especially the wheat fields, of the surrounding plains. As far as society in Hippo is concerned, we shall see that Augustine's sermons provide unparalleled information on every aspect of his congregation's everyday life and concerns.[12]

CHRISTIANITY IN AFRICA

We know, in fact, very little about early Christianity in Africa. Our first real evidence is the account of the seven men and five women from Scilli, somewhere in Numidia, who were brought before the Proconsul Saturninus in Carthage, in AD 180, for 'refusing to swear by the genius of the Emperor' and who were subsequently martyred. Towards the end of the second century Victor I (189–99) became the first African Bishop of Rome. Of course, we also have the work and witness of Tertullian (*c.* 160–*c.* 225) during the early, unsystematic period of persecution, and later, that of Cyprian (d. 258) who, after ten eventful years as Bishop of Carthage, including the periods of systematic persecution by Imperial edict, was martyred under Valerian. That Cyprian was able to assemble 85 bishops to meet in council at Carthage is some indication of the contemporary extent of Christianity, at least in Numidia and the Proconsular Province. But even in Augustine's day, when Christianity had spread rapidly following Constantine's conversion, and enjoyed official protection and support, it is difficult to know exactly why people became Christian or to estimate just how widespread it was, especially where, for reasons of class, language, culture or geography, paganism, or the old cults of Saturn and Ceres still held sway in people's minds (and were, indeed, sometimes syncretistically mixed up with Christianity[13]).

We possess a statement of the number of bishops, and sermons provide us with some idea of the social spread of Christianity, but this information is of limited value. So too is the undoubtedly rhetorical statement of Tertullian, in AD 197. He defiantly claims, 'We are of yesterday, yet we have filled all that is yours, cities, islands, villages, free towns, market towns, the camp itself, tribes, town councils, the palace, the senate, the forum; we have left you your temples alone . . . If we abandoned you for some far country you would shudder at your solitude, at the silence, the stupor of a dead world,'[14] or indeed, Augustine's similar, but rather more tempered

---

[12] The classic book in this respect is Van der Meer (1961). Also useful are the first three papers in Veyne (1987).

[13] In *cons. eu.* 1.21.29–30 Augustine observes that many Christians thought they were worshipping Saturn. See Frend (1952), 77–83; 104–6.

[14] *Apologeticum* quoted by Raven (1993), 151.

observation in a sermon, that 'You will find many households in this city in which there is not a single pagan; while there is no household to be found in which there are no Christians. And if you were to examine the matter carefully, there is no household to be found in which there are not more Christians than pagans' (*s.* 302.19).

Whatever the degree of Tertullian's rhetorical excess, Lepelley is convinced that Augustine and his contemporaries did not live in what we might call a 'Christian society' (*une chrétienté*). By this he means that Christianity had almost no impact on municipal life in the Roman city in Africa. Whereas the institutions and offices of the Roman State had been grounded in paganism, Christianity failed to assume its functions when the traditional religion was officially proscribed. Instead, what we see is a virtual secularization of municipal life, in which the Church seems to have had little influence or meaningful place. There are no documents to suggest that a city ever funded the erection of a Christian building, as it had built temples and shrines in the past,[15] rather inscriptional evidence suggests that the Church financed its own buildings from contributions made by the faithful. Conversely, there is no evidence to suggest that the Church had any part to play in the construction of public buildings, statues or dedications.[16] Nor did it play any part in the secular institutions: bishops were not called upon to bless new magistrates, the inauguration of public buildings, or the opening of the curia; the Christian symbol was not displayed on public buildings.[17] Pagan civic rites came to an end but were not replaced; the city was secularized and de-sacralized but did not turn to Christianity to sanction new rites and practices. Instead both pagans and Christians almost unthinkingly kept the titles of the ancient priesthoods of the Imperial cult (such as the *flamen perpetuus*), continued to attend pagan schools and followed the pagan calendar for their everyday lives.[18] Even if it is the case that Christianity succeeded in wiping out paganism (and we will discuss this below) the Christianization of the city was never more than partial. This is no doubt why it could be regarded, as it were, as neutral ground in debates between the Church and schismatics.[19]

ORDINATION

When Augustine returned to Africa in AD 388 he headed immediately for his native town of Thagaste with the intention of setting up a small lay

---

[15] Lepelley (1975), 32.   [16] Ibid. 35; (1979), 374.   [17] Lepelley (1979), 374.
[18] Ibid. 375.
[19] Lepelley (1975), 25—for example, the Council of Carthage in 403 decided that official encounters between Catholic and Donatist bishops should be held in the presence of the city magistrates.

community of men who agreed to hold everything in common and devote themselves to the Christian life. It was while he was in Hippo in 391, visiting someone who was interested in joining the community, that he was forcibly ordained. Augustine tells us that he had been careful to avoid places where he knew the bishopric was vacant, for fear of this very event (*s*. 355.1.2. Cf. *vita* 4). In fact, Hippo did possess a bishop, the aged Greek, Valerius, but he and his congregation had come to the conclusion that he needed a priest to relieve him of some of his onerous ecclesiastical duties. So Augustine was not allowed to leave Hippo until he had been ordained, as was the practice in the early Church, after the acclamations of the people and the choice and consent of the clergy. Possidius tells us that he wept, not, as some thought, because he aspired to a bishopric, but because he feared the dangers to his way of life which church duties would impose (*vita* 4).

This procedure might seem strange, but it was not at all unusual: Ambrose, a provincial governor, had similarly been chosen by clergy and people, was duly baptized, and eight days later, was consecrated bishop.[20] What was irregular was that Valerius, contrary to African practice,[21] encouraged Augustine to preach, on the grounds that, as a Greek, he was not himself as proficient in the Latin language, and doubtless because of Augustine's obvious gifts in this respect. Furthermore, in ignorance (perhaps) or disregard of the Nicene canons, he arranged with the primate of Carthage, Aurelius,[22] to have Augustine ordained co-adjutor bishop in 395, presumably because he anticipated his succession in the not too distant future and wanted to be sure that, in the meantime, he did not lose his new and promising priest to a neighbouring parish when a bishopric became vacant (*vita* 8).[23]

Augustine had no choice but to accept, but he did so, to a certain extent, on his own terms; Valerius acceded to his request for time free to study the Scriptures (*ep*. 21), and made available to him a house in the grounds of the basilica where he could continue to live in community as a priest-monk. Like teachers and doctors, as a priest he would be included among those whom Constantine had ruled immune from municipal duties. Despite successive laws which attempted to ensure that priests of curial

---

[20] Ramsay (1997), 19–20—see his account of the even more extreme case of Paulinian, who was bound and gagged so that he could not resist his ordination.

[21] Though the practice did subsequently become established in the light of the success of Valerius' experiment, Possidius *vita* 5.

[22] It was initially opposed by Megalius of Calama, Primate of Numidia, the consecrating bishop, because of Augustine's links with the Manichees and fraudulent rumours about his personal conduct—*c. litt. Pet.* 3.16.19; *Cresc.* 3.80.92.

[23] Augustine, who was doubtful about this procedure from the outset, later became aware of the Nicene ruling and ensured that it was endorsed by a conciliar ruling and thus brought to people's attention so that it should not happen again.

rank should not escape their fiscal duties,[24] Augustine seems to have somehow managed to give his inheritance and property to the church at Thagaste.[25]

His ecclesiastical duties as priest should not have been onerous, since, where a bishop was present, it was not usual for a priest to celebrate, baptize or preach, he simply assisted him and acted as assessor in the bishop's court.[26] But, as we have observed, Augustine began to preach almost immediately. He confronted Fortunatus, the Manichee, in public debate in 392 (*c. Fort.*). Late in 393 he addressed the assembled bishops of Africa, at the Council of Hippo, on the subject of faith and the creed (*De fide et symbolo*). Meanwhile he was at work on a series of works refuting his former co-religionists, the Manichees (*util. cred.*; *duab. an.*; *lib. arb.*), on a popular song against the Donatists (*Psalmus contra partem Donati*), a commentary on the Sermon on the Mount, the beginnings of a commentary on Genesis (*De Genesi ad litteram liber imperfectus*), the first 32 sermons of the massive *Enarrationes in Psalmos* and a number of works on Paul (*Ex. prop. Rm.*; *ep. Rm. inch.*; *exp. Gal.*), which, as we have seen, were dramatically to change his theological worldview. In these different respects Augustine's years as priest at Hippo laid the foundations for his ministry as bishop and began the work which he was to continue to the end of his life. They also mark a watershed which leaves behind his earlier life of ascetic aspiration and philosophical speculation. Commentators too many to mention have observed the change in subject, tone, and audience of the works following his ordination. To a large extent these changes were brought about by force of circumstance and one can only speculate how Augustine's thought might have developed, free from the demands of ordained ministry, free to choose his own subjects and pursue his own thoughts, as we find him but rarely able to do in the moments snatched from his ecclesiastical duties.[27]

THE ROLE OF THE BISHOP

Following the conversion of Constantine the role of the bishop changed dramatically. Not only did he baptize, preach, and celebrate (the latter two often daily) but he also assumed the burdensome and demanding duties of

[24] E.g. *Cod. Theod.* XII.1.121 ruled that they should nominate someone to take over their worldly goods and fulfil their curial duties.

[25] *ep.* 126.7. Lepelley (1979), 286   [26] Chadwick (1994), 140.

[27] Possidius *vita* 24: 'He got through all this by living laborious days and working far into the night.' The fact that his great works, the *City of God* and the *De Trinitate*, for example, took so long to write is an indication of this. His congregation later agreed to allow him five days out of seven to do his own work, but were obviously unable to abide by it—*ep.* 213.5.

administrator and legal arbitrator. The Church was now a legally recognized institution, able to receive donations, gifts, and bequests. It fell to the bishop to administer these goods, which often included land, estates, and buildings, for the benefit of the Church and for the needy to whom it had traditionally ministered—the widows, foundlings, orphans, and homeless who had figured on the Church's 'list', and benefited from its care, since the time of the apostles. Augustine seems to have been unwilling to adopt any long-term building or investment projects to maximize the resources which became available to the Church, but rather, Possidius tells us, preferred to delegate the administration of property and the keeping of accounts, and to use, or more accurately, give away money, as it came in, for the relief of the needy (*vita* 23–4). For other, less disinterested bishops, however, the evidence suggests it could become a cause of corruption and conflict.[28]

The bishop also became the public face of the church when any of its members sought employment, got into difficulties with the law or had to negotiate with state officials. A good deal of his energies were therefore taken up in the writing of recommendations, in interventions and representations to the powers that be on behalf of his congregation. Augustine was wary of this practice, repeating the maxim that he had too much regard for his own reputation to vouch for his friends. Moreover, his experience was that officials who were asked favours generally became intolerably overbearing. When he relented, Possidius tells us that he wrote with 'such dignity and reasonableness' that he frequently aroused admiration and his recommendations were followed (*vita* 20, 27).

The greatest demand a bishop faced was in his capacity as legal arbitrator for any two parties who chose to consult him and who agreed to abide by his judgement. Constantine's laws had, in fact, given the bishop power to hear, and to make final decisions, in the area of both criminal and civil law, to try pagans and Christians immune from municipal intervention (save to request the authorities to carry out his decision) and beyond appeal.[29] In reality the Church does not seem to have grasped the free hand Constantine's ruling offered, but rather appears to have preferred to delimit its areas of jurisdiction—encouraged and confirmed by subsequent, more restricting, Imperial laws under Constantine's successors—to specifically religious matters such as Church doctrine, practice, and organization, the trial of its own clergy (even in criminal proceedures[30]) and to legal arbitration between two consenting parties.

Whereas Constantine's far-reaching law was no doubt motivated by a

---

[28] The most notorious example is that of Antony of Fussala. For references to other cases in Augustine's correspondence, church canons, and records of councils see Courtois (1955), 140. [29] *Cod. Theod.* I.27.1.

[30] Ibid. XVI.2.12 (AD 355) for bishops; XVI.2.41 (AD 412) and XVI.2.47 (AD 425) for priests.

desire to enable Christians to be tried by Christian judges, rather than face a hostile pagan judge, its subsequent restrictions were made in the knowledge that many high-ranking civil officials were now Christian. Despite the fact that he bitterly resented the demands made upon his time by such business, Augustine no doubt reflects the general feeling among Christian authorities, inspired by Paul's injunction in 1 Cor. 4: 6,[31] when he encourages his congregation to resort to episcopal arbitration rather than use the civil authorities to resolve their difficulties (*en. Ps.* 80.21). It appears that they hardly needed encouragement. It must have seemed as if the bishop had taken over the role of *defensor ciuitatis* (a civil officer, created by Valentinian I, who was elected by each city to protect its poor, especially in the collection of taxes, and who had the right to hear small trials[32]).

In an Empire which had no police force and no organized system of legal advice or representation,[33] episcopal jurisdiction—the *episcopalis audientia*[34]—was attractive: it was open to everyone, rich and poor, pagan and Christian; it was free, speedily expedited and relatively impartial.[35] Although limited to religious and civil cases, and accessible only when the two parties agreed to abide by the final judgement without appeal, bishops found themselves inundated with business. In Hippo it took place in the hall, or *secretarium*, adjoining the basilica, where, practically every weekday, from morning, frequently until late afternoon (*vita.* 19.1–5), Augustine and his notaries heard family arguments, wranglings over inheritances, property, land, debts, children. They were minor cases, tedious petty disputes, which Augustine could not but wish to be free of. His feelings are very near the surface in *On the Work of Monks*, when he observes, 'If it were up to me to choose, I would much rather perform some manual work at certain hours each day, as these are laid down in a well-run religious community, so as to have the rest of the time free to read, to pray, or to study ... than to have to sit through the turbulent and confused court cases of people I do not know' (37).[36] Although he was dealing directly with the problems his congregation brought to him according to Christian principles, it must still often have been difficult to justify to himself the time he was obliged to spend in court.

The 'privilege' of *episcopalis audientia* was not restricted to Christians.[37]

[31] Chadwick (1994), 143.

[32] Lepelley (1979), 193. This was not, of course, strictly the case, but under Honorius bishops were allowed to participate in his election, though the role of the office subsequently underwent considerable change.   [33] Cameron (1993), 106.

[34] For further information and bibliographical references see Lepelley (1979), 389 f.

[35] Brown (1967), 195.

[36] For similar complaints see *ep.* 139.3; *en. Ps.* 98.24.3; *s.* 340.1; 302.17.

[37] Brown (1972), 317 observes: 'The privileges of the *episcopalis audientia* should not be exaggerated. They were enjoyed by Jews and by non-Catholic bishops when they were in the majority, as in Egypt.'

Moreover, the bishops' powers were strictly limited; he was dealing with what was marginal (even though it might seem of burning importance to the appellants). Serious cases had to be transferred to the provincial governor. Indeed, Augustine regards the civil authorities with unfailing respect and deference and, as we have seen, treated them as neutral ground where the Catholic Church could dispute with a heretical faction and their differences be heard. When a rather inexperienced and rash fellow-bishop, Auxilius, excommunicated a high-ranking official, Classicianus, and his family, because he had arrested criminals who were seeking sanctuary in the Church, Augustine was quick to make clear to Auxilius that he had exceeded his canonical rights (*ep.* 250), and to assure Classicianus that he would make every effort to have his excommunication lifted as soon as possible (*ep.* 250A).

Nor did the *episcopalis audientia* help in any way to integrate the Church into municipal structures. As we have seen, it in no way impinged upon their workings, and from the evidence Augustine provides,[38] bishops seem to have had very little authority or influence when it came to episcopal interventions or representations to its officials. In a sermon he complains, '. . . you all know that it is your needs which compel me to go where I would rather not; to dance attendance, to stand outside the door, to wait while the worthy and unworthy go in, to be announced, to be scarcely admitted sometimes, to put up with little humiliations, to beg, sometimes to obtain a favour, sometimes to depart in sadness. Who would want to endure such things, unless forced to?' (*s.* 302.17). One cannot but agree with Lepelley that this is further evidence of the Church's marginal role in civil life and of the limited nature of the Christianization of the city structures in North Africa.[39] This is not to say that Augustine did not have some influence with high-ranking Roman officials. He corresponded with a number of them as personal acquaintances, for example the proconsuls Apringius and Donatus, the *vicarius* of Africa, Macedonius, the tribunes and *notarii* Dulcitius and Marcellinus (a Christian who was to play an important role in the Council of 411 against the Donatists), and the tribune, then *comes domesticorum*, Count Boniface.[40] It was in imposing imperial legislation against heretics that the bishop did, in fact, come to play a key role in the affairs of his town and the surrounding country estates. He was uniquely placed to identify heretics and, as we shall see below, to send representations concerning them to the Emperor, to act for

[38] E.g. *ep.* 22* (Divjak). This is endorsed by Basil, *ep.* 72–3; 112. References from Chadwick (1994), 145.

[39] Lepelley (1975), 18; (1979), 398.

[40] Van der Meer (1961), 246. See *vita* 20 where Possidius describes Augustine's frequent success in writing recommendations or making interventions to the powers that be. He cites a highly complimentary letter from Macedonius to this effect.

their coercion or dissolution and to administer their property. In this respect, the bishop's power should not be underestimated.[41]

CHURCH CANONS AND COUNCILS

The Church also advanced its own system of self-government during this period, in the form of conciliar meetings and the promulgation of canon law, which secured for it a significant degree of freedom and independence from the municipal authorities of the State. Canon law in Africa began with Cyprian and the councils he held at Carthage in the third century. In the second edition of his collection of canons, the sixth-century monk, Dionysius Exiguus, jumbled together the canons of some twenty African councils under the heading 'Councils convened at Carthage'. These were untangled in 1961 by F. L. Cross[42] whose work prepared the ground for C. Munier's compilation of all the extant African canons from 345–525 in his *Concilia Africae*.[43]

At the first council Augustine attended at Hippo in 393, where he addressed the assembled clergy on *Faith and the Creed*, it was agreed that a general council should meet annually, with authority to resolve all matters of church law, practice, and discipline, and that each of the six African ecclesiastical provinces should (with the exception of Tripoli) send three representatives. This proposal obviously proved rather too optimistic, for in 407, we find a canon which rules that the council should only meet when there were matters to discuss which affected all African clergy, and that otherwise cases should be heard in their own province (Canon 95). As one might expect, most of the canon law deals with matters of clerical discipline, church practice, and procedures for appeal. As such, it gives us an invaluable insight into the nature, workings, and perceived failings of the churches in Africa during Augustine's time.[44]

THE CHURCH IN HIPPO

But what of the church in Hippo? The Christian basilica at Hippo was situated away from the centre of the town, in the prosperous area where splendid villas overlooked the harbour, and within uncomfortably close hearing distance of the large basilica of the Donatists (*ep.* 29.11). With its gardens and related buildings (the garden monastery, the bishop's secre-

---

[41] Brown (1972), 327–9.   [42] Cross (1961), 227–47.

[43] *Corpus Christianorum* 1974.

[44] I am indebted to J. Merdinger (1997a) for these observations—see Ibid., Chapter 6 for a careful review of the canons in their historical context, against the difficulties of the records.

tarium, the baptistery, the clerical monastery or bishop's house, a chapel and various storerooms and pilgrims' rooms) the basilica took up no more than a third of the space of the Roman forum in the heart of Hippo.[45] The interior of the church would probably appear to modern eyes as rather bare since it had no seats, apart from the bishop's *cathedra* in the centre of the apse, but was rather divided into separate sections for men, women, consecrated virgins, and penitents. A square wooden altar stood in the nave, surrounded by a barrier, together with the reader's pulpit. The vestments of the clergy were likewise simple and servicable. Augustine would wear a plain cloak (*birrus*) but none of the regalia (mitres, cross, ring, staff) which we now associate with a bishop.[46] His priests, who stood on either side of him in the apse, would be clothed in a similar fashion. Nor was there any special distinguishing dress for the other ranks of clergy, the deacons, acolytes, and lectors.

The congregation would stand throughout the long services. Their bishop's sermons give us a startlingly life-like picture of their individual habits, superstitions, weaknesses, failings, and foibles and a good insight into their social backgrounds and context. They were a microcosm of society as a whole: the vast majority were poor, largely illiterate, and engaged in work upon the land. A good number were what we might call the urban middle-classes; traders, shop-keepers, craftsmen. A small percentage belonged to the nobility, though, as we shall see, this was the group most resistant to Christianity and most tenacious of the old pagan traditions. Most were married; a minority, who were set apart behind a balustrade, were vowed celibates or virgins.[47] There were also a group of senior laymen, or elders (*seniores*), who were appointed because of the high respect in which they were held within the community (as in the traditional village hierarchy) and who held an authority independent of the bishop, which could be exercised in his absence and appealed to in a semijuridicial way, through the elders' council. They provide an interesting insight into the overlap between church structures and traditional village structures, which is also evident in the African system of appointing primates according to seniority rather than position or qualifications.[48]

Augustine was a tremendously popular preacher. He was often invited to be a guest preacher and at home his congregation was far from passive in its response to his sermons, which reveal that the people were accustomed to demonstrating their approval, puzzlement, enthusiasm, or

[45] Brown (1967), 190.

[46] Possidius tells us that 'His clothes and food, and bedclothes also, were simple and adequate, neither ostentatious nor particularly poor,' *vita* 22.

[47] See Van der Meer (1961), Chapter 7 on Day-to-Day Pastoral Work.

[48] I owe these insights to Shaw (1995b).

enjoyment with acclamations, applause, or groans, as the case may be. His simple style, his training as a rhetor and teacher, together with his innate skill, combined to enable his simple congregation to follow him in his investigation of the meaning of a given passage of Scripture, to tease out its theological problems, and to take to heart its moral lessons, with little problem. He takes them by the hand, as it were, anticipates their questions and problems, discusses them through an imaginary interlocutor, repeats what he has found in a number of ways, and uses all the exegetical tools and verbal skills he possesses to enable them to grasp what he wants to convey. Using these methods, and sensitive to their capabilities, he does not seem to spare them, either in respect of the length of time they were to stand to listen to him (anything between twenty minutes and two hours), or in respect of the theological problems he sets before them—indeed he often expresses appreciation of their support of him during an especially arduous sermon, on a hot day. He would preach almost every day, so that it has been estimated he would have preached about eight thousand times![49] In fact, we only have 546 extant sermons, all of them on texts of Scripture set by the liturgy, in addition to the Enarrations (or Discourses) on all 150 Psalms, the 124 Tractates on St John's Gospel, and the 10 Homilies on the First Epistle of John, which are made up of sermons preached on various occasions, over a period of time, but which together cover every verse of the works involved.[50]

His interpretation of Scripture, as we saw in Chapter 2, has little in common with modern exegetical methods, precisely because it took place in this liturgical, exhortatory, spiritual context. Its key is the unlocking of the mystery of the Christian life and the life of the Church which is found in its Head, Christ.[51] It is therefore fundamentally christological (the whole of the *Enarrations on the Psalms*, for example, is presented as Christ, the Head of the Church, speaking to His body). Augustine's understanding of Christ as offerer and offering (*trin.* 4.4.19), Head and body, the one priest and shepherd of all—bishops, priests, and laity—also guarded against any 'clericalization' in his conception of the Church; the Church receives its unity and holiness from Christ, not from its ministers.[52]

We have very little evidence for the actual liturgy of Augustine's church apart from what he reveals in sermons and letters.[53] The fate of the church in North Africa following the Vandal, and then Arab, conquests means that,

---

[49] Madec (1989), 115.

[50] On Augustine's preaching see Chapter 2 above; Pontet (n.d.); Van der Meer (1961), 405–67; Brown (1967), 251–8.   [51] Harrison (1992), 224–30.

[52] Chadwick (1994), 148. For a full discussion of this idea see Madec (1989), 85–153 and Mandouze (1953)—it becomes especially prominent in the Donatist controversy.

[53] The most important material is to be found in Van der Meer's classic book on *Augustine the Bishop* (1961), 277–402, which also contains useful bibliography.

in comparison to say, Gaul or Italy, very little liturgical material, such as sacramentaries or breviaries, survives.[54] We can, however, deduce the order and content of the service, the cycle of lessons and the form of the creed from incidental remarks Augustine and his contemporaries make, and sermons,[55] letters,[56] and treatises[57] tell us much about his sacramental theology.

From what one can gather, the clergy of Africa were often criticized for their lack of education (*ep.* 22.3.7). Since each town had its bishop, and a bishop required priests, deacons, acolytes, and lectors (in 427 we know that Augustine had seven priests and four deacons), the number of clergy required was not insubstantial. Furthermore, country priests who could minister to the masters and *coloni* of the enormous estates, and who could preferably speak Punic, were also needed. When we also bear in mind that ordinations were simply a combination of perceived need and force, that there was no organized system for training clergy, that levels of illiteracy generally were staggeringly high, and that primates were appointed by seniority rather than ability, we should not be surprised that their intellectual level left something to be desired. Augustine was sensitive to the criticism; he had himself been repelled by the crudity of the Church's Scriptures and the literal, credulous nature of North African Christianity. His *Confessions* were in large part an apologia of his own educational credentials and literary culture, to his cultured detractors. Chadwick further suggests that they are also a defence of the high calling of the clerical ministry.[58]

The monastery at Hippo, where clergy were educated and trained, and which supplied a number of the major sees in Africa with their bishop, did much to raise the level of clergy: Severus of Milev, Possidius of Calama, Alypius of Thagaste and Profiturus of Cirta were all prepared for their ministry in this way.[59] The fact that they were also personal, and much missed (*ep.* 84), friends of Augustine lent a distinctive collegiality to the African Church in his time which was furthered by their regular meetings at Church Councils in Carthage or elsewhere. Augustine also got on well with his older, though less intellectual, colleague, Aurelius, primate of Carthage, the senior bishop of Africa. Their different characters seem to

---

[54] Barnes (1971), 275–6.

[55] Notably his Easter sermons, which are collected together, in parallel text, with an excellent introduction, notes, and bibliography by S. Poque (1966). Also *cat. rud.* He no doubt draws on the catechetical instruction he received from Ambrose in Milan, the content of which is found in Ambrose's *De Mysteriis*.   [56] Notably *ep.* 54 and 55 to Januarius.

[57] Notably *ciu.* 10 and his work on the sacraments against the Donatists, e.g. *bapt.* 67; *cat. rud.* 9.13; *doctr. chr.* prologue.   [58] Chadwick (1994).

[59] Possidius tells us that at least ten men were supplied to the churches in Africa in this way, and that, in founding new monasteries, they prepared new priests—*vita* 11.

have complemented each other: Aurelius the energetic administrator; Augustine the learned preacher and writer. The fruits of their partnership are clearly evidenced in the series of councils they organized together, beginning with the Council of Hippo in 393, where Augustine preached to the assembled clergy and a large number of canons were passed to deal with clerical discipline.

Communications between the clergy were, however, slow and difficult. Distances within Africa, never mind the Empire, were vast, and letters delivered by individual travellers could be very late in arrival. Nevertheless, Augustine maintained frequent correspondence with churches throughout the Christian world in Italy, Spain, Gaul, Dalmatia, the Holy Land, and Egypt. It was relations with the Roman See, the only Apostolic see in the West, that were perhaps the most frequent and most highly charged.

AFRICA AND ROME

In North Africa, Augustine was heir to a long tradition of reflection on the status and authority of Rome, stretching back to Tertullian, Cyprian, and Optatus.[60] All three were eager to present the Roman Church as the source (*origo*) of the Catholic Church throughout the world, since it was established by Peter, the apostle chosen by Christ to found his Church (Matt. 16: 18). The see of Rome was the fount of the Church's unity, continuous with the apostles from the time of Peter by the unbroken succession of duly appointed bishops in apostolically founded sees. Among these sees, Rome, founded by Peter, was pre-eminent. Any schismatic group which established its own Church, and conducted its own ordinations and baptisms, was separating itself from the one Church, throughout the world, which originated in Rome, and could not claim to be Catholic.[61] These are ideas which Augustine takes over without question. They would have been endorsed in his mind by the increasing pre-eminence of the see of Rome during his lifetime, in bishops such as Siricius, Innocent, and later, Leo. Of course, African synods had their own canon law, and their own authority and procedure for appeals. J. Merdinger's careful study of African appellate legislation in relation to Rome portrays a double-sided reality: Rome was at once a court of appeal, a source of advice and support, a final authority for decisions in serious cases, and also an interfering, ill-informed, authoritarian threat to African autonomy. The situation depended very much on the Bishop of Rome in question and the way in which he chose to deal with a particular situation.

[60] The following section is greatly indebted to J. Merdinger (1997a) where chapters on each of the incidents mentioned below can be found.   [61] See Merdinger (1997a), Part 1.

The case of Honorius, a Mauritanian bishop who had attempted to transfer his see to the bishopric of Caesarea during a contested election, shows the African bishops consulting Pope Boniface for advice and help.[62] Similarly, driven to thoughts of resignation, Augustine appealed first to Boniface, and later to Pope Celestine, concerning the case of Antony of Fussala, an under-age priest from his monastery whom he had appointed in a difficult and urgent situation to a vacant bishopric, but who had turned out to be a rapacious, corrupt, and immoral piece of work (*ep.* 209). We also find Augustine in 418, being sent, along with Alypius and Possidius, as a papal legate for Pope Zosimus, to investigate some difficulties in Mauretania Caesariensis.[63]

Zosimus was, however, to prove to be the occasion for a good deal of friction between Africa and Rome. As we saw in Chapter 3, he had already been shunned by the African bishops for his support of Pelagius's follower, Caelestius, when they had appealed over his head directly to the Emperor Honorius. When an excommunicated priest named Apiarius chose to ignore the African appeals procedure and to appeal to him directly a year after the Caelestius incident was resolved in 418, Zosimus, who presumably by then had little good will to spare for the African bishops, justified his intervention by citing, quite innocently, two canons of the Council of Serdica (343) as canons of the Ecumenical Council of Nicaea. The officious legate whom Zosimus had sent to Africa only served to exacerbate the situation and to provoke the African bishops to tighten up their legislation to prevent similar cases in the future.

But Apiarius did astonishingly resurface in 425, this time to appeal to Pope Celestine, and by lies and deception he got himself reinstated. After his trial, when he had broken down and confessed the truth, the African bishops dispatched a strongly worded letter of opposition (the *Optaremus*) to what they saw as Rome's incursions upon their rightful autonomy, in contravention of Nicene and African canon law. They requested the Pope, in no uncertain terms, to refuse to hear appeals from Africa which should rightly have been heard at home, to refrain from reinstating those whom the African Church had excommunicated, to stop sending papal legates, and most especially, to abide by the canons of Nicaea. The Africans felt they had Nicaea on their side and that it obviously took pre-eminence over papal opinion or decisions. This should, however, not obscure the numerous cases in which Africa did, in fact, appeal to, and rely upon, Rome as the primary see in the West. It does, however, clearly demonstrate a significant degree of African independence.

---

[62] *ep.* 22*; 23*; 23A* (Divjak), dated AD 419–420.
[63] Though see Bonner (1964) for the difficulties concerning the nature of this visit.

CHRISTIANS AND PAGANS

The Emperor Constantine's conversion to Christianity in AD 312 was a watershed in the history of the Church. What it meant immediately was the end of the persecutions which the Church had sufferered intermittently from the time of Christ, and which, by Imperial edict, had assaulted it with increased rigour from the 250s.[64] Now the Church found its interests protected and furthered by Imperial law; its concerns became those of the State, and the Emperor convened councils at which representatives of the Church throughout the Empire could meet and discuss Church organization, discipline, and doctrine.

The ambiguity of the relationship between Church and State is perhaps the dominating feature of the history of their relations during the fourth century.[65] Imperial intervention did not go unchallenged; Catholic Christianity did not always win the day against heretical factions, such as the Arians. The Emperor's interests did not always coincide with those of the Church. The early enthusiasm—one might say, wild optimism—of theologians like Eusebius, who described the advent of a Christian Empire, the *tempora christiana*, the defeat of paganism under an almost messianic Emperor figure, was a strand of thought with a long tradition, encouraged and furthered by later Emperors such as Theodosius. For Augustine, however, this ideal increasingly failed to bear the weight of the evidence. For the first ten years or so of his episcopate he had shared the Eusebian ideal, but his personal experience and the evolution of his theology, which we have already witnessed in previous chapters, meant that the ideal of a fully realized Christian Empire, victorious over paganism and triumphant over evil, became for him a dangerous and unattainable illusion.[66]

From the very beginning Christians had found reflection on their place within the world an unavoidable aspect of their faith. It posed itself in the starkest and most urgent terms during the times of persecution. Christianity, the religion of the One God, was alien to the many pagan gods and cults, but how far could one compromise with the world, with pagan customs and rites? Was sacrifice to the gods to avoid the death penalty an unforgivable sin? On a more everyday level, both before and after Constantine's conversion, questions such as what allegiance a Christian owed to the authorities, what occupation he could blamelessly pursue in a society permeated by pagan customs, traditions, and practices, were unavoidable. Was he being unpatriotic, uncivil, and anti-social in refusing to have a part in them? How was he to educate his children? Could he allow them to marry a pagan? Could he observe the festivals, attend the games,

---

[64] Jones (1948).   [65] Greenslade (1954).
[66] Markus (1970c). See Chapter 6 below.

theatre, and spectacula which together gave identity, meaning, and cohesion to life in society. In order to respond to questions such as these Christians were forced into conscious self-appraisal and an examination of precisely what conversion to Christianity meant. For some, like the North African Tertullian, writing in the second to third century, a total separation from, and rejection of, all things pagan was called for by the faithful Christian. For others, the majority, the precise details had to be worked out in the course of their everyday lives—a faltering, ambiguous process of accommodation or separation and quite often, confusion as to what was simply part of 'secular' life and what was 'sacred' to either paganism or Christianity. The boundaries were certainly nothing like as clear cut as Tertullian liked to believe. Rather, they were being established, slowly, erratically, without any real uniformity, wherever a particular problem arose in the life of the individual Christian, the local Church, or the theological reflection of its bishops.

We have seen this process at work in the first half of this book in our consideration of Augustine's relation to various aspects of late antique culture. That culture was unquestionably pagan; how far it could be legitimately taken over and used, in what respects it had to be modified or rejected, was, we saw, a far from straightforward process. In the following chapter we will see that one response to the blurring of the boundaries between Christianity and paganism in the post-Constantinian era was the institution of monasticism—an extreme attempt to separate Christian life and faith from compromise and contamination with the world. But we will also see that for Augustine, in contrast to his Eastern counterparts, the monastery is no isolated haven; the monastic vocation is in no way immune from the difficulties which characterize life in the world. This is of a piece with his rejection of the Eusebian ideal: Christianity was too caught up in a world where the pagan past was still very much part of the present; the Church itself was made up of men and women who came from and were moulded by it. Their conversion did not—could not—bring about a final and decisive break with it, just as it could not obliterate the insidious inheritance of original sin. This was no ground for optimism.[67]

Just how far can we speak of a christianization of Roman society? We have already observed in this chapter what little impact the Church had made upon the municipal identity and organization of the average Roman town in Augustine's day, how the Imperial cult and its priests survived (albeit presumably secularized) without provoking any comment or opposition, how limited the powers of bishops actually were and what little influence they had on officers of State.

---

[67] Markus (1990) is an invaluable discussion of these themes.

The fact that Chrisitianity provided no real alternative to the traditional link between paganism and civic duty and patriotism perhaps accounts for paganism's extraordinary persistence among the noble, aristocratic members of society who were as tenacious of the old order as of the old traditions which had secured the gods' preservation of it. Noble senators such as Symmachus, Flavianus, and Praetextatus were therefore pushed into what might be called a self-conscious paganism in order to articulate what had hitherto been ancient tradition but which was in danger of being overthrown—quite literally in the case of the statue and Altar of Victory in the Senate House in Rome. Despite moving pleas[68] following the removal of this altar under Gratian, upon which the offerings of twelve generations of senators[69] had been made, Symmachus was defeated by the overbearing authority and influence of Ambrose upon Valentinian II, Gratian's successor—a salient example of the sort of power a Christian bishop could wield.[70]

Paganism also persisted at a rather less exalted or obvious level in the everyday lives of the citizens of the Empire. Repeated references in Augustine's sermons to what he regards as a sort of vestigial paganism among his congregation are a good indicator of the prevalence of pagan superstitions—astrology (*exp. Gal.* 35), amulets and charms (*ep.* 245), the swearing of oaths (*s. dom. mon.* 1.17.51), divination (*en. Ps.* 93.3), the popularity of traditionally observed pagan festivals (especially the Kalends of January), of the games, theatre, and spectacles (*ep.* 22; 29), and the persistence of dances and processions, even when they were officially proscribed. It was almost impossible to avoid pagan tradition; even the days of the week still bore the names of the gods (*en. Ps.* 93.3); funeral customs, meals at the graveside, and feasts on the cult of the martyrs were taken over directly from pagan practice (*ep.* 22; 29.8–9). Thus Augustine laments that 'the man who enters [the Church] is bound to see . . . people wearing amulets, assiduous clients of sorcerers, astrologers . . . He must be warned that the same crowds that press into the churches on Christian festivals, also fill the theatres on pagan holidays'.[71]

But would his congregation have been as sensitive as their bishop to these lingering remnants of paganism? Would they have even seen them in this way? So much of what Augustine definitively labels, and categorically rejects, as 'pagan' would probably have appeared to them as activities which they had always pursued, which everyone practiced, which were simply part of how things had always been done, but not as hostile to, or

---

[68] Symmachus *Rel.* 3.   [69] Dill (1898), 25.
[70] See 'The Pagan Revival in the West at the End of the Fourth Century', in Momigliano (1963), 193–218.
[71] *cat. rud.* 25.48 quoted by Brown (1967), 213.

detracting from, their Christian faith, nor even as overtly or identifiably pagan. As Robert Markus has made clear, this lingering paganism would be regarded by Augustine as yet another example of the immense force of habit, the crushing weight of custom, the way in which the past cannot just be sloughed off in conversion as so much unneccesary baggage, but rather makes the individual what he is in the present, and forever burdens him, whether he wills it or not.[72] In other words, as we have seen in the last chapter, it is the Augustine of the Pelagian controversy arguing from experience for the unavoidable vitiation of human nature and the unattainability of perfection in this life. It is Augustine the bishop conscious of the very rudimentary nature of his congregation's grasp of what really constitutes a Christian life and the weight of ancient traditon which shapes them. It fell to bishops, therefore, authoritatively to identify, clarify, distinguish, and separate what was pagan from what was acceptable Christian behaviour—to thereby 'invent' a paganism which had not hitherto been recognized as such in order to reject it; to draw the outlines of a Christian culture and society by distinguishing it from the everyday, the traditional, and the customary. It is this process which Peter Brown has briefly outlined in his *Authority and the Sacred*.[73]

As repeated edicts testify, there were obviously many Christians who lapsed back into paganism; conversion, under a Christian emperor, and especially in the face of persecution, was often merely a means to avoid penalties, to advance one's career or to open up opportunities, rather than a matter of religious conviction.[74] Furthermore, there were many pagans who remained faithful to their religion.[75] Augustine's correspondence witnesses to the numerous occasions on which he had to deal with pagan objections to Christianity (*ep.* 102; 135; 136). Indeed, throughout his work, as Pierre Courcelle has noted, there are numerous references to—and refutations of—pagan objections to Christianity,[76] which together give us a very clear picture of just how absurd, illogical, bizarre, and credulous Christianity could appear to pagans: crudely written and contradictory Scriptures, unquestioning reliance upon faith, confusing Christology and trinitarian theology, an absurdly odd doctrine of the resurrection of the flesh, their dubious morality, vestigial paganism, self-glorifying, avaricious clergy, divisions, heresies and feuds within their Church, the fact that things did not get better in the fortunes of the Empire following the advent of

---

[72] Markus (1997b); Cf. Wetzel (1992) on the time-bound nature of human willing.

[73] Cambridge, 1995. See further reflection on this in Markus (1997b).

[74] E.g. Faustinus, whose opportunistic conversion Augustine urges his congregation to accept. *s. Morin* I (reference from Brown (1967), 231).

[75] See e.g. *ep.* 232 to the decurions of Madura, since almost all the members of the civic *ordo* there remained pagan—cited by Lepelley (1979).

[76] Courcelle (1958).

Christianity, but worse, were all common criticisms which confirmed pagans in their rejection of Christianity and their traditional devotion to the gods.

CHRISTIANITY V. PAGANISM

Although laws were passed to protect the Church, the traditional Roman policy of toleration was, for a long while, effectively extended to include paganism. In the past it had ensured a degree of unity, loyalty, and peace which enabled the incredibly diverse geographical, ethnic, and religious aspects of the Empire to coexist without friction. Even when laws were passed to limit pagan practices, their imposition was at first patchy, not only because long-standing tradition had made them part of the fabric of society, but because the officials to whom it fell to impose them probably lacked conviction[77] and had more pressing concerns, such as the collection of taxes, where goodwill was paramount.[78] But this state of affairs did not last. As the century drew to a close, so Theodosius' anti-pagan legislation gained momentum and urgency—for it seems that the Emperor now placed his hopes of unity and cohesion in a fully Christianized State, rid of the taint of paganism.[79] The tables were now completely turned in contrast to the first three centuries of Christianity, and it was now paganism which a Christian emperor sought systematically to obliterate through laws which undermined and proscribed every aspect of its existence.[80]

In Africa this change in Imperial policy was cogently manifested by the arrival in Carthage, in 399, of two Imperial agents, the *comites* Gaudentius and Jovius, who had been instructed 'to upturn temples and break idols' (*ciu.* 18.54). The age of (relatively) peaceful coexistence between the Church and paganism was over.[81]

Pagan reaction to persecution rarely flared up into violence, but two cases in Augustine's letters attest to how inflamed pagans could become by Christian interference. In 399, at Sufes, in Byzacena, the Christians had destroyed a statue of Hercules and in the riots that ensued sixty of them were killed (*ep.* 50). When the town council added insult to injury by requesting the Christians to meet the cost of regilding Hercules' silver beard they, not surprisingly, met only with severe rebuke from Augustine. In another incident in 408, at Calama, a riot seems to have been precipitated when Christians attempted to halt a pagan ritual procession. Church buildings were burnt, the monastery plundered, a monk killed and

---

[77] Dill (1898), 24.   [78] Brown (1995), Chapter 2.

[79] For this interpretation of Theodosius' activities see Cochrane (1940), 324–38.

[80] For details of the laws see Cochrane (1940), 329 f.   [81] Markus (1997b), 38.

Possidius, the bishop, narrowly escaped with his life (*ep.* 90–91;103–104). Similar, isolated incidents, are recorded in Northern Italy.[82]

Bishops were eager to support Imperial policy, to encourage its enforcement and suggest further measures to ensure its total success.[83] We saw earlier that they were not reluctant to use their episcopal authority to 'define' paganism, and to clearly mark out boundaries for their congregations' everyday lives. In the early fifth century these boundaries became more delimited as they were moved inwards to exclude ever-increasing areas of life which had hitherto been tolerated as having only limited religious significance, but which were simply part of the common, social life, of all townspeople, pagan and Christian.[84] Foremost among the bishops' exclusions were the festivities and banquets, games (especially animal baiting in the amphitheatre and chariot racing in the hippodrome / circus), theatre performances, spectacles, and combats which were tremendously popular with all citizens, and frequently emptied their churches on particularly splendid days (the *munera*) of public entertainment (*en. Ps.* 50.1; *s.* 19.6).[85]

Just how far these games and performances had hitherto been perceived to be bound up with paganism is difficult to gauge. Certainly, they had frequently been accompanied by pagan rites and ceremonies (until these were outlawed), and Christian theologians, such as Tertullian, in his *De Spectaculis*, had wholly denounced them as the work of the devil, but as Markus has shown,[86] the evidence is ambiguous. Christian congregations do not seem to have chosen to be particularly conscious of the link between paganism and the various festivities they continued to enjoy. Bishops, if Augustine is anything to judge by, seem, at first, to have tolerated, though not condoned, their attendance—presumably because they were very much at the heart of a town's identity, unity, and cohesion, and in terms of social function, their existence was not necessarily wholly to be disapproved of:[87] he significantly lists them in *On Christian Doctrine* among the

---

[82] Three priests were murdered in the Val di Non following attempts to halt a pagan ceremony. Vigilius *ep.* 11.

[83] E.g. Canon 84 of the Canons of the Church in Africa (AD 401) demanded of the emperor not only the destruction of statues of the gods but also of the sacred places, woods, and trees of paganism.

[84] As Chadwick (1985), 9 comments, 'The pagans did not know they were pagans until the Christians told them they were'.

[85] For further discussion of the various forms the entertainments took and Augustine's attitude to them see Van der Meer (1961), 47–56.

[86] Markus (1990), Chapter 8, to which I am much indebted for this section.

[87] Markus (1990), 111 cites e.g. *s.* 104 (*Morin Guelf* 29) 7 where Augustine remarks in reference to a banquet in honour of Venus, 'these things are to be tolerated, not loved'.

ways in which men communicate with one another, albeit in a useless and extravagant way, rather than among the ways they communicate with demons, such as sacrifice, divination, and magic.[88] The Emperor too, while legislating to obliterate the latter, carefully guarded the games, performances, and banquets as civic events, separated from specifically religious rites,[89] so long as—no doubt prompted by concerned bishops—they did not coincide with Sundays or Christian festivals.[90] Both the bishops and the Emperor concurred in outlawing gladiatorial shows.

But what had been a matter of shared, mutual participation in civic life, became, as we have noted above, a matter for increased episcopal attention—and censure—when attempts to obliterate paganism were initiated towards the end of the century. Now the pagan aspects of the festivities were stressed more forcibly than before, and episcopal toleration was worn away by what they increasingly saw was their congregations' inveterate attachment to them despite the now overt identification with paganism. The fact that they often found their churches empty on the occasion of the spectacles led Augustine to make frequent references in sermons to the rival attractions of the Christian cult and its festivals.[91] The latter were 'a truth offered to the eyes of the heart and not a vanity displayed to the eyes' (*Io. eu. tr.* 7.6).

The games, performances, and banquets were traditionally financed by civic notables, who donated funds to provide lavish entertainments. This was very much a matter of family tradition, but was primarily motivated by the popular understanding that high public office carried with it the commensurate obligation to enhance the status and unity of the city for the benefit of all its citizens by providing the means for civic entertainments and the construction of civic buildings. Public offices, such as that of magistrate, could therefore not, in practice, be held by anyone who did not have the requisite private funds. Such giving, which is usually referred to as evergetism, was therefore not primarily charitable or philanthropic. Although it did coincidentally benefit the town and its citizens, it was rather characterized by a large degree of calculated self-interest; it was a way of buying honours.

We find a good example of this, but at the same time a somewhat exceptional one, in Augustine's early reference in *Against the Academics*, to his benefactor Romanianus, who had made possible his higher studies. He is depicted in 1.2 as the typical Roman evergete, who, because he provided the citizens of Thagaste with their desires—bear-fights, spectacles, banquets—was rewarded with popular acclamations, inscriptions, statues, and

---

[88] Markus (1990), 112.   [89] *Cod. Theod.* XVI.10.17   [90] *Cod. Theod.* XV.5.5.
[91] E.g. *en. Ps.* 32. *s.* 2.25; 80.23. See Markus (1990), 118 for further references and discussion.

public office with extensive powers. However, Augustine's obvious affection for him as a father figure in whom he could confide his future plans, and find warm-hearted support, gives a more human face than is usual in rhetorical descriptions of the grand gestures of evergetic giving (2.2).

The largely calculated, self-seeking, municipal level of evergetic giving had little to do with the Church. There is no evidence that such money was ever used to finance church buildings in Africa,[92] and bishops obviously found it an up-hill task to persuade local notables to give money in a form which was so novel, which was not established by tradition, and which did not carry the same personal rewards. There was indeed a tax, or *munus*, which the great Carthaginian landowners (and those of other cities) were obliged to pay as part of the municipal *annona*,[93] which provided food to distribute to the people, but this enforced giving has little in common with Christian almsgiving or charity, which was, by definition, freely willed, disinterested, and unostentatious, motivated only by generosity and compassion for anyone in need. As a theological concept, it could simply mean granting forgiveness to a sinner (as in *ench.* 72), or having mercy upon oneself (*ench.* 76); it could be a way of propitiating one's sins by having mercy on others, especially the poor, in the same way as one would desire God to have mercy upon oneself—the poor became a cogent symbol of the sinner in need of mercy.[94] The bishops also constantly called for practical almsgiving, for the wealthy to give to those who have nothing. Possidius tells us that Augustine gave to the poor from the funds that supported him and his fellow monks, that is, from the income from the church's property and the offerings of the faithful; when funds were short Augustine did not hesitate to melt down church plate to realize the money needed (*vita* 23–24). The Church's care for the needy, for foundlings, orphans, widows, the poor, although it had Jewish roots, was a new and striking affirmation of a common humanity shared by all, rich and poor, in the traditionally hierarchic context of late antique society.

This does not mean that Christian noble families did not give to the Church in the same manner as their pagan counterparts gave to the city, or that their giving was not received by popular acclamation or commemorated by inscriptions very similar to those which record traditional evergetic giving.[95] Whether they were motivated by ascetic renunciation

---

[92] Lepelley (1975), 35. Though Lizzi (1990) suggests that in Northern Italy bishops successfully persuaded rich landowners to give to the Church, as they had to the city, in order to finance large building programmes.

[93] *Cod. Theod.* XIV.25.1—referred to by Lepelley (1979), 382.

[94] Brown (ed. Veyne) (1987), 227.

[95] Lepelley (1979), 384–5. Brown (1992), 95 mentions mosaic floors in churches inscribed with the name or even portrait of their donors.

and concern for the poor, or by the desire for honour, prestige and status (in contradistinction to the clergy) we can only speculate. That the minds of Augustine's congregation were still moulded by the tradition of classical evergetism is well evidenced in what must have been the highly embarrassing occasion of Melania and Pinianus' visit to Hippo. Melania, granddaughter of the celebrated ascetic, Melania the elder, belonged to the well-known, noble family of the Valerii. With her young husband, Pinianus, she had fled Rome after 410, and on arrival in North Africa, the couple continued to give away their vast fortune to charity, churches, and monastic communities—in this instance, to the great benefit of the church at Thagaste. When they visited Hippo Augustine's congregation obviously saw an opportunity and at the Sunday liturgy decided to attempt to ordain Pinianus priest. Their acclamations turned to an ugly riot when Pinianus did not show willing and their anger was only exacerbated when Augustine threated to resign his bishopric. They were eventually quelled by Pinianus' undertaking that, if he ever should be ordained, it would be at Hippo (*ep.* 125; 126). By honouring Pinianus the congregation obviously anticipated a large donation for their church and they went about securing it in exactly the same way as they would in the forum.[96]

The question of just how far the Roman Empire was 'christianized' in Augustine's time is therefore not an easy or straightforward one to answer. We have seen just how limited Christianity's influence was in some instances, especially in respect of its place in the traditional Roman town. In its organization, jurisdiction, municipal offices and even its sense of identity, coherence, and public events, the Church seems to have played but a marginal role. Legislation against paganism seems to have done little but secularize what was once understood on the basis of ancient religious traditions, but not to have Christianized them. As this book will hopefully demonstrate, the Church, as seen in Augustine's church at Hippo, came to affirm its identity and self-understanding, its sense of the sacred and its place in relation to the world, in a rather different manner than Theodosius' systematic attempt to establish Christianity and wipe out paganism by legislation.

THE IDEA OF THE HOLY

We need only look to the Church's developing sense of holy places, in contradistinction to the Roman town, and the expression of popular piety which this affirmed and encouraged, to see this process of independent

---

[96] Lepelley (1979), 385 f.

self-definition at work.[97] For whatever reason, the Church, quite unlike its pagan neighbours, seems to have had no real sense of particular places as sacred, or holy, sanctified because of their position or their associations, until the emergence of the cult of the martyrs and their relics, and of interest in the holy sites and topography of the Holy Land, in the fourth century.[98]

Why these developments should have taken quite so long is unclear. The reason seems to partly lie in what we have already seen of the Church's attempt to recover something of its earlier identity and spirit, to hold on to the glorious past which had made it very much what it aspired to be in the present, in other words, to retain and foster the martyr spirit against the compromising forces of the world. The Church felt this acutely in the century after Constantine's conversion, when the Roman State took it in its embrace and thereby threatened to immerse it in the privileges of the secular. If it had hitherto been sufficient to hold that the members of the Church themselves constituted the temple of God, in the fourth century it became increasingly necessary to provide a more tangible focus for Christianity's presence and its continuity with the heavenly communion of saints. The saints were brought down to earth, so to speak, and made the focus of particular devotion, by the erection of shrines over the body of a martyr (*memoria*), of stone *mensa* or tables, for martyrs' relics, and by the burial of martyrs under the floor, or under the altar, of churches.

This movement seems to have originally been popular, rather than clerical, in inspiration, and the Church obviously felt the need to regulate and control its easy propensity for excess: it ruled that only genuine martyrs, rather than fictitious ones who may have appeared in dreams or revelations, should be so honoured[99] and the number of *mensae* should be similarly restricted.[100] The long-standing tradition, to which all congregations were passionately devoted, of rowdy celebrations (or *laetitiae*) to accompany the anniversaries of the martyrs were forbidden.[101]

But nothing would stem what Markus has described as 'the tide of relics flowing into the cities'.[102] For the saints were not only brought down to

[97] The following section is greatly indebted to Markus's work on the Christian idea of holy places in his articles of 1994 and 1990, Chapter 10. See also Saxer (1980).

[98] See Taylor (1993), though other scholars argue that interest in the Holy Land predates Constantine.

[99] Canon 83 of the Council of Carthage 401, cited by Markus (1990), 148.

[100] Ibid. repeated in Canon 14 of Council of Carthage 438 cited by Van der Meer (1961), 438.

[101] Most notably *ep.* 96 where Augustine recounts his attempts to dissuade his congregation from holding a meal on the occasion of the feast of the first martyr bishop of Hippo, St Leontius. The congregation's weeping reduced Augustine to tears. Van der Meer (1961), 516–25. [102] Markus (1990), 148.

earth, they were brought in from outside, from the dead; from the traditional burial places outside the towns, into the very heart of the city, to be enshrined in a church or specially constructed building. The most famous instance of this was Ambrose's placing of the relics of Saints Gervasius and Protasius in the basilica in Milan, in 386, which Augustine himself probably witnessed. They were also brought in from far-flung areas of the Empire; a compelling symbol of the universal Church and the communion of saints, present within the local church. Initial reserve to these developments on Augustine's part, seems to have been gradually transformed, between 401 and 422, into enthusiastic endorsement.[103] Markus notes a parallel, and no doubt, connected, change in Augustine's attitude to miracles during this period. Although at first rather dismissive and uninterested,[104] he did not later question the miracles performed by the relics of Saint Stephen, brought to Africa by Orosius in 416, and enthusiastically had the miracles performed at the shrine erected in his honour at Hippo, by Eraclius, in 424, meticulously recorded, with carefully verified statements (*libellus*) by witnesses which were stored in the Bishop's library and read out on appropriate occasions in Church.[105]

CHRISTIANS AND JEWS

As well as pagans, the population of Hippo would also count a significant Jewish community, second perhaps only to Carthage. The Jews had come to Africa before the end of the Jewish State in Palestine and were ethnically and linguistically close to the indigenous population.[106] They had found converts among both pagans and Christians (especially during the persecutions) and had been a subject of reflection for the most notable African Christian authors; Tertullian's, *Against the Jews*, Cyprian's *Testimonies* and Lactantius' *Divine Institutions*. The Jews had always been an exception to the Empire's requirement of allegiance to the gods; the Romans respected their antiquity and understood their claim to be practising the religion of their fathers. They were therefore tolerated, even though they did not pay cult to the gods; the Jews, in return, were not above naming synagogues after the emperor or dedicating their own sacrifices to the gods. This policy continued under Theodosius: the Jews were excepted from his assault upon paganism and their religion was recognized

---

[103] Markus (1990), 149 and note 32 for bibiography.
[104] E.g. *util. cred.* 16.24; *ver. relig.* 25.47; *ep.* 78.3; *s.* 88.2. De Vooght (1939).
[105] *ciu.* 22.8. Cf. *s.* 286.5; 316.1; 319.6. Van der Meer (1961), 527–57.
[106] Blumenkranz (1958).

as licit, though restrictions were imposed with regard to their possessing or attempting to proselytize Christian slaves, intermarriage with Christians, the construction of new synagogues, or entry to the imperial service.[107]

Augustine unfailingly demonstrates an unusually (among Christian authors) positive, tolerant, and respectful attitude towards the Jews. This was no doubt in part based upon his shrewd appreciation of the profound complexity and ambiguity of their situation in relation to the Christian Church; the wild olive of the Church/Gentiles is grafted onto a Jewish root (*s.* 21.8.7), Christ left his mother (the Jews) in order to cleave to his wife (the Church) (*Io. eu. tr.* 9.10) and Christians and Jews have the same father in Abraham (*Io. eu. tr.* 42.5).[108] It was also determined by his attempts to identify the Jewish God of Israel, of the Old Testament, with the God of the Christian Church, in frequent polemics against the Manichees' rejection of all things Jewish. Most especially, however, it was obviously rooted in the theology of man's fallenness, of the unmerited, unfathomable, hidden workings of God's will, which he developed in the 390s, which effectively placed Jews and Christians in the same position under God's justice and necessitated the conclusion that Jews, even after the coming of Christ, have a providential role to fulfil in God's order of salvation.[109] His main concern, therefore, was to reflect on the lessons which might be drawn from this situation, following the witness of Scripture (especially Romans 11), to enlighten the position of Jews, pagans, and Christians in the present.[110] The first and most obvious is that the history and fortunes of the Jews have been providentially ordained both as a fulfilment of prophecy and as a witness to, and prophecy of, Christ and his Church (*Io. eu. tr.* 35.7; 54.1; *ep.* 137.4.16). They are the forerunners, the preparers: like slaves carrying their master's books, they faithfully guarded the Christian Scriptures;[111] like the carpenters of Noah's ark they construct salvation for others but themselves perish in the flood (*s.* 373.4): like a blind man with a lantern they show others the way but do not see it themselves (*en. Ps.* 56.9; *s.* 121.1 in relation to the Gentiles). Their antiquity and their fierce opposition to Christianity were both used by Augustine to refute pagan

---

[107] Cochrane (1940), 334–5.

[108] These references are taken from Borgomeo (1972), 46.

[109] These observations are indebted to Fredriksen (1995), who modifies Blumenkranz's (1973 and 1958) theory that Augustine's teaching on the Jews stems from personal contact with them.

[110] His three main works are the *adu. Iud.*; *s. Caillau* 2; *ep.* 196. Other observations are scattered throughout his work.

[111] *en. Ps.* 40.14; 56.9; 136.18; *s.* 5.5; *c. Faust.* 12.23—cited in *BA* 73A, 461–2.

criticisms of the newness of Christianity (*ciu.* 18–37) and the veracity of the Jews' witness.[112]

CHRISTIANS AND HERETICS

As well as other religious traditions, such as paganism and Judaism, Augustine, as we have seen, had to contend with heretical schools of thought which threatened the Christian faith from inside.[113] We have already encountered his work against Manichaeism and Pelagianism. In his *On Heresies* of 428, he lists eighty-eight different heresies which have been reported throughout the Empire—though by no means all were manifest in Africa. Indeed, in comparison to the rest of the Empire, it seems to have been strongly orthodox.[114]

In the province of Hippo itself, he had to deal with a rather odd sect who called themselves Abelites; male and female couples practised celibate cohabitation and ensured the future of their community by adopting a boy and girl child who would eventually live in the same way (*haer.* 87). At Carthage he persuaded the Tertullianist (Montanist) community to rejoin the Catholic Church (*haer.* 86).[115]

Arianism had determined the theology of the Eastern empire since the time of Constantine. In the West, as D. Williams has demonstrated in relation to Homoianism in Northern Italy, its significance and threat to Nicene supremacy has perhaps been generally underestimated. The anti-Arian work of the likes of Eusebius of Vercelli, Zeno of Verona, Filastrius of Brescia, and Hilary of Poitiers reveal the strength of the opposition and the tensions between the two sides which intensified during the 360s and 370s in Northern Italy, culminating in the council of Aquileia, under Ambrose, in 381[116] and Ambrose's dramatic victory in resisting the dowager Empress Justina's demand for an Arian basilica in Milan (Ambrose, *ep.* 20).

In Africa, however, Arianism had few representatives and made very little impact.[117] This does not mean that the theological issues were ignored—Augustine's *On the Trinity*, and frequent references to the equality of Father and Son in sermons, is evidence of that—but controversy was rare. There are only two letters which witness to Augustine's contacts with Arians: one to Elpidius (*ep.* 242) who had sent him some Arian works in

---

[112] *en. Ps.* 40.14; 56.19; 58.[*s.* 1.22; *s.* 200.2.3; 201.3.3; 373.4.4; 374.2; *ep.* 137.4.16; 149.19; *ciu.* 4.34; 18.46–47.]   [113] See Zeiller (1941).
[114] As Monceaux (1922), IV.165 comments 'L'Afrique latine était la terre classique de l'orthodoxie.'   [115] Van der Meer (1961), 119; de Labriolle (1913), 470 f.
[116] Williams (1995).   [117] See Zeiller (1934).

the hope of converting him; the other (*ep.* 171) to a doctor who had been converted from Arianism by Augustine's sermons and wanted to persuade his family to follow him. In addition, there are references to two public debates which Augustine held, the first with the theologically illiterate—he thought *homoousios* was someone's name!—but distinguished *comes domesticorum*, Pascentius, at Carthage (*ep.* 338–241) and the second with the Arian bishop, Maximin, when he visited Hippo in 428. Maximin and Pascentius' groundless boasting that they had got the better of Augustine also occasioned treatises finally to refute them.[118]

DONATISM

The main threat to the Catholic Church in North Africa and the one move-ment that did most to shape the identity and self-understanding of this church was not another religious tradition, such as paganism or Judaism, nor was it strictly a heretical deviation from it, such as Manichaeism, Pela-gianism, or Arianism. It was a schism which happened within the Catholic Church itself, and which was unique to North Africa (though it had representatives in Rome)—the Donatist schism, so called after its main founder, Donatus, bishop of Carthage (313–55).

The schism originated during the 'Great Persecution' of AD 303–5. Those clergy who had compromised, by obeying Diocletian's edict that all copies of the Scriptures should be handed over to the Roman authorities, were regarded by rigorists as *traditores*—literally, those who had 'handed over' the Scriptures—in other words, those who had betrayed their faith and were therefore understood to have excluded themselves from the true Catholic Church in Africa.

When the *traditor* Mensurius, Bishop of Carthage, died (311–12), the Carthaginian Church elected his unpopular archdeacon, Caecilian, to take his place. The rigorists, represented by Secundus of Tigisi, Primate of Numidia, who had recently acquired jurisdictional rights over the Carthaginian Church and the privilege of consecrating its bishop, opposed the election, no doubt partly motivated by traditional rivalry between Numidia and Carthage, but more strongly by their conviction that any compromise of the faith was wholly unacceptable, especially in one of its most prominent, ordained, representatives, who had, by his action, nulli-fied his ministry. With the support of seventy bishops, therefore, Secundus

---

[118] *ep.* 238–41 (Pascentius); *conl. Max.*; *c. Max.* (Maximin). See *vita* 17 where Possidius makes much of these examples. These examples of Arianism in north Africa are cited and discussed by Van der Meer (1961), 119–25 on whom I rely here.

opposed the election on the technical ground that one of the consecrating bishops, Felix of Apthungi, was himself a *traditor* and therefore his ministry was invalid. They elected their own candidate, Majorinus, a lector, whose candidature was financed and furthered by Lucilla, a wealthy noblewoman, following a personal slight by Caecilian. He was quickly succeeded by Donatus, an able, forceful, eloquent individual who remained bishop of Carthage for the next forty crucial years of the schism.

The African Church, in common with the Catholic Church throughout the Empire, had, of course, experienced numerous schisms based on rigorist ideals of perfection and purity, most especially during the persecutions. Donatism was exceptional, however, in its localized character, its social, political aspect, and its fierce tenacity over a number of centuries.

Despite Imperial opposition—the Catholic Church immediately appealed to Constantine following his conversion—the schism soon became entrenched in North Africa. It had its own churches—some of them quite magnificent buildings—its own clergy and a bishop in Rome (Victor of Gaba, who thus established a rival Donatist list in the apostolic see). In 336 Donatus was able to call a council of 270 Donatist bishops. Repressive measures (e.g. under the Imperial commissioners, Paul and Macarius, from 347 on, when Donatus was exiled) proved ineffective in halting the growth of Donatism and the brief period of toleration under the Emperor Julian (361–3) only added further fuel to its fire. In 355 Parmenianus succeeded Donatus at Carthage and it was he whom Augustine faced as the leader of the Donatist church, on his ordination at Hippo. In Hippo itself, the Donatist church, under their bishop Proculeianus, had a definite majority over the Catholics. The two churches had coexisted for well over eighty years, with the result that Donatism, for many individuals, had simply become the obvious and accepted representative of the Catholic Church in Africa, attended because of established tradition and custom. Indeed, it might be argued, as the Donatists did, that this tradition and custom stretched back to the time of the apostles, that it represented the true tradition of the Catholic Church in Africa, which the so-called Catholics had abandoned, thus placing *themselves* in a position of schism. Imperial edicts and church canons, history, and scholarly tradition have ensured that the real schismatics were the group of African Catholics who held to the uncompromising, rigorist, separatist line which was described as 'Donatist' by the Catholic bishops. Whether in fact they were more representative of earlier African tradition and custom is another matter.[119]

It is certainly the case that when one begins to attempt to explain the

---

[119] For a timely reminder that history is written by the victors and that an unthinking use of labels such as 'Donatist' fails to do justice to the facts, see Shaw (1995a).

extraordinary tenacity, inflexibility, and determination of Donatism it is those elements which attach it to the earlier tradition of the African church which seem to carry more weight than other explanations based upon geographical, political, economic, or social factors. Scholarship in this area is a complicated surfeit of thesis and counterthesis, based on differing assumptions derived from different types of evidence. It is difficult to conclude anything with any degree of certainty. What is clear is that what the Donatists held to, and thought they stood for, was the true African church of the apostles, the church of the martyrs, of Tertullian and Cyprian, which saw the hostile, demonic world represented in the State, and any compromise with it as apostasy ('What has the Emperor to do with the Church?'[120]). They would not accept the Constantinian settlement, which for them compromised the integrity and purity of the Church and placed it in a subservient position to a false authority. Rather they were the successors of the martyrs, those who refused to bow to the secular authorities, who set themselves apart, and were prepared to defend their holiness and purity untainted—without spot or wrinkle—and suffer for their true, separate identity, with their lives. In this sense, of course, they could claim to perpetuate the stance of the great African fathers of the persecuted Church, of Tertullian and Cyprian.[121] The Catholic Church, in contrast, appeared to them to have not only compromised with the world, but to have placed itself under its patronage and protection in order to oppose and undermine the true Church in Africa. On this, most scholars agree.

Other explanations of the origin and persistence of Donatism are more divisive. It has been argued that the origin and large concentration of Donatism in the poorer, less fertile, predominantly Berber inland areas of southern Numidia and Mauretania Sitifensis is explained by their rural character; the fact that ancient traditions are more tenacious in villages than in towns; that the more Romanized and economically significant, richer towns of the coastal areas of Proconsular Africa were more likely to support Imperial policy and receive Imperial favour[122] and that it was here that the Catholic Church was strongest.[123] The economic and

---

[120] Donatus in Optatus *de schismate* 3.3.

[121] See Frend (1952), Chapters 9 and 10 on Tertullian and Cyprian in this respect; Merdinger (1997a), Chapters 2 and 3; Markus (1970c), 105–32.

[122] E.g. Frend (1952), Chapters 2–4.

[123] This has been undermined by Brown (1972), 237–59; 279–300, who questions the village, peasant, Berber element of Donatism, its hostility to the State, the idea of a 'nationalist' movement, and the role of local grievances or of a social/political motivation in the rise of Donatism. Rather he sees religious dissent as primarily arising from questions centring on the place of religion in society. He refers to Jones (1959) and Tengström (1964) who are similarly critical of some of Frend's theses. See also Brown's review of Tengström in (1972), 335–8.

political implications of these divisions have also been used to explain the extremes of Donatist disaffection and resistance. A strong sense of social injustice, it has been suggested, was fostered by the increasingly heavy taxes (due to Diocletian and Constantine's reforms) which were mercilessly extorted from the rural poor by the *curiales* of the towns, in order to meet the Roman goverment's unremitting demands. This is thought by some to lie behind the rise (from 340 on) of the extreme and violent wing of Donatism, represented by the fanatic Circumcellions—disaffected itinerant, seasonal, agricultural workers[124]—and of their support of political revolts such as those by Firmus (372) and Gildo (398). Since the Roman State was perceived as allied with the Catholic Church, one way of expressing nationalist opposition based on economic greivances was to align oneself with those who opposed it on religious grounds—hence the alliance between the so-called Circumcellions and the Donatists, two groups with different grievances but the same oppressor.[125]

In fact, this explanation is rather too neat to do justice to the evidence, for the Circumcellions seem to have had an undeniable religious consciousness and motivation, however fanatical and violent its manifestation. Although they were popularly referred to as Circumcellions (from *circum*, around, and *cella*, cells, tomb, or hut; in other words those who dwelt among the tombs, or plundered the houses of the peasants) they referred to themselves as soldiers of Christ, *Milites Christi Agonistici*; their leaders went under the name of *duces Sanctorum*, they carried clubs called Israels and used war cries such as *Deos laudes, Deos gratias*, or quotations from the psalms, adopted an ascetic type habit, and travelled in the company of *sanctimoniales* (consecrated virgins). Furthermore, their *raison d'être* was to achieve martyrdom by whatever means they could, even if it meant persuading others, at knife point, to kill them, offering themselves as human sacrifice at pagan festivals, or throwing themselves *en masse* off precipitous cliffs or into water or fire (*ep.* 185). Otherwise they attacked other people, rather in the manner of highwaymen (Augustine himself narrowly escaped

---

[124] Brisson (1958), 28; Tengström (1964), 24–78; Frend (1952), Chapter 5. These ideas have been especially favoured by soviet historians of Donatism, who see in the movement the reaction of an exploited peasant class against an oppressive social and economic order represented by the landowners and the State—see Gacic (1957). For a balanced view see Lepelley (1979), 328.

[125] Again, note the reservations of Brown and others in note 143. One must beware of confusing or identifying Circumcellions and Donatists and attributing the characteristics of the former to the latter: 'We may not safely or wisely assume that almost all North African Catholics were Latin-speaking, respectable, bourgeois, and urban, and that almost all Donatists were alienated, Punic-speaking rustics who struck first and asked questions afterwards.' Chadwick (1985), 14.

such an ambush by losing his way and taking another route (*ench.* 17; *vita* 12)). They looted and burned houses and robbed granaries (*ep.* 111.1) and were particularly brutal with Donatist apostates and Catholic clergy, thinking nothing of kidnap, assault, and murder (*ep.* 134.2; 138.7), of blinding their opponents with lime and vinegar (*ep.* 138.8), burning down churches and destroying sacred books (*breuic.* 3.8.13), or forcing people to be rebaptized by intimidation (*ep.* 111.1).[126]

But only a minority of Donatists were Circumcellions. The former counted members from across the social spectrum, from peasant *coloni* to noble landowners, from illiterate labourers to educated, cultured scholars. Their leaders shared the same education and culture as their Catholic counterparts (e.g. the laymen, Cresconius and Vitellius Afer and the bishops, Petilian and Parmenian), and some, like Tyconius, were distinguished intellectuals who both inspired Augustine's admiration and influenced his theology. (In fact, Tyconius' teaching that the true Church could not be identified with any particular group or place but was made up both of individuals destined for salvation who were obedient to God's will, and of sinners destined for damnation, who would only be separated at the end, proved to be very close to Augustine's ideas in the *City of God*, but rather too advanced for his Donatist confrères who excommunicated him.[127])

THE BATTLE AGAINST DONATISM

From the moment of his ordination Augustine began to tackle what must have seemed the most pressing, but long-standing, problem in the African church with a number of works and a popular rhyming poem against the Donatists.[128] One gets the impression that, prior to Imperial intervention, he was working almost single-handed. There were laws, such as Theodosius' edict of 392, which subjected heretical clergy to fines, confiscated their churches and forbade them to make or receive bequests (*Cod. Theod.* 16.5.21), but as Augustine comments, 'There were laws but we allowed them to sleep in our hands, as though they had never been made at all':[129] Donatism was perceived primarily as a schism, not a heresy.

His main source of knowledge for the history of the movement and for earlier Catholic polemic and anti-Donatist theology was Optatus of Milev's

---

[126] See Possidius' description in *vita* 10.
[127] See Frend (1952), 204. He did not, however, join the Catholic Church.
[128] *c. ep. Don.* (no longer extant); *ps. c. Don.* Possidius *vita* 9 tells us that Augustine was occupied day and night with plans for their conversion.
[129] *Cresc.* 3.47.51 cited by Van der Meer (1961), 85.

On the Donatist Schism (two editions of 365–7 and 385).[130] This was invaluable but not without factual errors and flaws in interpretation. Later on, as a bishop, and aware that so much of the controversy hinged on factual details and their interpretation, Augustine set about establishing the facts for himself. He carefully and meticulously compiled dossiers of evidence, travelled to towns to hear first-hand evidence, and corrected and revised Optatus in the process. Aware that in criticizing the Donatists it was of the utmost importance that his own church and clergy be beyond reproach and any hint of scandal, he took energetic measures to enforce clerical discipline through canons such as those promulgated at the first of the reforming councils he organized with Aurelius of Carthage in 393.[131] He preached innumerable sermons against the Donatists, wrote at length to their lay and clerical leaders (Petilian, Cresconius, Gaudentius, Parmenian), composed treatises in order to respond to their works[132]—he quotes them section by section, thereby providing us with an invaluable record of their work[133]—and attempted to engage them in public debates or in conferences through the neutral offices of the local magistrates. His efforts met largely with defiance and non-co-operation.

In 405 the Emperor Honorius, seeing that the situation showed no signs of improvement, and petitioned from all quarters to act to preserve the Catholic Church in Africa, issued an edict ordering unity between the two churches. Whereas Augustine had hitherto simply identified schism as the grounds for the division between Donatist and Catholic, and had attempted to stress the features which the two sides had in common as a basis for reconciliation, the edict, for the first time, branded the Donatists not only as schismatics (there were no effective laws against schism) but as heretics, and therefore directly subject to anti-heretical law (*Cod. Theod.* 16.5.38; 6.4–5; 11.2). The Catholic Church was given military protection, Donatist property was confiscated, meetings or services were forbidden, clergy were threatened with exile, the giving or receiving of legacies was prohibited, landowners who allowed Donatist services on their estates were fined, any resistance was regarded as sedition and judges were fined if they failed to carry out the edict. Most significantly, the practice of rebaptism, which was identified as heresy, was forbidden.

Augustine, by contrast, simply seems to have regarded as heretical what he calls their 'inveterate schism' (*ep.* 87.4; *haer.* 69; *Cresc.* 2.9)—their long-standing refusal to back down even in the face of incontrovertible evidence. Nevertheless, he seems to have welcomed the edict as a means of enforc-

---

[130] Translated and edited by Edwards (1997).   [131] See Crespin (1965), Chapter 4.

[132] See Monceaux VII, 275–92 for chronological tables of works.

[133] See Monceaux IV, 487–510 and Maier (1987–9) for lists of Donatist documents.

ing the law, of controlling Donatist violence and their disturbance of civil and ecclesiastical peace, and both justified it (see *Cresc.*) and acted upon it, with alacrity and rigour. In Hippo itself he ejected the Donatist bishop Proculeianus from his basilica and pasted its walls with his own anti-Donatist works.

When the Emperor seemed to err towards a policy of renewed toleration in panic following the fall of Rome in 410, Augustine and Aurelius immediately sent a delegation to request its abrogation and to ask him to use his authority to call a conference at which the two sides could be heard and predetermined penalties imposed. A conference was duly held in Carthage in 411, for which we possess an extraordinarily full and accurate record.[134] In fact, the conference was not so much an occasion for debate as a last chance for the Donatists to be made to recognize and recant of their errors or to continue to suffer the penalties. The Donatists attended, nevertheless, because it was made clear that if they did not, they would continue to be proscribed.

The presiding Imperial representative was Marcellinus, a devout Catholic and long-standing friend of Augustine's. The proceedings did not go smoothly, as the Donatists, no doubt intent on challenging the legitimacy of the meeting, did everything they could to be obstructive and to demonstrate their discontent—they turned up *en masse*, rather than providing the requested eighteen representatives, insisted on a rather farcical identity parade so that each bishop could be identified by his local counterpart (thus, in passing, giving us a good idea of the distribution of Donatist and Catholic sees) and, perhaps most annoyingly of all, given the heat and the tortuous length of the proceedings, they refused to sit in the presence of the ungodly.

It is clear that the two sides were almost equally balanced in terms of numbers—385 Donatist bishops to 386 Catholic bishops (when false contenders and those who were already dead had been discounted)—but that otherwise the Donatist cause was lost from the outset. Marcellinus's final decision almost four weeks later was a foregone conclusion. In 412 the edict of unity was renewed, Donatism became a criminal offence, with a scale of fines according to rank, clergy were exiled, property was to be surrendered and handed over to the Catholics. Although the Donatists did not give in, and continued where they could to avoid exile, perform new ordinations, and hold on to churches,[135] their strength was inevitably broken. It had for a long time been subject to internal schisms and divisions (among

---

[134] It is recounted in the *Gesta Coll. Carth.* Augustine also composed a summary of the Conference in three books for later circulation and wrote to the Donatists, *Ad Donatistas post Collationem.*   [135] Notably Gaudentius in Thamugadi—see *c. Gaud.*

them the Rogatian and Maximinianist schisms—whose contradictoriness the Catholics had of course not been slow to point out). Its leaders were weak, its rich and landed members could not afford not to relent, and the combined forces of the Catholic Church under Aurelius and Augustine and of the Imperial edicts, enforced and supported by all the chief military and administrative officials in Africa, meant that its future could not but be severely restricted. Nevertheless, as Gregory the Great's correspondence rather surprisingly attests, there were Donatists and Catholics in Africa, living in relative harmony within a single community, at least until the sixth century.[136]

COERCION

It is in the coercion of heretics that we find one of the most cogent effects of the Constantinian settlement. The Church was now part of the State, the State became its protector and defender, and the question of the Church's attitude to, and role in, the persecution of heretics became a pressing one. Theodosius's laws of 392 and Honorius's edicts of 405 and 411 had effectively brought the bishops to the front line of battle; it was they who were in a position to identify heretics, to inform or summon the imperial officials or specially appointed commissioners or *executores*; it fell to them to administer the property, land, churches, and fines that were handed over. The Donatist might protest that the Church was now obedient to Caesar, rather than to God, but Augustine is not slow to point out that they too were evidently not reluctant to appeal to the authorities for support; they had called upon Constantine (*ep.* 88.1–5), Julian (*ep.* 93.12), and civil tribunals (*ep.* 51.3) when it suited them.

Augustine's own attitude was, however, ambiguous, and seems to have moved from an initial distaste and unease concerning coercion to a final endorsement of it in the face of the facts and its evident effectiveness. At first he seems to have felt that a person should best be free to seek the truth in peace, at his own pace, to be able to listen to reasoned arguments and to finally embrace it in love, free from fear and coercion.[137] The violent outrages of the Circumcellions, the seemingly inconquerable defiance and

---

[136] Markus (1997a), 193–9; (1983), VI; (1964). Frend also cites archaeological evidence which suggests that Donatist churches in villages were continuously occupied until the seventh century—(1952), 299.

[137] *ep.* 23.7; 34.1; 35.4; 93.17 cited by Kirwan (1989), 214. 'For originally my opinion was, that no one should be coerced into the unity of Christ, that we must act only by words, fight only by arguments, and prevail by force of reason, lest we should have those whom we knew as avowed heretics feigning themselves to be Catholics' (*ep.* 95.17).

hostility of the Donatists, despite all his efforts, and the evident effectiveness of the Imperial edicts in breaking their force (*ep.* 93, 16–17), all seem
to have contributed to his later support of State intervention.

He explains and justifies his position in a number of works written after
405.[138] As one might expect, his mature theology of the fall, the impotence
of man's will, and the role of God's grace led him to see the operation of
grace in the 'benevolent' discipline, correction, and pressure of coercion
(*ep.* 93.3; 185.2 and 6; 3.13 and 19–20; *en. Ps.* 118.2), which worked in fallen
man to break the chains of unthinking habit and custom (*ep.* 93.17;
185.2).[139] Coercion might move him beyond his long-held prejudices to
seek the truth, and perhaps even to hold to it in love, rather than fear (*ep.*
93.16–17; 185.25). Just as parents discipline, correct, and punish their children through love, so the Church should act to bring back those who had
erred from it,[140] 'the truth is, that always both the bad have persecuted the
good, and the good have persecuted the bad: the former doing harm by
their unrighteousness, the latter seeking to do good by the administration
of discipline; the former with cruelty, the latter with moderation; the
former impelled by lust, the latter under the constraint of love' (*ep.*
93.5–10). Even if coercion did not result in repentance, and the Donatists,
like so many pagans, merely feigned conversion in order to avoid penalties, he was aware that God's grace was unfathomable and might well work
in electing and bringing to faith an, at first, feigned conversion (*c. Gaud.*
25.28), just as a sincere and devout member of the Church might not be
elected. Likewise, as bishop, he says he felt bound to attempt to bring the
Donatists into the Church rather than allow them to face eternal damnation, even if this could only be done by force.[141] Indeed, he had himself
seen such forced conversions become genuine ones.

But all this reads like special pleading when one sets it against what we
have seen of Augustine's work against Pelagius. One suspects that Augustine was himself very much forced to adopt this position because, as a
bishop, he had to do something more than simply establish the historical
details, write letters and treatises, or preach. The Donatists were not just
a religious heresy to be refuted in the manner of the Pelagians, but a source

---

[138] *c. ep. Parm.* 1.8.13 f; *Cresc.*; *ep.* 77; *en. Ps.* 101.iii; and especially *ep.* 93 to Vincentius;
ep. 143; *ep.* 185 to Boniface.

[139] He gives the example of Paul's conversion in *s.* 129.4 and *ep.* 93.5, who 'was compelled,
by the great violence with which Christ coerced him, to know and to embrace the truth'.

[140] *ep.* 138.15; *c. litt. Pet.* 2.94.217 'However we treat you we do so out of love for you . . .
even when we are acting contrary to your own desires. Our aim is to have you change your
outlook volunarily and to live a reformed life . . .'.

[141] *ep.* 185.3.14; 143.4–6 cited by Kirwan (1989), 215 who does not have much time for
Augustine's 'paternalistic' arguments.

of totally unacceptable public outrages; of theft, arson, assault, and murder. The force of the imperial authorities was needed to control them and he could not, in all justice, hinder their operation. What he did do, however, was unfailingly to attempt to moderate the extremes of the law and most especially, to avert the death penalty[142] (it did not allow for repentance) for he wanted to avoid the creation of more Donatist 'martyrs' (*ep.* 139.1–2).

THE NATURE OF THE CHURCH

As we saw earlier, the Donatists very much thought of themselves as preserving undefiled, and untainted by corruption and compromise, the true Catholic Church in Africa, the Church of the martyrs, of Tertullian and Cyprian, where God's sacraments could be truly administered. They saw themselves as the righteous remnant of Israel, preserving God's law in holiness and purity amidst an unclean people. For Augustine, however, brought up in the Catholic stronghold of Thagaste and well acquainted with the Catholic Church abroad, as he had experienced it in the cosmopolitan atmosphere of Milan and Rome, they were in a state of schism from the whole of the rest of the universal Catholic Church throughout the world (*ep.* 49.2–3; 93.20–23)—*securus iudicat orbis terrarum* (*c. ep. Parm.* 3.4.24). Their position was an absurd one: 'the clouds roll with thunder, that the House of the Lord shall be built throughout the earth: and these frogs sit in their marsh and croak—We are the only Christians.'[143]

Furthermore, Augustine was convinced that the holiness or purity of the Church does not depend upon the moral integrity and uprightness of its individual members—on these grounds no Church, including that of the Donatists, could ever hope to attain it (*ep.* 44.4). Not only do they too count immoral, drunken, violent people among their members, they have polluted their integrity by the most grievous sin of all, a sin far worse than *traditio*: they have placed themselves in schism.[144] No one, Catholic or Donatist, can say he is without sin (*c. ep. Parm.* 2.14 quoting 1 John 1: 8); everyone must pray 'Forgive us our sins' (ibid. 2.20). We have seen Augus-

---

[142] E.g. *ep.* 100.1, 'We "love our enemies" and we "pray of them" [Matt. 5: 44]. It is not their death, but their deliverance from error, that we seek to accomplish by the help of the terror of judges and of laws . . .'. Cf. *ep.* 133, 1–2 where he exhorts Marcellinus to perform his judicial duties as 'a tender father'; 139, 1–2; 153. Bonner (1987) VII, 240–1 agrees with Markus (1970c), that coercion, for Augustine, was always 'part of a pastoral strategy'.

[143] *en. Ps.* 95.11 cited by Brown (1967), 221.

[144] Here, as so often, Augustine is probably drawing upon Optatus. Cf. *De Schismate* 1.21; 7.2.

tine moving towards the conviction that in this life the Church will forever be a mixed body, containing wheat and tares, the good and bad, who will only finally be separated at the Last Judgement (*ep.* 93.28; *Cresc.* 2.34.43; *c. litt. Pet.* 3.2.3). Meanwhile, sinners must be tolerated, as they have been tolerated throughout history—indeed as the Donatists themselves have tolerated notorious sinners and schismatics within their own church (*ep.* 23.6; 87.8; 93.31–33).[145] The Church has only one source of holiness and unity and that is Christ in His Holy Spirit (*s.* 71). No one merits salvation, that he achieves it is wholly due to God's grace.

The Donatists, on the other hand, held that it was not they who were in schism, but the Catholic Church; that their bishops were *traditores*, their priestly ministry, their prayers, and the sacraments they administered were invalid (*c. ep. Parm.* 2.10–27)—indeed, not just invalid, but actively corrupting with the contagion of their sin those to whom they ministered. They therefore maintained that any Catholic seeking to enter their Church should be rebaptized, since their first baptism, administered by one who was effectively dead, could not give life and was without any value or effect (*c. litt. Petil.* 1.10–12; 2.14; 3.64).[146] In this, as in so many ways, the Donatists could appeal to African tradition for authority, and in particular to Cyprian. He too had taught that an apostate bishop's ministry was ineffective, that he contaminated his congregation with his sin and must be removed.[147] Most famously, he had defended the practice of rebaptism of heretics against Stephen, Bishop of Rome, on the grounds that only the one true apostolic Church possesses the Holy Spirit, and therefore only within it can true, effective baptism take place (*ep.* 74). Schism from the one apostolic Church was the gravest of sins for Cyprian since it shatters the unity, the source, from which it derives its life and faith (*de unit:* 19.5–6).[148] In order to preserve this unity he did not excommunicate those who, like Stephen, disagreed with him, and was prepared to soften his original rigorism and readmit, on certain conditions, those who had lapsed during the persecutions, rather than exclude them from the Church or force them into schism. Only the Novatianists, who, like the Donatists, insisted upon uncompromised perfection and sinlessness, and who would not tolerate the readmission of the lapsed, remained excluded by placing themselves in schism. It is this latter aspect of Cyprian's teaching that Augustine emphasized against the Donatists.

But what was he to make of Cyprian's teaching on rebaptism? In *On*

---

[145] See Crespin (1965), 153, n. 2 for further references.
[146] A criminal cannot impart innocence (1.8) or a bad tree good fruit (1.9).
[147] Cyprian *ep.* 65; 67; 70   [148] See Merdinger (1997a), Chapter 4.

Baptism against the Donatists Augustine argues that, in fact, rebaptism was not the practice of the Church until Cyprian's predecessor, Agrippinus, in the late second, early third, century;[149] that Cyprian's confirmation of it against Stephen was a break with ancient tradition (*bapt.* 3.17); and that the Catholic Church had subsequently approved the practice of the Roman Church and recognized baptism outside the Church (*bapt.* 3.14; 4.8–9): the Council of Arles in 314/15 had stated that if a heretic professes faith in the Trinity it is enough to lay hands on him.[150]

Augustine was well aware, not only that the members of the Donatist Church failed to meet their own rigorous criteria for holiness and purity, but that they were thoroughly inconsistent when it came to questions of baptism, or rebaptism, of former heretics or schismatics. The Donatists themselves suffered a number of internal schisms but invariably failed to rebaptize those who sought to rejoin the main Church (*c. litt. Pet.* 2.120). Their theology of priestly integrity and purity also began to falter: when pushed on this point in order to defend Petilian, Cresconius suggested that a priest's ministry was not defiled or undermined by hidden failings in his personal morality; what mattered were sins which might destroy unity within the Church, such as heresy, schism, and *traditio* (*c. ep. Parm.* 2.21). This, of course, conveniently salvaged the ministry of most Donatist priests but effectively wrote off all Catholic ones.

Augustine's theology of baptism cuts through these uneasy distinctions by attributing the efficacy and grace of the sacrament wholly to its source in Christ (*ep.* 108.3), and by making them entirely independent of the one who administers it. Like Optatus, whom he follows closely here (see *de schismate* 5.2; 5.4; 5.7), he attributes to the sacraments an objective value independent of the person who administers them; 'they are holy in themselves' (*per se ipsa sancta sunt*) (*bapt.* 4.18) and this holiness has its source only in Christ who instituted them and who works in them (*c. litt. Pet.* 2.88). In order to be valid they must be in the name of Christ, and the correct form of words must be used (*bapt.* 4.18; 5.4). If these conditions are fulfilled the sacrament confers what Augustine calls a *consecratio*, an indelible, definitive, unrepeatable sign or character, which cannot be lost (*c. ep. Parm.* 2.29; *bapt.* 6.1). The character and standing of the one who baptizes are really of no consequence: light is not dulled when it passes through the shadows; water is not contaminated by the stone canal it passes through (*bapt.* 3.15). Nor, in fact, is the faith of the recipient crucial; a believer can

---

[149] Cyprian too cites this as evidence in *ep.* 73.3. Firmilian (*ep.* 75.7) also refers to a Council at Iconium (c. AD 230) which agreed on the practice—see Merdinger (1997), 46.

[150] Mansi II.427A. This was reiterated at Nicaea, Canons 8 and 19, Mansi II.671 B; 675B.

grow in faith without needing rebaptism. What *is* crucial is charity, without which faith serves for nothing (*bapt.* 3.19).[151]

Augustine therefore maintains that the sacraments of the Donatists can indeed be validly administered and received in schism; they do not need to be repeated on entry to the Catholic Church (*bapt.* 6.7). However, they are not effective and cannot lead to salvation (*bapt.* 1.8; *un. bapt.* 13)[152] because in schism they have cut themselves off from the One Catholic Church, which is the only place where the Holy Spirit can be given and received (*s.* 71.28; *bapt.* 5.33). Their separation from the Church is a sign of their lack of charity and without this, like a tree without roots, all they do is fruitless (*bapt.* 1.7; 4.25; *Io. eu. tr.* 13.16).

The divisions which the Donatists wished to impose, between pure and tainted, saint and sinner, holy and profane, were, Augustine saw, not ones which were served by schism or by physical separation, they were rather a matter of divine grace and election, a loving response to God's will made possible by the action of His Holy Spirit within the heart of the believer. Baptism, and the unity of the Catholic Church, provided the necessary ground and context, but that is all. The Church evidently consisted of both good and bad, elect and reprobate, of those who love God and those who love the world, and any attempt to separate them, in this world, was both impossible and premature; only God can do this, at the Last Judgement, according to his providential purposes. As we will see in the final chapter, the Donatist controversy contributed a great deal to the substance of the *City of God*.

---

[151] Crespin (1965), 275.

[152] He distinguishes between baptism *ad utilitatem* and *ad salutem*—*c. ep. Parm* 2.13.28; *Cresc.* 1.29.34—Crespin (1965), 88.

5

Marriage and monasticism

*There is nothing so social by nature and so discordant by its perversion as
the [human] race* (City of God 12.28.1).

In *City of God* 19.13 Augustine describes the ideal form of human society
as, 'a perfectly ordered and perfectly harmonious fellowship in the enjoyment of God and mutual fellowship in God.' The idea of order is one which
is carried over from his early thought; the concept of harmonious, mutual
fellowship in God as characteristic of this order is one which gradually
evolved as his thought became more immersed in Scripture, especially
St Paul, and as his life and experience in the world led him to reflect on the
nature of human society, its foundation, characteristics and goals.

In order to trace this evolution we might begin with Augustine in 386,
at the moment of his conversion. In *Confessions* 8 he presents it to us in
uncompromising terms as a choice between two different social identities:
either celibacy or marriage. At this stage nothing less than celibacy would
do—only one distinctive form of life would meet the high calling of Christianity—he must renounce his arranged marriage, his temporary mistress,
and henceforth embrace celibacy as a life-long companion.

Why are marriage and celibacy so sharply contrasted here? Is it simply
a question of sexual continence or did it have more to do with a rejection
of the duties of family and civil life? Is it attributable to philosophical influence (continence, though not necessarily celibacy, had traditionally been
the ideal of the true philosopher) mediated to Augustine through
Ambrose[1] and Neoplatonism? Is it a last vestige of Manichaeism—that the
highest religious life was reserved for the continent elect? Is it symptomatic
of the strong emphasis on asceticism prevalent in Church circles in the
fourth century, especially at Rome? Is it inspired by Augustine's first
encounter with the monastic life—with Ponticianus' account of the Life of
Antony and the conversion of the two civil servants in Trier? Is it indica-
tive of the rather low esteem in which marriage was held—a relationship
which was generally thought, like the sexual relationship which defined it,

[1] Ambrose had made celibacy the acme of the devout live in late fourth-century Milan—
McLynn (1994).

to be a direct result of the fall, fraught with temptations and difficulties, to be entered into only as a last resort—better to marry than to burn?

These, and perhaps other reasons too, were probably in Augustine's mind in 386, but viewed retrospectively, in the light of his later theology, the picture is a rather different one: though the celibate life will always be given a higher place by Augustine, the contrast with the married life will become less antithetic, to the point where the two can be seen as two different social identities which are yet characterized by the same ideals, the same goals, and the same temporal ambiguities. It is this evolution which I would like to trace in this chapter.

THE THREE 'GOODS' OF MARRIAGE

As we shall see, patristic reflection on marriage tends to lurk in the dark shadows cast by the glorious ideal of virginity: we learn more about it in treatises exhorting the reader to virginity where it appears as a definite second-best—a good, but a relatively low one on the scale of perfection, and preferably to be avoided—than anywhere else. When we try to look beyond this to historical, sociological investigations of the Greco-Roman family, the evidence is similarly limited, this time by the sheer size and diversity of the Roman Empire which does not allow for generalizations. The sources are also limited to a cultured élite, the wealthy upper classes of the Empire for whom documentary and inscriptional evidence exists— in other words to 10–20 per cent of the population who are probably not at all representative of the remaining 80–90 per cent given the very stark distinction between slave and free. Moreover, we only hear from men, from lawyers, doctors, writers, theologians, writing from a male perspective, for other men—marriage and family life from a woman's or child's perspective can only be glimpsed, rather inadequately, through what is said on other subjects.[2]

Augustine's first discussion of the marriage relationship is a rather odd one. It appears in his first attempt at interpreting Genesis, *On Genesis against the Manichees* (AD 389), which, like a number of his early works, is directed against the Manichees. But whereas one would therefore expect him to defend the goodness of the body and sexual reproduction, he continues the allegorical approach of the commentary and offers a spiritual

---

[2] Perhaps the best book in this respect is G. Clark (1993b). For a theological perspective see E. A. Clark (1986a); (1986b). Other studies of marriage and the family, which generally only take one up to the second century but nevertheless provide a very valuable context in which to place later Christian reflection on these ideas include, Shaw (1987); Veyne (1987); Rawson (1986); Dixon (1988); Bradley (1991); Gardner and Wiedemann (1993); Grubbs (1994); Arjava (1995).

interpretation of the command to 'increase and multiply': Adam and Eve, he suggests, would have brought forth 'spiritual offspring' of 'intelligible and immortal joys' rather than children (*Gn. adu. Man.* 1.19.30). Theirs would have been a 'casta coniunctio'; there would have been a 'copulatio spiritualis' giving birth to 'good works of divine praise' (*Gn. adu. Man.* 2.11.15).[3] His defence of marriage comes only twelve years later in one of a pair of treatises attempting to steer a middle way amidst the storms created by Jerome and his outright denigration of marriage on the one side, and Jovinian, the Roman monk, who had dared to interpret the Song of Songs in relation to Christian marriage and to put marriage on a par with virginity, on the other. For Jerome a first marriage is a regrettable weakness—its only purpose being the conversion of other members of the household, the education of a new Christian generation and the production of Christian ascetics (*ep.* 107.1);[4] second marriage is only one step from the brothel, like a dog returning to its vomit. Jerome's views were obviously felt to be extreme by his contemporaries and we see him attempting to moderate or defend them in letters written to a certain Pammachius: he points out that he is no Marcionite, Manichee, or Encratite, he does not condemn marriage even though he does not praise it, rather it is like wood and pottery, in contrast to gold and silver in a household: it is of lower value but still necessary (*To Pammachius* 49.1). What *he* has said about marriage is no more or less favourable than most Latin authors, 'Read them' he urges 'and in their company curse me or free me' (ibid. 49.17). And of course a comparative reading supports him.

Most fathers, including Augustine, would, however, add procreation and the controlling of lust to the purposes of marriage: it 'makes us chaste and makes us parents', as Chrysostom puts it.[5] But then they usually add that procreation, which, in the beginning, necessitated the creation of Eve (Augustine *Gn. litt.* 9.3.5; 5.9) and justified the Patriarchs' taking of a number of wives (Augustine *b. coniug.* 19; 21), is now no longer necessary. This was either because, like Tertullian, they thought the end to be near— Christians, 'for whom there is no tomorrow', need no longer be concerned

---

[3] It seems strange that scholars should suggest that Augustine was unaware of thus giving ground to the Manichees and that his interpretation only moved to being a literal, 'earthier' one in *Gn. litt.* (3.9.5) where he felt directly challenged by the charge of Manichaeism when it was levelled at such ascetical interpretations by the likes of Jovinian (e.g. E. A. Clark (1986b), 353). Augustine specifically rejects this spiritual interpretation in *retr.* 1.10.2. The reason he pursues a thoroughgoing allegorical interpretation here is to counter the Manichees' insistence upon a crudely literal interpretation which they then used to demonstrate the absurdity, inconsistency, and contradictory nature of the Genesis account. Augustine is making the point that much of the text *is* allegorical and should be read in its own terms.

[4] Cited by Yarbrough (1976), 162.

[5] *Sermon on Marriage*, in Roth and Anderson (1986), 85.

about posterity[6] he observes—or because hope in the resurrection makes the desire for children superfluous. Now that, as Augustine comments, 'there is a vast crowd from all nations to fill up the number of the saints', what was at first a duty for man—the begetting of children—is no longer necessary and is at best a healing remedy for those who are sick (*Gn. litt.* 9.7.12; *b. coniug.* 5–6)[7]—in other words to control lust. It is in this context that Augustine steers a middle way between Jerome and Jovinian in *On the Good of Marriage* (AD 401), by maintaining that marriage is good but virginity is better. The three 'goods' of marriage he enumerates as progeny (*proles*), fidelity (*fides*), and the sacrament (*sacramentum*) (*b. coniug.* 4.3; 4.4; 7.6). In this treatise he is still uncertain concerning the exact nature of procreation before the fall and simply admits that there are a number of different views. But he has more to say about the last two goods.

First, fidelity (*fides*): for Roman citizens, the ideal of *concordia* represented the highest expectation and greatest achievement of marriage—that the partners should live in harmony and unity, holding all things in common. *Concordia* in the family constituted the basis for harmony and unity in the city and in the State.[8] As Cicero writes, 'The origin of society is in the joining (*coniugium*) of man and woman, next in children, then in the household (*una domus*), all things held in common; this is the foundation (*principium*) of the city and, so to speak, the seed-bed of the State (*seminarium rei publicae*)'.[9] In *On the Good of Marriage* Augustine takes over, and christianizes these ideas, describing a *concordia religiosa* (13.15). Referring to Acts 4: 32—a text which will also be determinative of his description of the common monastic life—he suggests that the union of man and wife in marriage, with one heart and one mind towards God, signifies the unity of the heavenly city (18.21).[10] Augustine makes clear at the very beginning of the treatise that the married relationship is above all one of reciprocal friendship, fellowship, and love: 'Since every person is part of the human race and human nature is something social and has in itself the power of friendship as a great good, God willed for this reason to create all humans from one person, so that they might be held fast in their society not only

---

[6] Tertullian *Exhortation to Chastity*, 12. Cf. Augustine *b. coniug.* 32. See pp. 166–7 below for further discussion of *sacramentum*.

[7] Cf. Chrysostom *On Virginity*, 19.1–2.

[8] There is much artistic evidence for the ideal of *concordia* on, for example, marriage belts and rings (see Vikan (1990)) and also on sarcophagi where Adam and Eve are depicted adopting the formal Roman figure of the married couple with clasped right hands—the *dextrarum iunctio*.

[9] Cicero, *De Officiis* 1.17.54, quoted by Shaw (1987), 11 who notes that these ideas are heavily Stoic in tone.

[10] Cf. Aristotle *Politics* where he describes the building block of human society as man and woman bonding to raise children.

by likeness of descent, but also by the bond of relationship. Thus the first tie of natural human society (or fellowship—*societas*) is husband and wife.' He goes on to describe the married couple as those who are 'joined one to another side by side, who walk together, and look together where they walk' (1.1).[11]

FRIENDSHIP

It has justly been observed that Augustine never seems to be alone; he is always in the company of family, friends, or a community. His character was a gregarious one and he evidently needed someone to share his thoughts, with whom he could discuss and debate (e.g. *conf.* 4.18.13; *ep.* 130.4, to Proba, *ep.* 258). That he valued these friendships highly is more than evident,[12] and that he reflected upon the familiar classical ideals of friendship to reshape them in a Christian mould is unsurprising but also revealing of his thought on life in society—both married and celibate. He finds nothing to disagree with in Cicero who can in fact be seen as the source of many of his descriptions of the married or monastic life: friendship is, 'an agreement on all things human and divine with goodwill and love' (*Laelius* 6.20; Aug. *ep* 258), Cicero comments in the *Laelius de amicitia*, 'so that many should, as it were, become one soul' (*Laelius* 25.92).[13] But Augustine adds that the source of such friendship lies in God's grace (*conf.* 4.4.7); that unity in the body of Christ provides the solidest base for friendship (*diu. qu.* 71.6–7; *ep.* 208; 142.1), and love of God in one's friend is the best way to love him properly (*s.* 336.2.2; *conf.* 4.9.14)—this is the meaning of the double commandment to love God and neighbour: God is to be loved above all else; one's neighbour is to be loved in and for him.[14] He describes such friendship as a natural good, like health, which is essential to human existence and any form of human relationship.[15] It was through friendship, or friendly benevolence (*amicalis benevolentia*), that Adam fell in not abandoning Eve (*Gn. litt.* 11.42.59). His emphasis on friendship in relation to the married couple goes beyond traditional Roman expectations of

---

[11] There are numerous passages in Augustine which refer to the mutual affection between the two partners—see Schmidt (1983), 280–1. He observes that 'L'amour dont Augustin se fait ici l'avocat est une intimité profonde entre deux âmes, pure de toute recherche égoiste et passionnelle, une sorte de chasteté amoureuse du coeur, condition de toute véritable chasteté du corps' (181).

[12] E.g. his account of the death of his friend in *conf.* 4.6.11.

[13] Friends who share the same interests and wishes love each other as much as they love themselves (*De Officiis* 1.17.56).

[14] See the rather convoluted and ultimately rather inconclusive discussion of this in *doctr. chr.* I.　　　[15] *s. Denis* 16.1; *f. inuis.* 2.4—cited by Van Bavel (1989), 48.

the married relationship as revealed in law codes and funerary epigraphs, which are more likely to mention the more mundane virtues of devotion, modesty, thrift, chastity, fidelity, hard work, reliability . . . but has more in common with Tertullian's encomium of married life in his treatise *Ad Uxorem*. Contrasting the distinctive life of the Christian married couple with that of pagans, he describes how they should pray, fast, and attend Church together, take communion together, discuss the meaning of the prayers and readings, instruct and encourage one another, sing psalms to one another, give alms, have no secrets from one another, and have no fear about fulfilling their Christian duties. 'How beautiful, then', he observes, is 'the marriage of two Christians, two who are one in hope, one in desire, one in the way of life they follow, one in the religion they practice . . . Nothing divides them either in flesh or spirit' (*ad Uxorem* 9).

It is in the context of friendship, significantly, that in *On the Good of Marriage*, Augustine places the sexual aspect of marriage—not as a result of the fall, but as part of the 'friendly fellowship' of marriage (9).[16] When he speaks about *fides* he includes sexual relations which are not motivated by the desire for procreation but which are simply part of the duty which spouses owe to one another (*b. coniug.* 4.4);[17] in other words he entertains the idea of the marriage as a sexual relationship, but at the same time, one which exists independently of any desire for procreation. Rather it is a social bond (*societas*) which serves to order, or 'socialize' the otherwise disordered and anti-social movements of concupiscence (*b. coniug.* 5.5).[18] We shall see the same independence of the social bond of the marriage from procreation being established in a rather different form in what Augustine has to say about its sacramental aspect.

Meanwhile, his understanding of *fides* foreshadows Augustine's later treatment of the question of intercourse in his *Literal Commentary on Genesis* of AD 410. In Book 3 he again opts for a spiritual interpretation and emphasizes the marital love and accord of will between Adam and Eve, which would give birth to children without any concupiscence—*piae caritatis adfectu*—an idea which should be seen in the context of classical ideas of friendship to be rightly understood.[19] But in Book 9, Augustine finally decides in favour of the possibility of the presence of sinless sexual intercourse *before* the fall (although the fall took place before it occurred). As is often the case, it is in reaction to various extreme forms of asceticism that the fathers can be seen defending marriage and the married life. In the early centuries it fell to theologians such as Clement of Alexandria to defend the

---

[16] Cf. *s.* 9.6.7—babies are born in marriage 'from the parents' friendship'.
[17] I owe this insight to Hunter (1994), 153–77. Though this view will be revised in his work against Julian of Eclanum in the second and third decades of the fourth century.
[18] Quoted by Hunter, ibid. 162.   [19] See Doignon (1982), 25–36.

goodness of marriage and procreation against the asceticism of those Gnostics who condemned marriage. Their hostility to creation, which they regarded as the work of an alien, evil, Creator God, and their consequent extreme asceticism, distancing themselves from the body and matter as much as possible, and especially from intercourse which would only serve to propagate evil matter, undermined the Christian notion of a Creator God responsible for a fundamentally good creation. Augustine, in turn, gives marriage perhaps its most positive evaluation among the fathers, against the Gnostics' fourth-century successors, the Manichees, whose ideas, we have already seen, are very similar.

In his *Literal Commentary on Genesis*, he maintains that Adam and Eve were a married couple and would have had children by sexual intercourse *before the fall*. Others, with the exception of Ambrosiaster, to whom we will return, held that Adam and Eve were either a virginal couple[20] or sexless[21] and that there was no marriage, no intercourse, no children in Paradise— these are all a result of the fall and symptomatic of man's fallenness: 'where there is death, there is marriage' Chrysostom observes in an admittedly uncharacteristically sombre mood.[22] For those who thought in this way intercourse and children were simply measures to counter man's loss of immortality at the fall[23]—they are a sort of solace for man's loss of virginity,[24] a concession to his weakness.[25] What would have happened in Paradise if Adam and Eve had not fallen is obviously a matter of pure speculation, especially since God foresaw the fall, but some of the fathers do comment either that Adam would have reproduced in some sort of non-sexual way,[26] or that God could have created other human beings in the same manner as the angels and archangels;[27] marriage and children are not envisaged. Although, as we have seen, Augustine also, at first, interpreted the command of God in Genesis to 'increase and multiply' in a spiritual sense, rather than in reference to human intercourse, Elizabeth Clark I think rightly suggests[28] that he was moved to temper these early, seemingly ascetic leanings, by the debate between Jovinian and Jerome already mentioned. Jovinian, reacting against a mounting tide of enthusiasm for asceticism in the fourth century, had attacked extreme ascetics such as Jerome by calling them 'Manichees'—indeed, it has been suggested that the main thrust of Jovinian's work was, in fact, motivated by and directed

---

[20] E.g. Jerome, *Adversus Jovinianum* 1.16.

[21] Gregory of Nyssa, *De Opificio Hominis* 12.9 (quoted by Brown (1988), 294).

[22] *De Virginitate* 14. 6.   [23] E.g. Gregory of Nyssa, *De Uirginitate* 12.

[24] Chrysostom, *De Uirginitate* 14. 5.

[25] Ibid. 15.2; Methodius of Olympus, *Symposium* 3.10.78–13.89 (quoted by Brown (1988), 185)   [26] Maximus the Confessor, *Ambigua* 41.

[27] Chrysostom, *De Uirginitate* 14.6.   [28] See E. A. Clark (1986a); (1986b).

against distinctively Manichaean ideas[29]—and Augustine could see that there was some substance in this. A more literal interpretation of Genesis, in which marriage is seen as part of man's original condition, even in Paradise, served Augustine to counter this extremism and defend *himself* against charges of remaining a Manichee (as we have seen, he had been one, and was known as one, for almost ten years before his conversion).[30]

From now on intercourse, like marriage, for Augustine is part of man's original and intended state; he is intended to live in fellowship, to found a society. Woman was created for this purpose and when God blessed them He said 'Increase and multiply and fill the earth and subdue it'. So, although Scripture says that it was after their expulsion from Paradise that sexual intercourse and children happened (Gen. 4: 1), Augustine writes, 'I do not see what could have prohibited them from honourable nuptial union and the bed undefiled even in Paradise . . . so that without the tumultuous ardour of passion and without any labour and pain of childbirth, offspring would be born from their seed' (*Gn. litt.* 3.6. Cf. *ciu.* 14.26). If this had happened, he comments, there would be no death; rather, all the inhabitants of paradise would have remained in the prime of life until the determined number was complete, when they would be transformed into spiritual bodies. Offspring would have been desired, not as a remedy against death, but as companions for life (*Gn. litt.* 9.14.).[31] As far as I know, Augustine had only one other predecessor for these ideas, the Roman priest commonly known to us under the name of Ambrosiaster. He too was probably reacting against what he perceived to be the unacceptably extreme ascetic stance of various individuals in the Roman Church, such as Jerome, and probably represents a current of Christian resistance to asceticism among what D. G. Hunter describes as 'the socially conservative and theologically traditional Roman Church'[32] in the last few decades of the fourth century, similar to that of Jovinian and which is also present

---

[29] Hunter (1987)—for a thorough and convincing re-evaluation of Jovinian. He argues that 'each of Jovinian's positions can be seen as directed against distinctively Manichaean ideas: a Manichaean Docetic Christology, an exaltation of virginity and fasting which implied the denigration of the Old Testament and married Christians, and a Manichaean view of the authority of the devil in the created world and denial of the efficacy of baptism: Jovinian is best understood, I suggest, when he is seen not as the opponent of monasticism or asceticism per se, but rather as a kind of ecclesiastical watchdog wary of the influence of extreme dualistic views on the community at Rome' (49–50).

[30] Though this suggestion still does not explain why Augustine failed to make this point in the earlier commentary, which was itself directed against the Manichees—unless his spiritual interpretation was determined by the allegorical form of the commentary.

[31] So, commenting upon 'male and female created he them' in *Gn. litt.* 3.22, Augustine makes it clear that God created their different bodies not just *in potentia* or as some sort of damage limitation after the fall, but *before* the fall.   [32] Hunter (1989).

in the other two authors whom Jerome had occasion to write against in this context, Helvidius and Vigilantius.[33]

In his little-known treatise, *On the sin of Adam and Eve* (*De Peccato Adae et Euae*), Ambrosiaster puts forward a number of arguments to defend marriage and childbearing which one cannot help but think give voice to the otherwise largely unarticulated views of the 'silent majority' of married Christians with children who were seeking to lead a life in society. Hunter has analysed this treatise in some depth and highlights a number of arguments in favour of procreation. The most important is the appeal to the 'innate power' for procreation which all living things possess and which was present from the beginning in man who was commanded to 'increase and multiply'. Read literally, Genesis suggests that marriage and sex belong to man's original paradisal state and preceded the fall. Nor is the time for procreation over: so long as creation continues it is part of a larger whole and must also continue. To reject it is to impugn the value of creation. Secondly, Ambrosiaster will admit no link between the fall and sex: sexual relations took place before the fall and continue, unaffected, after it. What did change was what Genesis tells us changed: the addition of pain in the labour of childbirth and the difficulty Adam experienced in farming the soil. As we shall see, of course, for Augustine, after the fall, concupiscence destroys the untroubled control of the will and fundamentally undermines and vitiates the married relationship—which to a large extent explains his preference for chastity—but it by no means destroys it or its ultimate value.

Having thus established the place of sexual relations in the context of *fides* and *proles*—of marriage as a relation of friendship and fellowship in society which includes procreation but is not defined by it—we might now turn to consider the third 'good' of marriage, the sacramental aspect.[34] The fathers held that marriage was sacramental in the broadest sense—as a human institution which disclosed profound truths about the Christian faith. (Although Augustine's use of the word *sacramentum* is extraordinarily wide, ranging from 'sacred sign' to 'rite', he never uses it in the latter sense in relation to a nuptial liturgy.) It is on such texts as Ephesians 5 and Genesis 2 (the creation of Eve from Adam's rib while he slept, likened to the blood and water which issued from Christ's pierced side at his death) that their teaching hinges (*nupt. et conc.* 1.10.11; *b. coniug.* 17; 21). Augustine maintains that there is an enduring 'quiddam coniugale', an enduring marital 'thing' which survives the breakdown of marital relations, just as the 'sacramentum fidei' of baptism survives apostasy (*nupt. et conc.* 1.11). Marriage

---

[33] In his *Against Helvidius* and *Against Vigilantius*. I am indebted, for this section, to the excellent article by Hunter (1989).

[34] For Augustine's understanding of the sacramental aspect of marriage see Reynolds (1994), Ch. 13—to whom I am indebted in the following section.

is a smaller but identical sacrament to the great sacrament of union which is between Christ and his Church (ibid. 1.23; 31–32). So, even in a case of sterility, the marriage cannot, as in Roman law, be dissolved (*b. coniug.* 7; 21).

DIVORCE AND REMARRIAGE

The doctrine of the indissolubility of marriage which emerged in the West in the fourth century, and especially with Augustine, sharply distinguished the Church's teaching from Roman divorce law—where the dissolving of the marriage bond was quite straightforward and simply required notification of intent—and was the key to the Church's 'Christianization' of marriage in contradistinction to Roman, pagan, and Jewish customs. Reynolds notes that Augustine developed his theory of marriage during an especially lax time, when divorce was allowed for any reason whatsoever following the Emperor Julian's (the Apostate) removal of Constantine's restrictions.[35] But even Christian emperors did not, and did not wish to, legislate to cover the strict and rigorous views of the fathers: these could not, for example, be imposed on pagan citizens, nor were they helpful in a society which, given its shockingly high mortality rates, could not afford to forbid remarriage.[36] Their legislation simply gives us 'a fair, though indirect, indication of prevailing attitudes in the Church as they knew it'.[37]

Christian emperors do not seem to have been motivated by theological or doctrinal reflection and in general simply reflect the prevailing Roman assumption that marriage is a life-long relationship and that divorce and remarriage fall short of this. How 'Christian' their legislation is, either in intention or content, is therefore a matter for debate, not least because cultural and juridicial attitudes differed widely in East and West irrespective of Christian influence.[38] One can simply observe that they do not contradict Christian standards. Indeed, the vast majority of Christians, as Augustine's sermons frequently witness, found it extremely difficult to change traditional moral customs, either in their own lives or in society at large. Householders still slept with their female slaves, wives still turned a blind eye to their husband's infidelities. In theory, however, Christian teaching on marriage was radically new in that it got rid of the double standard whereby the actions of an adulterous husband would be overlooked but

---

[35] Reynolds (1994), 304. Constantine's restrictions were not imposed again until AD 421.
[36] Arjava (1996), 189.
[37] Reynolds (1994), 417 referring to J. T. Noonan, 'Novel 22' in W. Bassett (ed.), *The Bond of Marriage* (1968), 41–90.
[38] Arjava (1996), 191.

those of an adulterous wife punished.[39] These were the only grounds on which divorce was allowed for either party and Augustine calls upon wives to hold their own and not to ignore or tolerate their husband's conduct (e.g. *s.* 9.4). Fourth-century Western Christianity also saw a hardening of ideas on remarriage: whilst the fathers always discouraged second or further marriages, they did not forbid them. Augustine's doctrine of the indissolubility of marriage, however, meant that even after divorce the marriage bond in some sense remains, so that remarriage would constitute adultery.

In one respect, however, Augustine reflects the changing times by acknowledging that whereas intermarriage between a pagan and Christian was once regarded as a sin (for example, by Cyprian), it is now tolerated.[40] (The official line, however, remained unchanged: the Council of Chalcedon in 451 still forbade marriage between a Christian and a non-Christian or heretic unless the latter converted to Christianity (Canon 14)). What was uniformly condemned by the Church was the Roman practice of concubinage. Although a 'common-law' marriage, with no legal status, and therefore entailing no legal rights for the children of such partnerships, it allowed a stable relationship for males either before marriage, or following widowhood, most often with a woman of lower social status, which avoided the redistribution of property consequent upon marriage or remarriage. Augustine too later condemned it, but his own experience of it during fifteen years with his unnamed, but evidently well-loved partner, the mother of his son, Adeodatus, leads him to see it in perhaps a more positive light than others.[41]

Perhaps the most important aspect of what Reynolds describes as the Western Church's 'radical and decisive form of Christianization by identifying the "sacramentality" of marriage with indissolubility'[42] is the reconfirmation of the essence of marriage as a mysterious bonding of two individuals, a holy, sanctifying union of mutual love, friendship, and fellowship irrespective of the sexual relations or procreation which were elsewhere definitive of it. There is a 'natural association between the sexes' (*b. coniug.* 3.3), Augustine observes, which is independent of procreation, or the age of the partners. Against Julian, who argued that there can be no marriage without intercourse, Augustine cites the example of the old and

---

[39] see G. Clark (1993b), ch. 1 on the double standard. She also makes clear just how difficult it was for Christians to change traditional moral customs in their own lives and society at large (something we have seen in the previous chapter) and how the legislation of Christian emperors, for pagans and Christians, could not, and did not intend to, keep pace with the Church.   [40] *f. et op.* 21.37 cited in Brown (1972), 172.

[41] *b. coniug.* 5—which states that concubinage can—if regarded as a permanent relationship which will embrace children if they are conceived—be viewed as marriage.

[42] Reynolds (1994), 417

infirm, observing that one becomes the friend and companion of one's spouse to the extent that sexual desire no longer intrudes (*c. Jul.* 5.12): they are bound not 'by the voluptuous ties of their bodies but by the voluntary affections of their minds' (*nupt. et conc.* 1.12). He develops these views most especially in relation to Mary and Joseph, who were married even though there was no sexual relation between the partners. They are called husband and wife because, as he puts it, 'intercourse of the mind is more intimate than that of the body' (*c. Faust.* 23.8).[43]

THE STATUS OF WOMEN

The question of woman's status, both before and after the fall, is a vexed one, not least because Augustine himself is far from being consistent on this point; so much of what he says seems to be determined by ulterior factors which, though they often contradict his own independent thinking, are unthinkingly reiterated and allowed to influence his work, with no attempt to reconcile, or even articulate, the resulting contradictions. It therefore remains for us to invesigate just what factors were at play and what Augustine has to say in different contexts, noting the loose ends and irreconcilables as they arise.

The main theoretical distinction Augustine makes is between a woman's mind and body: in the mind, intellectually, woman is created, like man, in the image of God (*c. Faust.* 24.2; *Gn. litt.* 3.22.34; *trin.* 12.3.10). Here there is no sexual differentiation—this occurs only at a physical and social level—so that intellectually and morally, as Plato held, men and women are equal.[44] Nor are women, for Augustine, defective males in their physical bodies, lacking the male's vital energies, as many late antique thinkers believed.[45] In body too, they are equal to men. But this physical and intellectual equality does not mean that they are not inferior to men.

When speaking about women in any context other than the purely theoretical, which we have just outlined, the language of inferiority is insidious. Although Augustine will allow that inferiority is not natural (*natura*),

---

[43] Quoted by E. A. Clark (1986b), 139–62, who also refers to *cons. eu.* 2.1.2–3; *s.* 51.13.21.

[44] *Meno* 71E–3B; *Republic* 451D–7B, cited by Gould (1990), who also gives references for the same ideas in the Cappadocians, e.g. Basil, *The Creation of Man* 1.18. Cf. *conf.* 13.32.47 'In her mind, regarding intellectual understanding the woman possesses a nature equal to that of the man.'

[45] See Brown (1988), 10 where he observes that it was generally held that it was precisely the female's lack of vital heat which enabled the surpluses necessary to nurture and contain the male seed, and thus produce children, to build up. Women were therefore necessarily 'defective'. Augustine does not hold the views of his predecessors that at the resurrection women will be changed into men, *ciu.* 22.17–18.

it is now part of women's lot (*condicio*)[46] as helper and childbearer. Eve, the woman, was created for the sake of procreation, even in paradise (*Gn. litt.* 9.3.5; 9.5.9; *ciu.* 14.22).[47] If it had been God's intention to provide Adam with a companion, Augustine rather unfortunately, but self-evidently adds, then of course God would have created another man (*Gn. litt.* 9.5.9). Before the fall she was oriented towards the man through love, which knows no domination; after the fall she is subjected to him as a servant to her lord (*Gn. litt.* 11.37.50).[48] This was reinforced in Augustine's mind by Scripture and by the traditional customs and practices of his society—as Rist comments, 'an aura of (often symbolic) "inferiority" envelops the female, which takes different forms at different times'.[49]

A literal understanding of 'increase and multiply' would obviously lead to an understanding of woman as created for procreation, not to mention the fact that it was Eve who was taken in by the serpent and caused Adam's fall; whereas Eve was lacking in knowledge and was to be taught by Adam, *he* fell knowingly, through 'the good nature of a friend' (*amicali benevolentia*) (*Gn. litt.* 11.42.59). Paul's comments on women in the New Testament would do nothing to enhance their status: his injunction that they should be veiled in Church led readers such as Augustine to conclude that women could not physically be held to represent God's image (whereas men of course could)[50]—and so on, the scriptural passages are too numerous to reiterate.

Everyday experience of traditional social attitudes to women and the literature of classical paganism[51] would also do much to confirm Scripture's presentation of women in Augustine's mind: his hierarchical view of society carried over into the family or household (*domus*), which was virtually a State in miniature, its unity and harmony ensuring the well-being of the State. Here the rule of the *dominus*, usually the *paterfamilias*, was unquestioned—over wife, children, slaves, and any other members of the household, who were all, in Augustine's time, regarded as members of the *familia*. It was he who stood between, and mediated between, the household and the larger society in which the household had its place. In this

[46] See van Bavel (1989), 12 for these distinctions.

[47] Cf. Ambrose *De Paradiso* 10.47, who also comments, ' for the sake of human reproduction, woman had to be added to the man'.

[48] Cf. *exp. Gal.* where slaves are included.

[49] Rist (1994), 118. I am very much indebted to the excellent section 'Soul, Body and Personal Identity' for the following section.

[50] See Rist (1994), 117; van Bavel (1989), 20–9; Børresen (1990); Power (1995). It is important to appreciate that Augustine's interpretation is figurative, rather than literal (as some commentators have erroneously supposed).

[51] See E. A. Clark (1986a), 29–30 for references to classical authors and the Old Testament against women.

context marriage, and the subjection it entailed, was (at least until the advent of Christian asceticism) the only real option for women. They passed their lives under the authority or *potestas* of males—usually of a father or guardian, who would choose a marriage partner for her (the only grounds on which she could reject him was bad moral character). Although practices changed throughout the fourth century, it had traditionally been the case that, even when married, she usually remained very much a member of her original family, under the *potestas* of her father, and kept her maiden name. Her children, however, were legally under the *potestas* of her husband, and unless freed by Augustus' *ius liberorum* for having produced three or more children, she had no rights over them and could only act as their guardian after her husband's death if she did not remarry.

The woman's sphere was therefore the private one of the household; the man's, the public one of the city. The fathers tended to see this state of affairs, in which again women are implicity 'inferior', as divinely ordained: Ambrose traces it to Eve's original creation when he writes on Genesis 2: 21–22:

'God built (*aedificavit*) the rib he took from Adam into a woman.' 'He built', is well put in that verse where he was speaking of woman's creation, because the domestic edifice of man and woman seems to be rich in a certain kind of perfection. The man who is without a wife is accordingly considered to be without a home. Just as a man is thought to be more skilful at public duties, so a woman is thought more skilful in domestic services.[52]

FEMALE ASCETICISM

In general the fathers seem to suggest that a married woman's lot is a highly unenviable one. Long rhetorical descriptions of the trials of marriage—the *molestiae nuptiarum*—are a recurrent literary theme or *topos* in their works—especially on virginity. Indeed, it is an odd fact that we learn more about the fathers' attitude to marriage through treatises which urge the reader to adopt the celibate, ascetic life, than anywhere else. Here, they depict the appalling reality of married life (especially for women): the shame and sorrow of infertility, the discomforts of pregnancy, the risks of childbirth, worry about one's children, the sheer drudgery of childrearing and housework, problems with servants, family quarrels, the death of family members, abusive, violent, jealous husbands, constant worry about

---

[52] *On Paradise* 11.50, quoted by E. A. Clark (1983). Cf. Chrysostom *How to Choose a Wife*; *The Kind of Women Who Should be Taken as Wives*, 4; Tertullian *An Exhortation to Charity*, 12.

a husband's fidelity, his health and safety, and finally widowhood.[53] Marriage, in effect, becomes servitude. Prefacing a similar catalogue in his *On Virginity* (3) Gregory of Nyssa comments, 'If only, before experience comes, the results of experience could be learnt . . . then what a crowd of deserters would run from marriage into the virgin life.' Just how rhetorical such descriptions were and to what degree they were governed by the ulterior motive of literally frightening someone into the celibate life—especially among its most extreme advocates—is worth consideration. Augustine's description of his own mother's married life certainly rings true to such language: Monnica was the only wife in Thagaste not to bear the marks of blows from a violent husband because she accepted, and advised other women to accept, that the marriage contract was one which entailed slavery for the wife. Her practice had been to remain silent and not to argue with, or oppose her husband, but to explain herself quietly when the moment was opportune (*conf.* 9.9.19).

It is undeniable that the ascetic, virgin life, would appear an attractive option to married women, not just for its own sake, but as freeing them from the *molestiae nuptiarum* so vividly described by the fathers in this context. It offered their only chance of standing on an equal footing with educated men, of forming close friendships with men (e.g. Rufinus's companion, Melania and Jerome's companion, Paula), of exercising religious functions as deaconesses, of travelling on pilgrimage (like Egeria), or of establishing and living in a women's religious house. Virginity broke the bonds of subjection which fettered women as a result of Eve's sin and enabled them to become brides of Christ. Whether this was a deliberate protest against patriarchy, as some feminist critics might have us believe, is another matter.

ASCETIC MODELS

As we have already seen, language and imagery describing the trials and tribulations of marriage, intercourse, and the family, are the fathers' preferred way of exhorting virgins to embrace the ascetic life. However, they are also used, rather tellingly, in a very positive way, to describe the virgin or celibate state itself (e.g. *b. coniug.* 21; *uirg.* 2; 11; 48; 55).[54] Not only is the Church the Bride of Christ and Christ her Bridegroom, the virgin is Christ's wife and lover; He is her husband and unites Himself to her in a spiritual marriage bond. The spiritual fruits of this union are 'the offspring

---

[53] See Amand and Moons (1953); *uirg.* 5; E. A. Clark (1986a), 261 n. 140 for references to lists of *topoi* on this theme.

[54] Gregory of Nyssa *De Uirginitate*, 20; Jerome *Ep.* 22 to Eustochium.

of devotion', born of the spirit: 'If, therefore, you despise marriages of sons of men, from which to beget sons of men, love you with your whole heart Him, who is fair of form above the sons of men; you have leisure; your heart is free from marriage bonds. Gaze on the beauty of your lover . . .' (*b. coniug.* 55). In a letter to the virgin Eustochium Jerome goes so far as to refer to her mother as the 'mother-in-law of God' in virtue of Eustochium's marriage to Christ. The marriage is described in highly charged erotic language taken from the Song of Songs: Eustochium flies to Jesus her lover and united with him cries 'Many waters cannot quench love, neither can the floods drown it'.[55] Augustine's own *Rule* talks of a father and brothers; the father having power (*potestas*) and authority (*auctoritas regendi*) to rule (*reg.* 5.3; 6.3), to discipline and care for his sons (7.3), who must render him obedience (7.1). The relationships of the monastery, Augustine stresses, should take precedence over natural family relationships.[56]

The household and the life of the virgin ascetic also often overlapped in the case of a daughter (or even a son) who remained at home, under the protection of her father (who is in one text referred to as 'priest of the Most High'), to dedicate her life to virginity.[57] In this way, either as a solitary or in a larger community, scholars have frequently maintained, women freed themselves from the constraints of family and child-rearing and attained a significant degree of freedom and independence in a society largely under male control. But one might well ask just how much 'freedom' and 'independence' they did, in fact, gain, and how significant the fathers' use of marital, sexual, and familial imagery is. The very language and imagery which served to illustrate women's subjection is also used to describe the virginal state. How many of the negative overtones, of obedience, of being under *potestas*, of subjection and even slavery, are not carried over in describing the woman's relation to her new family, the Church, and her new spouse, Christ? Graham Gould notes the fathers' stress on the modesty, charm, and self-restraint of virgins, 'as though everyone needed reassuring that no departure from convention was intended'.[58] On the other hand, it might be asked how far their use of marital, sexual imagery to describe the highest calling of the Christian life reflects their positive appreciation of these institutions. Whatever the case, it is difficult to get behind conventional, traditional language when it is used of virginity, to evaluate just how much the

[55] *Letter* 22.41—quoted by E. A. Clark (1986a), 28–9.

[56] See e.g. *ep.* 243 to Laetus—on leaving his mother; *uirg.* 3, on Matt. 12: 48–50, 'who is my mother, brother, sister . . . ?'—which Augustine interprets as setting spiritual relationships above blood relationships. This obviously challenged traditional notions of *pietas*, or loyalty to ones family and ancestors, as Rousseau (1978), 109, observes in reference to Jerome. On such alternative models of asceticism see Elm (1994).

[57] On this subject see Amand and Moons (1953).   [58] Gould (1990), 9.

fathers' estimate of women was changed by their aquaintance with women who had adopted the virginal life.

AUGUSTINE'S RELATIONS WITH WOMEN

The concrete examples we have from Augustine's own life leave us with conflicting impressions: to a woman named Edicia, who desired to lead an ascetic life and who had tried to persuade her reluctant husband to take a vow of celibacy, he writes to caution and rebuke her for overzealous asceticism which has led her husband into adultery: he writes, 'he [your husband], ought not to have been cheated of the debt of your body before your wills were joined in that good that surpasses marital chastity (*ep.* 262.2)'. Furthermore, Edicia ought to have consulted him before giving away her clothes, gold, silver, and money; she should have sought his agreement to give alms and devote her possessions to the poor. In other words, a wife is subject to her husband, even in matters of asceticism. But as Gerald Bonner observes,[59] to other female correspondents such as the highborn Proba and Melania, the girl Florentina (*ep.* 266) and the religious Sapida (*ep.* 263) he displays great sensitivity: he 'treated his correspondents as intellectual equals and never shrank from theological exposition on the highest level because of the sex of his correspondent.'

As well as to Augustine's very positive teaching on marital friendship and fellowship, and his theological reflections on marriage as sacramental, which we have already discussed, Bonner also points to the influence of Augustine's mother and concubine as possible correctives to his seemingly negative estimate of women in other contexts, and especially in his rather radical interpretation of Genesis—that woman was created for procreation rather than as a companion. It is also noteworthy that Augustine attaches positive significance to Christ's birth of a woman (*diu. q.* 11)[60] and uses feminine, maternal imagery for God (*en. Ps.* 26.2.18). Perhaps most interestingly, he generally seems to have held that women were emotionally stronger than men. This is the reason he gives for the fact that Mary Magdalene was the first to see the risen Lord.[61] Unfortunately Augustine failed to develop this rather promising insight except in the context of sermons, where it is treated as a self-evident fact to rebuke and chastise the men of his congregation and to exhort them to emulate the integrity and chastity of their wives.[62]

---

[59] Bonner (1987b), 260. Van Bavel (1989), 8–9 for further examples.

[60] See Madec (1989), 197 for other references.

[61] Rist (1994), 119 and note 84 where he refers to *Sermo Guelf.* 14.1 = 229L.1; 45.5; 51.3; 232.2; 245.2; *trin.* 4.3.6; *Io. eu. tr.* 121.1.

[62] *s.* 392.4.4–5.5; 132.2.2; 280.1.1—quoted by van Bavel (1989), 16–17.

We are thus left with tantalizing hints of a more positive theology of women, and isolated instances of equal treatment of men and woman, against a background largely determined by negative scriptural and social understandings. There are at least two other factors which must be considered, one of personal temperament and the other of theological reflection, which may also go some way to explaining Augustine's failure to paint a more balanced picture of women.

In considering why Augustine failed to develop what she terms a 'companionate' (what we have referred to above as marriage characterized by friendship and fellowship) rather than a predominantly sexual understanding of marriage, Elizabeth Clark suggests that as well as Augustine's general estimate of woman's secondary status, the absence of a close circle of female friends such as Jerome and Chrysostom enjoyed[63] (his mother and concubine being uneducated and unable to meet him at an intellectual level), were also significant.[64] In a similar vein Gerald Bonner laments Augustine's lack of sensitivity, demonstrated in the absence of any appreciation of *feminine*, as opposed to female, qualities in women[65] and suggests that in later life, Augustine probably found such satisfaction in male friendships, in the male community and environment of the monastery—the episcopal 'familia' (he certainly uses familial language to describe it)—that he tended to undervalue relationships with women.[66]

SEXUALITY AND CONCUPISCENCE

The second factor is more theological: although Augustine develops a predominantly sexual understanding of marriage, rather than the companionate, sacramental understanding we have noted above, he still fails to satisfactorily consider the place of sex in marriage and the affective bonds of the partners at a sexual level, whether in Paradise, this life, or the life to come. Rist maintains that if he had, and there are features of his work which lead in this direction, he could have developed a sophisticated account of the sexualized person which would have entailed a far more sensitive appreciation of the feminine and the female. For example, the mutual affection, which we have seen in some contexts he makes the essence of marriage, is, Rist points out,[67] a condition of the soul and could therefore have led to an increased appreciation of femininity, or for that matter, masculinity, but Augustine fails to develop this. Similarly, his

---

[63] Though the latter is exceptionally positive and deeply perceptive in what he has to say about the married life, and at times closely parallels Augustine in his ideas (see e.g. Roth 1986), the former's female friends do not seem to have had any significant effect on his estimate of marriage. [64] E. A. Clark (1986b).

[65] Bonner (1987) I, 263. [66] Rist (1994), 271. [67] Ibid. 115.

assertion at the end of *City of God* (22, 17) that in the resurrected body sexual differences will remain leaves open the question as to why there should be sexual differentiation, which Augustine held was only at the bodily level, given that procreation is no longer necessary. What the relation between the soul—which cares for and fosters the body—is with a male and female body, in Heaven, or for that matter elsewhere, is also left unexamined.[68]

His treatment of sexual concupiscence, or lust, might also, Rist convincingly maintains, have led to a more developed understanding of the sexualized person, and therefore of women. Augustine maintains that before the fall sexual activity was controlled by reason, or the will, and was untroubled by carnal passions (*Gn. litt.* 9.3.6; *ciu.* 14.26; *pecc. mer.* 2.22); there was no *libido* or *concupiscentia* (the two are used synonymously in this context)—or at least, if present (as he later concedes to Julian), they operated in order and obedience (*nupt. et conc.* 2.35.59),[69] entirely under the control of the will and solely for the purposes of procreation. The genital organs would be like any other bodily organ, operating directly in obedience to the will (*Gn. litt.* 9.10.18; *ciu.* 14.24). As Augustine puts it in *City of God,*

between the marriage partners there was a trusting community springing from chaste love; there was a peaceful alertness of mind and body and an easy keeping of the commandment. In such an easy situation, in such human happiness, we are far from suspecting that it was impossible for offspring to be begotten without the malady of lust. Rather, those bodily parts could have been moved by the same command of the will as the other members are (*ciu.* 14.26).

After man's fall, however, lust, or concupiscence, is the punishment for his disobedence: the will is no longer in control and concupiscence works in the act of intercourse in disorder and disobedience, characterized by violent and irrational carnal feeling (*nupt. et conc.* 1.24.27).[70]

The Pelagians, and especially Julian of Eclanum, forced Augustine to rehearse these ideas incessantly in order to refute their belief that there was no difference between the sexual act before and after the fall. For Augustine, marriage and intercourse are now different, not in nature, but in quality, because of the 'illness' of concupiscence which characterizes man's life after the fall (*nupt. et conc.* 1.6.7; 8.9; 2.22.37). In only one passage (which is unfortunately rather difficult to date), Augustine distinguishes

---

[68] Rist (1994), 119–20.

[69] Rather than in disobedience and disorder as after the fall. The same ideas are reiterated in *c. Iul.* and *c. Iul. imp.*

[70] Although Augustine thinks of desire, or concupiscence, as operating in the same way in males and females, he does suggest that it has different effects: females are generally more vulnerable to their desires and especially to how they look; males are more vulnerable to anger and the desire to dominate others.

between the concupiscence which is an inevitable result of the fall—
concupiscentia carnis—and the concupiscence, or desire, which is present
in marriage—*concupiscentia nuptiarum*, which includes desire for conjugal
chastity, the desire to have children, and desire for a common life (*concu-
piscentiam vinculi socialis*).[71] But while it can be used positively in other contexts, in the context of sexual intercourse after the fall, concupiscence is
otherwise invariably used pejoratively. But Rist's point is that while Augustine can maintain that concupiscence derives from the mind or soul, not
the body, and is thus aware of the importance of eroticism, he fails to
develop these insights, as he might well have done, to give 'a more sophisticated account of the sexualized person', of the affective bonds between
partners at a sexual level, and which would have included a more sensitive
treatment of women and femininity.[72] Although he shares the standard
philosophical assumption that there is no sexual differentiation at the level
of reason (thereby raising the interesting possibility of talk in terms of
'human', rather than male or female, beings), we are still left to wonder
what the importance of sexual differentiation was in Paradise and why it
was the chosen means of procreation; what the importance of sexual differentiation is in Heaven, where there will be no procreation; what is the
significance and implications of sexual differentiation at the level of mind
or reason, as well as body.

ASCETICISM AND MONASTICISM

However, as we have seen, Augustine himself chose not to pursue this ideal
of marriage, in friendly fellowship and oneness of mind and heart, but
rather regarded celibacy—later monasticism—as the only possible form his
conversion to Christianity could take. In order to appreciate his choice,
which was by no means an obligatory one in order to embrace Christianity, elements of Augustine's philosophical, religious, and social background
need to be considered.

Augustine would have been long acquainted with classical, philosophical notions of withdrawal (*otium*) from the world, of the 'inclination to
retirement',[73] asceticism and celibacy as intrinsic to the true philosopher's
search for truth. They seem to lie behind the account in *Confessions* 4. 14.

---

[71] *ep. 6*.5 (BA 46B).* It probably dates to *c.* AD 420–1. (Augustine does concede, in other
places, that there may have been libido in Paradise, but of a different sort to the one we now
know, e.g. *c. ep. pel.* 1.34 (i.e. against the Pelagians, here, rather than the Manichees). Note
also *Gn. litt.* 3.21.33 where Augustine writes of generation occuring 'solo piae caritatis
adfectu' rather than by concupiscence.

[72] Rist (1994), 119–20 who refers to Fredriksen (1988). See also Markus (1994a) XIX, 922–3
for similar reflections.   [73] Analysed by Festugière (1954), lecture 4.

24 of his first attempt to set up a community in 386, in Milan, with a group of friends, 'remoti a turbis otiose vivere'—to live a life of contemplation apart from the crowds. They planned to hold everything in common, to live in one household, as friends, and to appoint two men, chosen like magistrates for one year, to undertake practical, administrative responsibilities. The plan fell at the first hurdle, with the problem of wives and fiancées, but the passage is important as providing a first sounding of ideals—common life, friendship—which never disappear in Augustine's work and find their fullest outworking in the communities at Hippo.

Meanwhile, the philosophical ideals we have mentioned would have been brought to sharp focus for Augustine by his reading of the 'books of the Platonists', and especially Plotinus, which were so instrumental in his conversion in 386. Indeed, the influence of the Neoplatonists was so great in this respect that although scholars generally disagree with Alfaric's famous assertion that Augustine was converted to Neoplatonism rather than Christianity,[74] some still concede that his understanding of Christianity was so highly coloured by the revolution which Neoplatonism had recently effected in his thought that the retreat which he undertook immediately after his conversion, and prior to baptism, at Cassiciacum, was in social, organizational, ascetic terms, primarily a philosophical one— albeit a Christian philosophy—rather than a first example of a Christian community which was to find its final outworking in the monastery at Hippo. (There is no evidence, at this stage, of a rule, a pattern of communal prayer, of manual labour or of the authority structure so characteristic of Christian monasticism.) We cannot enter into an examination of Augustine's life and work at Cassiciacum here. It can, of course, easily be made to conform to the long-established practice of philosophical retreat and simply be seen as a realization of the earlier, failed attempt at communal living mentioned in *Confessions* 6, but the unwillingness which scholars such as Halliburton[75] and Folliet[76] demonstrate in refusing to allow even an embryonic monastic community, or what Lawless describes as a 'monastic impulse', at Cassiciacum, is curious, especially when one takes into account the striking similarities between the precepts or rules for attaining the happy life in *De Ordine*, one of the works written at Cassiciacum, and those of the *Rule*.[77]

More important still is the significant role Augustine assigns in his conversion to what he surprisingly acknowledges was his first encounter with Christian monasticism in his conversation with Ponticianus in Book 8 of

---

[74] Alfaric (1918), 380–1.   [75] Halliburton (1962), 339.

[76] Folliet (1961), 35–6 and note 46 citing Courcelle and Marrou.

[77] Verheijen (1980), 239 observes that 24 of the precepts in *De Ordine* 2.8.25–19.51 anticipate the precepts for the common life in the *Regula*.

the *Confessions*. Ponticianus, a high-ranking official and fellow-African, paid him a surprise visit in Milan. Amazed to find that Augustine was reading St Paul, and already a Christian himself, Ponticianus began to talk about the story of Antony, the most well-known and influential Eastern ascetic, and was even more amazed that Augustine and Alypius had not heard of him. After mentioning the Christian monastery on the outskirts of the very city in which they stood, under the care of Ambrose, of which they were also ignorant, he went on to recount a related story which involved himself and three other friends while they were in the service of the Emperor at Trier: they had some time free and went for a walk in the gardens adjacent to the walls. They divided into pairs and the other pair happened upon a dwelling occupied by monks ('servants' of God). There they read the life of Antony and such was the effect of their reading that they were converted on the spot, deciding to 'serve God'—in other words, become monks, too. (When their wives later heard of this, they also dedicated their virginity to God.) Augustine took Ponticianus' words to heart; they gave him an appalling vision of his own vileness from which he could not escape except by heeding them and suffering their judgement upon his own situation. The subsequent passages recount Augustine's attempt to embrace the celibate, ascetic life, and are followed by the famous conversion scene. The importance of this passage cannot, I think, be underestimated in any evaluation of Augustine's subsequent attempts to live a Christian life in the world—least of all at Cassiciacum when he would still be feeling the full force of its impact. To suggest that it was a purely philosophical retreat and that Augustine's asceticism was entirely philosophical at this stage is to willfully ignore it, even though the Cassiciacum works betray little of the later, formal structures of Christian monasticism.

CHRISTIAN MONASTICISM

Augustine was to learn much more of this type of monasticism in the following year. He had planned to return to Thagaste with his mother and friends to carry out their 'holy enterprise' (*placitum sanctum*) (*conf.* 9.9.2)—presumably the establishing of a community there—but they were prevented, first of all by Monnica's death at the seaport of Ostia in 387, and then by a blockade of the Mediterranean due to Emperor Maximus's invasion of Italy and his defeat of the young Emperor Valentinian. Augustine spent this year in Rome, which we have already had cause to note was very much at the centre of strong ascetic movements and debates in the 380s and 390s. Athanasius had spent seven years in Rome, from 339, during his second exile. Peter, his successor and brother, had also stayed in Rome after

Athanasius' death, from 373 to 378. Jerome had been in Rome from 382 to 385. Evagrius of Antioch had translated the *Life of Antony* into Latin *c.* 370.[78] Through these channels, and many others which are impossible to trace (as one might expect with a popular and not just a literary movement) Eastern monasticism influenced the emerging monastic movements of the West.

In Rome, therefore, Augustine was able to visit a number of monasteries[79] and learn more about Eastern asceticism. He records his impressions in *On the Morals of the Catholic Church and the Manichees*, written against Manichaean ascetic practices: 'For who does not know that the multitude of Christian men of perfect continence is daily speading farther and farther, throughout the entire world, and especially in the East and in Egypt' (*mor.* 1.65). He describes with admiration the organization of the monasteries, both in Rome and the one Ponticianus mentioned in Milan as well as the practices of Eastern asceticism in general: of manual labour (which he regards as an Eastern tradition), the common life and sharing of possessions, chastity, the rule of the 'father' who cares for his 'sons'. He mentions female communities, widows and virgins living together, who support their common life by spinning and weaving, and he defends the anchoritic life from criticism whilst admitting that its rigours put it beyond the reach of the average man. How much of all this comes from direct experience and conversations with others, and how much is an idealized description taken over from Jerome is debatable[80]—but what matters for our purposes is Augustine's growing awareness of forms of Christian communal life which will inform the community at Thagaste (and therefore confirm it, in our eyes, as at least monastic in character, if not in name) and which will later be included in his *Rule*.

AUGUSTINE'S PATH TO MONASTICISM

Augustine was able to return to North Africa, to his native town of Thagaste, in 388, to the family house and land he had inherited there. Here he established the community of *serui dei*, or servants of God, which he had intended to set up the year before. Just what sort of community was this? The words Augustine uses to describe it should not mislead us: *seruus dei*, or *deo seruiens* have a wide range of meaning, from a devout layman who

---

[78] See Lawless (1987), 41 f. for these and further examples.

[79] See Zumkeller (1986), 22 note 109 for bibliography on Roman monasteries at this time, especially Lorenz (1966).

[80] Verheijen (1979), 40–2 suggests it is taken from Jerome's *Letter* 22.35 whereas Lawless (1987), 42 thinks this claim 'strains the existing evidence'.

simply serves God to a monk. His failure to use the technical terms *monasterium* and *monachus* is neither here nor there—they are translations from the Greek and, being relatively new in the West, both as words and phenomena (the former only began to be used *c.* 370) took time to become established. There are certainly occasions when Augustine is referring to individuals or groups which are obviously monastic but fails to use them: we have seen this already in the passage from *Confessions* 8 referred to above and it is also the case throughout *On the Morals of the Catholic Church* when he is referring to Eastern monasticism or the monastery at Milan.

The diversity of monastic forms in the West, from house asceticism and house communities, to anchorites, wandering monks, and coenobitic monasteries,[81] together with the thin line between ascetic and monk in the fourth century in the West,[82] also adds to the confusion. We must look beyond terminological distinctions to establish the character of the community at Thagaste. For this, we might do well to examine the account of Possidius (Augustine's first biographer and a contemporary) in his *Life*: 'He had abandoned all worldly cares, and served God with those who were with him, in fasting, praying, and good works, while day and night he meditated upon the law of the Lord, passing along in what he wrote whatever God had revealed to him in study and prayer' (*vita* 3).

At Thagaste Augustine wrote the dialogue *The Teacher*, *83 Diverse Questions* (many of which are responses to questions asked by his fellow *serui dei*), finished *On the Morals*, and wrote *On True Religion*, *On Genesis Against the Manichees* and *On Music*, all works (with the exception perhaps of *The Teacher*) which evidence his emerging preoccupation with distinctively Christian concerns—Scripture, the Church, faith, incarnation. It is therefore odd to find that Folliet[83] and Halliburton[84] persist in seeing Thagaste as a philosophical retreat, in which Augustine was primarily concerned with philosophical questions. Possidius' description, Augustine's avowed intention, the subject matter of the works written there, and the fact that Augustine would later take 'brothers' from there to the lay monastery at Hippo (*ep.* 31 and 33.2) and that the community continued as a religious one even after he had left, all militate against this conclusion. Indeed, Augustine went on his fateful journey to Hippo in 391 to see someone who he thought might be persuaded to join the community at Thagaste and to examine possibilities for the site of a new monastery (*s.* 355.2). Instead,

---

[81] see Lorenz (1966) on these various forms.

[82] see Lienhard (1977), introduction, on this transition.

[83] (1961), 38 'La demeure d'Augustin ressemble plus à une maison de philosophes, de lettrés, qu'a une monastère.'

[84] (1962), 339 who, like Folliet, argues from the absence of the use of the word *monasterium*.

although he reports that he had been careful to avoid places which had a vacant episcopal see, for fear of being commandeered into the post (which was not at all unusual), he was seized by the congregation in the basilica at Hippo and immediately ordained priest and successor to the ageing bishop Valerius of Hippo. Augustine's response was to ask for time to study the Scriptures and to be allowed to continue his monastic life as a priest. Valerius granted both of these requests and provided a plot of land in the garden of the basilica where the monastery could be built. Thus, Augustine began life in community at Hippo and adopted the way of life in which he was to remain until his death.

THE *RULE*

It is through Augustine's *Rule* that we get our clearest picture of this community. I do not, however, wish to enter here into the complicated questions of philology and textual criticism concerning the different versions and exact date of the Rule[85] but accept Verheijen's conclusions that only the male version of the Rule (*Praeceptum*), written around 395/6, can with certainty be attributed to Augustine and that this was probably soon after re-edited in a form for nuns (*Regularis informatio*) in the convent where Augustine's own sister was superior.

Possidius strikes a new note in describing the Garden monastery when he alludes to Acts 4: 32, 35, 'all things must be held in common, and there was given to everyone as he had need' (*vita* 5). Augustine explicitly confirms this modelling of the monastic life at Hippo on the first Christian communities of Acts at the beginning of the Rule, when he writes, 'The first object of our common life is to live together in unity, and to have "one heart and soul" directed towards God' (*reg.* 1.2). The use of this text is not at all uncommon in other monastic writings before Augustine;[86] most monastic communities would base themselves on it in some form or another,[87] but for Augustine, as is evident in his use of it throughout his works, it becomes central and informs every other aspect of the monastic life in a way which is absolutely distinctive and which makes the monastic community intrinsic to the unity of the Church as a whole.[88] It is present

---

[85] For this see the definitive work of Verheijen, especially (1967); Zumkeller (1986), 283–300 contains a useful summary of research and bibliography on this question; Lawless (1987).

[86] See Zumkeller (1986), 36 and notes 106–9 for references and Verheijen's (1975) discussion of this text where he traces possible sources for its use in Jerome *Letter* 22.35 (albeit by oral account) and Paulinus of Nola *Ep.* 30.3 (which he believes brought the community implications of the text to Augustine's attention).   [87] Van Bavel (1975), 87.

[88] Verheijen (1979) for Augustine's use of Acts 4: 32–35, where he traces a gradual use of the whole text, concluding, 'one can read the whole monastic history of Saint Augustine and of those around him in this gradual increase of the use of the Acts of the Apostles.' (80).

in his famous definition of the monk in the *Enarrationes in Psalmos* (132.6; cf. *en. Ps.* 131.4; 132. 10.), 'Those who live in unity in such a way that they form but one person are rightly called "monos", one single person [in contrast to *monachos*, the solitary]. They make true to life what is written, "of one mind and one heart", (Acts 4: 32) that is, many bodies but not many minds, many bodies but not many hearts.'

The emphasis upon oneness through charity informs all the precepts for communal living in the *Rule* and in the closing prayer is explicit given as the spirit in which the precepts are to be carried out. Indeed, as many scholars have noted, the Augustinian *Rule* is characterized by its emphasis upon the motivation for an action—why something is done, what is going on within—rather than on laying down regulations to be observed. Augustine's main aim is embodied in his quotation of 1 Cor. 13: 5 in Chapter 5 of the *Rule* which says of love that 'it is not self-seeking'. It is love which puts the interests of the community before personal interests which is to be the goal of the individual monk: 'The degree to which you are concerned for the interests of the community, rather than your own, is the criterion by which you can judge how much progress you have made' (5.2). This is, of course, a classical idea which Augustine first mentions in *On Free Will* (1.6.14) using classical terminology (*publicus, privatus*). Here the same ideas are expressed with a more markedly Christian colouring derived from their use in Acts 4: 32–35, which speaks of that which is one's own (*proprius*) and that which is in common (*communis*).[89] Putting the good of others before oneself means, on a practical level, the acknowledgement that community does not mean uniformity: concessions must be made to individuals within the community in view of their social background; slaves, peasants, and manual labourers would probably enjoy a better life within the monastery than they had in the world; those accustomed to a more luxurious life-style, Augustine allows, may need different food and bedding—at least for a while (3.3–5). The sick, too, are to be believed and provided with everything they need, for example, special food or visits to the baths (5.6–7).[90] Although everyone was expected to sell their possessions and give them to the poor or the monastery, where everything was held in common and clothes kept in a common store, provisions were to be made, and clothes distributed, according to individual need (5.1). Gifts, too, were to be given to the superior and likewise passed on to those in need of them (5.3). Relations within the community were likewise to be characterized by selfless mutual service and regard. The superior, or *praepositus*, is not, for Augustine, the same figure as

---

[89] Verheijen (1974), 5–9 (and esp. 8–9); (1984), 97–100; Madec (1994), paper 13: 'Le communisme spirituel'.

[90] These precepts for mutual tolerance and help are closely paralleled and prefigured in *diu. qu.* 71, which probably represents Augustine's response to questions asked by members of the community at Hippo.

the Eastern *abba*, placed above the community and concerned with spiritual direction, rather, he is, literally, one put forward from within the community, who does not stand above it, but remains part of it, to serve it in everyday administration. He is superior because of the esteem in which he is held, but the least of all the brethren because of his responsibility to God (7.3). Much space is given to dealing with an erring brother who, Augustine urges, must not be ignored but gently warned, and if he persists in his sin, treated with the compassion due to a sick person by referring his illness to one or two others who should try to convince him of his state. If this does not work, the situation should be brought to the attention of the superior and if he cannot convince him to mend his ways, he should be sent from the community, not through heartlessness, but through love, so that his sickness does not spread and cause others to fall: one must act 'always with love for the offender but with aversion for their faults' (4.10). In the same spirit, the monks must render each other mutual service without grumbling or delay (5.9), refrain from quarrelling (6.1), and be ready to apologise and forgive (6.2).[91]

THE LAY AND CLERICAL MONASTERIES AT HIPPO

It is from the Rule that we learn most about the character of the first lay monastery in the Garden of the Basilica at Hippo which Augustine founded in 391. Sermons and letters fill in the accidental details of daily life, the lay-out of the monastery, the offices, manual work, and so on, but these need not concern us here.[92] What is of interest is the establishing of another monastery specifically for clergy in the bishop's house, following Augustine's consecration as Bishop of Hippo in 396, in succession to Valerius. In a later sermon he explains: 'I saw that a bishop had to show constant courtesy to all those who came or went . . . Yet if this practice should be allowed in a monastery, it would not be fitting. On this account I wanted to have a monastery of clerics in my bishop's house' (*s.* 355.2).

The only precedent for such an arrangement in the West is the clerical community established by Bishop Eusebius of Vercelli following his return from exile in the East in *c.* 363, for his cathedral church, a fact Ambrose mentions,[93] but of which Augustine may have been ignorant. Indeed, it is difficult to know exactly which models, if any, Augustine would have in

---

[91] See Madec (1994), XIII 'Le communisme spirituel' for illuminating comments in this respect.　　　　　[92] Zumkeller (1986), 35–40.

[93] Lienhard (1977), 90 cites Ambrose's *ep.* 63, where Ambrose observes that Eusebius was the first bishop in the West to join 'monasterii continentia' with 'ecclesiae disciplina'.

mind in establishing and organizing the lay and clerical monasteries at Hippo.

Throughout the Christian Empire, and especially when persecution came to an end with the conversion of the Emperor Constantine, asceticism was linked with, and often expressed in terms of, or held to replace, martyrdom—the martyrs had been the Christian élite, those who had denied the world and battled with the forces of evil. Celibacy, asceticism, and the common life were later viewed within the same frame and motivated by the same ideals.[94]

African theologians, such as Tertullian and Cyprian, foreshadow Augustine's emphasis on Acts 4: 32–35 and the oneness of charity expressed in the holding of goods in common in a life in community, when they speak of Christian perfection.[95] They, and numerous witnesses before them, provide evidence for the long-standing practice of chastity in the African Church, by women (*uirgines*) and men (*spadones, continentes*), and also clergy.[96] We learn more about this from Acts of the Councils of Carthage and Hippo, and the Theodosian Code, where we find, for example, regulations for the age of admission to the ranks of consecrated virgins,[97] regulations for house asceticism,[98] and laws against the cohabitation of continents and virgins.[99]

We have already had occasion to touch on the life of consecrated virgins[100] earlier in this chapter. Here we might mention one other phenomenon of early Christian asceticism, that of wealthy, noble Christian converts or *conversi*—often women—who, because of their family or public responsibilities, were unable to enter communities but instead undertook to live an ascetic life in the world and to give up as many worldly goods as possible. Many came from old senatorial families, with enormous estates, which were used to benefit the Church. As Ladner observes, 'Melanias and Marcellas, Paulas and Paulinas, Blesillas and Eustochiums and Demetrias and Pammachius, Pinianus, Ponticianus, Romanianus, and Marcellinus and many others became models of an inner reform of Christian society, though some of them retained permanently, others for a long time, a non-monastic way of life'.[101] Augustine met or corresponded with a good number of such *conversi* and the Church at Hippo benefited from their bequests.[102]

---

[94] See Malone (1950), referred to by Markus (1990), Ch. 4 which is itself very interesting on this subject.

[95] Tertullian *Apologeticum* 39; Cyprian *De opere et eleemosynis* 7; 25—both cited by Folliet (1961), 26.   [96] Folliet (1961), 27 f.

[97] Council of Hippo AD 393, Mansi 3, 919—Folliet (1961), 32 n. 36.

[98] Ibid.   [99] *Cod. Theod.* 370, Folliet (1961), 31 n. 33.

[100] Whom Augustine also refers to as *uirgines Christi* (*serm.* 355.2) or *sanctimoniales* (*ep.* 254.1).

[101] Ladner (1959), 371.   [102] See Ch. 4, 140 on Melania and Pinianus.

As far as organized female asceticism was concerned, we have noted the common practice of house asceticism where a consecrated virgin would live in her family house, guarded by her father or another male guardian, and also the practice of groups of virgins, living a common life together and supporting themselves by spinning and weaving. Often, too, they lived in the house of, or under the patronage of, a wealthy convert. How much these resembled later convents it is difficult to tell. Augustine established a convent at about the same time as his clerical monastery, in Hippo, with his widowed sister as its Mother (it also included a number of his nieces and female cousins) and a priest to provide spiritual direction (*ep.* 210).

There is, however, no early evidence for communities of men, or *continentes*, though Folliet does not wish to rule out the possibility.[103] We have seen that Western monasticism, in terms of communities of monks, was a relatively recent phenomenon, dating back only to the last third of the fourth century. From this period, Augustine had first-hand knowledge of the community outside the walls of Milan under Ambrose,[104] of various houses, for men and women, in Rome, and would have some knowledge of the monasteries established by St Jerome in the Holy Land through the correspondence with him begun while he was still a priest and from Alypius's visit to Jerome in Bethlehem.

A letter from Paulinus of Nola (who was to establish his own monastery at Nola in 395[105]) to Alypius (*ep.* 24), testifies that as early as 394 there were monasteries in Hippo and Carthage, as well as in Thagaste, alongside those founded by Augustine. According to Pope Siricius, there were monasteries in Spain in 385, and there is evidence for a chain of monasteries in Gaul in this period: Augustine would later read Sulpicius Severus' *Life of St Martin*[106] (written *c.* 400) where Martin's enthusiasm for the monastic life is recounted in his founding of a number of communities, including the one outside Tours, in 373, while he was bishop there, and Hilary's founding of a monastery in Poitiers in 360 is mentioned. He would also correspond and build up a close friendship with that other monk-bishop, Paulinus.

Indeed, the elevation of individuals like Martin, Augustine, and Paulinus, who had previously been monks, to the status of bishop, and their subsequent founding of a clerical monastery to enable them to continue their monastic life, is a notable feature of Western monasticism during this period and explains some of its distinctive characteristics—the 'monas-

---

[103] (1961), 34.

[104] Ambrose's influence in this respect, and his writings on virginity should not be underestimated—see Ramsay (1997).

[105] See Lienhard (1977) for a detailed treatment of this which illuminates the nature of Western monasticism in general.   [106] Lorenz (1966), 38 n. 6.

ticization of the clergy', its orientation towards the city,[107] involvement in public affairs, and emphasis on study and writing rather than manual labour.[108] The figure of the monk-bishop had, of course, a forerunner in the East, in the figure of Basil of Caesarea, and although his *Rules* were probably not known to his Western counterparts[109] the similiarities, especially in respect of Basil's primary emphasis upon common life and charity, rather than asceticism, are striking.

Augustine's clerical community presumably included all the clergy in Hippo (*s.* 355 suggests that if a priest is not prepared to live the common life he is prohibited from orders[110]). As pastoral activity replaced manual labour, its costs were met from ecclesiastical lands (which Augustine would have preferred to dispose of but was not allowed to (*ep.* 125.2; 126.9. *uita* 23)) and donations from the faithful. The clerical monastery continued alongside the lay monastery in the Garden and became, as we have seen in the previous chapter, very much a seminary for training priests and seedbed for future bishops. Possidius records that it provided ten men for vacant episcopal sees (*uita* 11) during Augustine's lifetime, and others from its members founded more monasteries in North Africa, and so its influence spread.

CLERICAL CELIBACY

As we have noted above, the origins of clerical celibacy can be traced well before the 'monasticization of the clergy' and the founding of clerical monasteries in the West. It was observed by many clergy from an early date, not because it was a law but because it was commonly regarded and widely practised by lay men and women, as well as clergy, as an ideal of Christian perfection.[111] We have already noted the martyr ideology which informs this type of Christian asceticism. Christianity's austere sexual morality, which rejected divorce, disapproved of remarriage and of intermarriage with pagans, and increasingly expected celibacy in its clergy, Peter Brown suggests is also partly due to its consciousness of lacking other clear

---

[107] Markus (1990),160.

[108] For parallel movements in the East see Rousseau (1971), 380–419 (though I am inclined to disagree with his analysis of the concept of 'authority' in the West).

[109] Lawless (1987), 42, following Kelly *Jerome* (1975), 228, 280–1, assigns the Latin adaptation of Basil's *Rules* by Rufinus of Aquileia to the years 397–400. Brown 1972, 196 n. 7 refers to 'the general reception of oriental monastic traditions in the late fourth century, made available in the translations of Rufinus'.

[110] *adult. coniug.* 2.20.22 suggests that celibacy was imposed on all African clergy.

[111] See e.g. Tertullian *De exhortatione castitatis* 13.4; Pontius *Vita Caecilii Cypriani* 2—Folliet (1961), 29.

markers, such as the dietary laws and circumcision of Judaism, to set it apart from the pagan world: 'In the very centuries when the rabbinate rose to prominence in Judaism by accepting marriage as a near-compulsory criterion of the wise', he writes, 'the leaders of the Christian communities moved in the diametrically opposite direction: access to leadership became identified with near compulsory celibacy.'[112]

For clergy, this was often a 'post-marital' celibacy, undertaken in middle-age, after having children, and therefore not as dramatic as Jerome's life-long virginity. The Council of Elvira (*c.* 303) ruled that 'bishops, priests, deacons and all members of the clergy connected with the liturgy must abstain from their wives and must not beget sons'.[113] That the situation was the same in the 380s is reflected in Ambrose's wish that clergymen should 'have had sons, and not continue to make sons'.[114] Augustine's founding of a clerical monastery in effect reversed the process of making monks priests, but rather made priests monks, thereby ensuring that clerical celibacy was indeed a life-long vocation. It is in this context that one should read the precepts of the *Rule* forbidding women in the monastery and advising on behaviour towards them when they are encountered.

VIRGINITY AND MARRIAGE: ONENESS OF MIND AND HEART

But it is important to examine Augustine's understanding of exactly what celibacy or virginity entails. He is far from assuming that it is simply a matter of an uncorrupt body. As one might expect it is much more a matter of an uncorrupt mind, a heart single-mindedly devoted to God and undistracted by any worldly attachments (*uirg.* 2.2; 11.11),[115] which might apply to all Christians who have an integrity of faith, hope, and love (*uirginitas fidei*[116]). Nor is it something which the individual attains, rather, it is a grace which

---

[112] Veyne (1987), 266.

[113] *Canon* 33, ed. Jonkers, 12–13—quoted by Brown (1988), 203.

[114] *De officiis* 1.50.258: 105A cited by Brown (1988), 357—see 357–8 on developing ideas of clerical celibacy.

[115] Augustine distinguishes between *uirginitas carnis, uirginitas in carne, uirginitas corporis* and *uirginitas cordis, uirginitas in corde, uirginitas mentis*.

[116] *en. Ps.* 90.2.9; *s.* 93.3.4; 213.7—cited by Zumkeller (1986), 241. This is also present in the Eastern tradition, e.g. Gregory of Nyssa (*On virginity*) who also describes virginity as single-ness of mind and heart, and Chrysostom who, as so often, resembles Augustine when he writes: 'virginity does not simply mean sexual abstinence. She who is anxious about worldly affairs is not really a virgin. In fact, he [that is, Christ] says that this is the chief difference between a wife and a virgin. He does not mention marriage or abstinence, but attachment as opposed to detachment from worldly cares' (*Homily 19 on I Cor. 7*—Roth and Anderson (1986), 41).

he receives.[117] Augustine's examination of his attempt to achieve *continentia* in *Confessions* 10, in terms of the various temptations which hinder its attainment, listed in 1 John 2: 16 as the lust of the flesh, the lust of the eyes, and the pride of life—together with his opening plea to God which would so incense Pelagius, to 'grant what thou dost command and command what thou wilt'—is a good example of this broader understanding.

What is revealing in Augustine's understanding of the celibate life, or virginity, is that it evidently evolved along much the same lines as his reflection on marriage: from the proposed, but never realized community of friends at Thagaste (386—*Conf.* 6,14,24), to the Christian reading party-cum-philosophical retreat of Cassiciacum (386), through the common life of the lay *serui Dei* at Thagaste (388) to the lay and then clerical monastery at Hippo (391; 395/6), his idea of the celibate life was invariably of one lived in *community*, with friends, or later, with individuals who sought a common life: to be, again in the words of Acts 4: 32, 'of one heart and mind' in loving fellowship and by sharing of goods. It is as if he sought a temporal alternative to the post-lapsarian, vitiated ideal of the married, social life of paradise, in monastic life in the world, which he saw as the closest approximation to it man could now hope to achieve. This was not simply because the monastic life was distinguished by celibacy and therefore avoided sexual concupiscence and the perpetuation of original sin through procreation. Concupiscence had a much wider range of reference in Augustine's thought than the purely sexual, and was, as we shall see below, just as likely to be at work in the monastery as in the home. Rather, Augustine saw in the attempt of the monks to live a harmonious common life 'intent upon God in oneness of mind and heart' the true antidote to fallen man's self-referential pride, and his best chance of retrieving what was destroyed in the married relationship of Adam and Eve after the fall, that is, the centring of the relationship upon God rather than upon themselves. This suggestion is borne out in reading Augustine's *Rule*. Its primary concern, as we have seen, is not so much with asceticism, the attainment of holiness or perfection, as in the East, or, indeed, with celibacy. Its main concern is with the social aspect of life lived in common and the moral, ethical aspects of such a life. His ideal of the monastic life, like that of marriage, is of one characterized by unity and *concordia or harmony*, which, like the harmony between a married couple, makes it the basis of harmonious life in the Church, the city—God's heavenly city (*en. Ps.* 105.34), and thereby of the State—God's *res publica* (*op. mon.* 25.32).

---

[117] See e.g. his letter to Juliana, Demetrias' mother, criticizing the letter which he later learned was by Pelagius, to her daughter, in which the author had suggested that 'justice, continence, piety and chastity we have of ourselves'. Augustine replies, 'These are God's gifts, and they are yours, but they are not from you' (*ep.* 188.2.6).

These ideals underline Augustine's thought from soon after his conversion and at least from 400 onwards when, as R. A. Markus has made clear,[118] he began to define sin not so much in terms of a breach of right order as in social categories, in terms of sin against the community in self-referential pride and self-seeking, turning away from the common good to one's own private good.[119] This is made explicit in the *Literal Commentary on Genesis* (11.15.20), where Augustine speaks of

These two loves—of which the one is holy, the other impure; the one sociable, the other private; the one concerned for the common good for the sake of the heavenly society, the other subordinating the common good to self-interest for the sake of a proud lust for power . . . the one given to friendship, the other to envy; the one wishing its neighbours what it would wish for itself, the other wishing to subject its neighbour; the one ruling its fellows for the good, the other for its own . . .

Sin is henceforth understood as a failure of the love, fellowship, and friendship which lies at the heart of human society and which defines it in relation to God—hence the pivotal emphasis we have noted upon oneness, harmony, and love in his treatment of married life and of monastic life in the *Rule*.

For the monastic life, in Augustine's experience, often fell far short of the ideal of unity and harmony to which it aspired, and failures of love, in instances of proud, selfish actions, seemed to be inherent in any attempt to live in community. It is telling that even Augustine's work *On Virginity* is more occupied with the problem of pride and the virtue of humility than with the nature of virginity as such: 'It is much better to be married and humble than celibate and proud' (*virg.* 51.52).[120] This seems to represent a rethinking of the virtue of virginity in the light of his theology of the fall and grace similar to his rethinking of the married relationship, rather than a reordering of it on the scale of the virtues. It will always be a greater good than marriage, but it is just as susceptible, indeed, more susceptible, given its higher place, to the sin of pride—of self-reliance and self-congratulation and failure to acknowledge that all is of grace.

The subject matter of *On Virginity* is perhaps also symptomatic of the absence of any real emphasis on asceticism in Augustine's thought either here, or in the *Rule*: it was obviously of little importance to him either in a lay, monastic, or clerical context, again, presumably, because whatever the individual achieves is a gift of God and ascetic striving so easily lends itself to self-referential pride. Similarly, the monastic life, into which his celibate vocation inevitably developed was not, as it often seems in patris-

---

[118] Markus (1994a) III.   [119] *Gn. litt.* 11.15.20 quoted by Markus (1994a) III, 256.
[120] Cf. *ep.* 266 to Florentina.

tic writings, that of an élite of holy men who consequently possessed immense authority and stood in sharp contrast to the silent majority of married couples. (This is something Augustine had wanted to avoid from as early as *On the Good of Marriage*, and makes him very similar, in many respects to Jovinian while moving him further away from Jerome.[121]) Both modes of living in society were, for Augustine, characterized by the unavoidable ambiguity of Christian life in the world inherent in man's fallenness. The monk, Augustine observes, is like Daniel in the lions' den—dwelling in the face of the Lord, in the middle of wild beasts, yet seated in deep peace. Daniel's decidedly ambiguous position is brought home in another image Augustine uses to describe life in the monastery:

Far from the roar of the people, from the noise of the great crowds, from the stormy waves, they are in a harbour, as it were . . . Then is the promised rejoicing already there? Not yet. There are still laments and worry over temptations . . . even a harbour has an entrance somewhere . . . sometimes the wind rushes in from that open side. And even where there are no roads, the ships are dashed against each other and are shattered. (*en. Ps.* 99.10)

The context of this passage is a sermon which appears to be directed against those who enter a monastery, expecting it to be a perfect haven, only to leave it disillusioned, and full of criticism and slander, on finding that life 'inside' is very much the same as life 'outside': there are still objectionable and sinful brothers to tolerate within the confines of the monastery, just as there are in the outside world: 'lilies must grow among thorns and wheat will be hidden in the chaff.'

There are numerous instances in Augustine's works where we find him dealing with specific problems within the monastery: vicious accusations (*ep.* 6; 8); quarreling brothers (*ep.* 78); quarreling nuns (*ep.* 210; 211); a monk who died leaving a will (*s.* 355; 356); backsliders and grumblers (*en. Ps.* 132.12; *op. mon.*); those who had to be expelled from the monastery (*perseu.* 15.38). So, just as there was no room for spiritual élitism in the Church, so also in the monastery and in the home—both are states of friendship, fellowship, and love striving for unity and concord, but cannot, in this life, be immune from the failures of love, the self-interest and concupiscence symptomatic of man's fallenness. Both, to various extents, anticipate the perfect community of unity, mutual love, and friendship which will be the heavenly city, but neither can realize it in its fullness here.[122]

We are perhaps in a better position now to answer the question which

[121]　Hunter (1994).

[122]　Markus (1990), Ch. 11, where these ideas are considered and Augustine is contrasted with Cassian in this respect. See also Verheijen (1979), 95–97; White (1990), 204 who observes that Augustine's view of friendship—that human relationships can only be perfect eschatologically—diverged from the classical view.

we raised at the beginning of this chapter, as to why Augustine chose celibacy, which for him was to mean monasticism, rather than marriage, as his preferred way of living a Christian life in society, but any suggestions we make will be partly anachronistic. The choice seems clearer in the light of Augustine's developed theology but would have presented itself to Augustine rather differently in 386 before he had immersed himself in reading St Paul, especially Romans, and worked out a theory of the fall which reflected the vitiated nature of man's willing. The far-reaching repercussions of the fall would later echo hauntingly through every aspect of human society, but in 386 the choice would have been rather less ambiguous and more clear-cut, determined more by philosophical ideas of perfection and the attainment of truth by freely willed ascetic renunciation,[123] than Pauline ideas of human weakness and divine grace.

Having traced the development of Augustine's thought on the fall and its effects on life in society, as well as the various influences which moulded the final form of his monastic life, we can now appreciate, as Augustine would have done, retrospectively, that the choice which faced him at conversion between marriage and celibacy was by no means one between perfection and compromise, as he had once seen it, rather it was, as he later puts it, one between that which is good and that which is better.

We have also noted the very positive approach to marriage which characterizes his work when he considers the relationship in a theological context—not only to rebut its extreme detractors, such as Jerome, or to moderate its extreme supporters, such as Jovinian, but in presenting it as the original and intended destiny of human society, in Paradise and in the life to come—a relationship of unity, harmony, fellowship, friendship, and love. It is a relationship which is in essence sacramental, defined by its indissolubility, but which includes a sexual relationship, on a secondary level, in order that human society might indeed *be* social, that is, made up of a community of beings. The sexual aspect might be secondary but it is undeniably constitutive of marriage, and although Augustine, almost alone among the Fathers, theoretically avoids a theology of marriage and sex which makes them a *result* of the fall and allows for sex for its own sake as part of *fides*, his close association of sex with concupiscence as one of the main effects and prime examples of man's fallen nature has had a damaging effect, especially on twentieth-century evaluations of the relationship in his thought. This too, then, is a factor in explaining, at least retrospec-

---

[123] E.g. *sol.* 1.10.17: 'I feel that there is nothing which can so undermine the defenses of a manly spirit as the blandishments of women and that contact with their bodies without which no wife can be contented. For this reason I fully believe it proper and useful for the freedom of my soul that I have commanded myself not to wish for, not to look for, not to marry, a wife.' *uera rel.* 3.3, cited by Zumkeller (1986), 240.

tively, why, despite his extremely positive treatment of marriage, his choice of celibacy would later be confirmed in his adoption of the monastic life.

The positive attraction of the monastic life is, of course, significant: community, friendship, intellectual companionship, order—all things which the early works and the *Confessions* make clear Augustine was seeking from the beginning. The ascetic environment in North Africa, fostered by Tertullian, Cyprian, and Ambrose, the martyr ideal and the classical, contemplative, philosophical mould into which the Christian monastic ideal so easily fitted, together with Augustine's own profound personal inclination towards the values of the monastic life—Lawless develops the thesis, *anima Augustiniana naturaliter monastica*[124]—all create a context in which Augustine's choice would appear to be a natural and inevitable one, irrespective of his attitude to marriage, women, or indeed the fall. The latter, of course, would, as we have seen, profoundly alter his understanding of any form of life in society, making both marriage and the celibate life wholly dependent on God's grace, and only fully realizable in their perfection in the life to come.

---

[124] Lawless (1987), 36.

6

The two cities

We shall be in a city, of which, my brethren, when I speak, I find it
difficult to leave off. (*en.Ps.* 84.10)

When Rome fell to the Goths in AD 410 a crisis of understanding, opening
up questions which had long been rumbling beneath the surface of late
antique thought, erupted to engulf both pagan and Christian thinkers.
Rome was the heart of pagan civilization and tradition; in it pulsed the still
vigorous blood of the ancient religions, the life-source of the Empire.
Christianity may have attempted to diminish its flow; the Constantinian
revolution, the removal of the altar of victory, Theodosius's anti-pagan legislation were all significant outward signs of its demise. Rome, the eternal
city, was now the burial place of the apostles, Peter and Paul, the seat of
the Bishop of Rome, the ancient centre of the new Christian Empire. At
least, this is how it seemed until Rome fell into the hands of Alaric and his
Arian Goths.

Christians, who had taken so much for granted—had not history led
them to do so?—now stood aghast in incomprehension. Was the Christian
proclamation of triumph premature? Had they misinterpreted what had
happened? Had the God of the Christians failed to protect the Empire
which he seemed so recently, so triumphantly, to have favoured and promoted? Was the catastrophe the first sign of the trials and tribulations which were expected to accompany the end? Was the millennium
approaching? Was Rome's senescence, its sixth age, now to give way to
death? Such questions, which clamoured like deafening bells in the eternal
city, echoed and re-echoed throughout the Empire. In Jerusalem Jerome
was (rhetorically) robbed of speech: 'After the most radiant light of all the
nations had been extinguished . . . after the head of the Roman Empire had
been cut off and . . . in one city the entire world perished, I fell silent and
was humiliated and unable to speak of goodness' (*In Ezekielen praefatio*).
His bewildered cry, 'If Rome can perish, what can be safe?' (*ep.* 123.17)
voiced the feelings of many.[1]

---

[1] Cf. Pelagius *Ad Demetriadem* 30.

The pagan reaction was rather different. The fall was indeed a vindication, proof of their determined and long-standing insistence that in neglecting the gods, in failing to propitiate them by sacrifices, the Empire was hurtling headlong into disaster. And so it had proved. It was Christianity, the Christian emperors, who had so ruthlessly attempted to wipe out the old religion, who were responsible.[2]

In fact, Alaric was merely a clever and ambitious profiteer. He held Rome for only three days. What he seems to have had in mind was promotion within the Imperial service, rather than any grandiose plan of conquest. He lacked the expertise and the resources for anything more. To rescue the reaction he inspired from bathos we must remember that individuals like Jerome were hundreds of miles away and may well have had alarmist information. Alaric's limited ambitions were not known to his contemporaries, and, more importantly, we must be sensitive to the essentially symbolic nature of what happened and the significance of the questions it inspired, irrespective of their immediate context.

The questions were by no means new, at least on the pagan side. As we saw in chapter four, Rome was the stronghold of traditional, conservative paganism, represented by the likes of Symmachus, Praetextatus, and Albinus. As with any attempt to resist change in the present, they looked to the past to define and endorse their identity—in this case, to the literature of ancient paganism, to the classic authors who (as we saw in Chapter 2) formed the backbone of the education of every cultured man of position in the Empire, its bishops included. Such works carried the unquestioned authority of antiquity and undying tradition, custom, and civilization. The fact that this paganism found its most prominent contemporary representatives in wealthy, highly articulate, influential members of the senatorial aristocracy, in a time of crisis which suggested that there was more to their ideas than dusty antiquarian meanderings, ensured that it could not be ignored. Rather, they were thrown into the limelight; they were forced out of their beloved city, exiled throughout the Empire, and looked to as those who could explain what had happened: Rome had fallen because, through Christianity, the city had been robbed of its cult, that which had always ensured its security and protection.

One such exile was the young senator Volusianus, a member of one of the most prominent and wealthy Roman families, which counted among its number such illustrious Christians as Albina and the younger Melania (whom we encountered at Hippo in Chapter 4). Taking refuge in Carthage he, like the Christian Marcellinus, wrote to Augustine with questions concerning paganism and Christianity.

---

[2] See Courcelle (1958).

Augustine, meanwhile, was in the midst of one of the most pressing crises of the Donatist controversy. Panic following the fall of Rome had meant that toleration was being extended to them at the very moment he felt that significant progress was being made after the edict of 405. But he could not but feel the tremors which the erupting crisis in Italy had initiated and, when refugees, letters, and questions eventually reached Africa, he responded quickly with a series of letters and sermons intended to console the Christians of Rome, to answer their concerns, and to counter pagan accusations. Unlike Jerome, he seems to have reacted practically, rather than dramatically, and refused to attach undue significance to Rome itself, or to its fall; rather he regarded the matter *sub specie aeternitatis* with a marked ascetic detachment. It was simply yet another military coup, a temporal disaster, a trial for sinful men, a sign that no earthly kingdom is eternal, and ultimately insignificant when compared to the eternal reward promised to faithful Christians (*s.* 81; 105; 296).[3]

When the Spanish priest Orosius arrived in Hippo in 414, a refugee from Vandal invasions, Augustine took the opportunity to commission him to write a history which would refute the pagan claim that the disaster was due to neglect of the gods, and to demonstrate that similar disasters did, indeed, befall Rome before the advent of Christianity or a Christian emperor. Orosius' chronicle of world history, from Adam to the present, completed in 417/18 and entitled, *Seven Books of History Against the Pagans*, was dedicated to Augustine, who himself pursued the same arguments— with rather more scholarly expertise and critical reserve—in the *City of God*, which he had begun in 413.

THE PLAN FOR *CITY OF GOD*

We have a clue to his plans for writing this enormous work in the letters he wrote to his friend and fellow Christian, Marcellinus, after the fall of Rome. So much of these letters (137 and 138) seems to anticipate the arguments of the *City of God*, both in general outline and in details.[4] Moreover, Augustine ends letter 138 by telling Marcellinus that if he would still like to hear more, he will reply with a letter or a book. That reply, dedicated to Marcellinus, was to be the *City of God*, completed in 426.

As his letter to Firmus[5] indicates, and as numerous summaries in the *City of God*,[6] together with the final review in the *Retractations* (2.43; 2.69)[7] confirm, Augustine had a very clear idea of the structure and contents of

---

[3] *De excidio urbis Romae sermo* (CCL 46.249–62). Lauras and Rondet (1953), 99–162.

[4] O'Meara (1961), 10 f.

[5] Ed. Lambot (1939). It was written some time after the completion of the work.

[6] Book 6, preface and ch. 1; 11.1; 12.1; 15.1; 22.30.   [7] See Guy (1961).

this huge 22-book work—although these are all texts which post-date its completion. It could be argued that the first ten books were written in immediate response to the fall of Rome, in order to answer pagan criticisms (that Rome fell because the gods had been neglected (1–5) and that only the worship of the gods would guarantee an immortal and happy existence hereafter (6–10)) whilst the remaining twelve, which detail the origin (11–14), historical course (15–18), and ends (19–22) of the city of God and the city of the world were added later, once he realized the potential for development in the idea of the two cities. Taken in isolation the work would certainly suggest this. However, the structuring idea of the *City of God* was not, as we shall see below, a new one in Christian tradition or in Augustine's thought; it is present in numerous earlier allusions to two groups of men, two cities or two societies, in contexts very similar to the *City of God*.[8] It rather seems that Augustine used the occasion of the fall of Rome to articulate and bring to fruition ideas which he had long reflected and written upon and which he now saw were immediately relevant to a particularly pressing historical event. The fall of Rome seems to have provided the catalyst, but not the inspiration or ideas for the *City of God*.

BOOKS 1–10: THE REFUTATION OF PAGANISM

He addresses immediate concerns first and is obviously acutely conscious of his audience. They are not just pagans, they are cultivated, learned, noble pagans, those fervent antiquarians and upholders of the ancient traditions who were exiled from Rome across the empire. He writes both to refute and to impress; cogent and cutting argument accompanies highly stylized prose. He knows his audience because he too shares their culture; he has read his Virgil, Varro, Sallust, Cicero . . .[9] He is prepared to meet them on their own ground, and to argue his case in their terms: by appeal to their authorities, their literature, history, and philosophy. The first ten books of the *City of God* might therefore, on first encounter, read rather oddly. There is no reference to contemporary events, literature, or persons; anything and anyone of importance belongs in the past.[10] In this way, following the well-established tradition of Latin Christian apologetical writing against the pagans,[11] he demonstrates that Rome did indeed suffer wars, civil wars, and various calamities under the gods, well before the

---

[8] See note 15 below.

[9] *BA* 33, 98 for a list of classical authors whom Augustine cites in the *City of God*.

[10] Brown (1967), 300–11 is a brilliant evocation of this.

[11] E.g. Tertullian *Apologeticum*; Minucius Felix *Octavius*; Cyprian *ad Demetrianum*; Lactantius *Divinae Institutiones*.

coming of Christianity, and that the gods, mere jumped-up men, were incapable of averting disaster (Books 2–4). What has happened in the past has, rather, been the work of God's providence. That Rome at first prospered and its empire grew, is due to God's reward for the Roman's (relative) virtues—their self-sacrificing love of Rome, their lack of avarice, their courage and bravery for the sake of praise, freedom, glory, and fame. That they suffered defeat and hardship is similarly the work of God's providence and the consequence of their vice, which Augustine sums up as a 'desire to dominate', a *libido dominandi*,[12] which perverted all their good actions and turned them into a cruel, self-glorifying lust for power (Book 5). They were convicted in this respect by their own highly regarded historian, Sallust, who saw, even in the glorious early Republic, the first signs of this corruption in the Roman character.[13]

In order to refute the pagans' claim that worship of the gods secures a happy and immortal existence hereafter, Augustine reviews their religious philosophy and practice in order to demonstrate, as we saw in Chapter 1, the superiority of Christianity as the unique and universal way of salvation. It is this demonstration of Christianity as the one true religion, constitutive of the one true *ciuitas*, which the second half of the *City of God* confirms in its examination of the origin, course, and end of the city of God as opposed to the city of the world.[14]

BOOKS 11–22: THE TWO CITIES

But as we suggested above, the idea of two cities was not original or new to Augustine.[15] In *On True Religion* (AD 390) he divides the human race, 'stretching from Adam to the end of the world', into two classes (*genera*); one, the 'multitude of the impious', the other, those 'devoted to the one God', which will be separated on the day of judgement (50). A short while afterwards in *On Free Will*, he similarly distinguishes two *genera* of men corresponding to two *genera* of things, 'those who love and pursue eternal things and those who pursue temporal things' (1.16.34). In *On Teaching the Uninstructed* (c. 400) he refers for the first time to two cities (*ciuitates*), 'one

[12] Ruokanen (1993), 96–100 for a survey of Augustine's use of this term.
[13] Sallust *Bellum Catalinae*. 2 cited in *ciu*. 3.14.
[14] Madec (1994), 208. He notes, referring to Studer (1991), that the *confirmatio* follows the rules of rhetoric and that in describing the origin, development, and ends of the city of God, Augustine was inspired by a pattern suggested by the epidictic genre.
[15] See Lauras and Rondet (1953) for list of early texts, in particular some of the *en. Ps.* and *sermones* concerning the two cities, Jerusalem and Babylon, composed before *ciu*. Also Duchrow (1970), 186–243; Cranz (1954) (esp. 272 n. 58 for references to the heavenly Jerusalem and the city of God).

of the ungodly, and another of the holy, which are carried down from the beginning of the human race even to the end of the world, which are at present commingled in respect of bodies, but separated in respect of wills, and which, moreover, are destined to be separated also in respect of bodily presence in the day of judgement' (19.31).

His description of the characteristics of the city of the ungodly has much in common with his depiction of the Romans in *City of God* 5 ten or more years later, further suggesting that the specific ideas he would use to respond to, and interpret the fall of Rome, were already well established in his thought in a general way in relation to human society:[16] 'For all men who love pride and temporal power with vain elation and pomp of arrogance, and all spirits who set their affections on such things and seek their own glory in the subjection of men, are bound fast together in one association.' The members of the city of the holy, in contrast, 'seek the glory of God and not their own, and . . . follow him in piety'. The same ideas are found in the *Literal Commentary on Genesis*, begun in the year following the fall of Rome. What Augustine says here, and his tentative indication (here and to Marcellinus in *ep.* 138) that he will develop the ideas in another work, suggests that the *City of God* was taking firm shape in his mind at this time:

There are, then, two loves, of which one is holy, the other unclean; one turned towards the neighbour, the other centred on self; one looking to the common good, keeping in view the society of saints in heaven, the other bringing the common good under its own power, arrogantly looking to domination . . . These two loves started among the angels, one love in the good angels, the other in the bad; and they have marked the limits of the two cities established among men under the sublime and wonderful providence of God . . . With these two cities intermingled to a certain extent in time, the world moves on until they will be separated at the last judgement. The one will be joined to the holy angels and, being united to its King, will attain eternal life; the other will be joined to the wicked angels and, being united with its king, will be sent into eternal fire. Concerning these two cities I shall perhaps write more at length in another book, if the Lord is willing. (11.15.20)

This passage closely parallels *City of God* 15.28.

That these ideas are present in Augustine's work from the very beginning suggests that they were probably common currency. Certainly, he writes as if they need no explanation, and with an assurance that in using them he will be readily understood. Where did they originate, and what can this tell us about their meaning in Augustine's works?[17]

---

[16] Markus (1970c), 46.

[17] In examining this question I am much indebted to the painstaking work of Van Oort (1991).

SOURCES FOR THE IDEA OF THE TWO CITIES

Beginning the second part of the *City of God* Augustine refers to Scripture, and in particular the Psalms, as the source of his ideas on the city of God, Jerusalem, the heavenly city. This is confirmed by his earlier *Explanations of the Psalms* where he frequently encountered and used these ideas (e.g. *en. Ps.* 61; 86; 136). He was also well aware of Paul's references to 'our commonwealth . . . in heaven' (Phil. 3: 21), the 'Jerusalem which is above' (Gal. 4: 26) and the Letter to the Hebrews' allusions to ' Mount Sion . . . the City of the Living God, the heavenly Jerusalem' (12: 22), that 'here we have no lasting city' (13: 14). But the contrast between two opposed cities is absent from these scriptural references and Augustine rarely refers to the Apocalypse, perhaps the most obvious place to find a contrast between Jerusalem and Babylon. This leads Van Oort to suggest that Augustine obtained the idea of two opposed cities from Christian tradition and read it back into Scripture[18]—and as he demonstrates, there was certainly a rich seam of traditional ideas to be mined. The predominant feature of this strand of ancient thought was its dualism, a feature well attested in Platonism, Stoicism, and Philo, in all types of Gnostic thought, and not, as S. Pètrement has cogently demonstrated, absent from New Testament authors, such as Paul and John.[19] Indeed, Augustine had been a member of the dualist sect *par excellence*, of his time, during his years as a Manichee. Their doctrine of the two kingdoms, of the exile of the soul in this world, the kingdom of darkness, and its return to the heavenly kingdom of light, at first seems very similar to the idea of two opposed cities, of the righteous elect and the sinful damned. Of course, as we saw in Chapter 1, Augustine's antitheses are not dualistic at an ontological level; the two cities are determined and opposed by man's use/misuse of his will, and both are under God's providence and judgement.[20] Nevertheless, one cannot eliminate the influence of Manichaean, or general dualistic ideas, upon his thought. In fact, as one critic has suggested, they may have inspired the shape of the doctrine of the two cities in his polemic *against* them: he emphasizes their confusion, inseparability, and interwovenness in this life, in contrast to the Manichees' (and the Donatists') attempt to separate them into two clear and distinct, readily identifiable groups.[21] As we saw in Chapter 4, this was certainly a feature of the apostate Donatist, Tyconius' thought with which he could openly sympathize.

Tyconius' *Commentary on the Apocalypse*[22] unfortunately only survives in

---

[18] Van Oort (1991), 356.   [19] Pétrement (1990), 127–214.
[20] See Van Oort (1991), section 4 A on Manichaeism.   [21] O'Donnell (1979), 75.
[22] Augustine mentions it in *doctr. chr.* 3.30.42. Edition by Lo Bue (1963). For MS and later commentaries see Ladner (1959), 260 notes 92–3. On Augustine and Tyconius see Chadwick (1991), 49–55; Monceaux (1922) V, 165–219.

fragments, pieced together by later commentators. As such it cannot carry much weight as an accurate indicator either of the views of its author or of what Augustine may have found there. Nevertheless, it is worth noting that in the editions we possess Tyconius does seem to use the idea of two cities to interpret Revelation; the city of God and the city of the Devil, Jerusalem and Babylon, Abel and Cain, serving Christ and the world, destined for salvation and damnation, respectively.[23] Whether these are later Augustinian interpolations, or whether Augustine could have derived some of his key ideas for the *City of God* from Tyconius, we cannot know. What we do know is that Augustine read another work of Tyconius which contains rather similar ideas, *The Book of Rules*.[24] Augustine refers to this work, a collection of seven rules to interpret difficult passages of Scripture, in *On Christian Doctrine* (3.30.42–37.56), where he expounds and discusses the rules in turn and obviously regards them as extremely useful exegetical tools. In the first, second and seventh rule Tyconius uses the term body (*corpora*) rather than city (*ciuitas*) in order to refer to the 'Lord and His Body' (Christ and His Church), to the 'Bipartite Body of the Lord' (the good and evil members of Christ's body, the Church), and to the 'Devil and His Body' (the Devil and the impious). Augustine objects, however, to the expression 'bipartite' in reference to Christ, since it cannot be said that his body includes the impious in heaven: 'Rather it should be called "Of the True and Mixed Body of the Lord", or "the True and Simulated" or something else, because hypocrites should not be said to be with him either in eternity or even now, although they seem to be in His Church. Whence this rule might have been named in such a way that it designated the "mixed Church"' (3.32.45). Such, we shall see, is Augustine's doctrine in the *City of God*.

Earlier Latin tradition also provided the thought-world in which the ideas for the *City of God* could evolve. As members of a persecuted Church, African theologians such as Cyprian and Tertullian inevitably juxtaposed the Church, the community of the righteous, the elect, and its persecutors, represented as the world, the forces of evil, the State.[25] We saw how this influenced the Donatists' rigorous perfectionism, separatism, and exclusivism in relation to all who were not members of their sect. But it must also have influenced Augustine's less dualistic, less realized, and more eschatological conception of two antithetical groups, with different priorities, allegiances, and ultimate ends. The antithesis of two, at present intermingled, cities, which will be separated eschatologically, is also found, at a more spiritual

---

[23] Dulaey (1986) concludes that the influence of Tyconius' commentary is particularly striking in the last few books of the *City of God*, for example on points of exegesis or interpretation of symbolic expressions, but that Augustine shows no evidence of having read or used it before this.

[24] Burkitt (1984); S. Babcock (1989).   [25] Van Oort (1991), 293–301.

level, in Origen and Ambrose, for whom Jerusalem, the city of God, primarily signified man's soul at war with Babylon, the forces of evil.[26]

But it is in early Jewish-Christian works, such as the *Shepherd of Hermas*, the *Doctrina Apostolorum/Didache* and *Barnabas*, and later works such as the *Apostolic Church Order*, the *Didascalia*, and the *Apostolic Constitutions* that Van Oort sees the real source for ideas of the two ways, the two cities, which were influential throughout Christian tradition and were ultimately developed by Augustine in the *City of God*.[27] Not only do they contain the closest parallels in terms of content (the two cities, the earthly exile of the heavenly city, the eschatological separation of the elect from the reprobate . . .), but they also possess very much the same form: they are (at least partly) concerned with catechesis, and Books 11–22 of the *City of God* follow closely the catechetical narration of sacred history in, for example, *On Teaching the Uninstructed*, which in turn evidences close parallels with the *Didache* and the *Doctrina Apostolorum*. Whether Augustine himself knew these works—and Van Oort does not rule this out[28]—or whether their content and form were mediated to him through the tradition, the parallels are illuminating.

CHRISTIAN TIMES?

But there are other strands of ancient thought which must also be examined in order to evaluate Augustine's use of the idea of two cities. Theologians were generally agreed in regarding the conversion of Constantine as the inauguration of a new period of sacred history in which the Empire and the Church were providentially allied in order to convert the empire to Christianity and to bring the Church under Imperial protection. An 'Imperial theology' which, at its most enthusiastic, regarded the Emperor as an almost messianic figure, a representative of the logos on earth, divinely ordained to deliver the Empire from the forces of paganism and to ensure its salvation in the Christian Church, was first propounded by Eusebius of Caesarea. It was based upon earlier beliefs, held by the likes of Philo, Melito of Sardis, and Origen, in the providential coincidence of the Pax Romana and peace in a single unified Empire under Augustus with the birth of Christ. Under Constantine and his successors this had been fully realized; monotheism and monarchy went hand in hand: the worship of the One God under one Emperor. It was a view shared by almost all of Augustine's contemporaries—Ambrose, Orosius, Jerome, Prudentius, Rufinus—and determined their attitudes to the Emperor, the Empire, and

---

[26] Van Oort (1991), 277–81.   [27] Ibid. 300–57.   [28] Ibid. 345.

the Church's place within it.[29] There was little sense of the old hostility between the persecuted Church and the pagan empire, which had been so vivid in Tertullian, and which had assumed apocalyptic dimensions in Hippolytus. Rather, it was generally assumed that men now lived in 'Christian times'—*tempora christiana*—a term which served for Christians to refer to the era following Christ's incarnation and especially to the time of Christianity's triumph, and pagans to sum up the reasons for the ills and sufferings of the present age.[30]

There are a few hints in Augustine's earlier work that he shared, or at least, did not question, the prevailing 'imperial theology' of his day, that he saw the fulfilment of prophecy ('and all the kings of the earth shall adore him, and all the nations shall serve him' Ps. 72: 11) in the victory of Christianity over paganism.[31] It was obviously not something which particularly interested or concerned him at this stage, apart from justifying persecution of pagans and coercion of Donatists: we find enthusiastic praise of Theodosius in *City of God* 5.26, for precisely these reasons. But following the fall of Rome, we find him impelled by urgent circumstances increasingly to re-evaluate received assumptions and opinions on the relation of the Church and the Empire—how could Rome, the heart of the Empire, fall in 'Christian times'?—and it was in this way that he arrived at a new, and rather different understanding, which breaks decisively with existing tradition.[32]

It is interesting that in breaking with 'imperial theology' he actually reaffirms his earlier reflection on the two cities, such as we have found in *On Teaching the Uninstructed* and the *Literal Commentary on Genesis*. It is as if these two incompatible ideas could stand in juxtaposition in his early thought until the crisis of the fall of Rome threw them together and showed them up as irreconcilable. I would agree with R. A. Markus that the Empire has no real place in Augustine's idea of the two cities: it is neither synonymous with the city of God, the predestined elect, as earlier Eusebian imperial theology might have held; nor can it be identified with the city of the world, the unrighteous damned, as Hippolytus held. It is, as Markus has cogently demonstrated, theologically neutral.[33] It is part of the context, the secular context, in which the life of man now takes place, in which the members of the city of God *and* the city of the world pursue their, at present, intertwined courses. In other words, it is part of the *saeculum*.[34]

[29] Markus (1970c), 42–51.

[30] *s. Denis* 24.11; *s.* 81.9; 105.6–8 referred to by Markus (1970c), 37. See Madec (1994), 233–59 and Markus 'Tempora Christiana Revisited' (forthcoming in the Festschrift for G. Bonner) for further references and discussion of this idea.

[31] *c. Faust.* 13.7; 13.9; 22.38; 44.2 (c. AD 400); *cons. eu.* 1.13.20 (c. AD 400)—Cranz (1954), 305. Also *cons. eu.* 1.14.21; 26.40; 34.52; *cat. rud.* 3.5—Markus (1970c), 30–1.

[32] See Lohse (1962).   [33] Markus (1970c), 54–5.   [34] Markus (1970c).

That the Empire happened to espouse Christianity in Augustine's day was not ultimately significant; divine providence had also been at work when it had persecuted, tortured, and killed Christians. The members of the city of God, the predestined elect, may find their temporal course running through the vicissitudes of Roman history, but they will ultimately leave it behind in the eschatological city which they will attain after this life.

THE IDEA OF HISTORY?

The same holds true of another strand of ancient thought which illumines the nature of Augustine's reflection on the city of God—the idea of history. It was commonly held, by pagans and Christians alike, that history, like the life of the individual man, was divided into six ages, stretching from infancy to old age, each age lasting a thousand years, and that the world had now reached the last age. Rome was therefore popularly depicted as in its old age. Although he shows little interest in either pagan or Christian historiography,[35] Augustine was happy to use these ideas to interpret the ages of man's life (*ver. rel.* 26.49) and the six days of creation (*Gn. adu. Man.* 1.23.35–25.43) in relation to God's progressive education of man (*ciu.* 10.14), and, as we have seen in the *Confessions*, to structure his theological reflection on conversion. Later, he uses it in *City of God* 11–18, as he had in *On Teaching the Uninstructed* 22.39, to divide up the account of Scripture, culminating with the sixth age—the present time between the incarnation and the end (although he does not think we can know how long this age will last (*ciu.* 22.30), he is clear that it does not fit the calculations of the millenarians[36]). However, he was acutely aware that ordered stages and patterns were of little use in making sense of fallen man's experience in the present (or of past history). In the place of ordered progress, achievement, or culmination he saw only an absolute antithesis between the city of God and the city of the world, the righteous and the unrighteous, the predestined elect and the reprobate. The only thing that makes sense of human history, he was convinced, is faith in the operation of divine providence and divine grace—attested in the inspired revelation and historical record of Scripture (see *ciu.* 11.1 and 3)[37]—that the elect will ultimately be saved.

[35] On these see Momigliano (1963), 79–99. He does, however, use Eusebius' *Chronicle*, translated into Latin by Jerome, and refers to it a number of times in *ciu.* 18.

[36] They thought the second coming would happen in 1,000 years. See *ciu.* 20; *ep.* 197; 199 to Hesychius.

[37] This is what Markus (1970c, ch. 1) refers to as Augustine's development of a theology of prophetic inspiration (fully worked out in *Gn. litt.* 12 (AD 414)) whereby he came to see 'sacred history' as confined to the history recounted in Scripture and all subsequent history as strictly 'secular'.

But the scriptural record ends with the coming of Christ. In the present age, man is faced with the intractable ambiguity of what is happening and will happen. The certainties, structures, ascents, and patterns of the early works tend to collapse into the mysterious and ambivalent workings of God's will to save fallen man.[38]

What we have already seen of Augustine's reflection on the fall of man in preceding chapters should explain the reasons for Augustine's divergence from these strands of ancient thought. He breaks with an 'imperial theology' like Eusebius', because he is all too aware that fallen man's pride, lust for domination, blindness to the truth and moral incapacity mean that he is incapable of realizing a perfectly just empire in which there is true order, peace, and justice. He abandons the idea of pattern, progress, and meaning in secular history, because the only order there is belongs to the unfathomable workings of divine providence and grace, without which man can do nothing but sin and create disorder and dissolution.

What Augustine therefore describes in the second part of the *City of God*,[39] when he turns to consider the origins and temporal course of the two cities, is not the history of the Empire as God's chosen vehicle for the triumph of Christianity, but the progress of the city of God, the predestined elect, from creation to the coming of Christ, as it is recounted in Scripture, alongside the course of the city of the world from Assyria to the rise of the Roman Empire. The city of God originates in heaven with the angels before creation (Book 11); the city of the world came into being when Satan and the rebel angels fell (Book 12), followed by the fall of man (Books 13–14).[40] The characteristics of the two cities are evident in two of their first members, Cain and Abel.[41] Though both belonged to the same condemned 'lump' of fallen men, God chose one for dishonour and the other for honour. Whereas Cain, like Romulus, murdered his brother in order to rule alone and fixed his love upon temporal things, Abel, in humble faith and hope, directed his love towards his Creator; whereas Cain founded a city, Abel was a 'pilgrim and stranger in the world . . . predestined by grace and chosen by grace, by grace a pilgrim below, and by grace

[38] See Marrou (1950). I am indebted in this section to Cranz (1954), who also cites Augustine's division of history into four ages in, for example *ex. prop. Rm.* 13–18, which we examined in Chapter 3. Scholars can be rather more optimistic in their evaluation of what Augustine has to say about history, see e.g. Ladner (1959), 239–83; Harrison (1992), 184–9 (there is an order and beauty to the workings of divine providence).

[39] For reflections on the second part of the *City of God* and especially Book 19, see Combès (1927); Baynes (1936); Markus (1970c) (this is the classic, and invaluable work, which has determined all subsequent research); Rist (1984); O'Donovan (1987); Ruokanen (1993).

[40] In *ciu.* 22.1 he therefore suggests that the elect make up the number of the fallen angels in the city of God—'God by his grace is gathering a people so great that from them he may fill the place of the fallen angels and restore their number.'

[41] For other general descriptions of the characteristics of the two cities see, for example *en. Ps.* 61.6 and 8; 64.2; 136.1; *ciu.* 14.1 and 28.

a citizen above' (15.1); whereas the evil, like Cain, 'make use of God in order to enjoy the world' and 'lust for domination over others', the good, like Abel 'make use of this world in order to enjoy God' and act with 'a loving concern for others' (15.7). The course of the city of God is traced from biblical history, from Noah, Abraham, and King David (16), the prophets and the exile (17), whilst the course of the city of the world is traced from secular history, from Assyria, Egypt, and Greece to the rise of Rome (18). In the present age the two cities are inextricably interwoven and intermixed, only separated morally, by the ends to which they aspire (Book 19). Their physical separation will only be fully realized in the last judgement (Book 20), in hell (Book 21), or in the blessed life of the city of God in heaven (Book 22).

Despite what we have said about Augustine's diminishing optimism and lack of conviction in expounding any sort of plan or pattern in human history apart from the providential and gracious actions of God recorded in Scripture and his mysterious, rather ambiguous work in the present, the *City of God* does most definitely seem to have an ordered pattern of composition, and I think one might argue, an ordered sense of human history, albeit working within the constraints we have outlined. In this respect, it is very similar to the *Confessions*, where in Books 1–9 Augustine uses the six ages of man to recount his own 'history' or biography, from birth to conversion, just as he recounts the origin and history of the city of God from the fall to the coming of Christ in Books 11–18 of the *City of God*. And just as Augustine then turns in *Confessions* 10 to examine his present life as a Christian in the sixth age of the world, and presents it very much as one wholly dependent upon God's grace, incapable of realizing the good or attaining the truth without it, so in Book 19 of *City of God* he turns to examine the lives of the members of the city of God in the present age, unable to realize true justice, peace, love, or order in this life but longing for their eschatological realization in the life to come. Both works also conclude with three books which anticipate the seventh age of eternal life in the life to come.

BOOK 19: THE CITY OF GOD IN THE WORLD

Book 19, then, like Book 10 of the *Confessions*, is crucial in any analysis of Augustine's views on the nature of man's present existence. In Book 19 he reaffirms that man's existence is originally, actually, and ultimately a social one. This is what he understands by the term *ciuitas*: it is not so much a city or a state as a *society* of individuals with a common origin, life and goal: 'how could that City have made its first start, how could it have advanced along its course, how could it attain its appointed goal, if the life of the saints were not social?' (19.5). What defines the nature of the society is its goal, its end, its ultimate good; that to which it directs its actions, to which it aspires, and which in turn, determines the way in which it lives its present life. In stating this, as we saw in Chapter 2, Augustine was reiterating a commonplace of ancient philosophy. The schools differed only in what they thought man's ultimate good consisted. Augustine therefore begins Book 19 by examining Varro's review of ancient philosophy and his 288 hypothetical sects or schools, based on their view of where the ultimate good, or happy life, was to be found (19.1–3). He notes that the philosophers also believed that the happy life is a social one, but that they mistakenly thought that it could be realized here on earth, by their own efforts. The first part of Book 19 is largely a demonstration, based on past history and present experience, of just how wrong they were. Augustine's two key concepts are peace and justice, the first because it is universally acknowledged that all men seek to attain it; the second because it had traditionally been held, by pagans and Christians, to be the defining factor of any human society. His arguments in respect of the two concepts are similar because they are both, he thinks, unrealizable in this world for very much the same reasons.

PEACE

For Augustine, peace is a natural law inherent in the order of nature, the absence of which moves even irrational creatures to seek to recover it (19.14). All rational creatures possess a certain degree of peace in the ordered subjection of the body by the soul. It is, in fact, a part of the natural order of human existence in society. Disorder and war are simply symptoms of its absence, of the dissolution of human society (19.12–14). The question is how man attempts to retain peace or to regain it when it is lost. For the Christian, Augustine observes, 'peace between mortal man and God is an ordered obedience, in faith, in subjection to an everlasting law . . . the peace of the Heavenly City is a perfectly ordered and perfectly harmonious fellowship in the enjoyment of God, and a mutual fellowship in God' (19.13). Order, subjection, law, society, enjoyment, fellowship—for the Christian these are the key to peace when God is recognized and loved as their author, object, and end. When temporal goods or earthly concerns take God's place in this equation, such as when the Romans waged war, not so much to attain peace, as through a lust to dominate and to subject men to their own temporal order, law, and society, then the peace attained is no more than a 'shadow peace', a 'semblance of peace' because God's order—of subjection to him in humility and love, of love of neighbour, and the use of all earthly goods towards enjoyment of Him—has been ignored: 'pride hates the just peace of God, and loves its own peace of injustice' (19.12). But it is this 'shadow peace', the 'peace of Babylon', obtained by war and subjection, which is the characteristic feature of the city of the world. It is essentially a 'compromise between human wills', irrespective of faith in God, an 'ordered agreement . . . concerning the giving and receiving of commands' so that human society might function as harmoniously as possible. And it is this 'compromise' which the members of the city of God, while they are on earth, respect and obey so long as it does not hinder their worship of God (19.17). (It is, in a sense, a very Roman compromise; a toleration of the customs, laws, and institutions they encountered in conquered territories so long as they did not threaten allegiance to Rome and its gods.)

But this 'shadow peace' is not simply a result of the Roman's *libido dominandi* and their failure to worship the Christian God. It has far deeper and more pervasive roots in the vitiated wills of all men following the fall. This is the real reason why peace, that harmonious order which pertained before the fall and which all creation desires, will never be fully realized in this life. In chapters 4–9 of Book 19 Augustine memorably evokes the 'miseries of this life', the bodily and mental weaknesses, the failures of virtue and justice so common to earthly life, in order to demonstrate the 'amazing folly' of those philosophers who thought it was possible to attain happiness in this life by their own efforts (4). He does so by working his way through the same levels of human society which he had enumerated to describe the 'friends' who made up the happy social life which the philosophers placed on earth (3): members of one's household, the city, the world, the universe, and the angels. The discord and division, darkness and moral ambiguity, so painfully obvious at each of these levels is a mark of just how much peace is lacking. In the household 'we do not know the hearts of those with whom we wish to maintain peace' (5); the city is corrupted by sedition, civil war, bloodshed, civil and criminal crimes and their resultant law suits, in which—such is the incapacity of even the fairest of judges—the innocent are tortured and killed and the guilty are freed (6); the world is likewise torn apart by wars while its inhabitants are divided from each other by different languages and tortured by fear and worry for their friends' well-being (7–8); among the angels the demons masquerade as angels of light and delude men into worshipping them in the pagan cults. 'Such blessedness as this life affords' Augustine concludes, 'proves to be utter misery when compared with that final bliss' (10).

JUSTICE

What he has to say about justice in 19.21 is a diptych of the long earlier section on peace. Here he is consciously taking up, and developing further, a subject which he had already raised in *ciu.* 2.21, where he first cites Cicero's definition of a commonwealth in order to use him to reiterate Sallust's conviction that the Roman State had sunk to such depravity that it had effectively undermined itself and ceased, in any real sense, to exist as a commonwealth. In this way he aligns two of the pagans' most respected authorities to buttress the Christian charge that Rome suffered its worst depradations under its own gods, and at its own hands, well before the advent of 'Christian times'. Cicero has the second-century hero and conqueror of Carthage, Scipio, define a commonwealth (*res publica*) as 'the weal of the community' (*res populi*), and the 'community' (*populi*) 'as meaning not any and every association of the population but "an association united by a common sense of right (*consensus iuris*) and a community of interest (*utilitatis communio*)"' (*De Rep.* 1.25; *ciu.* 2.21). Thus, Cicero argues, a commonwealth exists where there is a 'sound and just government'; where it is unjust, by definition it ceases to exist. The depravity of the Roman State which Sallust so vividly describes therefore effected its demise. As Cicero argues, 'For we retain the name of a commonwealth, but we have lost the reality long ago: and this was not through any misfortune, but through our own misdemeanours' (*De Rep.* 5.1).[42] It is in this context that Augustine's well-known comment 'Remove justice, and what are kingdoms but gangs of criminals on a large scale?' should be placed, for it demonstrates that he had in mind the all-pervading absence of justice at every level, not only in the Roman commonwealth, but in any social grouping, however small:

For it was a witty and truthful rejoinder which was given by a captured pirate to Alexander the Great. The king asked the fellow, 'What is your idea in infesting the sea?' And the pirate answered, with uninhibited insolence, 'The same as yours, in infesting the earth! But because I do it with a tiny craft, I'm called a pirate: because you have a mighty navy, you're called an emperor.' (*De Rep.* 3.14.24; *ciu.* 4.4)[43]

---

[42] On Augustine's agreement with Cicero and Plato on the unattainability of justice in this life see Fortin (1972), 12–14.

[43] It is not often noticed that he gives a very similar analogy for the universal quest for peace through lust for domination in *ciu.* 19.12, in the example of the robber who seeks peace through manipulative domination of his associates, his family, and if he were given the opportunity, would operate in the same way, as heads of state now do, in relation to the city or the nation.

WAS ROME A COMMONWEALTH?

Anticipating his return to this subject later on in *City of God* Augustine is well aware that definitions can merely be invented to fit the argument, that rhetoric can override reality. He concedes that the Roman commonwealth 'certainly was a commonwealth according to more plausible definitions; and that it was better ruled by the Romans of antiquity than by their later successors' (2.21). He is not, however, prepared to abandon Cicero's arguments, rather he reinforces them by setting them in a somewhat alien and anachronistic theological context: 'true justice (*ius*)' he insists, 'is found only in that commonwealth whose founder and ruler is Christ'. The context is more fitting to develop this insight when he returns to the argument twelve years later, in 19.21, to develop a definition of the justice (*iustitia*) on which the commonwealth hinges, as that which assigns 'to everyone his due'. The Romans have patently failed to do this, either in relation to other men—whom they have subjected and robbed in their lust for domination, and whom they have misled in worship of the gods—or, above all, in relation to God. Rather, they have perverted and vitiated the natural and just order of reality, whereby 'God rules man, the soul rules the body, the reason rules lust and the other perverted elements in the soul' by failing to give God his due, that is, to serve Him.[44] Thus they lack justice both as individuals, and collectively, as a commonwealth; there is no 'consent to the law' or 'community of interest' to define them as ever having been one.

In 19.24 he continues his theological reinterpretation and reapplication of Cicero by means of a revised definition which subsumes justice to love, as the defining factor of a commonwealth: 'A people is the association of a multitude of rational beings united by a common agreement on the objects of their love'.[45] It should be noted, however, that Augustine is not, as some commentators have suggested, rejecting the concept of justice and replacing it with love; rather he is reinforcing the point already made in 19.21 that justice, rendering to someone his/their due, consists—for the member of the only real commonwealth, the city of God—in rendering his neighbour and God their due, which, in Christian terms, means loving God, and one's neighbour as oneself. Love is therefore a more accurate definition of justice in a Christian context. As Augustine realized, it has the virtue of transcending temporal, necessarily partial and culturally relative,

---

[44] See the early work *mus.* 6.15.50 where Augustine describes justice as the order 'by which the soul serves none but God, by which it wishes to be equal to none but the purest souls and to dominate none but bestial and corporeal natures'—Cranz (1954), 266. It is axiomatic for Augustine that the righteous man is one who is a true judge of the nature of things and has an ordered love—see, for example *doct. chr.* 1.

[45] Augustine had already seen this in *mor.* 1.26.49, where he writes 'From this precept [of love for one's neighbour] proceed the duties of human society'—Quoted by M. T. Clark (1963).

legal definitions of exactly what constitutes justice, whilst still allowing the existence of other commonwealths. The Roman commonwealth was therefore a commonweath, but because it was founded upon essentially flawed and disordered loves lacked true justice. The two-fold commandment, as ever, for Augustine, is the defining factor and lowest common denominator for all Christian conduct in every age and every society.

Having established his definitions, Augustine is forced to acknowledge that, as with peace, true justice—a rightly ordered love of God and of one's neighbour—is unattainable, not only for the Romans but for all men in this life. We possess but a shadow, a vestige, of that ordered love which will reign in the city of God in Heaven. It is his conviction that true peace and justice, in rightly ordered love, are unattainable in this life, that determines what Augustine has to say about the life of the Christian within the world and the role of the Emperor and the Roman State in temporal government and politics. It is to this wider context, amidst the vestigial shadows of peace and justice, that we now turn.

CHRISTIANS IN THE *SAECULUM*

Augustine is unflinching in evoking the misery and wretchedness of the present age. It is, for him, 'a kind of hell on earth' (*ciu.* 22.22) in which the members of both cities are inescapably captive. Indeed, part of man's suffering is his uncertainty as to which city he will ultimately find himself to be a member, for the identity of the predestined elect of the city of God is unknown in this life. Here, the two cities are inextricably interwoven (*ciu.* 1.35),[46] they share the same society, the same city, the same occupations, the same laws, in some cases, the same family and the same worship. They are separated, as we have seen, not physically, but in will; in the manner in which their love is directed and ordered towards their desired goal. This means that the members of the city of God, like the exiles from Rome following its fall, find themselves in the position of captives, aliens, foreigners in a strange land, longing to regain the homeland from which they have been exiled.[47] One of Augustine's favourite images is that of pilgrims, *peregrini*—in the classical sense of resident aliens in a land which is not their own (*ciu.* 19.17). The psalms, where he found so much to shape his understanding of the city of God, were also a rich source of images of exile, of the Israelites longing to return to their native land and to Jerusalem.

---

[46] Markus (1970c), 71; Marrou (1957), who raises the possibility of a third 'city' made up of the temporally inextricable mixture of the two; Van Oort (1991), 153, who suggests that Augustine prefers to emphasize the antithesis of the two cities, rather than their intermingling.   [47] O'Donnell (1979).

In this life, therefore, Christians have no lasting city, no permanent home. There is nothing to distinguish or identify them in worldly society, rather they are an intrinsic part of it; they use and support the laws, institutions, and customs already in place, without seeking to revise, restructure, or overturn them, so long as they do not hinder their worship of God (*ciu.* 19.17). They are to be dutiful citizens, Augustine urges, and follow St Paul's exhortation to obey the powers that be, since, even if they are corrupt, they are willed by God's providence (*ciu.* 2.19; 5.19). In this way the faithful preserve and benefit from what shadow peace and justice there is: the laws, customs, and institutions which make them possible are to be used in such a way that the citizen of the city of God 'does not let himself be taken in by them or distracted from his course towards God, but rather treats them as supports which help him more easily to bear the burdens of "the corruptible body which weighs heavy on the soul"' (*ciu.* 19.17), just as the Israelite exiles, the righteous remnant, used the peace of Babylon and offered prayers for it, 'because in her peace is your peace' (Jer. 29: 7; *ciu.* 19.26). They are part of the structure which preserves a harmony between the two cities in, as Augustine puts it, 'the things that are relevant to this [temporal] condition' (*ciu.* 19.17).[48] The dress and manner of life of the faithful are likewise undistinctive and simply accommodated to the customs and structures of the society in which they find themselves (*ciu.* 19.19). Whether they pursue an active or a contemplative life, or a mixture of both, is also unimportant; what matters is the end to which they direct every aspect of their life and every encounter with the society in which they find themselves. It is a question, as we have already seen in the highly systematized first book of *On Christian Doctrine*, of 'use', of loving one's neighbour in God and of referring everything to Him; of not taking earthly things as ultimates in themselves. Only thus is the commonweal of the people promoted (*ciu.* 19.19). Above all, it is a question of love, of longing for the heavenly commonwealth, Jerusalem.

In his attitude to Christian life in the world Augustine is, rather strangely, very close to his predecessor Tertullian. Although Tertullian is perhaps best known for his total rejection of all things pagan, of all compromise with the world ('nothing is more foreign to us [Christians] than the State (nec ulla magis res aliena quam publica)' *apol.* 38), and his advocacy of total separation from everything to do with the State, in a treatise such as *On Idolatry*, he does, in fact, incline to be rather more accommodating when he attempts to defend Christians against the charge of being

---

[48] This is very much in line with what we found of Augustine's attitude to secular culture and institutions in *doctr. chr.* in Ch. 2: 'The Christians do not neglect those human institutions which are valuable for a common society in view of the needs of the present life' (2.39.58) Cranz (1954), 308.

useless, ineffective, or even seditious members of society. In answer he stresses the common life they share with pagans in their everyday dealings, 'we sojourn with you in the world, abjuring neither forum, nor meat market, nor bath, nor booth, nor workshop, nor inn, nor weekly market, nor any other places of commerce. We sail with you, and fight with you, and till the ground with you . . .' (*Apologeticum* 42). In the same text he likewise stresses the fact that Christians are law-abiding citizens, prompt to pay their taxes and debts and assiduous in their obedience to authority. The fact that they abstain from politics is a positive thing since it ensures they will not be a source of opposition. And he exhorts Christians to pray for the Empire so that it might be preserved and the end of the world, with its attendant calamities, averted (*Apologeticum* 32; *Ad Scapulam* 2).

In his portrayal of relations between the Christian and the world, or *saeculum*, Augustine stands firmly in this line of Christian apologetic, stretching from the New Testament onwards. Even the most radical apologists, such as Tertullian, did not diverge from the common emphasis upon the Christians' law-abiding support of the powers that be, in the interests of a peaceful and just common life.[49] But perhaps more than anyone else, Augustine was aware of just how much a *necessary* compromise this situation was, how the peace and justice thereby obtained are merely shadows of what will obtain after this life. Although he goes further than most in allowing Christians a role in politics, government, the army . . . he is more acutely aware of how important detachment was, not at the level of everyday life, but in terms of ultimate ends and loves.[50]

SLAVERY

What Augustine has to say about the institution of slavery and the role of the Christian household in Book 19 sheds a good deal of light on his general thinking about the nature of Christian life in the world.[51] As we saw earlier, he follows tradition in structuring social relations in an ordered pattern of rule and obedience which he regards as being natural, in the sense of being part of man's original and intended state. This is especially seen in the relations which should naturally order the family, or household, where the *paterfamilias* rules his wife, the parents rule their children, and the householder rules his servants, thus ensuring a harmonious, peaceful, and just order of rule and obedience for all its members (*ciu.* 19.14; *qu.*

---

[49] *Scorpiace* 14.1; *De Corona Militis* 13.4 on Rom. 13: 1; *Apologeticum* 30–33 on the Christian's obligation to pray for and support the Emperor as the guardian of peace, stablility, law, and order.

[50] I am indebted for these insights on Tertullian to Isichei (1964).

[51] On this see Klein (1988); Rist (1994), 236 f.

Hept. 1.153). The same relations pertained in the first couple, Adam and Eve, where Adam ruled and Eve obeyed. Her obedience, however, was not through fear or subjection, but through love (*Gn. litt.* 11.37.50). The institution of slavery, however, is the most obvious sign in the present age of how the original hierarchy of human relations has been subverted by fallen man. Instead of ruling in love, with the welfare of their charges at heart, those with authority, such as the Romans, have perverted the natural order by using their position in order to dominate and subordinate those in their care. The present subjection of slaves to their masters, in captive and enforced service, rather than freely willed, loving obedience, is a sign of and punishment for the fall.

Augustine's distinction between natural and voluntary providence (*providentia naturalis; providentia voluntaria*) in the *Literal Commentary on Genesis* (8.9.17–23.44) makes this situation clear:[52] having broken away from the natural and intended order of human relations man has created for himself a world in which human relations are fractured by disorder, cruelty, and fearful subjection—all men are, in fact, slaves (*ciu.* 19.15). Still, God's providence continues to work, a voluntary providence, inspiring the vitiated wills of fallen men within their self-inflicted constraints. It is a providence which does not seek to transform the structure of fallen society—this has been determined by man—but to reorientate it towards the eschatological city. It is the process of reorientation which makes life bearable for fallen man and begins the reformation which will be complete in the life to come. Thus, although he abhorred the institution of slavery, and did what he could to ameliorate it,[53] Augustine does not seek to abolish it. It is, as he puts it, 'ordained by the law which enjoins the preservation of nature[54] and forbids its disturbance' (*ciu.* 19.15). Rather, he suggests ways in which slaves and masters should behave within the constraints of this fallen world. Slaves should, as it were, create their own limited freedom, in freely obeying their masters with a good will and 'fidelity of affection' (*ciu.* 19.15; *en. Ps.* 125.7). They should be aware that they are probably better off in slavery than in many other 'free' occupations (*s.* 159.5) and that slavery to a master is infinitely preferable to slavery to lust (*ciu.* 19.15).

[52]   Markus (1970c), 87 f; 203–4.
[53]   E.g. in *ep.* 24* he insists that free-born men should not be sold into slavery. See Chadwick (1995), 102 who cites examples of Augustine using the Church chest to liberate slaves in bad households and of his congregation taking action to liberate slaves from a ship in Hippo harbour.
[54]   He does not, I think, mean the order of man's fallen nature (Rist (1994), 236), but rather the original order, now subject to God's voluntary providence, which demands just punishment for sin. Man's punishment, under this order, is slavery—both to sin and to other men. Augustine continues this quotation: 'in fact, if nothing had been done to contravene that law, there would have been nothing to require the discipline of slavery as a punishment.'

The master, on his side, should treat his slave with benevolence and compassion, try to ensure that he is encouraged either to become, or to continue as, a Christian, and be included, on a par with the rest of the household and 'with equal affection', in matters of worship (*ciu.* 19.16[55]). He should, as it were, become the slave of those whom he appears to command (*ciu.* 19.14). Again, love, in both the master and the slave, is the antithesis of, and antidote to, a desire to dominate and subject.

STATE AND HOUSEHOLD

But how far does the family analogy take us? Augustine is quite clear about the original and natural order of rule and obedience within the household. But what about the wider context of human relations, within the city, the country, the Empire? He seems to break with classical thought[56] when he suggests, in talking about slavery, that outside the family, man was originally created to exercise rule only over irrational creatures, the animals, *not* over other men: 'hence the first just men were set up as shepherds of flocks, rather than as kings of men.' (*ciu.* 19.15). It seems that the institutions of the State, that is the institutions of human government, the structures set up to order human society according to civil laws and enforced by military power, are not part of man's natural or intended state, and cannot, as was traditionally held, be regarded as analogous to natural rule and order within the family. They are, rather, a sign of man's subjection and symptomatic of his fall: man is naturally social, but not naturally political.[57] This is not to say that the household and the city or State are mutually opposed. As we saw in Chapter 5, the family is to some extent a microcosm of the State and its primary building block. Augustine makes clear the natural superiority of the family unit and its interdependence with the State in Book 19, when he observes that 'domestic peace contributes to the peace of the city—that is, the ordered harmony of those who live together in a house in the matter of giving and obeying orders, contributes to the ordered harmony concerning authority and obedience obtaining among the citizens' (19.16). The texts where he exhorts government officials to act as would a *paterfamilias*, especially in the benevolent correction of those for whom they are responsible, also witness to the way in which his ideal of the natural order of the family could contribute to shaping the wider order of the State.

---

[55] On ensuring slaves are converted and baptized see *ep.* 98.6, Rist (1994), 252.
[56] E.g. Cicero *De Rep.* 3.25 and 37; Plato *Rep.* IV.432a—Ruokanen (1993), 106–7.
[57] See the discussion by Markus (1970c), 197–210.

THE STATE AND THE CITY OF THE WORLD

However, as Markus notes, correction, in the sense of coercion, only enters the family and the State because of sin, but whereas it is not part of the family's original state, but a corruption of it, it is actually constitutive of the State's identity.[58] This is because Augustine believed that the State, in the sense of politically organized power and the institutions, laws, and officials which impose it, only came into being, and is only necessary, because of man's fall. Its characteristic features are like the symptoms of a fatal disease: coercion, violence, lust for domination and subjection, immorality, idolatry, corruption, warfare. It rests not upon God's eternal law, but upon a relative and shifting 'compromise between human wills about the things relevant to this life' (*ciu.* 19.17). This has led some scholars to identify the State and Augustine's 'city of the world' (*ciuitas terrena*) in the same manner as Augustine himself admittedly does in a number of texts. But Augustine, unlike these scholars, writes within a tradition of rhetoric which was not at all constrained by matters of general consistency and it is quite clear that, although the State and the city of the world do indeed resemble each other, and indeed overlap in many respects, and in numerous individual members, they are certainly not synonymous. For the State is in fact simply part of the *saeculum*, that age or context in which the members of both cities must live their lives on earth. Indeed, as we have seen, he is quite clear that the State, its institutions, officials, and laws, is one of the means which God has providentially provided to sustain human society after the fall and to preserve some degree—albeit vestigial and uncertain—of peace, justice, and order to restrain the anarchic and vicious onslaughts of the forces of sin unleashed by the fall. The State is, as it were, God's means of protecting human society against itself.

CHRISTIANS AND PUBLIC OFFICE

The Christian is therefore obliged not only to obey the State, but to actively participate in it by holding, or at least not shirking, civil, secular posts, such as those of governor, magistrate, councillor, or judge. The latter is the subject of one of the most disturbing passages of Book 19, for although fallen man is blind to the truth, both in himself and in the mind of another, and is consequently forced to reason in a context which makes clear insight and balanced judgement impossible, the judge, for the sake of whatever remnants of peace and justice might be salvaged, is still obliged to hear and try cases. His duty is invidious, and one from which any sensitive man

---

[58] Markus (1970c), 205–6.

with a passion for justice and public service would ordinarily recoil: such is the darkness which attends man's fall that the innocent are tortured and put to death whilst the guilty are set free (19.6). Many members of the city of God are in a similar position, for wherever public office is exercised, it is more a matter of stemming the tide of man's sin with the sandbags of authority, than of creating the perfect *ciuitas*. Nevertheless, they are thereby serving and loving their neighbour, and, as Augustine encourages two public servants, Caecilian and Macedonius,[59] what they do is pleasing to God.

The Emperor himself is simply another, more prominent example, of a public officer acting in the interests of temporal peace and security. He is distinguished by the extent of his powers and responsibilities, and if he is a Christian, by the ends to which he directs his actions and the manner (especially his humility) in which he performs them.[60] It has sometimes been remarked that Augustine's later support of coercion, as we saw it developing in relation to the Donatists in Chapter 4, is incompatible with his 'secularization' of the State and his emphasis on the Christian's obligation to simply accept and co-operate with the powers that be, without seeking to change or reform them, except in cases where he is hindered from worshipping. His strong advocacy of coercion, albeit in a predominantly pastoral context of concern and love for the reformation of the sinner, certainly breaks with the idea of a secular State and of passive acceptance of the *saeculum* by the Christian, in favour of vigorous action to transform a particular state of affairs in the Church. Markus[61] finds the key to this apparent incongruity in Augustine's emphasis on the fact that when a Christian official acts in matters related to the well-being of the Church, he acts, not as a representative of the State, but as a Christian individual. Nowhere is this more apparent than in the actions of a Christian Emperor, initiating and authorizing the coercion of schismatics and heretics: he is acting, not as Emperor, but as a Christian with special powers and responsibilities, for, and on behalf of, the Church: 'A man serves God in one way in that he is man, in another way in that he is also king. In that he is man, he serves him by living faithfully; but in that he is also king, he serves Him by enforcing with suitable rigour such laws as ordain what is righteous, and punish what is the reverse' (*ep.* 185.19[62]). Similarly, pleading with a proconsul for leniency with regard to the imposition of the law against Donatists, Augustine comments 'For when you act, the Church acts, for whose sake and as whose son you act' (*ep.* 134.3). It is therefore

---

[59] *ep.* 151.14; 152.2; 153.19; 155.7.17—Markus (1970c), 100.
[60] See *ciu.* 5.24–26 for Augustine's description of the Christian emperors.
[61] (1970c), Ch. 6.
[62] Cf. *c. litt. Pet.* 2.92.210; 2.97.224; *Io.eu. tr.* 11.14; *ep.* 95.19.

the Church, and not the State, which is acting through individual Christians, in their various offices, to coerce heretics and schismatics to repent and return to it. These observations should remind us that, in fact, the notion of a 'State', in the modern sense, is quite anachronistic.

WARFARE AND MILITARY SERVICE

The difficult problems surrounding the question of the appropriate actions of Church and State, or of individual representatives of them, were posed just as acutely for Augustine when he came to consider the question of military service and the Christian's involvement in warfare.[63] Although it recognized the need for armed combat to protect and defend the Empire, the attitude of the earlier Church was generally against the Christian serving in the military or engaging in war, though the reasons why are not absolutely clear. It seems that an abhorrence of bloodshed and murder, and in earlier centuries, the strong links between the army and pagan idolatry, were two of the main factors.[64]

The situation became more ambiguous, and attitudes gradually changed, following the conversion of Constantine. The army did not shake off its idolatrous connections overnight, but Constantine fought under the sign of the cross (the *labarum*) and attributed his victories to God's providence. Christian individuals were able to assume positions of State which were either supported and defended by the army, or even part of it. Church canons are ambiguous, but generally seem to envisage Christian participation in the military[65] and numerous scriptural texts were adduced to endorse the growing acceptance of Christian involvement in the defence and security of the Empire by participation in the army.[66]

It had always been appreciated that Christians depended upon the State to preserve peace, law, and order. Although, as Augustine recognized, it did so only very partially and ambiguously, it still needed to be supported in its efforts, otherwise human society would lapse into utter anarchy and ruin. It was for this reason that, like Ambrose,[67] he endorsed Christian mili-

---

[63] On this see Cadoux (1919); Harnack (1981); Swift (1983); Rist (1994), Ch. 6; Helgeland, Daly, and Patout Burns (1985); Langan (1991); Markus (1994a), V.

[64] E.g. Tertullian *De Idololatria* 19; *De Corona Militis* 11; *de pallio* 5.

[65] The most notorious is Canon 3 from the Council of Arles in 314 which reads 'Those who throw down their weapons in peace shall be excluded from communion'. Although numerous attempts have been made to avoid the obvious meaning, Harnack (1981), 100 argues for accepting it on face value.

[66] E.g. in defence of the Old Testament against the Manichees in *c. Faust.* 22.74–79; to persuade Boniface to remain in the army in *ep.* 189.4. See also *ep.* 138.15 (Luke's advice to the soldier, 'to be content with your wages' implies no prohibition against his profession).

[67] E.g. in the treatise *De Officiis*.

tary service and engagement in war, just as he had made it clear that Christians should not seek to avoid other offices and duties of State, however compromising and difficult they proved to be. Of course, there were wars which were unjust—those motivated by a desire for territorial expansion (*ciu.* 4.6), greed, revenge, a lust for power, glory, or domination (*ciu.* 3.14; *c. Faust.* 22.74)—and these he utterly abhorred. But wars fought *against* these motivations (*c. Faust.* 22.74), in order to prevent the annihilation of the State, and to secure peace and safety for human society, with the interests of the common good at heart, were to be approved and supported: Augustine writes to Boniface, 'Peace should be your aim; war should be a matter of necessity so that God might free you from neccesity and preserve you in peace' (*ep.* 189.6; cf. *ciu.* 3.10; 19.7; 22.6; *c. Faust.* 22.74; *qu. Hept.* 6.10). If soldiers are forced to kill in the course of duty they are not to be held guilty if they acted under the orders of a recognized authority (*lib. arb.* 1.5.11; *c. Faust.* 22.70 and 75; *c. Parm.* 2.20.45; *ciu.* 1.21 and 26), even if the war or the commander is unjust. It is not legitimate, however, for individuals or groups simply to take power into their own hands; this was no better than anarchy, whatever their motives (e.g. *s.* 302; *ep.* 47; *ciu.* 1.17).[68]

Although clergy were barred from military service,[69] Augustine was keen to encourage others to remain at their posts. He travelled many miles, for example, to talk with Count Boniface, in order to dissuade him from abandoning his military command in order to become a monk.[70]

At a theological level, Augustine evidently regarded war as part of God's providence in a fallen world. Like the rest of the machinery of State it served to control and order fallen man. Even when the evil were victorious he saw God's providence at work, humbling the pride of the defeated (*ciu.* 19.15). And like the duty of coercion, he believed that war does not exclude, but should be motivated by, benevolence and love; a concern for other human beings, that they might live in peace and security: ' . . . if the commonwealth observe the precepts of the Christian religion, even its wars themselves will not be carried on without the benevolent design that, after the resisting nations have been conquered, provision may be more easily made for enjoying in peace the mutual bond of piety and justice' (*ep.* 138.14. Cf. *ep.* 173.2; *s. dom. m.* 1.20.63–4).

This is not to say that Augustine advocated war, but rather that he recognized and lamented its necessity and encouraged any means which might avoid it whilst achieving the same ends. As he writes to the imperial ambassador Darius, who had been sent to negotiate a settlement with

---

[68] Rist (1994), 232.   [69] see Ambrose *De Officiis* 1.35.175; *ep.* 20.22.
[70] *ep.* 220.3; *ep.* 189.4–7 where he points out the similarities between the two vocations.

Boniface, 'Preventing war through persuasion, and seeking or attaining peace through peaceful means rather than through war, are more glorious things than slaying men by the sword' (*ep.* 229.2).

We can now appreciate that although the *City of God* (and especially Book 19) has often been read as a work of political philosophy, Augustine was obviously working with a rather different subject in mind: to demonstrate the unrealizability of classical ideas of the State, of the hierarchically ordered, harmonious working of human society, of the perfection and fulfilment of human life in the Greek city state (*polis*).[71] He had broken with these ideals very early on, when, in Milan, he relinquished his ambitions for high-ranking secular office—presumably having experienced its corruption and self-seeking desire for domination—and converted to Christianity.[72] His subsequent experience as priest and bishop merely served to confirm this.

THE CHURCH AND THE CITY OF GOD

There is one final question which any consideration of Augustine's reflections on the city of God inevitably raises, and that concerns the relation of the Church, the liturgical community of baptized Christians, to the city of God. Just as he often likens the State to the city of the world, without strictly identifying them, so he frequently likens the Church to the city of God (e.g. *ciu.* 13.16; 16.2; 20.11). Again, they must not be identified, for the Church too, contains members of both cities; those predestined for salvation and those who will suffer eternal damnation. Who the elect are, however, and who will not be saved, is unknown in this life. As Augustine repeatedly stressed against the Donatists, the Church is a mixed body, a *corpus permixtum* (*en. Ps.* 61.6) containing both good and evil, wheat and tares, which will only be separated at the end of the age, on the day of judgement. It does, however, seem that he thought that membership of the Church, through baptism, was a necessary prerequisite for membership of the city of God.[73] He also held, as we have seen, that a city is defined by its cult; the true city is identified by true worship, and this only takes place within the Church (*ciu.* 1.36).[74] The Church alone, therefore, contains the predestined members of the city of God in their temporal pilgrimage through this world, and in this sense prefigures and is continuous (though

---

[71] Markus (1970c), Ch. 4.   [72] Lepelley (1987), 245.

[73] *ciu.* 15.20; 21.16 'Let him, therefore, who wishes to escape eternal punishment, not only be baptized, but also justified in Christ and so pass from the devil to Christ.'; 21.24 'He who has not passed over to Christ, while he was in the body, is already counted as belonging to the Devil.'   [74] See Madec (1994), paper 12 for discussion and references.

not identified) with the *communio sanctorum*. The medieval identification of the Church and the city of God, however, whilst it butressed the authority of the Church, obviously betrayed Augustinian tradition.[75]

CONCLUSION

It is not often that an author is provided with such a fixed point to end their work: not only did Augustine die in 430, but the whole context of his life and thought was forever obliterated by the Vandal invasion of North Africa. The Western Empire had been increasingly destabilized by barbarian conquests; the Visigoths in Gaul, the Vandals, Alans, and Sueves in Spain, the Burgundians and Franks in the Rhineland. When the Emperor Honorius died in 423 it fell to his half-sister, Galla Placidia, the mother of his successor, the young Valentinian III, to assume rule on her child's behalf. In Africa, power was increasingly concentrated in the hands of foreign military commanders who protected the coast from attack. Such a man was Count Boniface, whom we have already encountered as the general who wished to embrace monasticism after his wife's death. Augustine, as we saw, was successful in dissuading him, but no doubt did not anticipate subsequent events. Boniface abandoned his posting on a remote provincial frontier and, returning from Ravenna, where he had his new post as Count of Africa (governor of the province of Africa) confirmed, brought with him an Arian wife, concubines, and a daughter who was subsequently baptized by the Arians (*ep.* 220). Worse was to come, for Boniface, ordered by Galla Placidia to return to Italy, was hoodwinked into defying her orders by the very person who had urged her to issue them, Aetius. Aware that he needed powerful support, he encouraged the Vandals to invade Africa. Under their leader Geiseric, 80,000 Vandals crossed the straits of Gibraltar, and joined by Alans and Goths on the way, seem to have met with no resistance when they entered Africa in 429–430.[76] As Possidius puts it, 'there poured into Africa from across the sea in ships from Spain a huge host of savage enemies armed with every kind of weapon and trained in war . . . They overran the country . . . everything they could they laid waste, with their looting, murders, tortures of all kinds, burnings, and countless other unspeakable crimes. They spared neither sex nor age, nor the very priests and ministers of God, or the ornaments and vessels of the churches, nor the buildings' (*vita* 28). Possidius continues to cite at length a letter in which Augustine gave strict orders to bishops and clergy not to abandon their churches and congregations by flight (ibid. 30).

[75] see Arquillière (1934); Gilson (1952).   [76] see Courtois (1955).

Boniface meanwhile, realizing Aetius' deception, transferred his allegiance back to Galla Placidia, who responded by sending him reinforcements. He moved to Hippo, a fortified town, and there resisted siege for fourteen months before admitting defeat and returning to Italy, leaving the town in the hands of Geiseric. In 431 the town was evacuated and burnt. Its subsequent history is unclear, though a township seems to have survived until the transfer of the site to Bone in the eleventh century.[77]

Three months into the siege of Hippo, on 28 August, Augustine died. Possidius describes the context in highly dramatic—almost apocalyptic— terms:

These days, therefore, that he lived through, or endured, almost at the very end of his life, were the bitterest and most mournful of all his old age. A man such as he had to see cities overthrown and destroyed . . . he saw churches denuded of priests and ministers; holy virgins and others vowed to chastity dispersed . . . He saw the hymns and divine praises ceasing in the churches, the buildings themselves in many places burnt down, the solemn sacrifices owed to God no longer offered in the appointed places, the holy sacraments no longer wanted, and, if they were wanted, ministers of them hard to find . . . (*uita* 28).

A whole world was coming to an end as the bishop of Hippo lay tearfully on his death bed, reading the penitential psalms, lamenting not these earth-shattering events, but his own sins.

What survived the devastation, quite extraordinarily, was not the towns, cities, and institutions of Roman society (he had always held that these were simply a passing context for the temporal pilgrimage of the city of God) but Augustine's carefully kept library in the *secretarium* at Hippo. He had spent the last year of his life re-reading, annotating, correcting, and commenting upon his life's work (*Retr.*).[78] This was not to be in vain, and with its preservation Augustine still speaks to us from his fourth/fifth-century context with a voice which evokes it better, perhaps, than any other survival of late antiquity ever can. As Possidius puts it, quoting the epitaph of a pagan poet:

> Traveller, would you like to know
> How poets live on after death?
> As you read aloud, it is I who speak;
> Your voice is sounded by my breath. (*uita* 31)

---

[77] Lepelley (1981), 124.   [78] See Madec (1996) I.

Bibliography

Abbreviations

Most reviews and journals are given their full title. The few that are not are:

BA   Bibliothèque Augustinienne.
Ét. Aug.   Revue des Études Augustiniennes.
HTR   Harvard Theological Review.
JTS   Journal of Theological Studies.
Rech. Aug.   Recherches Augustiniennes.
T&U   Texte und Untersuchungen.

Alfaric, P. (1918), L'Evolution intellectuelle de saint Augustin: I. Du manichéisme au néoplatonisme (Paris: Émile Nourry).

Amand, D., and Moons, M. Ch. (1953), 'Une curieuse homélie grèque sur la virginité', Révue Bénédictine 63: 211–38.

Arjava, A. (1996), Women and Law in Late Antiquity (Oxford: Clarendon Press).

Armstrong, A. H. (1970) (ed.), The Cambridge History of Later Greek and Early Medieval Philosophy (Cambridge: Cambridge University Press).

Arnold, Duane W. H., and Pamela Bright (1995) (eds.), De doctrina christiana: A Classic of Western Culture (Notre Dame/New York: University of Notre Dame Press).

Arquillière, H. X. (1934), L'Augustinisme politique (Paris: J. Vrin).

Ayres, L. (1995), 'The Discipline of Self-knowledge in Augustine's De trinitate Book X', in idem. ed. The Passionate Intellect: Essays on the Transformation of Classical Traditions (New Brunswick), 261–96.

——(1998), 'The Christological Context of Augustine's De trinitate XIII: Toward Relocating Books VIII–XV', Augustinian Studies 29: 111–39.

Babcock, W. S. (1989), Tyconius, The Book of Rules (Atlanta)

——(1991), 'Cupiditas and Caritas: The Early Augustine on Love and Human Fulfilment', in idem. ed. The Ethics of Saint Augustine, JRE Studies in Religion (Atlanta, Georgia), 39–66.

Baguette, Ch. (1968), Le stoïcisme dans la formation de s. Augustin (Louvain).

Barnes, M. R. (1993), 'The Arians of Book V, and the Genre of De Trinitate', JTS 44: 185–95.

——(1995a), 'Augustine in contemporary Trinitarian theology', Theological Studies 56: 237–50.

——(1995b), 'De Régnon Reconsidered', Augustinian Studies 26: 51–79.

——(1999), 'Exegesis and polemic in De Trinitate I', Augustinian Studies 30, forthcoming.

Barnes, T. D. (1971), Tertullian: A Historical and Literary Study (Oxford: Clarendon Press).

Baynes, N. H. (1936), 'The Political Ideas of Saint Augustine's *De Ciuitate Dei*', *Historical Association Pamphlet* 104: 3–17.

Blumenkranz, B. (1958), 'Augustin et les Juifs—Augustin et le Judaisme', *Rech. Aug.* 1: 225–41.

——(1973), *Die Judenpredigt Augustins* (Basel: Helbing and Lichtenhahn).

Bochet, I. (1982), *Saint Augustin et le désir de Dieu* (Paris: Études Augustiniennes).

Bohlin, T. (1957), *Die Theologie des Pelagius und ihre Genesis* (Uppsala: Uppsala Universitets Arsskrift).

Bonner, G. (1963), *Augustine. Life and Controversies* (London: SCM Press).

——(1964), 'Augustine's visit to Caesarea in 418', *Studies in Church History* 1: 104–13.

——(1987a), *God's Decree and Man's Destiny* (London: Variorum).

——(1987b), 'Augustine's attitude to Women and ⟨Amicitia⟩', in *Homo Spiritalis. Festgabe für Luc Verheijen, OSA, su seinem 70. Geburtstag* ed. C. Meyer (Würzburg: Augustinus Verlag), 259–75.

Børresen, K. E. (1990), 'In defence of Augustine: how *femina* is *homo*' *Collectanea Augustiniana—Mélanges J. T. van Bavel* ed., Brunning, B. (Leuven), 411–27.

——(1995), *Subordination and Equivalence: the Nature and Role of Women in Augustine and Thomas Aquinas* (Kampen: Kok Pharos).

Borgomeo, P. (1972), *L'Église de ce temps dans la prédication de saint Augustin* (Paris: Études Augustiniennes).

Bourassa, F. (1977), 'Théologie Trinitaire chez s. Augustin', *Gregorianum* 58: 675–725.

——(1978), 'L'intelligence de la foi', *Gregorianum* 59: 375–432.

Bradley, K. R. (1991), *Discovering the Roman family: Studies in Roman Social History* (Oxford: Oxford University Press).

Brisson, J. P. (1958), *Autonomisme et Christianisme dans l'Afrique Romaine* (Paris: E. de Boccard).

Brown, P. (1967), *Augustine* (London: Faber and Faber).

——(1972), *Religion and Society in the Age of Saint Augustine* (London: Faber and Faber).

——(1988), *The Body and Society: Men, Women and Sexual Renunciation in Late Antiquity* (New York: Colombia University Press).

——(1992), *Power and Persuasion in Late Antiquity* (Madison: University of Wisconsin Press).

——(1995), *Authority and the Sacred* (Cambridge: Cambridge University Press).

Burkitt, F. C. (1984) (ed.), *The Book of Rules of Tyconius* (Texts and Studies III, I; Cambridge: Cambridge University Press).

Burnaby, J. (1938), *Amor Dei: A Study in the Religion of Saint Augustine* (London: Hodder and Stoughton).

Cadoux, C. J. (1919), *The Early Christian Attitude to War* (London: Swarthmore Press).

Camelot, T. (1956), 'À l'éternel par le temporel: De Trinitate IV.18.24', *Ét. Aug.*, 164–72.

Cameron, A. (1991), *Christianity and the Rhetoric of Empire* (Berkeley-Los Angeles-Oxford: University of California Press).

——(1993), *The Later Roman Empire* (London: Fontana).

Carney, F. S. (1991), 'The Structure of Augustine's Ethic', in Babcock (ed.), 11–37.

Chadwick, H. (1959), *The Sentences of Sextus. A Contribution to the History of Early Christian Ethics* (Texts and Studies n.s. v) (Cambridge: Cambridge University Press).

——(1966), *Early Christian Thought and the Classical Tradition* (Oxford: Clarendon Press).

——(1985), 'Augustine on pagans and Christians: reflections on religious and social change', in *History, Society and the Churches*, ed. D. Beales and G. Best (Cambridge: Cambridge University Press), 9–27.

——(1994), 'On Re-reading the *Confessions*', in *Saint Augustine the Bishop: A Book of Essays*, ed. F. LeMoine and C. Kleinhenz (New York and London: Garland), 139–60.

——(1995), *Augustine* (Oxford: Oxford University Press).

Chevalier, I. (1940), *Saint Augustin et la pensée grecque. Les relations trinitaires* (Fribourg).

Clark, E. A. (1983), *Women in the Early Church* (Wilmington, Del.: M. Glazier).

——(1986a), 'Heresy, Asceticism, Adam and Eve: Interpretations of Genesis 1–3 in the Later Latin Fathers', in ead., *Ascetic Piety and Women's Faith: Essays in Late Antique Christianity* (Lewiston, NY).

——(1986b), 'Adam's Only Companion: Augustine and the Early Christian Debate on Marriage', *Rech. Aug.*, 139–62.

Clark, G. (1993a), *The Confessions* (Cambridge: Cambridge University Press).

——(1993b), *Women in Late Antiquity* (Oxford: Clarendon Press).

Clark, M. T. (1963), 'Augustine on Justice', *Et. Aug.* 9: 87–94.

——(1994), *Augustine* (London: Geoffrey Chapman).

Cochrane, C. (1940), *Christianity and Classical Culture* (Oxford: Clarendon Press).

Colish, M. (1985), *The Stoic Tradition from Antiquity to the Early Middle Ages*. Vol. II (Leiden: Brill).

Combès, G. (1927), *La Doctrine Politique de Saint Augustin* (Paris: Plon).

Comeau, M. (1930), *Saint Augustin: Exégète du quatrième évangile* (Paris: Beauchesne).

Courcelle, P. (1943), *Les Lettres grecques en Occident, de Macrobe à Cassiodore* (Paris: E. de Boccard) trans. Wedeck, H. E. (1969), *Late Latin Writers and their Greek Sources* (Cambridge Mass.: Harvard University Press).

——(1958), 'Propos antichrétiens rapportés par saint Augustin', *Rech. Aug.* I: 149–186.

——(1963a), *Les Confessions de s. Augustin dans la tradition littéraire. Antécédents et postérité* (Paris: Études Augustiniennes).

——(1963b), 'Anti-Christian Arguments and Christian Platonism: from Arnobius to St. Ambrose', in *The Conflict between Paganism and Christianity in the Fourth Century*, ed. A. Momigliano (Oxford: Clarendon Press).

——(1968), *Recherches sur les Confessions de saint Augustin*, 2nd edn. (Paris: E. de Boccard).

Courtois, C. (1955), *Les Vandales et l'Afrique* (Paris: Arts et Metiers Graphiques).

Cranz, E. C. (1954), 'The development of Augustine's ideas on society before the Donatist controversy', *HTR* 47: 255–316.

Crespin, R. (1965), *Ministère et Sainteté—Pastorale du Clergé et Solution de la Crise Donatiste dans la Vie et la Doctrine de saint Augustin* (Paris: Études Augustiniennes).

Cross, F. L. (1961), 'History and Fiction in the African Canons', *JTS* 12: 227–47.

De Bruyn, T. (1993), *Pelagius' Commentary on Saint Paul's Epistle to the Romans* (Oxford: Clarendon Press).

Delaroche, B. (1996), *Saint Augustin Lecteur et Interprète de Saint Paul* (Paris: Études Augustiniennes).

Dennis, H. V. M. (1970), *Hippo Regius from the Earliest Times to the Arab Conquest* (Amsterdam: Adolf M. Hakkert).

De Voohgt, D. P. (1939), 'Les miracles dans la vie de saint Augustin', *Recherches de Theologie Ancienne et Medievale* 11: 5–16.

Dill, S. (1898), *Roman Society in the Last Century of the Western Empire* (London: Macmillan).

Dixon, S. (1988), *The Roman Mother* (London: Croom Helm).

Dodds, E. R. (1951), *The Greeks and the Irrational* (Berkeley-Los Angeles-London: University of California Press).

Doignon, J. (1982), 'Une définition oubliée de l'amour conjugal édenique chez Augustin: *piae caritatis adfectus (Gen. ad litt.* 3.21.33)', *Vetera Christianorum* 19: 25–36.

Duchrow, U. (1970), *Christenheit und Weltverantwortung. Traditionsgeschichte und systematische Struktur der Zweireichelehre* (Stuttgart: E. Klett).

Dulaey, M. (1986), 'L'Apocalypse. Augustin et Tyconius', in *Bible de tous les temps: Augustin et la Bible* III, ed. A.-M. la Bonnardière (Paris: Beauchesne), 369–86.

Du Roy, O. (1966), *L'intelligence de la foi en la Trinité selon S. Augustin. Genèse de sa théologie trinitaire jusqu'en 391* (Paris: Études Augustiniennes).

Edwards, M. (1997) (ed. and trans.), *Optatus: Against the Donatists,* Translated Texts for Historians 27 (Liverpool: Liverpool University Press).

Eggersdorfer, F. X. (1907), *Der heilige Augustinus als Pädagoge und seine Bedeutung für die Geschichte der Bildung* (Freiburg im Breisgau).

Ellspermann, G. L. (1949), *The Attitude of the Early Christian Latin Writers Toward Pagan Literature and Learning* (Washington).

Elm, S. (1994), *Virgins of God: the Making of Asceticism in Late Antiquity* (Oxford: Clarendon Press).

Evans, R. F. (1968), *Pelagius: Enquiries and Reappraisals* (London: A. & C. Black).

Festugière, A. J. (1954), *Personal Religion among the Greeks* (Berkeley/Los Angeles: University of California Press).

Finaert, J. (1939), *Saint Augustin rhéteur* (Paris).

Folliet, G. (1961), 'Aux Origines de l'Ascétisme et du Cénobitisme Africain', *Studia Anselmiana* 46: 25–44.

Fontaine, J. and Pietri, C. (1985) (ed.), *Le monde latin antique et la Bible* (Paris: Beauchesne).

Fortin E. L. (1959), *Christianisme et Culture Philosophique au Ve Siècle* (Paris: Vrin).

——(1972), *Political Idealism and Christianity in the thought of Saint Augustine* (Villanova: Villanova University Press).

——(1974), 'Augustine and the Problem of Christian Rhetoric' *Augustinian Studies* 5: 85–100.

Fredriksen, P. (1980), *Augustine's early interpretation of Paul* (Ann Arbor/London).

—— (1986), 'Paul and Augustine: Conversion Narratives, Orthodox Traditions, and the Retrospective Self', *JTS* 37: 3–34.

—— (1988), 'Beyond the body/soul dichotomy: Augustine on Paul against the Manichees and the Pelagians', *Rech. Aug.* XIII: 87–114.

—— (1995), 'Excaecati Occulta Justitia Dei: *Augustine on Jews and Judaism*', *Journal of Early Christian Studies* 3.3: 299–324.

Fredouille, J. C. (1972), *Tertullien et la conversion de la culture antique* (Paris: Études Augustiniennes).

—— (1985a), 'Les lettrés chrétiens face à la Bible', in Fontaine and Pietri (eds.) (Paris: Beauchesne), 25–42.

—— (1985b), 'La bible et apologetique', in Fontaine and Pietri (eds.) (Paris: Beauchesne), 479–97.

Frend, W. H. C. (1952), *The Donatist Church* (Oxford: Clarendon Press).

Gacic, P. (1957), 'En Afrique Romaine: Classes et luttes sociales d'après les historiens soviétiques', *Annales Economies, Societés, Civilisations* XII.4: 650–61.

Gardner, J. F., and Wiedemann, T. (1993), *The Roman Household: A Sourcebook* (London: Routledge).

Geerlings, W. (1978), *Christus Exemplum: Studien zur Christologie und Christusverkündigung Augustins* (Mainz: Matthias Grünewald).

Gillespie, V. (1982), 'Mystic's Foot: Rolle and Affectivity', in *The Medieval Mystical Tradition in England* (ed.) M. Glasscoe (Exeter: University of Exeter).

Gilson, E. (1952), *Les métamorphoses de la Cité de Dieu* (Paris: Vrin).

Gould, G. (1990), 'Women in the Writings of the Fathers: Language, Belief and Reality', *Studies in Church History* 27: 1–13.

Greenslade, S. L. (1954), *Church and State from Constantine to Theodosius* (London: SCM Press).

Grillmeier, A. (1975), *Christ in Christian Tradition*, vol. 1 (Oxford: Mowbrays, 2nd revised edn.).

Grubbs, J. E. (1994), *Law and Family in Late Roman Antiquity* (Oxford: Clarendon Press).

Gsell, S. (1911), *Atlas archéologique de l'Algérie* (Algiers–Paris: Adolphe Jourdan, Fontemoing et Cie).

—— (1913–28), *Histoire ancienne de l'Afrique du Nord*, vols 1–8 (Paris: Hachette).

Guy, J.-C. (1961), *Unité et structure logique de la 'Cité de Dieu' de s. Augustin* (Paris: Études Augustiniennes).

Hadot, I. (1984), *Arts libéraux et philosophie dans la pensée antique* (Paris: Études Augustiennes).

Hadot, P. (1968), *Porphyre et Victorinus* (Paris: Études Augustiniennes).

—— (1979), 'La presentation du Platonisme par Augustin', *Kerygma und Logos. Festschrift für Carl Andresen* (Göttingen: Vandenhoeck und Ruprecht) 272–9.

Hagendahl, H. (1967), *Augustine and the Latin Classics* (Göteborg: Stockholm: Universitetet; Almquist & Wiksell International).

Halliburton, R. J. (1962), 'The Inclination to Retirement—the Retreat of Cassiciacum and the "Monastery" of Tagaste', *Studia Patristica—T&U* 5: 329–40.

228   Bibliography

Harnack, A. (1981), Militia Christi: The Christian Religion and the Military in the First Three Centuries (Philadelphia: Fortress Press).

Harrison, C. (1992), Beauty and Revelation in the Thought of Saint Augustine (Oxford: Clarendon Press).

——(1993), 'Delectatio Victrix: Grace and Freedom in Saint Augustine', Studia Patristica 27: 298–302.

Helgeland, J., Daly, R. J., Patout Burns, J. (1985), Christians and the Military: The Early Experience (London: SCM Press).

Henry, P. (1934), Plotin et l'Occident (Louvain: Spicilegium Sacrum Lovaniense).

Holte, R. (1958), 'Logos Spermatikos: Christianity and Ancient Philosophy According to St. Justin's Apologies', Studia Theologica 12: 109–68.

——(1962), Béatitude et Sagesse. Saint Augustin et le problème de la fin de l'homme dans la philosophie ancienne (Paris: Études Augustiniennes).

Howie, G. (1969), Educational Theory and Practice in Saint Augustine (London).

Humphrey, J. H. (1991) (ed.), Literacy in the Roman World (Ann Arbor Mi.: Journal of Roman Archaeology).

Hunter, D. (1994), 'Augustinian Pessimism? A New Look at Augustine's Teaching on Sex, Marriage and Celibacy', Augustinian Studies 25: 153–77.

——(1987), 'Resistance to the Virginal Ideal in Late-Fourth-Century Rome: The Case of Jovinian', Theological Studies 48: 45–64.

——(1989), 'On the Sin of Adam and Eve': A little-known Defence of Marriage and Childbearing by Ambrosiaster', HTR 82.3: 283–99.

Isichei, E. (1964), Political Thinking and Social Experience. Some Christian Interpretations of the Roman Empire from Tertullian to Salvian (Christchurch, New Zealand: University of Canterbury Press).

Jones, A. H. M. (1948), Constantine and the Conversion of Europe (London: Hodder and Stoughton).

——(1959), 'Were the ancient heresies national or social movements in disguise?', JTS X.2: 280–95.

——(1964), The Later Roman Empire, 3 vols (Oxford: Basil Blackwell).

——(1966), Decline of the Ancient World (London: Longmans).

Kannengiesser, C. (1995), 'The Interrupted De Doctrina Christiana', in Arnold and Bright (eds.), 4–14.

Kaster, R. A. (1988), Guardians of Language: The Grammarian and Society in Late Antiquity (Berkeley-Los Angeles-London: University of California Press).

Kevane, E. (1966), 'Augustine's De Doctrina Christiana: A Treatise on Christian Education', Rech. Aug. 4: 97–133.

Kirwan, C. (1989), Augustine (London: Routledge).

Klein, K. (1988), Die Sklaverei in der Sicht der Bischöfe Ambrosius und Augustinus (Stuttgart: Franz Steiner).

La Bonnardière, A.-M. (1986) (ed.), Saint Augustin et la Bible, Bible de Tous les Temps, vol. 3 (Paris: Beauchesne).

de Labriolle, P. (1913), La crise montaniste (Paris).

Ladner, G. (1959), The Idea of Reform. Its Impact on Christian Thought and Action in the Age of the Fathers (Harvard, Mass.: Harvard University Press).

Laistner, M. L. M. (1951), *Christianity and Pagan Culture in the Later Roman Empire* (Ithaca: Cornell University Press).

Lambot, C. (1939), 'Lettre inédite de s. Augustin relative au *De ciuitate Dei*', *Revue Bénédictine* 51: 109–21.

Langan, J. (1991), 'The Elements of Saint Augustine's Just War Theory', in Babcock (ed.), 169–89.

Lauras, A., and Rondet, H. (1953), 'Le thème des deux cités dans l'oeuvre de Saint Augustin', *Etudes Augustiniennes, Théologie* 28 (Paris: Etudes Augustiniennes), 97–160.

Law, V. (1997), *Grammar and Grammarians in the Early Middle Ages* (London: Longman).

Lawless, G. (1987), *Augustine of Hippo and His Monastic Rule* (Oxford: Clarendon Press).

Léon-Dufour, X. (1946), 'Grâce et libre arbitre chez saint Augustin. À propos de: *Consentire vocationi Dei . . . propriae voluntatis est*', *Recherches de Science Religieuse* 33: 129–63.

Lepelley, C. (1975), 'Saint Augustin et la Cité Romano-Africaine', in C. Kannengiesser (ed.) *Jean Chrysostome et Augustin*, Théologie Historique 35 (Paris: Beauchesne), 13–41.

—— (1979–1981), *Les cités de l'Afrique romaine au Bas-Empire*, 2 vols. (Paris: Études Augustiniennes).

—— (1987), 'Un aspect de la conversion d'Augustin: La rupture avec ses ambitions sociales et politiques', *Bulletin de Littérature Ecclesiastique* 88: 229–46.

Lienhard, J. T. (1977), *Paulinus of Nola and Early Western Monasticism* (Cologne: P. Hanstein).

Lieu, S. N. C. (1985), *Manichaeism* (Manchester: Manchester University Press).

Lizzi, R. (1990), 'Ambrose's Contemporaries and the Christianisation of Northern Italy', *Journal of Roman Studies* 80: 156–68.

Lo Bue, F. (1963), *The Turin Fragments of Tyconius' Commentary on Revelation*, Texts and Studies, New Series, 7 (Cambridge: Cambridge University Press).

Lohse, B. (1962), 'Augustins Wandlung in seiner Beurteilung des Staates', *T&U* 81: 447–75.

Lorenz, R. (1950), 'Fruitio Dei', *Zeitschrift fur Kirchengeschichte* 63: 75–132.

—— (1966), 'Die Anfänge des abendländischen Mönchtumes im 4 Jahrhundert', *Zeitschrift für Kirchengeschichte* 77: 1–61.

Louth, A. (1981), *The Origins of the Christian Mystical Tradition* (Oxford: Clarendon Press).

Madec, G. (1962), 'Connaissance de Dieu et action de grâces: Essai sur les citations de l'Epître aux Romains 1:18–25 dans l'oeuvre de saint Augustin', *Rech. Aug.*, 273–309.

—— (1970), 'Une lecture de *Confessions* VII.IX.13—XXI.27 (Notes critiques à propos d'une thèse de R. J. O'Connell)', *Et. Aug.*, 16: 79–137.

—— (1974), *Saint Ambroise et la philosophie* (Paris: Études Augustiniennes).

—— (1975), 'Christus, Scientia et Sapientia nostra', *Rech. Aug.*, 77–85.

—— (1989), *La Patrie et la Voie* (Paris: Desclée).

230   *Bibliography*

Madec, G. (1994), *Petites Études Augustiniennes* (Paris: Études Augustiniennes).

——(1996a), *S. Augustin et la philosophie* (Paris: Études Augustiniennes).

——(1996b), *Introduction aux 'Révisions' et à la lecture des Oeuvres de saint Augustin* (Paris, Études Augustiniennes).

Maier, J. L. (1960), *Les missions divines selon saint Augustin* (Fribourg: Editions Universitaires).

——(1987–9), *Le Dossier du Donatism, T&U* 134–5.

Mallard, W. (1980), 'The Incarnation in Augustine's Conversion', *Rech. Aug.* 15: 80–98.

Malone, E. A. (1950), *The Monk and the Martyr* (Washington: Catholic University of America).

Mandouze, A. (1953), 'Notes sur l'Organisation de la Vie Chrétienne en Afrique à l'époque de saint Augustin', *L'Année Theologique Augustinienne* XIII: 151–71; 201–31.

Markus, R. A. (1964a), 'Donatism. The Last Phase', *Studies in Church History* 1: 118–26.

——(1964b), '"Imago" and "similitudo" in Saint Augustine', *Ét. Aug.* 10: 125–43.

——(1970a), 'Augustine, Human Action: Will and Virtue', in A. H. Armstrong (ed.) *Cambridge History of Later Greek and Early Medieval Philosophy* (Cambridge: Cambridge University Press), 380.

——(1970b), *Marius Victorinus and Augustine*, in Armstrong (ed.), 327–419.

——(1970c), *Saeculum: History and Society in the Theology of Saint Augustine* (Cambridge: Cambridge University Press).

——(1983), *From Augustine to Gregory the Great* (London: Variorum).

——(1990), *The End of Ancient Christianity* (Cambridge: Cambridge University Press).

——(1994a), *Sacred and Secular* (Aldershot: Variorum).

——(1994b), 'How on Earth Could Places Become Holy? Origins of the Christian Idea of Holy Places', *Journal of Early Christian Studies* 2:3: 257–1.

——(1996), *Signs and Meanings: World and Text in Ancient Christianity* (Liverpool: Liverpool University Press).

——(1997a), *Gregory the Great and his world* (Cambridge: Cambridge University Press).

——(1997b), 'L'autorité Épiscopale et la définition de la chrétienté', *Studia Ephemeridis Augustinianum* 58: 37–43.

Marrou, H. I. (1950), *L'ambivalence du temps de l'histoire chez s. Augustin* (Villanova: Villanova University Press).

——(1949), *Saint Augustin et la fin de la culture antique* (Paris: E. de Boccard).

——(1955), *Histoire de l'Éducation dans l'Antiquité* (Paris: Seuil, 3rd edn.).

——(1957), 'Ciuitas Dei, Ciuitas Terrena: num tertium quid?', *T&U*, 242–350.

Marrou, H. I., and La Bonnardière, A. M. (1966), 'Le Dogme de la résurrection des corps et la théologie des valeurs humaines selon l'enseignement de saint Augustin', *Et. Aug.*, 111–36.

McGuckin, J. (1990), 'Did Augustine's Christology depend on Theodore of Mopsuestia?', *The Heythrop Journal* XXXI: 39–52.

McLynn, N. B. (1994), *Ambrose of Milan: Church and Court in a Christian Capital* (Berkeley-Los Angeles-London: University of California Press).

Merdinger, J. E. (1997a), *Rome and the African Church in the Time of Augustine* (New Haven-London: Yale University Press).

——(1997b), 'Augustine and Church Authority: The Developing Role of the Provincial Primate' *Studia Patristica* 33: 183–9.

Meynell, H. (ed.) (1990), *Grace, Politics and Desire* (Calgary: University of Calgary Press).

Mohrmann, C. (1951), Review article of P. Courcelle *Recherches sur les Confessions de saint Augustin in Vigiliae Christianae* 5: 249–54.

——(1958), *Etudes sur le Latin des Chrétiens* (Rome).

Momigliano, A. (1963) (ed.), *The Conflict between Paganism and Christianity in the Fourth Century* (Oxford: Clarendon Press).

Monceaux, P. (1922), *Histoire Litteraire de l'Afrique Chretienne* IV–VII (Paris).

Moreau, M. (1986), 'Sur un commentaire d'Amos 6,1–6', in la Bonnardière (ed.), 313–23.

Nock, A. D. (1933), *Conversion* (Oxford: Clarendon Press).

O'Connell R. J. (1968), *Saint Augustine's Early Theory of Man* (Cambridge, Mass.: Harvard University Press).

——(1978), *Art and the Christian Intelligence in Saint Augustine* (Oxford: Basil Blackwell).

——(1984), *Saint Augustine's Platonism* (Villanova: Villanova University Press).

O'Daly G. (1987), *Saint Augustine's Philosophy of Mind* (London: Duckworth).

O'Donnell, J. J. (1979), 'The Inspiration for Augustine's *De Ciuitate Dei*', *Augustinian Studies* 10: 75–9.

——(1992), *Augustine: Confessions*, 3 vols. (Introduction, Text and Commentary) (Oxford: Oxford University Press).

O'Donovan, O. M. T. (1980), *The Problem of Self-Love in Saint Augustine* (New Haven-London: Yale University Press).

——(1987), 'Augustine's *City of God* XIX and Western Political Thought', *Dionysius* XI, 89–110.

O'Meara J. J. (1954), *The Young Augustine* (London: Longmans, Green and Co.).

——(1961), *Charter of Christendom: The Significance of the City of God* (New York: Macmillan).

Patout Burns, J. (1980), *The Development of Augustine's Doctrine of Operative Grace* (Paris: Études Augustiniennes).

Pépin, J. (1955), 'Le "challenge" Homère-Moïse aux premiers siècles chrétiens', *Recherches de Science Religieuse*, 105–122.

——(1976), *Saint Augustin et la Dialectique* (Villanova: Villanova University Press).

Petitmengin, P. (1985), 'Les plus anciens manuscrits de la Bible latine', in Fontaine and Pietri (eds.), 89–127.

Pétré, H. (1948), *Caritas. Étude sur le vocabulaire Latin de la charité chrétienne* (Paris).

Pétrement, S. (1990), *A Separate God: The Christian Origins of Gnosticism* (New York: HarperCollins).

Pizzolato, L. F. (1968), *Le 'Confessioni' de sant' Agostino: Da biografia a 'Confessio'* (Milan: Vita e Pensiero).

Primmer, A. (1995), 'The function of the *genera dicendi* in *De doctrina christiana* 4', in Arnold and Bright (eds.), 68–87.

Pollmann, K. (1996), *Doctrina Christiana: Untersuchungen zu den Anfängen der christlichen Hermeneutik unter besonderer Berücksichtigung von Augustinus De doctrina christiana* (Freiburg Schweiz: Universitätsverlag).

Pontet, M., *L'Exégèse de saint Augustin prédicateur* (Paris: Aubier n.d.).

Poque, S. (1966), *Sermons Pour La Paque*, Sources Chrétiennes 116 (Paris: Cerf).

Power, K. (1995), *Veiled Desire: Augustine's Writings on Women* (London: Darton, Longman and Todd, 1995).

Ramsay, B. (1997), *Ambrose* (London: Routledge).

Raven, S. (1993), *Rome in Africa* (3rd edn. London: Routledge).

Rawson, B. (1986) (ed.), *The Roman Family* (London: Croom Helm).

Rees, B. R. (1991), *The Letters of Pelagius and his Followers* (Woodbridge: Boydell Press).

Rémy, G. (1979), *Le Christ Médiateur* (Lille).

Reynolds, P. L. (1994), *Marriage in the Western Church: The Christianization of Marriage During the Patristic and Early Medieval Periods* (Leiden: Brill).

Rist, J. M. (1969), 'Augustine on Free Will and Predestination', *JTS* 20, 420–47.

——(1994), *Augustine* (Cambridge: Cambridge University Press).

Roth, C. P., and Anderson, D. (1986), *Saint John Chrysostom on Marriage and Family Life* (Crestwood, NY: St Vladimir's Seminary Press).

Rousseau, P. (1971), 'The Spiritual Authority of the "Monk-Bishop": Eastern elements in some Western Hagiography of the Fourth and Fifth centuries', *JTS* 22: 380–419.

——(1978), *Ascetics, Authority and the Church* (Oxford: Clarendon Press).

Ruokanen, M. (1993), *Theology of Social Life in Augustine's City of God* (Göttingen: Vandenhoek & Ruprecht).

Sage, A. (1964), 'Praeparatur voluntas a Domino', *Et. Aug.* 10: 1–20.

Saxer, V. (1980), *Morts, Martyrs, Reliques en Afrique Chrétienne aux Premièrs siècles* (Paris: Beauchesne).

Schaüblin, C. (1995), 'De doctrina christiana: A Classic of Western Culture?', in Arnold and Bright (eds.), 47–67.

Schindler, A. (1965), *Wort und Analogie in Augustins Trinitätslehre* (Tübingen: Siebeck).

Schmaus, M. (1927), *Die psychologische Trinitätslehre des hl. Augustinus* (Münster).

Schmidt, E. (1983), *Le mariage chrétien selon saint Augustin* (Paris: Études Augustiniennes).

Shaw, B. (1995a), 'African Christianity: Disputes, Definitions and Donatists', in *Rulers, Nomads and Christians in Roman North Africa* (Aldershot: Variorum), XI.

——(1995b), 'The Elders of Christian Africa' Ibid. X.

Shaw, B. D. (1987), 'The Family in Late Antiquity: The Experience of Augustine', *Past and Present* 115: 3–51.

Simmons M. B. (1995), *Arnobius of Sicca. Religious Conflict and Competition in the Age of Diocletian* (Oxford: Clarendon Press).

Simonetti, M. (1994), *Biblical Interpretation in the Early Church* (Edinburgh: T & T. Clark).

Solignac, A. (1958), 'Doxographies et manuels dans la formation philosophique de saint Augustin', *Rech. Aug.* 113–48.

——(1988), 'Les exces de "l'intellectus fidei" dans la doctrine d'Augustin sur la grâce', *Nouvelle Revue Theologique* 110: 825–49.

Spanneut, M. (1973), *Permanence du Stoïcisme* (Gembloux: Duculot).

Studer, B. (1972), 'Consubstantialis Patri, Consubstantialis Matri', *Et. Aug.* 18: 87–115.

——(1975), '"Sacramentum et Exemplum" chez saint Augustin', *Rech. Aug.*, 87–141.

——(1991), 'Zum Aufbau von Augustins *De ciuitate Dei*', *Augustiniana* 41: 937–51.

Sullivan, J. E. (1963), *The Image of God. The Doctrine of Saint Augustine and its Influence* (Dubuque: The Priory Press).

Swift, L. J. (1983), *The Early Fathers on War and Military Service* (Wilmington, Delaware: Michael Glazier).

Taylor, J. E. (1993), *Christians and the Holy Places. The myth of Jewish-Christian Origins* (Oxford: Clarendon Press).

Tengström, E. (1964), *Donatisten und Katholiken: soziale, wirtschaftliche und politische Aspekte einer nordafrikanischen Kirchenspaltung* (Studia Graeca et Latina Gothoburgensia XVIII, Göteborg: Elanders Boktryckeri Aktiebolag).

Teselle, E. (1970), *Augustine the Theologian* (New York: Herder & Herder).

Testard, M. (1958), *Saint Augustin et Cicéron* I & II (Paris: Études Augustiniennes).

Theiler, W. (1953), Review of P. Courcelle *Recherches sur les Confessions de saint Augustin*, in *Gnomon* 25: 116–17.

Tugwell, S. (1984), *Ways of Imperfection* (London: Darton, Longman and Todd).

van Bavel, T. J. (1954), *Recherches sur la Christologie de saint Augustin: L'Human et le Divin dans Le Christ d'après saint Augustin* (Fribourg).

——(1975), 'The Evangelical Inspiration of the Rule of Saint Augustine', *Downside Review* 93: 83–99.

——(1989), 'Augustine's View on Women', *Augustiniana* 39: 5–53.

Van der Meer, F. (1961), *Augustine the Bishop* (London: Sheed and Ward).

Van Oort, J. (1991), *Jerusalem and Babylon. A Study into Augustine's City of God and the Sources of his Doctrine of the Two Cities* (Leiden: Brill).

Vanderspoel, J. (1990), 'The Background to Augustine's Denial of Religious Plurality', in Meynell (ed.), 179–93.

Verbeke, G. (1958), 'Augustin et le stoïcisme', *Rech. Aug.* I: 67–89.

Verheijen, L. M. J. (1967), *La règle de saint Augustin*, 2 vols (Paris: Études Augustiniennes).

——(1974), 'Le De Doctrina Christiana de saint Augustin: Un manuel d'herméneutique et d'expression chrétienne, avec, en II,19 (29)–42 (63), une charte fondamentale pour une culture chrétienne', *Augustiniana* 24: 10–20.

——(1974 and 1984), 'Eléments d'un commentaire de la Règle de saint Augustin. IX. Le Praeceptum et l'éthique classique', *Augustiniana* 24: 5–9; XX. La charité ne cherché pas ses propres intérêts', *Augustiniana* 34: 97–100.

——(1979), *Saint Augustine's Monasticism in the Light of Acts 4.32–35* (Villanova).

——(1980), *Nouvelle Approche de la Règle de saint Augustin* (Bégrolles-en-Mauges: Abbaye de Bellefontaine).

Verwilghen, A. (1985), *Christologie et spiritualité selon saint Augustin: L'Hymne aux Philippiens* (Paris: Études Augustiniennes).

Veyne, P. (1987) (ed.), *A History of Private Life, From Pagan Rome to Byzantium* (Cambridge MA/London: The Belknap Press of Harvard University Press).

Vikan, G. (1990), 'Art and Marriage in Early Byzantium', *Dumbarton Oaks Papers* 44: 143–63.

Vogel, C. J. (1985), 'Platonism and Christianity: A Mere Antagonism or a Profound Common Ground?', *Vigiliae Christianae* 39: 1–62.

Wallis R. T. (1972), *Neoplatonism* (London: Duckworth).

Westra, H. J. (1990), 'Augustine and Poetic Exegesis', in H. Meynell (ed.), 87–100.

Wetzel, J. (1992), *Augustine and the Limits of Virtue* (Cambridge: Cambridge University Press).

White, C. (1990), *The Correspondence (394–419) Between Jerome and Augustine of Hippo* (Lewiston-Quennston-Lampeter: The Edwin Mellen Press).

Williams, D. H. (1995), *Ambrose of Milan and the End of the Arian-Nicene Conflicts* (Oxford: Clarendon Press).

Williams, R. D. (1989), 'Language, Reality and Desire in Augustine's *De Doctrina Christiana*', *Literature and Theology* 3: 138–50.

——(1990), '*Sapientia* and the Trinity: reflections on the *De trinitate*', in B. Bruning et al. (eds.), *Collectanea Augustiniana: Mélanges T. J. Van Bavel*, vol. 1 (Leuven: University Press), 317–32.

Yarbrough, A. (1976), 'Christianisation in the Fourth Century: The Example of Roman Woman', *Church History* 45: 149–64.

Zeiller, J. (1934), 'L'arianisme en Afrique avant l'invasion vandale', *Revue Historique* 173: 535–41.

——(1941), 'Les hérésies en Afrique entre la paix constantinienne et l'invasion vandale', in *Mélanges Fr. Martroye* (Paris: Société nationale des antiquaires de France) 100–6.

Zumkeller, A. (1986), *Augustine's Ideal of the Religious Life* (New York).

Index